SAT®

Victory!

• The Simple & Easy Guidebook

for Overnight Success

on the **SAT** •

(Mastering the SAT in a

step-by-step game-plan format)

Raymond Karelitz B.A., Ed. B., M.A.

© 2007

Hi-Lite Publishing Company

www.Hi-LitePublishing.com

Copyright © 2007
Raymond Karelitz

Hi-Lite Publishing Company
P.O. Box 240161
Honolulu, Hawaii 96824

This book may be purchased in quantity for classroom use. For a complete listing of titles available, contact the publisher.

SAT® is a registered trademark of the College Board, Princeton, New Jersey 08541

Computer-Processing & Layout:
Toni Shortsleeve

Cartoons:
James Makashima

Cover Design:
Doug Behrens

Library of Congress Catalog Card Number: 2007930158

Karelitz, Raymond, 1952-

SAT Victory

1. Scholastic Assessment Test – **Study Guide**.

I. Title

ISBN 978–1–56391–033–3

Printed in China

Fifth Edition

Table of Contents

WHAT IS THE **SAT**?

For decades the **SAT** has been used as a college entrance requirement, with score-requirements as varied as the colleges themselves. But all colleges share in one objective: to accept students who will reflect favorably upon the college through either academic, athletic or other personal strengths. Colleges therefore are seeking people who excel in their field, whether in band, ROTC, drama, academics, or of course in sports.

As a prospective student of higher learning, your primary objective should be to impress upon colleges your potential contribution to their success. Once colleges become aware of your individual excellence, they'll eagerly seek to recruit you. The only thing preventing you from being accepted are the entrance requirements, of which the **SAT** is usually one of them.

THE BEST WAY TO BE NOTICED

There is a very important first step you can take to let colleges see who you are, and that's by taking the **PSAT**. Although the test-score is not of any importance other than to serve as a practice test evaluation, the profile-information you provide could open doors to colleges if they like what they see. The questionnaire gives you the chance to detail your sports background, academic strengths, as well as other significant details including ethnic status and your field of future interest. Dollar-for-dollar, the **PSAT** is the best value to get your name out into the college "marketplace."

WHAT SCORES DO YOU NEED?

Colleges have differing GPA (Grade-Point-Average) and **SAT**-score minimums, but there are general score-ranges that are consistent throughout the U.S.:

- General Admission:
  - 2.8 – 3.0 Minimum GPA
  - 1450 – 1600 **SAT** total score

◆ ◆

- Academic-Scholarship Range:
  - 3.5+ GPA (minimum)
  - 650 minimum per **SAT** section (Reading/Math/Writing)
  - (Generally, 2000 Total minimum)

◆ ◆ ◆ ◆ ◆ ◆ ◆ ◆ ◆ ◆ ◆ ◆ ◆ ◆ ◆ ◆ ◆ ◆ ◆ ◆

- Sports (NCAA) Participation:
  - 2.0 minimum GPA
  - 450 – 480 **SAT** minimum per section: Reading & Math *

*(NCAA eligibility-requirements are determined by an inverted scale correlating GPA and **SAT**. Check with your high school counselor to see exactly what **SAT** scores you must achieve to be NCAA-eligible.)*

---

* Although, for eligibility requirements, the NCAA only reviews the scores of the Critical Reading Section (also referred to as the "Verbal" Section) and Math Section, it behooves all athletes to take the Writing Section (Essay + Grammar) seriously. Meeting NCAA requirements does not guarantee immediate college acceptance – an exceptionally low score on the Writing portion of the SAT could undermine the entire test. Therefore, consider all three sections of the SAT of equal significance, even though the scores of only two sections comprise the NCAA-acceptance requirement.

✳ ✳

The above information is very general but useful insofar as it emphasizes the need to keep your grades up and to have a "ballpark figure" as to how well you will need to score on the **SAT**. If you are being scouted by a college, take the initiative to find out if you meet all their qualifications. After all, they want you but you've got to be sure you meet their basic requirements for acceptance.

CHECK OUT THE COLLEGE

Before you begin to "play the **SAT** game," decide which colleges you are interested in attending. Winning the **SAT** challenge but winding up at a place you don't feel comfortable in isn't winning at all. The college you attend wants you to stay, so no one wins if you don't like it there. Look beyond the glitter of the video hype – visit the campus and see if it's the right place for you.

If you find a particular college that you really would like to attend, let the right people know. Don't play "hard ball" by pitting colleges against one another. Once you've found that perfect college, let the admissions counselors and relevant coaches know that they are your #1 choice. The ball will then be in their hands, and it will be up to them to make your educational experience there affordable and worthwhile. Be honest and sincere with them, and they'll treat you with due respect as well. After all, it is a "team game" and you need to be following the same game plan if you want to be on the winning team!

A PARTING COMMENT REGARDING COLLEGE

Before you begin the **SAT** "game," take a moment to remember why you are going to college: it's to advance yourself academically, socially and professionally. Once you begin attending college classes, you'll notice that people are there because they want to be there, not because they have to be there. Class-schedules are flexible because *you* make them – there is no set time you must be in school; you may have two hours of class one day, four hours the next. Students in general love this freedom, but beware that with freedom comes responsibility. Don't slack off, procrastinate or make excuses about attending classes. Too many students drop out of college because they don't take it seriously, so be careful that you don't let yourself get caught up in such a "party" mentality or else you'll lose everything you've fought so hard to attain in this once-in-a-lifetime opportunity. College is nothing like high school – it's a new world filled with unique experiences. Be there to experience it!

THE GAME IS ABOUT TO BEGIN

Every chapter in this book will adhere to the analogy that the **SAT** is like a sport, not a test. Whether basketball, football, baseball or golf, the strategy is the same and the goal is the same. Once you see the **SAT** in this light, you'll find it much easier to understand; and once you learn how to "play the game," you will see your scores rise to new heights!

You Can't Study For The **SAT***, But You Can Prepare*

Many people feel that preparing for the **SAT** is like studying for a biology or history exam. They're wrong, and it's because the **SAT** contains different questions on each test. Like a sport, the rules are constant – but as in sports, you never know who you will be playing next. It's "academic" basketball: you've got the ball and you know what you need to do, but that's all you know. You've got to prepare a game-plan for winning, but no studying of the game can guarantee you success. Victory will only come on the field, when you put your game-plan into action and see how it succeeds against the unknown enemy.

There is one foolproof way to emerge victorious in the **SAT** game, but as with its sports-counterpart it isn't always feasible unless you've got the time and the commitment.

"LIFTING WEIGHTS"

Strength oftentimes ensures success, which is why every athletics complex includes a weight room. Given a few months of rigorous training, you can excel in practically any sport. Such is the case with **SAT**-training. If you have several months time and a commitment to "work out" a couple hours per day, you can raise your **SAT** scores far beyond your wildest dreams. Included in this daily regimen should be vocabulary-building exercises, intensive reading, developing critical thinking skills by engaging in games such as chess and crossword puzzles/logic puzzles, and **SAT**-practice. If you can dedicate yourself to such a training program, you will be at peak performance when you take the real **SAT**.

But although sports programs give students months of training for the upcoming season, few take the **SAT** anywhere near as seriously. Instead, there is usually a sudden need to prepare for an **SAT** that is a month, perhaps even two weeks away. If you are in this dilemma, then what you need to learn are the rules of the game so you can develop a strategy. (A "strategy" is a plan of attack when you haven't had the proper training to guarantee success.) With a consistent game-plan strategy, you may surprise yourself at just how well you can score without having put in the long-term commitment.

> Remember: It's not *what you know* but *how you use what you know*.

THE BALL IS IN YOUR COURT: WHAT TO DO NEXT

If you've never looked at a **PSAT** or an **SAT**, do it *now* before you read any further. Simply put, you've got to know how to dribble the ball before you can even hope to play the game.

♦ ♦

If you're reading this, then it's assumed you know what the **SAT** looks like, so let's briefly review the general format of the **SAT** and outline a sound overall approach:

Format

There are several sections, but they all fall into the categories of: Critical Reading (inc. Vocabulary); Mathematics; and Writing/Grammar. You need to know how each section is "played," because you can't afford to fall apart on one section and still expect to win the game.

Practical Approach

1) Your score is determined by the number of questions you answer correctly. There is a fractional penalty for incorrect answers, but this should not stop you from answering any questions. After all, if you never shoot you'll never score. And if you never score, you'll never win.

2) The test is multiple-choice (except for the essay and a brief portion of the Math section), which means that there is an answer somewhere within the five choices. Your goal is to find the correct answer, which necessitates the fundamental principal of *eliminating* choices that are not correct.

3) Every section has a time-limit. When the bell rings, the game is over. Your game-plan is to answer all the questions you can before time runs out. But more importantly, you want to get as many *correct* as possible during that time.

These pointers present a thumb-nail sketch to taking the **SAT**. There aren't many rules – the game is quite simple – but (because it is a national/standardized test comparing your score with thousands of others taking the same test) you've got to know how to outplay the competition. As in a game of golf, your score is only as good as when compared with everyone else's. But then again, as in golf there's only one score you should worry about: *your own*.

The strategy game-plan you'll be learning will help put you at the top of your performance, so pay particular attention to the advice given in this book. It has been responsible for hundreds, perhaps even thousands of sports-related scholarships for students whose counselors counted them out of the game. Two players who followed these strategies are in fact even now playing for the NFL. That's success!

MAXIMIZE YOUR SCORE BY MAKING THE LAY-UPS (NOT THE "PRAYER SHOTS")

Have you taken a sample **SAT** or **PSAT** lately? If not, then stop reading and ask your high school college/career counselor for a sample **SAT** test-booklet. Unless you've had some actual hands-on practice with the **SAT**, it will serve no purpose to introduce a workable game-plan.

♦ ♦

If you're reading this, you've had some recent experience with the **SAT**. Let's first clarify how the test is organized so you'll better understand how our game-plan will work. It's comparable in sports to analyzing the game itself first so you know why a game-plan is needed.

Every section of the **SAT** (except for the Critical Reading portion) is arranged so that the EASIEST problems are at the beginning and the HARDEST at the end. Although many people say that each problem is worth the same, they are wrong! Here's why:

The **SAT** assigns difficulty-levels to each problem:

Level 1 = EASY (almost everyone gets the problem correct)

Level 2 = Somewhat Easy (most get the problem correct)

Level 3 = MEDIUM (half of the people get the problem correct)

Level 4 = Somewhat Hard (not many get the problem correct)

Level 5 = HARD (very few get the problem correct)

SPORTS-ANALOGY (basketball):

Let's equate it to basketball:

Level 1 = a Lay-Up

Level 2 = a Short Shot

Level 3 = a Free Throw

Level 4 = a "Long Shot"

Level 5 = a Half-Court Shot ("Prayer-Shot")

All the above shots are supposedly worth the same points, but would a coach say to shoot them all? Of course not! A coach would expect you to take (and make) the Lay-Ups and the Short Shots. But any coach would add that Half-Court shots rarely win games, and anyone who takes them regularly is sure to **lose!** As a player, your goal is to shoot those shots you can make, and you know which ones they are – surely not those from "way out."

GET THE EASY ONES CORRECT.

DON'T WASTE YOUR TIME AND ENERGY ON THE HARD ONES.

This doesn't mean that you should automatically skip all the harder problems; it simply means that you should be sure to get the easy ones correct. If you make a "long shot," that's great! But if you miss the easy ones, you're setting yourself up for defeat.

In a nutshell, your game-plan should reflect your goals. If you are trying to score a 500, you should concentrate on getting the easy ones and the medium ones correct, placing all remaining time into double-checking your answers.

If you are seeking a 600+ score, you need to get all the easy and medium problems correct as well as many of the harder problems. This presumes that you will be answering every question and that you have strong **SAT** basic skills, too.

Let's now look more closely at each section of the **SAT** so we can put our game-plan into operation.

The game begins here.

SAT

Critical Reading

Section

CRITICAL READING SECTION: SENTENCE COMPLETIONS

The Critical Reading section of the **SAT** actually consists of Reading and Vocabulary. There are 19 fill-in-the-blank sentences, the object of which is to fit in the word (or word-pair) that makes sense. The easy ones are at the beginning, and your immediate goal should be to get the first half correct. The last couple of problems are HARD; don't waste your time and energy trying to make the impossible shots. Instead, use your time wisely to ensure that you make those lay-ups and short shots.

Here are several easy sentence-completion samples to get you familiar with the problem-type. You should be able to get at least 15 of 20 correct.

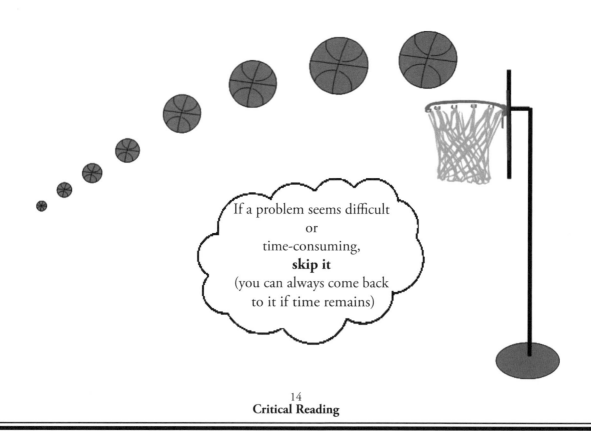

If a problem seems difficult
or
time-consuming,
skip it
(you can always come back
to it if time remains)

Directions: circle the letter whose words *best* complete the meaning of the sentence
[answers on page 182]

1. Having broken the glass bowl, Stan ___ it with an identical ___.
   A) revived…adjustment
   B) bartered…artifact
   C) replaced…duplicate
   D) repaired…substitute
   E) removed…clone

2. She suffered several ___ as a result of the ___ with another car.
   A) bruises…collision
   B) shrieks…impact
   C) obstacles…incident
   D) contusions…liberation
   E) hallucinations…mishap

3. While backstage, the crafty adolescent caught a ___ of the starlet ___.
   A) thrill…yearning
   B) glare…contemplating
   C) glimpse…disrobing
   D) portion…conversing
   E) reaction…reposing

4. An additional sample was necessary to ___ the success of the ___.
   A) discount…remainder
   B) schedule…tempest
   C) evaluate…interim
   D) determine…experiment
   E) supplement…debacle

5. After ___ the area for several hours, the party ___ that the search was futile.
   A) managing…concluded
   B) sheathing…verified
   C) surpassing…analyzed
   D) analyzing…deduced
   E) scouring…realized

6. The homeless lad was discovered to be the ___ ___ to the eccentric's fortune.
   A) prohibited…possession
   B) sole…heir
   C) prescribed…vagrant
   D) unexpected…victim
   E) disadvantaged…doubter

7. Rather than a ___ burst of colors, the fireworks exploded in an ___ fashion.
   A) simultaneous…alternating
   B) fierce…untimely
   C) habitual…automatic
   D) pronounced…outstanding
   E) modest…erratic

8. Locked in ___ combat, each participant found survival to be the ___ concern.
   A) stubborn…irrelevant
   B) juvenile…cultivated
   C) tense…global
   D) frivolous…paramount
   E) mortal…fundamental

9. The countess would not ___ to assist the impoverished ___.
   A) assume…dolts
   B) demand…miners
   C) commence…bystanders
   D) stoop…immigrants
   E) fail…royalty

10. Despite the ___ effort, fulfillment of their desires did not ___.
    A) straightforward…oblige
    B) concentrated…prevail
    C) stampeded…alter
    D) impeded…materialize
    E) repeated…disappoint

11. To minimize the severity of the ___, the herders ___ the entire flock to another pasture.
   A) epidemic…transferred
   B) influenza…launched
   C) oversight…grazed
   D) drought…removed
   E) struggle…defended

12. The unsuspecting ___ became the ___ of vast treasures of the Brighton estate.
   A) tyrant…representation
   B) ignoramus… principle
   C) adolescent…beneficiary
   D) curator…prey
   E) vagabond…upholder

13. Above all else, the restaurateur valued the ___ of the ___.
   A) briefness…souvenirs
   B) welfare…patrons
   C) quality…fugitives
   D) solace…multitudes
   E) price…compliments

14. The compatriots swore ___ allegiance and a pact to ___ with one another whenever problems arose.
   A) indivisible…consult
   B) grudging…conduct
   C) mental…involve
   D) cursory…deliberate
   E) steadfast…quibble

15. Due to the velocity of the winds coupled with sizable wave action, the dinghy ___ before completing its ___.
   A) contracted…guidance
   B) capsized…rendezvous
   C) depreciated…expedition
   D) succeeded…mission
   E) floundered…fiasco

16. No matter how much ___ abuse was issued, the defiant lad refused to ___ with the mother's demands.
   A) meritorious…adjust
   B) mocking…grant
   C) persistent…argue
   D) virulent…cope
   E) repetitive…cooperate

17. Seeking the most equitable compromise, the ___ deliberated at length with his ___.
   A) talent…descendant
   B) disciplinarian…advisor
   C) dictator…minions
   D) protester…conscience
   E) employee…attorney

18. ___ life is truly a ___ aquatic paradise.
   A) Oceanic…baneful
   B) Rustic…fragrant
   C) Clerical…mere
   D) Marine…visual
   E) Watery…wondrous

19. His followers' ___ were somewhat ___ when the so-called prophet was defrocked.
   A) impulses…hastened
   B) interpretations…depressed
   C) convictions…tainted
   D) suspicions…suspended
   E) aspirations…realized

20. In a ___ display of ___, the aficionado kissed the performer's feet.
   A) mutual…sentimentality
   B) ridiculous…gratitude
   C) tactless…exertion
   D) portentous…concern
   E) magnificent…pride

The problem with the second half of the Sentence Completions lies in the vocabulary words themselves. If you don't know what the words mean, then there is only one reliable approach you can utilize: *Eliminate* choices from words you do know and take an *educated guess* from those choices that remain. What you don't want to do is waste valuable time and energy on such sentences you hardly understand.

Elimination is the single best approach to answering *any* multiple-choice question, whether it be on the **SAT** or on a college history exam, or even on a written driver's examination. If you can *eliminate* one or two choices that you don't feel make sense, you've greatly increased your chances for getting the problem correct.

SPORTS-ANALOGY (basketball):

The *elimination* approach is similar to a player breaking free from his defender. Once he has *eliminated* his opponent from the play, there's a much greater chance of scoring!

Here's a sample quiz to test both your vocabulary and your test-taking skills. If you can get at least 15 correct, you have a solid vocabulary foundation and should probably not skip any **SAT** Sentence-Completion problems.

Directions: circle the letter whose words *best* complete the meaning of the sentence
[answers on page 182]

1. After a brief ___, the miners resumed the ___ of the mountainside.
   A) celibacy…conflagration
   B) accord…laceration
   C) respite…detonation
   D) hiatus…condescension
   E) postponement…construction

2. Located on the island boasting the world's greatest precipitation, the community remained ___ at the mercy of unannounced ____.
   A) pathetically…espionage
   B) heedfully…harassment
   C) precariously…inundation
   D) gratefully…warmth
   E) hopelessly…droughts

3. In a recent ___ of memoirs, I discovered a ___ my grandfather had told to me many years earlier.
   A) whim…jargon
   B) perusal…maxim
   C) upshot…triviality
   D) analysis…contradiction
   E) reflection…lesson

4. The major ___ the reasons for the ___ of confidence in the ranks.
   A) pondered…erosion
   B) convened…infraction
   C) redressed…fluctuation
   D) disputed…intimacy
   E) lamented…upsurge

5. In his first ballgame, the ___ big-leaguer remembered the tips given to him by the player he so devotedly ___ as a boy.
   A) hardy…adhered
   B) virile…incited
   C) veteran…venerated
   D) novice…emulated
   E) reticent…detested

6. The beleaguered businessman was forced to ___ his assets to ___ existing debts.
   A) embellish…regress
   B) liquidate…accommodate
   C) extricate…eschew
   D) distribute…exorcise
   E) admonish…pacify

7. The ___ of the evening air reminded us of the ___ days of our childhood.
   A) permeability…heterogeneous
   B) redolence…futuristic
   C) rabble…rustic
   D) aroma…wayward
   E) progression…nostalgic

8. An integral ___ for successful management is ___ incentive.
   A) liability…fraudulent
   B) menace…fruitless
   C) element…digressive
   D) component…monetary
   E) ideal…practical

9. The professor's ___ explanation proved a ___ to our understanding of the concept.
   A) complacent…benchmark
   B) tranquil…cataclysm
   C) inconsequential…stimulus
   D) profound…barrier
   E) inane…detriment

10. His success was a ___ of sorts insofar as few scholars had considered the newcomer ___ in such an advanced field of research.
   A) reciprocity…consummate
   B) precursor…blasphemous
   C) paradox…competent
   D) victory…willful
   E) conundrum…lacking

11. Although not outright slander, the ___ was suggestive enough to warrant a subsequent ___.
  A) parley…repentance
  B) innuendo…retraction
  C) holocaust…lesion
  D) eulogy…reprisal
  E) implication…confirmation

12. Seeking ___ with the other members, the teenager soon became ___ with perfection.
  A) dalliance…effaced
  B) fraternity…dispossessed
  C) alms…belabored
  D) harmony…bereaved
  E) parity…obsessed

13. Constructed after years of toil, the structure was an ___ fortress destined to ___ any would-be assailant.
  A) impregnable…thwart
  B) autonomous…manipulate
  C) impending…entice
  D) inalienable…vanquish
  E) inaccessible…stupefy

14. Because he was friendless in the town, it was no surprise that his suggestion was ___ and subject to ___.
  A) gelid…kudos
  B) imperious…ridicule
  C) ignored…reevaluation
  D) lauded…commendation
  E) berated…derision

15. With his ___ wit and insight, the politician demonstrated how he was the ___ in the Senate.
  A) impeccable…nonpareil
  B) seasoned…proselyte
  C) intolerable…paradigm
  D) mordant…tyro
  E) ineffable…pariah

16. In their gaunt state, even a ___ of meat scraps looked ___.
  A) tittle…sumptuous
  B) pathos…profuse
  C) maelstrom…culinary
  D) modicum…derivative
  E) surfeit…minuscule

17. The ___ of her smile belied her inner ___ character.
  A) radiance…morose
  B) earnestness…facetious
  C) nonchalance…sinuous
  D) gaiety…ebullient
  E) beneficence…magnanimous

18. Taken off-guard by the ___ words of the guru, the youth abandoned his disinterest and instead sought enlightenment from this ___ oratory.
  A) soporific…dynamic
  B) plaintive…esthetic
  C) perfunctory…wry
  D) indelicate…discreet
  E) mellifluent…didactic

19. Both the warden and supervisors were ___ of the newest procedures set forth for ___ of the irreverent prisoners.
  A) savants…transgression
  B) apologists…castigation
  C) misanthropes…retribution
  D) adherents…adulation
  E) suffragists…enfranchisement

20. He ___ an air of ___ solicitude, though the jury knew he was guilty.
  A) placated…insuperable
  B) evinced…fecund
  C) feigned…ingenuous
  D) propounded…unwary
  E) portrayed…thespian

WHEN IS IT BETTER TO SKIP?

SPORTS-ANALOGY (basketball):

If you are close enough to the basket to score, then shoot the ball! But if you're too far away to even reach the basket, then shooting the ball is a waste of time and a poor decision.

· ·

In basketball, you can't score if you don't shoot, and this is also true on the **SAT**, especially so on the Critical Reading section. However, if you find yourself without a clue on a Sentence-Completion problem, it is better to skip the problem rather than take a wild guess and suffer the penalty for what will most likely be the wrong answer.

· ·

General Helpful Hints For Sentence Completions

1) In a two-blank sentence, if one blank doesn't seem to make sense, *eliminate* the choice immediately. *Both* sides must fit for the problem to be correct.

2) In a harder two-blank Sentence Completion, if one word seems to make sense but you have absolutely no idea what the other word means, *select that answer*. You have a 50-50 chance of getting it correct, pretty good odds on any of the harder fill-in-the-blank problems.

• Just remember not to spend too much time on the harder sentences. •

You'll need that time for the Critical Reading passages.

BUILDING **SAT** MUSCLES

As mentioned earlier, in athletics the weight room is the place where long-term strength can be developed. On the **SAT**, *studying* is comparable to the weight room.

If you want to build up **SAT** Verbal strength, there are two sure-fire ways to do so:

1) study **SAT** vocabulary lists

2) read vocabulary-building novels

Fortunately, there are books available that are excellent vocabulary-builders, and you may well want to look into them online at Amazon.com.

- **SAT** *High School* & *College Dictionary* (+ *Workbook*)
- **SAT** *Dictionary of One-Word Definitions* (Over 5000 key words)
- **SAT** *Vocabulary-Building Novel* Trilogy-Series

These books are excellent sources for long-term "muscle-building," but they should be considered only if you are seriously committed to the effort required to score ***high*** on the **SAT** Critical Reading section (650⁺). In general, the game-plan strategy approach in this book will help you raise your scores as high as the mid-500s, though fact is there have been unusual instances in which students have scored 700 just by following the advice in this book. In the long run, however, those with a stronger vocabulary and more advanced reading skills are sure to have a decided advantage over the rest of the playing field. So if you're willing to dedicate yourself to a regimen for long-term improvement, the tools are available and at your computer fingertips!

BUILDING VOCABULARY QUICKLY

Although the **SAT** vocabulary encompasses literally thousands of possible words, there are "power words" that tend to appear frequently, both in the Sentence-Completion portion and throughout the Reading passages.

If you wish to build key vocabulary but lack sufficient time necessary for long-term gains, consider the following "Top 200" Word List as an effective first step: These are the most frequently-appearing words on **SAT**s, words many refer to as those essential "power words"!

1)	ABRUPT	*- sudden*	51)	INFAMOUS	*- shameful*
2)	ACUTE	*- sharp*	52)	INFLAMMABLE	*- burnable*
3)	ADVOCATE	*- support*	53)	IRONIC	*- contradictory*
4)	AGILE	*- nimble*	54)	LAMENT	*- mourn*
5)	AMBIGUOUS	*- unclear*	55)	LETHAL	*- deadly*
6)	AMIABLE	*- friendly*	56)	LETHARGIC	*- sluggish*
7)	APATHY	*- unconcern*	57)	LISTLESS	*- unenthusiastic*
8)	ARCHAIC	*- ancient*	58)	LOATHE	*- hate*
9)	ARROGANT	*- snobby*	59)	LUCID	*- clear*
10)	AVARICE	*- greed*	60)	MALEDICTION	*- curse*
11)	AVID	*- eager*	61)	MALICIOUS	*- spiteful*
12)	BEGUILE	*- deceive*	62)	MEEK	*- humble*
13)	BELLIGERENT	*- warlike*	63)	MELANCHOLY	*- sad*
14)	BENEVOLENT	*- kind*	64)	METICULOUS	*- exact*
15)	BIASED	*- unfair*	65)	NOTORIOUS	*- shameful*
16)	CANDID	*- honest*	66)	NOVEL	*- new*
17)	CENSURE	*- criticize*	67)	NOXIOUS	*- harmful*
18)	CIVIL	*- polite*	68)	OBESE	*- fat*
19)	COMPETENT	*- capable*	69)	OBJECTIVE	*- unbiased*
20)	COMPLACENT	*- content*	70)	OBSCURE	*- unclear*
21)	CONCILIATE	*- pacify*	71)	OPAQUE	*- dark*
22)	CONCISE	*- brief*	72)	PACIFY	*- calm*
23)	CONDONE	*- excuse*	73)	PENSIVE	*- meditative*
24)	COY	*- shy*	74)	PLACID	*- peaceful*
25)	DESOLATE	*- lonely*	75)	PROFICIENT	*- skillful*
26)	DETER	*- restrain*	76)	PROVOCATIVE	*- stimulating*
27)	DETRIMENT	*- danger*	77)	PRUDENT	*- wise*
28)	DILIGENT	*- hardworking*	78)	RASH	*- reckless*
29)	DISDAIN	*- scorn*	79)	RELINQUISH	*- surrender*
30)	DIVERSITY	*- variety*	80)	RESERVED	*- shy*
31)	DOCILE	*- manageable*	81)	SOMBER	*- gloomy*
32)	DOGGED	*- stubborn*	82)	SPURN	*- reject*
33)	ECCENTRIC	*- odd*	83)	SQUANDER	*- waste*
34)	EFFERVESCENT	*- excited*	84)	STOIC	*- unemotional*
35)	ELOQUENT	*- persuasive*	85)	SUBTLE	*- faint*
36)	ERRATIC	*- abnormal*	86)	SUPERFICIAL	*- shallow*
37)	EXOTIC	*- unusual*	87)	TACTFUL	*- thoughtful*
38)	FUTILE	*- useless*	88)	TANGIBLE	*- touchable*
39)	GRAVITY	*- seriousness*	89)	TERSE	*- brief*
40)	GULLIBLE	*- overtrusting*	90)	TIMID	*- shy*
41)	HEEDLESS	*- careless*	91)	TORRID	*- sizzling*
42)	HOSTILE	*- unfriendly*	92)	TRANQUIL	*- calm*
43)	HUMILITY	*- modesty*	93)	TRITE	*- unoriginal*
44)	HYPOCRITICAL	*- phony*	94)	TRIVIAL	*- unimportant*
45)	IMMACULATE	*- spotless*	95)	VAIN	*- hopeless*
46)	IMPARTIAL	*- unbiased*	96)	VALID	*- logical*
47)	IMPOVERISHED	*- poor*	97)	VIGILANT	*- alert*
48)	INDIFFERENT	*- unconcerned*	98)	VOLATILE	*- explosive*
49)	INDIGNANT	*- resentful*	99)	WARY	*- cautious*
50)	INEVITABLE	*- unavoidable*	100)	ZEAL	*- enthusiasm*

1)	ABASE	- degrade	51)	LAUD	- praise
2)	ACME	- peak	52)	LITHE	- graceful
3)	ADROIT	- skillful	53)	LOQUACIOUS	- talkative
4)	AFFABLE	- friendly	54)	LUGUBRIOUS	- gloomy
5)	AMORPHOUS	- shapeless	55)	NEFARIOUS	- wicked
6)	ANIMOSITY	- hatred	56)	OBDURATE	- stubborn
7)	APEX	- peak	57)	OMNISCIENT	- all-knowing
8)	ASCETIC	- abstaining	58)	OSTENTATIOUS	- showy
9)	ASSUAGE	- soothe	59)	PARIAH	- outcast
10)	ASTUTE	- perceptive	60)	PARSIMONIOUS	- stingy
11)	AUGMENT	- supplement	61)	PENURIOUS	- poor
12)	AUSTERE	- stern	62)	PERFUNCTORY	- superficial
13)	BANAL	- unexciting	63)	PHILANTHROPIC	- charitable
14)	BANE	- poison	64)	PIOUS	- devoted
15)	CAPRICIOUS	- changeable	65)	PITHY	- concise
16)	CLANDESTINE	- secret	66)	POMPOUS	- snobbish
17)	CORPULENT	- fat	67)	PRAGMATIC	- practical
18)	COVERT	- secret	68)	PRODIGAL	- unthrifty
19)	CRAVEN	- cowardly	69)	PRODIGIOUS	- immense
20)	CULPABLE	- guilty	70)	PROFUSE	- abundant
21)	DEARTH	- scarcity	71)	PROLIFIC	- productive
22)	DEFERENCE	- respect	72)	PROSAIC	- unimaginative
23)	DEMURE	- shy	73)	PUERILE	- childish
24)	DIDACTIC	- informational	74)	PUGNACIOUS	- fighting
25)	DIFFIDENT	- bashful	75)	RAZE	- demolish
26)	DISCERN	- distinguish	76)	REFUTE	- disprove
27)	DISINTERESTED	- unbiased	77)	REPREHENSIBLE	- hateful
28)	DISPARAGE	- belittle	78)	REPROACH	- blame
29)	DOGMATIC	- opinionated	79)	REPROVE	- criticize
30)	ELEGIACAL	- mournful	80)	REPUDIATE	- disclaim
31)	EPHEMERAL	- brief	81)	RETICENT	- shy
32)	ETHEREAL	- delicate	82)	REVERE	- worship
33)	EULOGIZE	- praise	83)	RUE	- regret
34)	EUPHONY	- harmony	84)	SCRUTINIZE	- examine
35)	EXTOL	- praise	85)	SERVILE	- obedient
36)	FACILITY	- ease	86)	SLOTH	- laziness
37)	FASTIDIOUS	- fussy	87)	SOPORIFIC	- sleepy
38)	FLIPPANT	- disrespectful	88)	SPARTAN	- disciplined
39)	FRUGAL	- thrifty	89)	SPURIOUS	- false
40)	GARRULOUS	- talkative	90)	STRIDENT	- harsh
41)	GREGARIOUS	- sociable	91)	SUCCINCT	- concise
42)	IMPASSIVE	- unemotional	92)	SUPERFLUOUS	- unnecessary
43)	INCESSANT	- continual	93)	SURLY	- rude
44)	INDIGENOUS	- native	94)	TACITURN	- bashful
45)	INDIGENT	- poor	95)	VERITY	- truth
46)	INNOCUOUS	- harmless	96)	VILIFY	- slander
47)	INTREPID	- fearless	97)	VIRULENT	- poisonous
48)	INUNDATE	- flood	98)	WANE	- decline
49)	JOCULAR	- joking	99)	WAX	- intensify
50)	LANGUISH	- weaken	100)	ZENITH	- peak

"POWER WORDS" QUIZ 1

Directions: select the choice that *best* defines the word in CAPITAL letters
[answers on pages 23-24]

1.	ABASE	1. grow	2. degrade	3. strengthen
2.	ABRUPT	1. damaged	2. sudden	3. powerful
3.	ACME	1. peak	2. irritation	3. uncertainty
4.	ACUTE	1. attractive	2. sharp	3. supplementary
5.	ADROIT	1. skillful	2. cloudy	3. lofty
6.	ADVOCATE	1. release	2. freshen	3. support
7.	AFFABLE	1. puny	2. bizarre	3. friendly
8.	AGILE	1. dangerous	2. nimble	3. poor
9.	AMBIGUOUS	1. clever	2. unclear	3. boastful
10.	AMIABLE	1. kind	2. friendly	3. silent
11.	AMORPHOUS	1. shapeless	2. sluggish	3. improper
12.	ANIMOSITY	1. honesty	2. hatred	3. nuisance
13.	APATHY	1. regret	2. unconcern	3. infamy
14.	APEX	1. peak	2. exception	3. pest
15.	ARCHAIC	1. ancient	2. invulnerable	3. curved
16.	ARROGANT	1. honest	2. snobby	3. polite
17.	ASCETIC	1. bitter	2. abstaining	3. prosperous
18.	ASSUAGE	1. soothe	2. liberate	3. distort
19.	ASTUTE	1. mysterious	2. perceptive	3. rugged
20.	AUGMENT	1. supplement	2. restore	3. repeat
21.	AUSTERE	1. abnormal	2. stern	3. persuasive
22.	AVARICE	1. luxury	2. greed	3. diversity
23.	AVID	1. dry	2. eager	3. peaceful
24.	BANAL	1. unexciting	2. welcome	3. damp
25.	BANE	1. poison	2. limit	3. storm
26.	BEGUILE	1. deceive	2. request	3. commence
27.	BELLIGERENT	1. picturesque	2. resonant	3. warlike
28.	BENEVOLENT	1. kind	2. outspoken	3. dominant
29.	BIASED	1. overrated	2. unfair	3. shy
30.	CANDID	1. secretive	2. determined	3. honest
31.	CAPRICIOUS	1. changeable	2. hilarious	3. expensive
32.	CENSURE	1. criticize	2. theorize	3. overcome
33.	CIVIL	1. childish	2. polite	3. experienced
34.	CLANDESTINE	1. illegal	2. inevitable	3. secret
35.	COMPETENT	1. aggressive	2. important	3. capable
36.	COMPLACENT	1. spicy	2. financial	3. content
37.	CONCILIATE	1. pacify	2. represent	3. comprehend
38.	CONCISE	1. brief	2. large	3. connected
39.	CONDONE	1. criticize	2. unite	3. excuse
40.	CORPULENT	1. dead	2. poisonous	3. fat
41.	COVERT	1. secret	2. aware	3. exempt
42.	COY	1. young	2. fearless	3. shy
43.	CRAVEN	1. hungry	2. cowardly	3. heavenly
44.	CULPABLE	1. guilty	2. active	3. qualified
45.	DEARTH	1. scarcity	2. demise	3. pinnacle
46.	DEFERENCE	1. disagreement	2. analysis	3. respect
47.	DEMURE	1. fickle	2. shy	3. luxurious
48.	DESOLATE	1. fancy	2. lonely	3. heated
49.	DETER	1. redirect	2. reverse	3. restrain
50.	DETRIMENT	1. danger	2. highlight	3. compliment

"POWER WORDS" QUIZ 2
Directions: select the choice that *best* defines the word in CAPITAL letter
[answers on pages 23-24]

#	WORD	1.	2.	3.
1.	DIDACTIC	inactive	definitive	informational
2.	DIFFIDENT	dissimilar	steadfast	bashful
3.	DILIGENT	restless	polite	hardworking
4.	DISCERN	distinguish	disobey	recommend
5.	DISDAIN	contradict	exaggerate	scorn
6.	DISINTERESTED	different	placid	unbiased
7.	DISPARAGE	expel	belittle	topple
8.	DIVERSITY	variety	unity	skill
9.	DOCILE	calculating	manageable	candid
10.	DOGGED	hungry	stubborn	barbaric
11.	DOGMATIC	practical	opinionated	spiteful
12.	ECCENTRIC	odd	circular	relevant
13.	EFFERVESCENT	appreciative	neglectful	excited
14.	ELEGIACAL	praiseworthy	innocent	mournful
15.	ELOQUENT	wealthy	careless	persuasive
16.	EPHEMERAL	brief	weak	emotional
17.	ERRATIC	abnormal	clumsy	loving
18.	ETHEREAL	delicate	fragrant	lofty
19.	EULOGIZE	praise	erupt	repent
20.	EUPHONY	harmony	replica	oddity
21.	EXOTIC	lustful	unusual	humorous
22.	EXTOL	exclaim	participate	praise
23.	FACILITY	existence	failure	ease
24.	FASTIDIOUS	hasty	fussy	repetitious
25.	FLIPPANT	disrespectful	dreamlike	tame
26.	FRUGAL	fertile	thrifty	faint
27.	FUTILE	immense	useless	quick
28.	GARRULOUS	meaningless	talkative	warlike
29.	GRAVITY	seriousness	weightlessness	devotion
30.	GREGARIOUS	invincible	sociable	warlike
31.	GULLIBLE	bewildered	overtrusting	intellectual
32.	HEEDLESS	unnecessary	careless	imaginary
33.	HOSTILE	unfriendly	improper	confined
34.	HUMILITY	modesty	boastfulness	shame
35.	HYPOCRITICAL	phony	precise	substandard
36.	IMMACULATE	enormous	illogical	spotless
37.	IMPARTIAL	unfavorable	unbiased	complete
38.	IMPASSIVE	unemotional	sizable	active
39.	IMPOVERISHED	crushed	poor	desolate
40.	INCESSANT	noxious	traditional	continual
41.	INDIFFERENT	unique	unconcerned	commonplace
42.	INDIGENOUS	rare	native	brilliant
43.	INDIGENT	poor	rude	sluggish
44.	INDIGNANT	resentful	mournful	humble
45.	INEVITABLE	unfriendly	unavoidable	unimportant
46.	INFAMOUS	indifferent	shameful	unknown
47.	INFLAMMABLE	resistant	influential	burnable
48.	INNOCUOUS	harmless	unpopular	irregular
49.	INTREPID	curious	despairing	fearless
50.	INUNDATE	cancel	pursue	flood

Directions: select the choice that *best* defines the word in CAPITAL letters

[answers on pages 23-24]

		1.	2.	3.
1.	IRONIC	ancient	infamous	contradictory
2.	JOCULAR	joking	indirect	portable
3.	LAMENT	cleanse	interpret	mourn
4.	LANGUISH	complain	intimidate	weaken
5.	LAUD	yell	praise	plunder
6.	LETHAL	energetic	overweight	deadly
7.	LETHARGIC	skilled	restless	sluggish
8.	LISTLESS	unenthusiastic	forgetful	unpredictable
9.	LITHE	boring	graceful	hardworking
10.	LOATHE	hesitate	obey	hate
11.	LOQUACIOUS	amiable	talkative	cooperative
12.	LUCID	tame	inferior	clear
13.	LUGUBRIOUS	gloomy	restrained	healthful
14.	MALEDICTION	curse	blessing	impediment
15.	MALICIOUS	luscious	agonizing	spiteful
16.	MEEK	unkempt	extinct	humble
17.	MELANCHOLY	sad	determined	serious
18.	METICULOUS	exact	unclear	relevant
19.	NEFARIOUS	wicked	dignified	distant
20.	NOTORIOUS	shameful	quarrelsome	unaware
21.	NOVEL	long	royal	new
22.	NOXIOUS	upset	homesick	harmful
23.	OBDURATE	satisfied	stubborn	inquisitive
24.	OBESE	honest	fat	ambitious
25.	OBJECTIVE	authentic	unbiased	unfriendly
26.	OBSCURE	extinct	unclear	mighty
27.	OMNISCIENT	short-term	all-knowing	far-reaching
28.	OPAQUE	dark	expensive	endless
29.	OSTENTATIOUS	logical	showy	vigilant
30.	PACIFY	confuse	calm	destroy
31.	PARIAH	outcast	priest	storm
32.	PARSIMONIOUS	religious	stingy	skillful
33.	PENSIVE	affordable	meditative	powerful
34.	PENURIOUS	poor	disgraceful	sensitive
35.	PERFUNCTORY	obsolete	superficial	outstanding
36.	PHILANTHROPIC	ancient	geographical	charitable
37.	PIOUS	curious	devoted	warlike
38.	PITHY	concise	hardworking	secluded
39.	PLACID	clear	unflavored	peaceful
40.	POMPOUS	obese	elegant	snobbish
41.	PRAGMATIC	opinionated	eccentric	practical
42.	PRODIGAL	spirited	easygoing	unthrifty
43.	PRODIGIOUS	wasteful	popular	immense
44.	PROFICIENT	skillful	lacking	fortunate
45.	PROFUSE	abbreviated	worthless	abundant
46.	PROLIFIC	wise	native	productive
47.	PROSAIC	colorful	unimaginative	poetic
48.	PROVOCATIVE	stimulating	favorable	vigilant
49.	PRUDENT	precise	wise	curious
50.	PUERILE	original	savage	childish

Directions: select the choice that *best* defines the word in CAPITAL letter
[answers on pages 23-24]

#	WORD	1.	2.	3.
1.	PUGNACIOUS	fighting	submissive	wise
2.	RASH	reckless	cheerful	pale
3.	RAZE	demolish	renovate	erect
4.	REFUTE	thaw	disprove	replace
5.	RELINQUISH	surrender	accuse	conquer
6.	REPREHENSIBLE	absolute	authoritative	hateful
7.	REPROACH	near	attempt	blame
8.	REPROVE	criticize	support	persist
9.	REPUDIATE	clarify	disclaim	starve
10.	RESERVED	shy	simple	domineering
11.	RETICENT	aware	virtuous	shy
12.	REVERE	advise	worship	endure
13.	RUE	deceive	divide	regret
14.	SCRUTINIZE	repair	magnify	examine
15.	SERVILE	jolly	obedient	perpetual
16.	SLOTH	fellowship	laziness	cleanliness
17.	SOMBER	tired	interesting	gloomy
18.	SOPORIFIC	sleepy	crowded	outstanding
19.	SPARTAN	sophisticated	competitive	disciplined
20.	SPURIOUS	angry	false	pointed
21.	SPURN	cleanse	reject	flee
22.	SQUANDER	contemplate	roam	waste
23.	STOIC	unemotional	endless	playful
24.	STRIDENT	quick	shrill	harsh
25.	SUBTLE	faint	underground	quick
26.	SUCCINCT	concise	dependable	fortunate
27.	SUPERFICIAL	generous	famous	shallow
28.	SUPERFLUOUS	exaggerated	unnecessary	fundamental
29.	SURLY	rude	doubtless	optimistic
30.	TACITURN	miserly	considerate	bashful
31.	TACTFUL	thoughtful	persevering	theatrical
32.	TANGIBLE	irrelevant	edible	touchable
33.	TERSE	poetic	flexible	brief
34.	TIMID	sociable	honest	shy
35.	TORRID	hardworking	rapid	sizzling
36.	TRANQUIL	sleepless	calm	sharp
37.	TRITE	scattered	unoriginal	melancholy
38.	TRIVIAL	unimportant	enthusiastic	festive
39.	VAIN	significant	hopeless	persistent
40.	VALID	ingenious	dirty	logical
41.	VERITY	greenery	experience	truth
42.	VIGILANT	alert	arrogant	courteous
43.	VILIFY	guarantee	enlighten	slander
44.	VIRULENT	muscular	poisonous	boisterous
45.	VOLATILE	patient	inexperienced	explosive
46.	WANE	decline	protest	fulfill
47.	WARY	cautious	tired	belligerent
48.	WAX	intensify	suspect	demand
49.	ZEAL	enthusiasm	hatred	speed
50.	ZENITH	storm	rendezvous	peak

CRITICAL READING PASSAGES: PLAYING THE GAME ONE PARAGRAPH AT A TIME

SPORTS-ANALOGY (basketball):

You've got the basketball in your hand. What is your main goal?

Many people mistakenly believe that the main goal of the Critical Reading section is "to read and understand the passage," but that's like saying the main goal in basketball is "to dribble the ball." Dribbling is important but not the main goal!

SPORTS-ANALOGY Answer:

The main goal is to *score*!

The main goal on *any* part of the **SAT**, including the Critical Reading section, is to **get the correct answer** (to "score"!). Everything you do should be with the intent of getting the correct answer (or, at the very least, putting down an answer you think is correct).

- Unless you're a very good reader, do *not* read the entire passage first. *
- Unless you have time to burn, do *not* look over the questions first.

Instead, after quickly reading the introductory *italics*, look at those first/earliest questions that refer to or are related to paragraph 1. (In general, questions follow the **sequence** of the reading passage: the first question/questions cover material discussed in paragraph 1, the next question/questions cover paragraph 2, etc. The final questions often concern the passage as a whole.) **Be sure to know what the questions are asking.** Then read paragraph 1 with one objective: to **answer these questions** (and don't forget to *eliminate!*).

Then do the same with paragraph 2, etc. **Read each paragraph in its entirety**, because although line numbers may be specific the answer is often found elsewhere *in that same paragraph.*

* In shorter passages (usually found immediately after the Sentence Completion portion) questions are often based upon an entire passage, which necessitates a complete reading prior to answering any of the questions. The strategies outlined here are to better handle the longer passages, which are the primary area of weakness for many **SAT** test takers.

(A question may occasionally appear out of place and need to be answered when appropriate, but you will find that most questions are in sequential order and can be answered as you continue reading the passage.)

Once you have finished reading the passage, **you should also have answered all the questions**! You don't need to worry about re-reading the passage or going back after reading the entire passage to answer questions. As a result, you won't:

1) run out of time before being able to answer the questions

2) be forced to read a lengthy, boring passage and need to remember all that you read in order to answer the questions

3) become frustrated before you even begin this section

Important Note: Unlike any other part of the **SAT**, the Critical Reading questions do *not* necessarily go in order of EASY-to-HARD. Because they instead go in general order of the passage, you really can't be sure where the HARD questions are. In fact, the last few Critical Reading questions are usually MEDIUM questions, which – like Free Throws – are a valuable source of points! In other words, don't give up on the final few Critical Reading questions; they are usually *not* difficult!

VALUABLE STRATEGIC ADVICE

Elimination is especially crucial in the Reading portion of the **SAT**: Look for **any error** in either of the five choices, because all it takes is <u>one incorrect word</u> to invalidate the entire choice! If you look for **<u>wrong</u>** answers (and *eliminate* them), you will surely improve on your overall Reading score! The **SAT** testmakers love to include choices that sound perfect yet have one tiny glaring error – don't be fooled by them!

Look for (and *eliminate*) **<u>wrong answers</u>**, and you'll be amazed at the results!

Here are a few sample reading passages – a short reading passage followed by two longer reading passages, all of vastly different subject matter. Remember that it doesn't matter how interesting the passage is; what matters is whether you can answer the questions correctly in the allotted time.

Apply the appropriate reading strategy and see if it helps you stay focused on the task at hand. If you are a good reader, you may wish to see if you can do better by reading the passage first. Or you may find yourself adjusting your strategy to address each specific reading. After all, no game is played the same way throughout; you've got to be flexible in your approach to best confront changing conditions in the game.

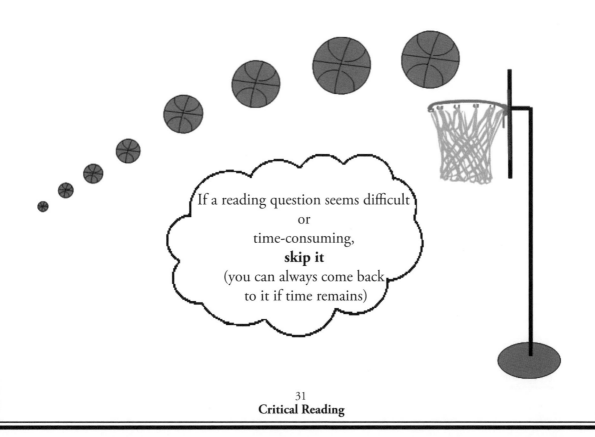

If a reading question seems difficult
or
time-consuming,
skip it
(you can always come back
to it if time remains)

The following passage briefly examines the validity and reliability of the **SAT**.

[answers on page 33]

The Scholastic Assessment Test has long been a controversial measurement of students' abilities. Counselors as well as administrators claim that its validity and reliability are suspect, that it measures little more than a student's ability to take tests under pressure and does not consistently gauge the level of verbal and math proficiency.

Validity and reliability are critical terms to consider in the judging of any examination. For a test to be valid, it must measure abilities relevant to the college experience that lies ahead. Reliability, on the other hand, indicates the consistency of the examination to produce similar results over a period of time. If a test lacks validity, the contents must be reviewed; if it lacks reliability, the test as a whole serves no predictable function.

Despite objections from its critics, the Scholastic Assessment Test continues to provide the country with a standardized benchmark upon which students' futures oftentimes depend. Whether one test can accurately measure a student's verbal and math proficiency is, for now, a moot point; suffice it to say that the Scholastic Assessment Test is the best we have, given our criteria for validity and reliability.

(circle your answer)

1. What is the author's tone in this passage?
   A) confident that the **SAT** is reliable and valid
   B) alarmed that the **SAT** has become too widespread in its administration
   C) indifferent to the test
   D) mixed feelings regarding the pros and cons of the test
   E) reckless disregard for the feelings of students

2. Which of the following is/are NOT discussed in the passage?
   I.   definition of terms
   II. specific scores
   III. advantages & disadvantages
   A) I only
   B) II only
   C) I and II
   D) I and III
   E) I, II, and III

3. How would the author best evaluate the merits of an examination?
   A) If it is not valid, it should be discarded.
   B) If it is not reliable, it should be discarded.
   C) If it is valid, it does not need reliability.
   D) Validity and reliability have no bearing on the merits of an examination.
   E) A good examination emphasizes reliability over validity.

4. It can be inferred in the final paragraph that the author
   A) is disgusted with the claims of the **SAT**.
   B) supports the **SAT** wholeheartedly.
   C) vocally seeks immediate change in the construction of the **SAT**.
   D) favors test-takers over non-test-takers in situations requiring academic⁻proficiency evaluation.
   E) questions the merits of any one examination for purposes of scholastic measurement.

5. The best title for this passage is
   A) Judging the Merits of the **SAT**
   B) The Future of the **SAT**
   C) Shortcomings of the **SAT**
   D) Test-takers Versus Non-test-takers
   E) Validity Versus Reliability

In the previous Critical Reading Quiz, you may have noticed a variety of questions being asked, with focus on:

- TONE (question 1)

- DETAILS in the passage (question 2)

- INFERENCE based on the author's attitude (question 3)

- INFERENCE based on information given (question 4)

- MAIN IDEA of the passage (question 5)

Although not every Reading passage contains one of each of these kinds of questions, most questions asked will likely fall into one of the categories. Some categories (such as exemplified in questions 1 and 5) can be answered quickly and efficiently, whereas others (such as questions 2-4) require more consideration. Questions concerning DETAILS are likely to consume the most time, and therefore you should caution yourself not to get too involved answering them. **Time is your most prized possession; don't use too much of it on any one question.**

Critical Reading
Quiz 1 **Answers**

1. **D**	4. **E**
2. **B**	5. **A**
3. **B**	

See how well your Reading strategies work on the following two passages. Allow no more than fifteen minutes to answer the questions. If you finish early, go back and more carefully read whichever passage you prefer. You'll be amazed at how manageable the **SAT** Reading portion can become with your step-by-step strategy approach!

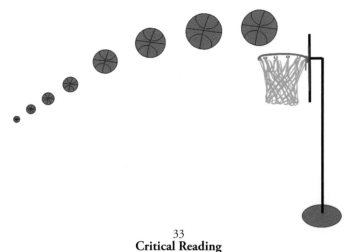

[answers on page 182]

The following excerpt is from a story about a couple who have found
their paths and ideologies quickly diverging.

Line

Billy tried to respond to her question, but Tom cut him off. "What on earth does it matter what he thinks?" Tom sneered. "He's only along for the ride."

Another evening altercation had begun, but Sandy knew this would be the climactic, decisive long-overdue one.

5   "So you're speaking for him now? Is that it, Tom?"

"I'll speak for me," Tom replied curtly. "I have no illusions, so say what you want about me. I don't pretend that a paintbrush and a canvas, or any of those other flower-power ideas you're so hot on, are any substitute for pulling your weight. I never meant for this to be a permanent live-in arrangement, you know. And by the way, he's no Matisse."

10   There was a long, cold silence. Tom had never said anything like that over the last four months, Sandy thought, but perhaps he had been thinking it all along. Perhaps his anger on the issue of "pulling one's weight" had as much to do with her as with Billy. Perhaps she was being sent a message. Sandy closed her eyes and rubbed them. When she opened them again, she realized Billy was gone.

15   "Now you listen to me," Sandy began in a low, threatening tone. "I didn't ask you to invest your time and your money in Billy's artwork. That was your idea. You were the one who said that we needed to add some color to our lives. And if you think I should get a job, why not do us both a favor and come out and say it? I don't mind work. Granted, I don't have any trust fund to coast on. But I don't mind work."

20   "I never wanted him to destroy us, Sandy," Tom responded softly.

"All he did was what you asked him to!" Sandy barked, "You're the one who lost your nerve since Amherst – and, of course, a little more."

Tom shot her a blank, uncomprehending look, amazed that she would, even in private, make open reference to a deep secret he had told her he never wanted to discuss under any 25 circumstances.

"Look," he said slowly. "It was my fault for inviting him to stay here. Now it's time for him to go. Let's leave it at that."

Sandy stared at him. "No," she said quietly, "let's not."

(circle your answer)

1. Which of the best describes the tone of the conversation between Tom and Sandy? A) belligerent and hostile B) sympathetic and searching C) unconcerned and dispassionate D) confused and responsive E) tranquil and sedate	2. What is the central issue being discussed? A) dropping Billy off after giving him a ride B) differing beliefs which have alienated Tom and Sandy C) Billy's longer-than-expected stay at the house D) authority and discipline E) the restoration of flower power

3. In what way can Billy's initial role in the couple's household best be described?
   A) he added conflict to their lives
   B) he provided stability to their financial affairs
   C) he provided the legwork for their endeavors
   D) he was there simply for the experience
   E) he was a hostage to their artistic inventiveness

4. What is the "deep secret" (line 24) Tom has been trying to guard?
   A) his inability to father a child
   B) his uncontrollable temper
   C) the loss of his creative faculties
   D) his obsession with the past
   E) the "secret" is not identified

5. It can be inferred from the final sentence in the passage that Tom and Sandy are most likely going to
   A) resolve the issue and resume their collective pursuits.
   B) continue to support one another but at a greater distance than before.
   C) ask Billy for future advice concerning their pursuits.
   D) discontinue their intimate association with one another.
   E) terminate their present pursuits while jointly initiating others.

In this passage, the Keynesian school of economic thought is touted for its resilience to and dependability amid the volatile world of modern economic trends.

Twentieth-century economics has introduced several new theories, counterbalancing technological innovations with equally innovative fiscal maneuvers, addressing new global competitiveness with theories of financial aggressiveness. The Keynesian analysis typifies one such bold attempt to quantify the chameleon-like mechanics of business life.

According to John Maynard Keynes, publisher of *The General Theory of Employment, Interest and Money* (1936), the level of effective demand for goods will at times exceed the production capacity, at other times fall below production levels. This shifting balance necessitates on the part of producers a keener understanding as to how key factors can be manipulated to affect demand and regain harmony. Foremost in the quest to keep the pendulum balanced is the role of government, whose policies risk rampant inflation on one extreme and severe unemployment on the other.

Several policy implementations may have a moderating effect on the pendulum of productivity. A tighter money supply and reduced government spending best serve to dampen demand, effect lower interest rates and thereby stem spiraling inflation. But when the one-time paper-prosperity turns to a dearth of spending capital and an inevitable increase in unemployment, an easing of the money supply becomes necessary. Once the economic footing appears solid, the pendulum again begins its motion towards the other side and resumed disharmony.

Keynesian theory is a theory of equilibrium, not static mathematics. It quantifies an elusive goal, adding sufficient variables to accommodate the necessary fluctuations prevalent in today's business world, yet not muddying the waters with variables too copious to allow consistency and predictability. Whether this theory will survive the 21st century is immaterial; it has placed economists in the battlefield, armed to combat new and unforeseen adversaries waiting on the horizon.

6. According to the passage, why was Keynesian analysis valuable to 20th-century economists?
   A) It helped explain the shifting of the economic cycle.
   B) It proved all other theories to be inaccurate.
   C) It allowed economists to precisely determine future business cycles.
   D) It placed responsibility for economic stability on the government.
   E) It encouraged producers to manipulate the market to maximize profitability.

7. It can be inferred from the passage that the government is most likely to curb the printing of cash in times of
   A) high unemployment, low productivity
   B) spiraling inflation, high unemployment
   C) severe inventory shortages, low unemployment
   D) high interest rates, excessive government spending
   E) low interest rates, uncontrolled inflation

8. The author treats Keynesian economics with
   A) unqualified reverence
   B) skeptical acceptance
   C) ambivalence and disregard
   D) investigative concern
   E) optimistic support

9. Which of the following future situations would most likely make Keynesian economics obsolete?
   A) a world-wide depression
   B) new technological advancements
   C) a socialistic world order
   D) a uniform worldwide monetary system
   E) international trade expansion

10. Which of the following pairs an advantage and disadvantage relating to Keynesian economics?
    A) security; ambiguity
    B) adaptability; mismanagement
    C) reliability; corruptibility
    D) universality; inexactness
    E) consistency; impracticality

There are also **2**-passage readings on the **SAT**, but your strategy-approach should not change. If you follow the questions as you read each paragraph, you'll find that the answers appear just as they do in a single-passage reading. This is because, once again, the questions go generally in order of the passage: the first questions cover the first passage, the next group covers the second passage, and the final few ask to compare the two readings.

The following sample readings should offer you the opportunity to see how well your approach works on the **2**-passage portion. In addition, each answer is explained in detail, offering a thorough defense of any questions you may have answered incorrectly. It is important to see why you may have answered a question incorrectly, because only by identifying your errors can you improve on and eliminate such mistakes in the future.

The following two passages concern the similarities between the lives and assassinations of two American Presidents. Passage 1 reflects upon events common to both; Passage 2 is a reaction to the phenomenon discussed in Passage 1.

PASSAGE 1

Line

Striking parallels exist between the lives of Abraham Lincoln and John F. Kennedy, two American Presidents whose terms were each cut tragically short by an assassin's bullet. Though politics usually shares nothing with parapsychology, the uncanny similarity of events surrounding the lives of these two men might well bolster one's belief in the supernatural.

5   Abraham Lincoln, elected in 1860 as the 16th President of the United States, was an active proponent of Civil Rights, issuing in 1863 the Emancipation Proclamation which liberated the slaves in the Southern states. Later in 1863, he delivered the Gettysburg Address which reaffirmed the principles of equality laid down a hundred years earlier by the nation's founding fathers.

10   John F. Kennedy, elected in 1960 as the 35th President of the United States, was also a social activist whose ambitious support of Civil Rights was evidenced by his innovative New Frontier program and his establishment of the Peace Corps to assist those oppressed abroad.

Of greater curiosity are the events surrounding each great man's death. Both occurred during public events, and each involved a shooting. Prior to the murders, each President was
15   advised not to appear at the site. Mr. Lincoln was so advised by his personal secretary, named Kennedy; Mr. Kennedy was given the precaution by his secretary, Mrs. Lincoln.

The lives of the assassins themselves also share eerie similarities. John Wilkes Booth, Lincoln's attacker, was born in 1839; Lee Harvey Oswald, Booth's counterpart, was born in 1939. In addition, neither of these two men ever went to trial for murder: each was himself
20   shot and killed shortly thereafter.

Even the aftermaths of the tragic deaths contain spine-chilling similarities. Andrew Johnson, born in 1808, assumed the Presidency upon Lincoln's death; Lyndon Johnson, born in 1908, assumed the Presidency upon Kennedy's death. Both Johnsons were Southern Democrats who had previously served in the U.S. Senate. Both served as Presidents during politically
25   turbulent times, and both declined to run for office in a subsequent election – Andrew Johnson in 1869, Lyndon Johnson in 1968.

A popular expression states that "Religion and politics don't mix"; however, an examination of the facts and circumstances surrounding the lives and deaths of both Presidents seems to suggest that otherworldly forces may at times interact with mundane ones. America can only
30   look with apprehension to the year 2060, when yet another statesman will rise to what may well be another ill-fated Presidency.

Perhaps more than ever before, religion and politics may need to mix; this future period of uncertainty could well be one in which a nation's prayers may best serve to ward off the spell of tragic events begun two centuries earlier.

Line

35   The so-called similarity between the presidencies of Lincoln and Kennedy reflects the
temperament of a nation that all too easily subscribes to mystical and superstitiously fallacious
logic. A further analysis of these two historical figures will expose this folly.

        Para-historians have noted that "Lincoln" and "Kennedy" each contains seven letters, of which
"N" is the only one in the alphabet common to both. In fact, the letter "N" is used twice in each
40   name. However, we can further analyze alphabetical correlations between these two beloved
leaders to such a degree that everything, even the obvious, begins to seem eerily coincidental.
The first letters of "Lincoln" and "Kennedy," L and K, are both consonants as well as adjoining
letters in the alphabet; more strikingly, one letter in each name is used exactly three times: "A" in
Abraham Lincoln"; "N" in John Kennedy." In an even more stupefying display of alphabetical
45   and numerical prestidigitation, each President's full name averages exactly seven letters: Abraham
Lincoln – two words, fourteen letters; John Fitzgerald Kennedy – three words, twenty-one letters.
The magic numbers three (mentioned earlier) and seven add up to 10, the number of letters in
JFK's middle name, Fitzgerald. The letter "J", amazingly, is also the tenth letter of the alphabet.

        Through a warped mirror of reflection, the assassinations of these two great figures also bear
50   a striking resemblance. Each man was sitting down as he was shot (and lying down, thereafter)
and each was shot by a bullet fired from a gun (though Kennedy was shot at several times with a
rifle). The name of each assassin – John Wilkes Booth and Lee Harvey Oswald – consists of three
words (Kennedy's predator could therefore have been Lyndon Baines Johnson, but that's another
theory) and each outlived the man he shot (a correlation that might include other greats such as
55   Julius Caesar and Mahatma Gandhi).

        With so many fascinating parallels so easily uncovered, it is no wonder that a gullible public
might interpret the events as preordained. But I submit that, as with television psychics and
stock market prognosticators, correlations are a product of reflection, not prediction: everything
is clearer with 20-20 hindsight. For example, it was reported that both Presidents were dissuaded
60   from attending the ill-fated public events, but so too are we all faced with daily decisions: should
we take the bus or car to work; should we eat eggs or cereal for breakfast; should we go through
the yellow traffic light or not? Were we to regard every decision as momentous and potentially
life-threatening, would it not behoove us to simply stay home and not venture out at all? With such
apprehension, who would ever wish to dare anything new, least of all aspire to such a tragically
65   lofty position as to one day become President of the United States?

        There comes a time in everyone's life when rabbit's feet and lucky socks need to be replaced
with personal responsibility and commitment. For those wishing to become President in the
year 2060, let no tales of witchcraft or divine voodoo derail your ambitions. In a land easily
mesmerized by occult nonsense and groundless phobias, it is all too easy for a person to be led
70   down a path of fear-induced anxiety. Two great Presidents gave their lives in defiance of such
narrow-mindedness; we should laud such rebel spirit and refute overtly offensive attempts by so-
called mystics to manipulate us through misguided, purposeless superstition.

1. Passage **1** is primarily concerned with
   A) philosophy
   B) democratic ideals
   C) famous people
   D) a tragic situation
   E) similarities of historical events

2. In line 9, "fathers" most nearly means
   A) heads of households
   B) political leaders
   C) architects
   D) teachers
   E) natives

3. In line 18, "counterpart" refers to
   A) a President
   B) a similar event
   C) a Vice-President
   D) an assassin
   E) an exception

4. Why does the author of Passage **1** look upon the year 2060 with apprehension?
   A) It may be the year an ill-starred person assumes office.
   B) It will climax a half century of societal depravity.
   C) It represents an arbitrary year in an uncertain future.
   D) It may be the year a tragic event takes place.
   E) It may mark the beginning of years of political upheaval.

5. Which of the following words from Passage **1** is the target of mockery in Passage **2**?
   A) parapsychology (line 3)
   B) equality (line 8)
   C) curiosity (line 13)
   D) religion (line 32)
   E) politics (line 3)

6. In which paragraph does Passage **2** begin to resort to overtly outlandish and ludicrous correlations?
   A) paragraph one (beginning on line 35)
   B) paragraph two (beginning on line 38)
   C) paragraph three (beginning on line 49)
   D) paragraph four (beginning on line 56)
   E) paragraph five (beginning on line 66)

7. In what manner does "stupefying" (Passage **2**, line 44) help convey the author's overall tone?
   A) The word implies both "amazement" and "dullness."
   B) The word is purposely misused.
   C) It has no "N"s in it, accentuating the meaninglessness of the argument.
   D) Its use conveys that the public is "stupid."
   E) It effectively exhibits the author's elitist attitude.

8. What information is revealed in Passage **2** that is not mentioned in Passage **1**?
   I. the year of the assassinations
   II. the names of the assassins
   III. a President's middle name
   A) I only
   B) I and II
   C) II only
   D) II and III
   E) III only

9. What is the primary purpose for the parenthetical comments (lines 50-55) in Passage **2**?
   A) They add critical information.
   B) They present the author's personal opinions.
   C) They ridicule the points being made.
   D) They question the reliability of the data.
   E) They bolster the arguments presented.

10. What word would best describe how the author of Passage **2** considers the author of Passage **1**?
   A) evil
   B) timid
   C) confused
   D) misled
   E) demented

11. In which of the following did the two Presidents <u>not</u> share a curious similarity?
   I.   the names of their secretaries
   II. the years of their birth
   III. the letters in their names
   A) I only
   B) I and II
   C) II only
   D) II and III
   E) III only

12. The topic being discussed in both passages most closely concerns
   A) the hereafter
   B) religion
   C) historical biography
   D) the occult
   E) politics

13. Which pair of words used in Passage **1** and **2**, respectively, best summarizes each author's attitude toward the subject matter that has been conveyed to the public?
   A) uncanny; gullible
   B) eerie; mesmerized
   C) spine-chilling; warped
   D) ambitious; offensive
   E) turbulent; purposeless

14. Which of the following do the authors each make reference to in the passages?
   I.   Civil Rights
   II. a saying
   III. the future
   A) I only
   B) I and II
   C) I and III
   D) II and III
   E) I, II and III

15. Both authors would most likely agree that
   A) numbers can be fascinating
   B) the future is unpredictable
   C) both Lincoln and Kennedy were destined to be shot
   D) religion and politics don't mix
   E) superstition is a powerful social force

1. **E** When a question asks what a Passage is "primarily" about, you need to identify what is <u>generally</u> being discussed. (Hopefully, you waited until later to answer this question – always answer the "general" questions after you've had a chance to read through the entire passage.) Some of the choices may be discussed in the passage, but the question is focused on the overall idea that runs throughout the passage. Passage **1** is primarily concerned with the similarities between the two Presidents, especially the assassinations of both. The focus of the argument is on the events surrounding the assassination – what happened before, during and after. **A** and **B** are not related to the essay. **D** is not the main focus of the analysis in Passage **1**, and although the passage does discuss two famous people (re: choice **C**), the main focus is on the events that have made the lives and deaths of both eerily similar in nature.

2. **C** When a question seeks the **in-context definition** of a given word, the best way to arrive at the answer is to substitute the choices in place of the word: Lincoln "reaffirmed the principles of equality laid down a hundred years earlier by the nation's founding _____."

        A) heads of household
        B) political leaders
        C) architects
        D) teachers ("founding teachers"?!)
        E) natives ("founding natives"?!)

It's clear from the paragraph that the reference is to those who initiated the "principles of equality." Only **B** and **C** remain viable candidates, of which **C** is precisely to whom the reference is alluding.

3. **D** This is a very easy question: it is easy to answer and easy to get correct. The reference-name (John Wilkes Booth) is actually in line 16. Take advantage of these simple line-number questions; they are quick and easy to answer.

4. **A** Unlike the previous two questions, this one is not easy to answer and therefore should be deferred until a closer reading* has taken place or quickly answered after preliminary elimination. According to line 30, 2060 is the year another statesman will assume the Presidency. **B** and **C** can be eliminated, leaving us with three choices to look at (or to guess from). A closer reading of the paragraph will reveal that not only is this the year the President is elected to office, but this may be the same person who will soon be assassinated. The year does not represent the "beginning of years of political upheaval" and is not the year that any assassination is expected to take place. It simply marks the start of the term for a President who may eventually become the victim of an assassination.

5. **A** At first glance, this looks to be an easy question. But further inspection will show that each choice must be carefully considered in comparison with a counterpart word mocking it in Passage **2**.

---

   * For advanced readers, the explanations occasionally refer to a "closer reading". If you are not seeking a 650+ score, you should answer the question without attempting to re-read. However, if you are very adept in reading and time-management, you may seriously wish to consider the option of a more thorough 'second reading'.

"Mockery" implies making fun of through ridicule, so the word must be the target of some verbal attack. "Equality" is not a word that is mocked in Passage **2**, nor is "religion" or "politics." "Curiosity" could be a word worthy of mockery, but there is no instance where the author of Passage **2** picks up on the word to mock it. "Parapsychology," however, is mocked on line 38; the author uses his own "para-" word "para-historians," whom he shortly thereafter exposes as nothing but charlatans displaying "alphabetical and numerical prestidigitation." There is a direct association between the two "para-" words – one used seriously in Passage **1**, the other word used mockingly in Passage **2**.

6. **C** This type of question is usually easy to answer. It is based on the essay's construction as much as its content. The key is to identify where the overtly "outlandish and ludicrous correlations" begin. Paragraph two hints at some underhanded trickery relating to letters in each President's name, but only in Paragraph three does the author resort to obvious silliness, clearly evidenced in the parenthetical comments.

7. **A** At first review this question looks easy to answer, but upon closer inspection you will see that it combines two very difficult elements: interpretation and vocabulary. You need to determine "What is the purpose for the author using 'stupefying'?" as well as "What does 'stupefying' mean?" Fortunately, even without a clue as to the true meaning of the word in question you can eliminate irrelevant or silly choices such as **C** and **E**. The question remains as to the definition of "stupefying" and whether the author has used the word correctly or incorrectly (and, if incorrectly, whether he has done so on purpose). Those with a well-grounded vocabulary know that "stupefying" has two definitions, one of which implies filling a person with "amazement" and the other which more closely means "dulling a person's senses," as alcohol might do. The word's double-entendre serves to better illustrate the author's sarcastic tone, on one hand suggesting that the number/letter correlations are "amazing" while at the same time implying that the public is so unaware as to be "dull" to the truth as if in a drunken stupor. The question is intriguing and simple-looking, but the answer is very difficult to get correct.

8. **E** Whenever a question lists possible choices which are incorporated into the answer-choices, you can be sure this question requires a more thorough review of the passage(s). You will need to examine each passage to see whether the points were discussed, then compare to see which of the points are contained within the choices. These are usually easy questions to answer correctly, though not necessarily questions that can be answered quickly. From a second and closer reading, you will notice that the years mentioned in Passage **1** include each President's year of birth, the year each was elected to office, the year each assassin was born, and the year the succeeding President was born. Passage **2**, however, lists no year other than 2060, which eliminates **I** (and therefore **A** and **B**.) <u>Both</u> essays mention the names of the assassins, eliminating **C** and **D** as possibilities. A deeper reading (which may not be necessary if four choices have already been eliminated!) will reveal that John Kennedy's middle name, "Fitzgerald," is mentioned in Passage **2**; reviewing Passage **1**, you will notice there is no mention of the full middle name, simply the initial "F". (By the way, Lyndon <u>Baines</u> Johnson is also mentioned only in Passage **2**, giving even more opportunity to get it correct!)

9. **C** This is a <u>focus question</u> – a question that refers to specific lines and is concerned <u>only</u> with the content of these lines. When you see a question that asks specifically what certain lines (or a specific paragraph) refer to, focus on that portion only — don't interpret unasked-for lines.

These questions are usually not difficult as long as you don't stray from the focused lines. At first glance, this focus question looks very easy to answer. In one sense it is (as are most focus questions), but in order to answer this question correctly the parenthetical comments must be interpreted as the author intended: as sarcasm. Then the words will begin to make more sense; they simply bring out the silliness of the original points. For example, it may be curious that both people were shot while sitting, but it seems obvious that after they were shot they would be lying down. The parenthetical remark makes the original observation trivial and seeks to expose it as just as absurd as the more tongue-in-cheek observation. Thus, the question can be answered quickly and easily but only with a proper understanding of the author's tone – which may require a second and more detailed review.

10. **D** This type of question is easy to answer once you've gotten a general idea what the passages are about. It may not be an easy question to get correct, but it is an easy one to answer quickly. Passage **2** has made fun of Passage **1**; the author of Passage **2** thus considers the other author as either a bit silly or simply ill-advised. The first author is not looked upon as "evil" or "timid," which eliminates **A** and **B**. You must now select from "confused," "misled" and "demented." Choice **E** means "crazy," a description that does not accurately reflect the tone of the second passage toward the author of Passage **1**. "Confused" implies that the first author does not know what he is saying, yet the second author does not question the facts at all. Rather, he feels the earlier author is stating facts that, though well-intended and acceptable at face-value, are misleading in assuming that these coincidences imply some greater forces are at work. He therefore looks upon the earlier author as a person misled by randomly-selected though admittedly-coincidental and curious information.

11. **C** Similar to question 8, this question requires a more-detailed review; answering it initially will use up more time than you care to give up after the first quick reading. But when you do eventually return in the remaining minutes to answer this question, you will find it straightforward and therefore quite easy to answer correctly. Because the question is not asking you to compare the passages, you need only read to locate if the two elements mentioned share a curious similarity. Passage **1** clearly mentions the curious similarity in the Presidents' secretaries' names, and both passages discuss the letter-formations in the names (Passage **2**, however, has done so in mocking fashion). But nowhere is there mention of the year of each President's birth, though the years of the birth of their successors have been stated. ***Elimination*** is once again the best strategic approach to determining the best answer.

12. **D** As with question 1, this question is general and therefore quick and easy to answer. The key is to eliminate what is <u>not</u> the most general issue being discussed. "The hereafter" refers to "heaven," which is not the topic of discussion, nor do the essays concern themselves with "politics" but rather the lives of two political leaders. "Religion" is never mentioned except as an afterthought in the expression "Religion and politics don't mix." Thus, **A**, **B** and **E** have been eliminated. The decision is between whether the essays are primarily concerned with "biography" or "the occult." Your first instinct will probably tell you that it is about those eerie coincidences in the two men's lives. <u>Trust your instincts; they usually will guide you to conclusions based on the reading itself, not on second-thought interpretations.</u>

The essays are historical in nature and are biographical in content, but the main topic is in the eerie similarities found common in both Presidents' lives. ("Similarities" is mentioned in the introductory italics, by the way.) In other words, the focus is on the "occult," those mystical forces beyond the normal world that have similarly affected the two historical figures.

13. **C** As with the last question, this one seems easy to answer but again requires a deeper understanding of the tone of each passage. The author of the first Passage is very serious about the subject; the author of the second Passage is equally as serious but in exposing the errors in logic of the earlier "occult" theory. *Elimination* is once again the key approach here: look for any word that does not answer the question. For example, the first author has not viewed the events as "turbulent," nor has the second author viewed the subject matter as "mesmerizing." You needn't worry about the other half of each choice: **B** and **E** are eliminated. Looking at the remaining three choices, you might feel hesitant selecting "ambitious" as a word summarizing the first author's attitude about the theory, and indeed you'd be correct in eliminating **D** as well. **A** sounds correct – "uncanny" surely fits the first author's perspective regarding the coincidental nature of the events surrounding both Presidents. However, though "gullible" describes how the second author views the public, it does not reflect how he views the *subject matter*. Instead, he calls the theory of coincidences a distorted theory which has been manipulated to deceive the public into believing such superstitions. In other words, the subject matter has been "warped" to bolster the "occult" theory. (By the way, "spine-chilling," "uncanny" and "eerie" could each be used to describe the first author's attitude toward the subject matter; it was the *second* word of the pair that eventually determined the best answer.)

14. **D** We have seen this type of problem twice before. By now you know this may be easy to answer, though not until after a more-thorough review. Passage **1** discusses the Civil Rights issue, but Passage **2** never mentions it. We can therefore eliminate **A**, **B**, **C** and **E**. That was quick! This question simply worked itself out without any deeper analysis needed. But for the curious, both passages do reflect on the future, each referring to the year 2060. The saying "Religion and politics don't mix" is mentioned in Passage **1**; and though never directly referred to as a saying, lines 58-59 in Passage **2** do allude to the saying that "everything is clearer with 20-20 hindsight." This could have been a difficult answer had it not been that the elimination of **I** settled the issue all by itself!

15. **E** This final question seems quite innocuous; it simply requires a general understanding of the tone of each passage. But the comparative nature of the question is deceivingly difficult. *Elimination* of obviously-wrong answers is imperative. **B** and **C** can be quickly eliminated: the author of Passage **1** would not agree that the future is unpredictable and the author of Passage **2** would not subscribe to any theory that predestiny plays a significant role in past or future events. **A** sounds feasible, but "fascinating" does not seem to be the appropriate adjective for either author – "eerie" would more closely fit as a description from the first author; "deceiving" would be a more appropriate adjective given by the second. **D** applies well to the author of the first passage, but the second passage's author offers no comment regarding whether religion and politics are related. Instead, he simply implies that occult theories and superstition have no logical validity and do not relate (except by sheer coincidence) with real events. Both authors would agree that superstition plays a major role in influencing society; the difference is that the second author does not believe the public should be so gullible.

CHANGING ANSWERS RARELY BENEFITS THE TEST-TAKER. MORE OFTEN THAN NOT, IN FACT, SUCH SECOND THOUGHTS CHANGE A CORRECT ANSWER TO AN INCORRECT ONE!

SO UNLESS YOU KNOW YOU SELECTED, BY MISTAKE, AN INCORRECT ANSWER, STICK WITH YOUR FIRST CHOICE!

GENERAL ADVICE: CRITICAL READING

To hone your skills on this portion of the **SAT**, it is highly recommended that you practice with actual sample **SAT**s (be sure they are *College Board* publications because the College Board are the **SAT** test-makers). See how well the answer-as-you-read strategy approach works for you – and if you answer a question incorrectly, check to see what level it was. If it was a Level 1, 2 or 3, be sure to review the question and correct your error. If it was a Level 4 or 5, then it was obviously a hard problem and may not be worth looking into any deeper.

SPORTS-ANALOGY

"Practice makes perfect" (Well, this may not be totally accurate, but practice sure does help make one better in the sport!)

On the **SAT**, practice and review will indeed help you become familiar with the type of questions asked and will also build confidence in all sections, including the Critical Reading portion. Especially important is that the answer-as-you-read approach will save you time and enable you to answer all questions with the least effort. And of course, narrowing the field through *elimination* of incorrect answer-choices will make your final selections even more likely to be the correct answers!

This approach does not ignore the fact that the key to getting good answers is by *reading* the passage, but it's sure a whole lot easier to do when you know what you're reading for: to *answer the questions* (and nothing else!). And although your score may not be "perfect," with this effective game plan <u>you'll be amazed at how well you can do!</u>

SAT

Mathematical

Reasoning

Section

SAT MATH SECTION: THE MOST IMPORTANT
5TH-GRADE TEST YOU'LL EVER TAKE!

Did you know that a major reason for poor **SAT** Math scores is that students think it's a high school test rather than a commonsense arithmetic test?!

SPORTS-ANALOGY (basketball):

It is very difficult to play against someone you think is 6' 5" when in fact they are only 5' 6" tall! By misjudging how to play against the competition, it is easy to fall victim to misplaced energies and serious miscalculations.

The same misjudgment repeats itself time and time again on the **SAT**, with a majority of errors occurring by:

1) misreading the problem

2) adding or multiplying incorrectly

3) filling in the wrong bubble by mistake

4) not answering what is being asked

These aren't "Math" errors; these are basic, commonsense silly errors. And they are easily avoidable by working slowly and carefully.

Let's now take a general look at the **SAT** Math section
and formulate a game-plan approach.

By all means, write down all computational work on the test booklet! Don't place

unnecessary strain on your brain – use all available space to compute, draw diagrams,

underline key words, and eliminate incorrect answers.

But don't forget to bubble your answers on the answer-sheet as soon as you solve

each problem!

SAT MATH: DO WHAT YOU KNOW, NOT WHAT YOU DON'T KNOW

On the **SAT** Math portion, the easy problems are predictably at the beginning, and these are the ones you want to get correct. But unlike the "elimination" game-plan approach effective in the Critical Reading section, Math problems generally need to be *solved*. Your approach is therefore to take whatever time you need to *solve* the problem correctly. <u>Do the problems you can; skip those you don't understand.</u>

| SPORTS-ANALOGY (basketball): |

If you can't make the shot, don't take the shot.

Unlike a question in the Critical Reading section – where you want to select the **best** answer – each problem in the Math section requires the *correct* answer. As a result, whatever Math problems you answer should be *correct*. If you have made an error, it will probably be due to either a silly mistake or a misunderstanding of the question. Therefore, work carefully to avoid making careless errors (and don't waste energy on problems you don't understand) and you will achieve your optimal score.

If your goal is to reach 500, all you need to do is get $^1/_2$ of the problems correct and skip all the rest. Therefore, <u>for scores in the 500-range the game-plan strategy is clear: do the "easy" half</u>, **but be sure you get them *correct!***

> When working on any **SAT** Math problem, a valuable suggestion is to <u>underline</u> key words such as <u>integer</u>, <u>greatest</u>, <u>must be true</u>, <u>positive</u>, etc. to avoid making careless reading errors. In addition, underline the specific question (e.g. What is <u>x + 10</u>; What is the measure of the <u>largest</u> angle; Which of the following is <u>not</u> possible . . .). Careless mistakes are the easiest to avoid <u>if</u> you take your time when reading the question and understand exactly what is being asked!

If your goal is to score in the 600⁺ range, then you'll really need to try to answer all the Math questions (and get most of them correct!). The following pages contain a basic review of math skills covered on the **SAT**. Though many **SAT** problems are dressed up to look more difficult or confusing, they all contain the basic elements covered in the next few pages. Use the provided samples as a "checklist" to be sure you understand how to do each type of problem. If you haven't learned a skill (or if you've forgotten the skill because it's from years past), take the time to become familiar with the problem. For some, it means going back and re-learning how to add and subtract fractions, while for others it may mean learning or reviewing basic algebra or geometry principles. But if you can master these basic skills, there's not a single problem on the **SAT** Math portion you won't be able to solve successfully. Of course, remember your game-plan – your goal may only be to do the easy ones, in which case this review should merely help strengthen your existing skills.

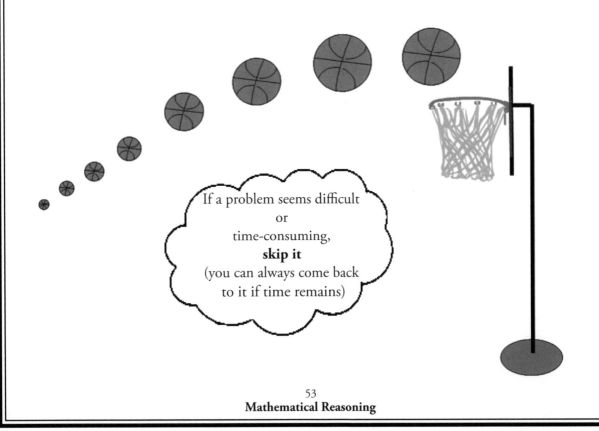

If a problem seems difficult
or
time-consuming,
skip it
(you can always come back
to it if time remains)

WHAT'S ON THE **SAT** MATH SECTION?

The average math problem on the **SAT** covers skills learned in the 5th and 6th Grades: fractions, decimals, and percents. There are some problems that include basic arithmetic, others that dabble in basic algebra and geometry; however, the average problem is around the 5th and 6th Grade range.

In addition, many of the **SAT** Math problems are geared to be solvable through a commonsense approach, thereby oftentimes bypassing the need for knowledge of algebra and geometry. In general, **SAT** problems most closely resemble **word problems** that you probably encountered in the 5th and 6th Grades, requiring careful reading and analytical (commonsense) thinking to answer each question correctly. It is important to be aware beforehand that these problems are very simple; otherwise, you'll be thinking too hard and will probably make the problems more difficult than they really are. Just remember: when working on an **SAT** Math problem, **think like a 5th Grader**!

MASTERING **SAT** MATHEMATICS SKILLS

There is a common misconception that the **SAT** Mathematics test is very difficult. In actuality, all you really need is a basic knowledge of fractions, decimals, percents, positive and negative numbers, and very elementary algebra and geometry. The key to increasing **SAT** Math scores is to practice, review and correct errors, then practice some more. The variety of problems on the **SAT** Mathematics section is very limited; indeed, several kinds of problems appear in similar form time and time again.

Should any of the following be unfamiliar, a more careful review or refresher course is highly recommended. Mastery of these basic ingredients will adequately prepare you for almost any problem on the **SAT**. Some of the more "difficult" problems are actually elementary problems disguised to look harder than they actually are. Occasionally a problem will appear that requires greater effort – in which case the time factor may be the primary reason to skip it – but in general the following **WHAT YOU NEED TO KNOW** should provide the necessary ammunition to achieve an optimal score.

✯ ✯ ✯ ✯ ✯ ✯ ✯ ✯ ✯ ✯ ✯ ✯ ✯ ✯ ✯ ✯

ARITHMETIC

1. WHOLE NUMBERS – adding and subtracting; multiplying and dividing
2. DIGITS – general operations
3. NUMBER LINES
4. FRACTIONS – adding and subtracting; multiplying and dividing
5. DECIMALS – adding and subtracting; multiplying and dividing
6. CHANGING FRACTIONS INTO DECIMALS; DECIMALS INTO FRACTIONS
7. CHANGING FRACTIONS INTO PERCENTS; PERCENTS INTO FRACTIONS
8. CHANGING DECIMALS INTO PERCENTS; PERCENTS INTO DECIMALS
9. RATIOS
10. ROUNDING OFF
11. POSITIVE AND NEGATIVE INTEGERS – adding, subtracting, multiplying, dividing
12. ORDER OF OPERATIONS
13. INTEGER MULTIPLES
14. INTEGER SQUARES/CUBES/ etc.
15. INTEGER SQUARE ROOTS/CUBE ROOTS
16. EXPONENTS

ARITHMETIC (Continued)

17. INEQUALITIES
18. MINIMUM/MAXIMUM
19. AVERAGES (incl. "weighted" average) / MEDIAN / MODE
20. PERCENT PROBLEMS
21. CHARTS
22. ARITHMETIC/GEOMETRIC SERIES
23. PATTERNS (inc. factorials)
24. VENN DIAGRAMS
25. PROBABILITY
26. LOGIC PROBLEMS

ALGEBRA

27. ALGEBRAIC EQUATIONS (inc. word-problem operations, consecutive-integer problems, and ratios)
28. ABSOLUTE VALUE
29. INTEGER FACTORS
30. PRIME/COMPOSITE NUMBERS
31. FACTORING, SIMPLIFYING AND ESTIMATING INTEGER SQUARE ROOTS
32. FACTORING SQUARE ROOTS INVOLVING VARIABLES
33. FACTORING AND EXPANDING QUADRATICS
34. COMBINING TERMS AND FACTORS
35. FUNCTIONS
36. DIRECT AND INVERSE VARIATION
37. COORDINATE AXIS
38. MIDPOINT FORMULA
39. DISTANCE FORMULA
40. LINE SLOPE
41. GRAPHS (linear/quadratic/translation)

GEOMETRY

42. PERIMETER OF POLYGONS
43. AREA OF SQUARES, RECTANGLES, TRIANGLES
44. VOLUME OF RECTANGULAR SOLIDS
45. AREA AND CIRCUMFERENCE OF CIRCLES
46. DEGREES IN A TRIANGLE, CIRCLE, STRAIGHT LINE
47. ANGLES AND ARC-MEASUREMENTS OF A CIRCLE
48. PARALLEL LINES AND TRANSVERSALS
49. SIDES AND ANGLES OF TRIANGLES
50. PYTHAGOREAN FORMULA
51. SPECIAL TRIANGLES
52. SPATIAL RELATIONSHIPS

BASIC ARITHMETIC SKILLS: Terminology

The following will help you translate word problems into workable arithmetic notation:

sum: +

difference: –

product: x

[Examples:

The sum of seven and nine = 7 + 9

The difference between eleven and six = 11 – 6

The product of eight and three = 8 x 3 (or 8 · 3)]

A few quick definitions will also help you greatly to master the terminology of the **SAT** Mathematics section. One of the most commonly used words is *integer*, a friendly word that will make any problem a lot less confusing. An *integer* is a **positive or negative whole number, or "0".** Examples include ⁻5, ⁻3, 0, ⁺4, ⁺76, etc. Any problem involving integers excludes fractions and decimals and is therefore likely to be easy to solve.

Arithmetic mean is used alongside the more common term, **average**. They both refer to the same operation, except that arithmetic mean satisfies the punctilious statisticians who claim that the word "average" is mistakenly used when "arithmetic mean" provides a more accurate description. They both refer to the same concept, and in any **SAT** the two appellations are likely to be used side by side to avoid any confusion.

Median is a mathematical term denoting the **middle number** in a set or series. Always remember, however, to **arrange the numbers in order** before determining which is in the middle.

Mode, another mathematical term, simply denotes the number that has appeared **most often**. You needn't rearrange them to identify the mode; simply look for the number that appears most frequently.

In geometry, *parallel* lines are two lines that **do not intersect** one another. *Perpendicular* lines, on the other hand, always cross one another at **90°** angles. In an intersection, if a line *bisects* a segment, it divides the segment into **two equal parts**. And if a line (or segment) is *tangent* to a circle, the line (or segment) intersects the circle at **one point**. In addition, this point, when connected to the center point, forms a radius that is **perpendicular** to the original line (or segment).

Each of three "end points" on a triangle is called a *vertex*. *Equilateral* triangles refer to triangles with three sides of equal length. Equilateral triangles also contain three angles of equal measure, each of which is 60°. *Isosceles* triangles refer to triangles with two sides of equal length. In a *right triangle* (a triangle containing an angle of 90°), the side opposite the right angle (90°) is called the *hypotenuse*; the hypotenuse is always the **longest side** of a right triangle.

Other key words to know are:

Prime Number (a number divisible only by 1 and itself): examples are 2, 3, 5, 7, 11, 13, 17, 19, 23…

Distinct ("different"): If x, y and z represent *distinct* numbers, then x ≠ y ≠ z.

Variable and *Constant*: A *variable*, identified by letters such as **x** and **y**, represent values that can change. For example, if **x = 2y**, the value of **x** will change according to **y**. A *constant*, on the other hand, does not change. For example, if **x = ky** (and **k** is a constant), and **x is 8** when **y is 2**, then we know **k = 4**. Then if we ask what **x** is when **y** is **3**, we know that **x = 4 · 3**, because **k** (which is a **constant**) cannot change values within the problem. (This problem is an example of DIRECT VARIATION, which is discussed together with INVERSE VARIATION in a later chapter.)

Coefficient: Any number or other variable alongside a variable is called the *coefficient*. For example, in the term 4**x**, **4** is the coefficient of **x**. In the term ⁻3ab**y**, ⁻**3ab** is the coefficient of **y**.

Respectively ("in that order"): If **A**, **B**, and **C** are **3, 7** and **8**, respectively, then it is understood that **A = 3, B = 7, C = 8**.

Former/Latter ("first"/"last"): If a family, for example, has two children whose ages are 10 and 12 years old, and if John is the *former* while Jason is the *latter*, then it is understood that John is 10, Jason is 12.

Having briefly reviewed the key terminology pertaining to the **SAT** Math test, let us now begin to analyze the Arithmetic Section:

WHAT YOU NEED TO KNOW.

Examples are provided to illustrate each heading.

1. WHOLE NUMBERS: adding and subtracting, multiplying and dividing

$$
\begin{array}{r}
341 \\
+557 \\
\hline
898
\end{array}
\qquad
\begin{array}{r}
468 \\
-189 \\
\hline
279
\end{array}
\qquad
\begin{array}{r}
245 \\
\times\ 12 \\
\hline
490 \\
2450 \\
\hline
2940
\end{array}
\qquad
\begin{array}{r}
189 \\
3\overline{)567} \\
-3 \\
\hline
26 \\
-24 \\
\hline
27 \\
-27 \\
\hline
0
\end{array}
$$

---

2. DIGITS: General Operations

Digits are simply single numbers that, when inputted, solve the problem. They are very simple and can be solved with basic arithmetic or with the assistance of a calculator.

Here are a few sample problems:

1.
$$
\begin{array}{r}
1X4 \\
+\ Y3 \\
\hline
23X
\end{array}
$$
$Y =$ _____

Solution:
$$
\begin{array}{r}
1X4 \\
+\ Y3 \\
\hline
237,\ X = 7
\end{array}
$$

$$
\begin{array}{r}
174 \\
+Y3 \\
\hline
237,\ Y = 6
\end{array}
$$

Answer: 6

- -

2.
$$
\begin{array}{r}
3XX \\
-\ 2Y \\
\hline
32X
\end{array}
$$
$X =$ _____

Solution: Because X–Y = X, Y = 0

$$
\begin{array}{r}
3XX \\
-\ 20 \\
\hline
32X
\end{array}
$$
X–2 = 2; X = 4

Answer: 4 (double check: 344 – 20 = **324**)

3.
$$
\begin{array}{r}
ZZY \\
\times\ 2W \\
\hline
335 \\
ABCC \\
\hline
7CZY
\end{array}
$$

What is the value of ABCC?

Solution: By common sense,
if W · ZZY=335,
then W = 1 and ZZY = 335.

Therefore, 2 · 335 = 670;
$$
\begin{array}{r}
335 \\
+6700 \\
\hline
7035
\end{array}
$$

Answer: ABCC = **6700**
(and Z = 3, Y = 5)

(it looks a lot harder than it really is!)

3. NUMBER LINES

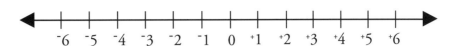

Example:

If point **P** corresponds with $^-1$ and point **Q** corresponds with $^+2$, what is the measurement of $\overline{PQ}$?

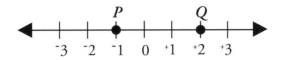

> **Answer:** the measurement of $\overline{PQ}$ is **3 units.**

4. FRACTIONS: adding and subtracting

[Note: *common denominator must be determined*]

(The simplest way to find a common denominator is to multiply the two denominators:

example, $^3/_5$ and $^4/_7$ yields a common denominator of **5 · 7 = 35**

$^3/_5 = {^?}/_{35}$ $^4/_7 = {^?}/_{35}$

To find the new numerator, simply cross-multiply:

$3 \cdot 35 = 105; 105 \div 5 = \underline{21}$ $^3/_5 = {^{21}}/_{35}$ $^4/_7 = {^{20}}/_{35}$ $^{21}/_{35} + {^{20}}/_{35} = {^{41}}/_{35} = 1^6/_{35}$)

$4 \cdot 35 = 140; 140 \div 7 = \underline{20}$

Examples:

$$
\begin{array}{l}
^2/_3 \quad ^2/_3 \quad = \quad ^8/_{12} \\
+ ^3/_4 \quad ^3/_4 \quad = \quad ^9/_{12} \\
\overline{} \\
\quad\quad\quad\quad\quad ^{17}/_{12}
\end{array}
$$

$$12\overline{)17} = 1^5/_{12}$$
$$\underline{-12}$$
$$5$$

$$
\begin{array}{l}
2^1/_4 \quad 2^1/_4 \quad = 2^5/_{20} \quad = 1^{25}/_{20} \\
- ^4/_5 \quad ^4/_5 \quad = {^{16}}/_{20} \quad = - {^{16}}/_{20} \\
\overline{\phantom{- ^4/_5 \quad ^4/_5 \quad = {^{16}}/_{20} \quad =}} \\
\quad\quad\quad\quad\quad\quad\quad\quad\quad 1^9/_{20}
\end{array}
$$

FRACTIONS: multiplying and dividing

[Note: *always change mixed numbers to improper fractions when multiplying or dividing fractions*]

(To change a mixed number to an improper fraction, multiply the whole number

by the denominator, and then add the numerator:

example, $2^1/_5 = 2 \cdot 5 + 1 = 11$. Then place this result over the original denominator: $^{11}/_5$.

Examples: $3^2/_7 = 3 \cdot 7 + 2 = {^{23}}/_7$ $5^1/_8 = 5 \cdot 8 + 1 = {^{41}}/_8$)

$$1^2/_5 \cdot 3^1/_2 = {^7}/_5 \cdot {^7}/_2 = {^{49}}/_{10}$$

$$\begin{array}{r} 4 \\ 10\overline{)49} \\ \underline{-40} \\ 9 \end{array} = 4^9/_{10}$$

$$3^3/_4 \div 1^2/_3 = {^{15}}/_4 \div {^5}/_3 = {^{15}}/_4 \cdot {^3}/_5 = {^{45}}/_{20} = 2^5/_{20} = 2^1/_4$$

or, a simpler step is to cross-cancel:

$$\overset{3}{\cancel{15}}/_4 \cdot {^3}/\underset{1}{\cancel{5}} = {^9}/_4 = 2^1/_4$$

5. DECIMALS: adding and subtracting
[Note: *always align decimal point*]

$$\begin{array}{r} 1.03 \\ .86 \\ +\ 2.432 \\ \hline 4.322 \end{array} \qquad \begin{array}{r} 8.161 \\ -\ 2.453 \\ \hline 5.708 \end{array}$$

DECIMALS: multiplying and dividing

$$\begin{array}{r} .03 \\ \times\ .6 \\ \hline .018 \end{array} \qquad \qquad .06\overline{)4.206}\ ^{70.1}$$

| (Move the decimal in the answer the same number of places as the total decimal places of the two numbers being multiplied.) | (Move the decimal in as many places as necessary to make the divisor a whole number; move the decimal the same number of places in the dividend.) |

---

6. CHANGING FRACTIONS INTO DECIMALS

$$3/4 = 4\overline{)3.00}\ ^{.75} \qquad\qquad 1^4/5 = {}^9/5 = 5\overline{)9.00}\ ^{1.80}$$

$$\begin{array}{r} -2.8 \\ \hline 20 \\ -20 \\ \hline 0 \end{array} \qquad\qquad \begin{array}{r} -5 \\ \hline 40 \\ -40 \\ \hline 0 \end{array}$$

CHANGING DECIMALS INTO FRACTIONS

$$.8 = {}^8/{}_{10} = {}^4/5 \qquad\qquad .25 = {}^{25}/{}_{100} = {}^1/4$$

---

7. CHANGING FRACTIONS INTO PERCENTS

$$3/5 = 5\overline{)3.00}\ ^{.60} = 60\% \qquad\qquad {}^2/{}_{25} = 25\overline{)2.00}\ ^{.08} = 8\%$$

CHANGING PERCENTS INTO FRACTIONS

$$20\% = {}^{20}/{}_{100} = {}^1/5 \qquad\qquad 45\% = {}^{45}/{}_{100} = {}^9/{}_{20}$$

8. CHANGING DECIMALS INTO PERCENTS
[*Move the decimal point two places to the right.*]

1.03 = 103%   .056 = 5.6%

CHANGING PERCENTS INTO DECIMALS
[*Move the decimal point two places to the left.*]

68% = .68   425% = 4.25

---

9. RATIOS (fractional relationships)
[also see PROBABILITY (page 74) and RATIO-PROBLEMS (page 85)]

Example: To express the relationship (ratio) of 5 boys to 7 girls:

5/7; 5:7; or 5 to 7

---

10. ROUNDING OFF
[*When the last digit is 5 or greater, round to the next highest number;*
if less than 5, do not change the number.]

nearest 100's	nearest 10's	nearest 1's *	nearest 10th's
1,473 = 1,500	246 = 250	146.4 = 146	1.035 = 1.0
21,625 = 21,600	315 = 320	35.52 = 36	8.35 = 8.4
4,858 = 4,900	1,272 = 1,270	6.87 = 7	16.79 = 16.8

(* note: "unit's digit" is another term for "**1**'s digit")

---

11. POSITIVE AND NEGATIVE INTEGERS: adding and subtracting
[*When faced with a subtraction problem, simply change the subtraction sign to a +, but*
be sure to also change the sign that follows. Then apply the rules of addition to solve.]

$$^-3 + {}^-5 = {}^-8 \qquad\qquad {}^-3 - {}^+2 = {}^-3 + {}^-2 = {}^-5$$
$$^-9 + {}^+4 = {}^-5 \qquad\qquad {}^+4 - {}^-6 = {}^+4 + {}^+6 = {}^+10$$
$$^+3 + {}^-2 = {}^+1 \qquad\qquad {}^+2 - {}^+3 = {}^+2 + {}^-3 = {}^-1$$
$$^-6 + {}^+8 = {}^+2 \qquad\qquad {}^-4 - {}^-2 = {}^-4 + {}^+2 = {}^-2$$

POSITIVE AND NEGATIVE INTEGERS: multiplying and dividing
[*The rule for multiplying and dividing positive/negative numbers is quite simple:*
If both signs are the same, the answer is "+"; if both signs are different, the answer is "−".]

$$^-6 \cdot {}^+3 = {}^-18 \qquad\qquad {}^-18 \div {}^-6 = {}^+3$$
$$^-7 \cdot {}^-8 = {}^+56 \qquad\qquad {}^+25 \div {}^-5 = {}^-5$$
$$^+4 \cdot {}^-6 = {}^-24 \qquad\qquad {}^-36 \div {}^+9 = {}^-4$$
$$^+8 \cdot {}^+9 = {}^+72 \qquad\qquad {}^+72 \div {}^+8 = {}^+9$$

12. ORDER OF OPERATIONS
[Perform all numerical operations in the following order:

1) parentheses operations

2) · and ÷

3) + and −]

$1 \cdot 3 - 2 + 8 \div 4 = 3 - 2 + 2 = 3$

$7 + 6 - 3 - (2 - 1) + 8 \cdot 2 - 6 \div 3 = 10 - 1 + 16 - 2 = 23$

$(^-2)(^-5) - 6 + (^+8)(^-2) = 10 - 6 - 16 = {}^-12$

13. INTEGER MULTIPLES

Multiples of 5 are {5, 10, 15, 20, 25 ...}

Multiples of 9 are {9, 18, 27, 36, 45 ...}

Multiples of $^-7$ are {$^-7$, $^-14$, $^-21$, $^-28$ ...}

14. INTEGER SQUARES/CUBES/etc.

$3^2 = 3 \cdot 3 = 9$

$8^2 = 8 \cdot 8 = 64$

$2^3 = 2 \cdot 2 \cdot 2 = 8$

$4^3 = 4 \cdot 4 \cdot 4 = 64$

$3^4 = 3 \cdot 3 \cdot 3 \cdot 3 = 81$

$5^4 = 5 \cdot 5 \cdot 5 \cdot 5 = 625$

$1^6 = 1 \cdot 1 \cdot 1 \cdot 1 \cdot 1 \cdot 1 = 1$

$2^6 = 2 \cdot 2 \cdot 2 \cdot 2 \cdot 2 \cdot 2 = 64$

15. INTEGER SQUARE ROOTS/CUBE ROOTS

$\sqrt{9} = 3$ (because $3^2 = 9$)

$\sqrt{49} = 7$ (because $7^2 = 49$)

$\sqrt[3]{8} = 2$ (because $2^3 = 8$)

$\sqrt[3]{27} = 3$ (because $3^3 = 27$)

16. EXPONENTS

Exponents on the **SAT** are very simple and easy to learn. Here are sample problems to reacquaint yourself with exponents, including positive, negative and fractional:

1. $3^2 =$ ___   5. $3^{-2} =$ ___   9. $6^{2/3} =$ ___

2. $^-2^3 =$ ___   6 $^-2^{-3} =$ ___   10. $5^{3/2} =$ ___

3. $2^2 + 3^2 =$ ___   7. $2^{-2} + 3^{-2} =$ ___

4. $5^4 =$ ___   8. $2^{1/2} + 3^{1/2} =$ ___

Answers:

1. **9**

(note: $3^{-2} = {}^1/_{3^2}$)

5. ${}^1/_{3^2} =$ **${}^1/_9$**

9. $\sqrt[3]{6^2} =$ **$\sqrt[3]{36}$**

10. $\sqrt{5^3} =$ **$5\sqrt{5}$**

2. $^-(2 \cdot 2 \cdot 2) =$ **$^-8$**

6. $^-{}^1/_{2^3} =$ **$^-{}^1/_8$**

3. $4 + 9 =$ **13**

7. ${}^1/_{2^2} + {}^1/_{3^2} = {}^1/_4 + {}^1/_9$
    $= {}^9/_{36} + {}^4/_{36} =$ **${}^{13}/_{36}$**

4. $5 \cdot 5 \cdot 5 \cdot 5 =$ **625**

8. **$\sqrt{2} + \sqrt{3}$**

17. INEQUALITIES

$12 < 16$ (12 is less than 16)	$14 > 2$ (14 is greater than 2)
$^-3 < ^-1$	$0 > ^-5$
$3^2 < 2^4$	$3^4 > 4^3$

18. MINIMUM/MAXIMUM

[To find the minimum or maximum value, determine which extreme numbers to use.]

Example: if X is a member of the set {1, 4, 6, 9}

and Y is a member of the set {3, 8, 9, 14}

1) the MINIMUM value of X + Y is 1 + 3 = 4

2) the MAXIMUM value of X + Y is 9 + 14 = 23

3) the MINIMUM value of X – Y is 1 – 14 = $^-$13

4) the MAXIMUM value of X – Y is 9 – 3 = 6

5) the MINIMUM value of Y – X is 3 – 9 = $^-$6

6) the MAXIMUM value of Y – X is 14 – 1 = 13

19. FINDING THE AVERAGE ("arithmetic mean")
[Determine the total and divide by the numbers of items.]

Average of 8, 14, 26 and 40 = $\dfrac{8 + 14 + 26 + 40}{4}$ = $\dfrac{88}{4}$ = 22

Average of ‾6, ‾3, 0, ⁺3, ⁺6 = $\dfrac{‾6 + ‾3 + 0 + ⁺3 + ⁺6}{5}$ = $\dfrac{0}{5}$ = 0

"WEIGHTED" AVERAGE
[Determine the total number of points and number of items, then divide.]

Example: If John averages 69 on his first three tests, how much must he score on his next two tests to raise his average to 73?

Solution:
$$\frac{69 + 69 + 69 + ? + ?}{5} = 73$$

[Note: *This problem can be solved most easily using* "**x**"*-variables, but because algebra is discussed later on, we have used* "**?**" *in place of* "**x**" *at this time.*]

$$207 + ? + ? = 73 \cdot 5$$
$$207 + ? + ? = 365$$
$$? + ? = 365 - 207$$
$$? + ? = 158$$

> **Answer:** John needs **158** points on his next two tests (or 79 points average per test).

Sample Problems:

1. If four people each weigh an average of 150 pounds, how much would each of the next two people need to average to make the group's total average weight 170 pounds?

   Solution: $150 \cdot 4 = 600$; $170 \cdot 6 = 1020$.
   $1020 - 600 = 420$ total pounds needed.

   > **Answer:** Each of the next two people would need to average **210** pounds.

---

2. If Sally knitted 8 sweaters in January, 9 in February and 14 in March, how many more sweaters would she need to knit to have an average of 5 sweaters per month for the entire year?

   Solution: $8 + 9 + 14 = 31$; $5 \cdot 12 = 60$; $60 - 31 = 29$

   > **Answer: 29** sweaters

FINDING THE MEDIAN

*[Arrange the numbers in order and identify the middle number – the **median**.]*
[If the set contains an even number of members, divide the middle two by 2]

Median of {⁻1, 3, 5, 8, 12} is **5**

Median of {3, 8, 10, 14} is $\dfrac{8 + 10}{2}$ = **9**

Sample Problem:

Median of {3, 8, 6, 2, 0, 1, 6} is ___

Solution:

Arrange in order: {0, 1, 2, 3, 6, 6, 8}

| **Answer:** Median is **3** |

Sample Problem:

Median of {0, 5, 1, 8, 3, 6} is ___

Solution:

Arrange in order: {0, 1, 3, 5, 6, 8}

| **Answer:** Median is $\dfrac{3 + 5}{2}$ = **4** |

FINDING THE MODE

*[Identify the number that **appears most frequently**.]*

Mode of {2, 4, 5, 5, 6, 6, 6,} is **6**

Mode of {1, 5, 3, 9, 3, ⁻2, 3, 18} is **3**

20. SOLVING PERCENT (%) PROBLEMS

Simply use this handy formula:

$$\frac{is}{of} = \frac{\%}{100}$$

Fill in the given information, cross-multiply, then divide to solve.

50 = what % of 200?

[Note: "=" is the same as "is"]

$$\frac{50}{200} = \frac{?}{100}$$

50 · 100 = 5000

5000 ÷ 200 = 25

| **Answer: 25%** |

30% of 80 is ?

$$\frac{?}{80} = \frac{30}{100}$$

80 · 30 = 2400

2400 ÷ 100 = 24

| **Answer: 24** |

21. CHART INTERPRETATION

Similar to problems you probably remember doing in the 6th Grade, these chart-problems involve simple understanding of chart-construction.

The following two examples will show how easy this problem-type is.

Monthly Family Expenditures

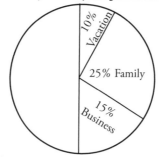

1. In the pie-chart above, how much would the family spend on business if they spent $240 on vacations for the month?

Solution: (Note: there are several different ways to solve this problem, including use of ratios):
10% of the total monthly expenditures = $240,
so total monthly expenditures were $2400. 15% of $2400 is $360

Answer: $360

2.

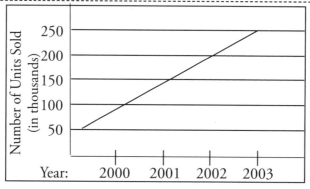

In the above chart, approximately how many more units were sold in the beginning of 2003 than in the beginning of 2001?

Solution: 2003: 250,000 units were sold (approx.)
2001: 140,000 units were sold (approx.)
250,000 – 140,000 = 110,000

Answer: approximately **110,000** more units were sold

22. SERIES (Arithmetic/Geometric)

Though there are formulas for solving Series problems, common sense is your best guide for all **SAT** Series questions. Here are a few sample problems to show you how manageable these questions really are:

1. In the series {1, 3, 6, 10...}, what would the 9th term be?

   Solution: 1, 3, 6, 10, 15, 21, 28, 36, 45

   (the difference of two consecutive terms is 1 greater than the difference
   of the former term and the term preceding it;
   $10 - 6 = (6 - 3) + 1$; $15 - 10 = (10 - 6) + 1$, etc.)

Answer: **45**

2. If in a series each term is 5 more than twice the previous term, what would the 4th term be if the 7th term is 699?

   Solution   (using commonsense approach and an algebra-preview):
   $699 = 2x + 5$, so $694 = 2x$; $x = 347$ (6th term)
   $347 = 2x + 5$, so $342 = 2x$; $x = 171$ (5th term)
   $171 = 2x + 5$, so $166 = 2x$; $x = 83$ (4th term)

Answer: **83**

3. If in a series in which the first term (**x**) is 0, what would the unit's digit of the 103rd term be if each subsequent term is defined as $2x - 2$?

   Solution (this problem also uses the concept of PATTERNS, discussed *next* in this text):

		0:	1st term
$2(0) - 2$	$=$	$^-2$:	2nd term
$2(^-2) - 2$	$=$	$^-6$:	3rd term
$2(^-6) - 2$	$=$	$^-14$:	4th term
$2(^-14) - 2$	$=$	$^-30$:	5th term
$2(^-30) - 2$	$=$	$^-62$:	6th term
$2(^-62) - 2$	$=$	$^-126$:	7th term

   Notice the pattern (especially in the unit's digit):
   0, $^-2$, $^-6$, $^-14$, $^-30$, $^-62$, $^-126$

   The unit's digit is: 0, 2, 6, 4, then repeating 0, 2, 6, 4 . . . Every 4th number ends in 4, so the series repeats after every 4 numbers.

   $$\begin{array}{r} 25 \\ 4\overline{)103} \\ \underline{-100} \\ r = 3 \end{array}$$

   The remainder is 3, which means that the unit's digit of the 3rd number of the series corresponds with that of the 103rd term in question.

Answer: **6**

23. PATTERNS (inc. FACTORIALS)

SAT Math problems are so often feared simply because they've been taught by teachers who take a hard-line approach rather than a commonsense approach to solving them. No problem is more misunderstood than Patterns problems – simple problems that can be solved either through a circuitous Math formula or by simple common sense.

Here are some sample problems with *simple* explanations!

1. A car can reach its destination to Town **H** via either of 3 roads, and from there can go to Town **J** via either of 3 roads. How many different paths can be taken on a round trip, provided that no road is traveled on more than once?

Solution: Draw a picture

Now let's label the different paths:

Then set up an organized pattern:

<u>ADE</u> (going) : returning can be via:

FDB
FDC
GDB
GDC

(4 routes without traveling on any path twice)

<u>ADF</u> (going) : returning can be via:

EDB
EDC
GDB
GDC

(4 routes)

<u>ADG</u> (going) : 4 routes returning

Starting at <u>B</u>, we have the same basic pattern:

BDE (going) : 4 routes returning
BDF (going) : 4 routes returning
BDG (going) : 4 routes returning

Starting at <u>C</u>, using the same pattern, there are also
4 + 4 + 4 = 12 total routes returning

Answer: 12 + 12 + 12 = **<u>36</u>** different paths

---

2. If a number consists of 4 distinct odd digits and the first and last digit are 1 and 3, respectively, how many different numbers can be formed?

Solution: 1 __ __ 3

only remaining usable digits are: 5, 7, 9

(Note: Single digits are the numbers 0 thru 9)

1<u>57</u>3

1<u>59</u>3

1<u>75</u>3

1<u>79</u>3

1<u>95</u>3

1<u>97</u>3

> **Answer: <u>6</u>**

(it's so simple when you solve these problems with a practical, commonsense approach!)

FACTORIALS

Occasionally, use of Factorials can save time on a Patterns problem, but only on certain ones. Here are a couple of problems that demonstrate when Factorials can be useful.

*   6 horses are kept in 6 different stalls. In how many different stall arrangements can the horses be kept?

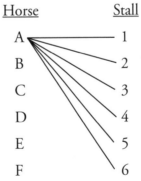

Horse	Stall

Solution:

Each horse can have 6 different stall arrangements.
Therefore, 6 horses · 6 different stall arrangements = 36

> **Answer:** There are <u>**36**</u> different stall arrangements.

Notice that this problem was easy to solve without using any algebraic formulas. The next problem, however, is not so obvious.

- If 6 horses can be kept in 6 stalls, in <u>how many different ways</u> can they be let out, one horse at a time?

Solution: This is not as simple as the previous question. Not only can the horses be kept in different stalls, but now there's also the question as to *who can be let out first, second, third, etc.*

Let's first solve this via PATTERNS:

Horse	Stall	Let Out
A	1	1st
B	2	2nd
C	3	3rd
D	4	4th
E	5	5th
F	6	6th

We need to know how many different stall-arrangements of horses there can be. If horse A is in Stall 1 and is let out 1st, here are the combinations of stall numbers in the order let out:

1 2 3 4 5 6
1 2 3 4 6 5
1 2 3 5 4 6
1 2 3 5 6 4
1 2 3 6 4 5
1 2 3 6 5 4

There are 6 combinations with 1 2 3 _ _ _

Beginning with 1 2 4 _ _ _ there are also 6 combinations.

Beginning with 1 2 5 _ _ _ there are 6 combinations

and beginning with 1 2 6 _ _ _ there are 6 combinations.

Therefore, beginning with 1 2 _ _ _ _ there are a total of <u>24</u> combinations.

If we begin with 1 3 _ _ _ _, there will again be 24 combinations.

If we begin with 1 4 _ _ _ _, there will be 24 combinations.

Beginning with 1 5 _ _ _ _ = 24 combinations.

And beginning with 1 6 _ _ _ _ = 24 combinations.

Therefore, there are 5 · 24 = 120 combinations with Horse <u>A</u> being in Stall 1 and let out 1st. If Horse <u>B</u> is in stall 1 and let out first, there are another 120 combinations. The same is true if Horse <u>C</u> is in stall 1 and let out first, and ditto for Horse <u>D</u>, <u>E</u>, and <u>F</u>.

Answer: There are 6 · 120 = **720** different ways the horses can be let out.

- -

FACTORIAL "shortcut": Since you know there were more than 6 · 6 = 36 combinations because of the additional "order in which they can be let out" problem, you could immediately switch to factorial mode:

6 horses = 6! ("6-Factorial") = 6 · 5 · 4 · 3 · 2 · 1 = <u>720</u>

(If the same problem involved <u>5</u> horses, the answer would be <u>5!</u> = 5 · 4 · 3 · 2 · 1 = <u>120</u>).

24. VENN DIAGRAMS

A mixture of visual and common sense, Venn diagrams are used to illustrate intersection and union of sets. Here are a couple of problems utilizing Venn diagrams.

1.

If 100 people selected two-scoop ice-cream cones, and if 60 included vanilla, 40 included chocolate and 30 included strawberry, how many chose only <u>one flavor</u> for their two-scoop cone?

Solution: 60 + 40 + 30 = 130; but because there are only 100 people, 30 took a <u>second scoop</u> of another flavor

> **Answer:** 100 – 30 = **70** chose only **one flavor**.

----

2. Which of the following diagrams most accurately reflects the <u>intersection</u> of the following three sets:

$$x = \{2,\ 4,\ 6,\ 8\}$$
$$y = \{1,\ 3,\ 6,\ 9\}$$
$$z = \{3,\ 5,\ 7,\ 9\}$$

A)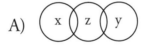

B) (x)(z) over (y)

C) (x)(z) over (y)

D) (x)(y)(z)

E) (z)(y)(x)

> **Answer: E** 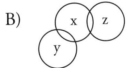 5, 7 (3,9) 1 (6) 2,4,8

25. PROBABILITY

Probability, or *odds*, is merely a fancy way to say *ratio*, which is simply another word for **fraction**. Therefore, these are elaborately-disguised *fraction* problems that are much easier to do than they at first appear.

Sample Problems:

1. What is the probability that, in a bag filled with 20 blue jelly beans, 35 red jelly beans, 15 green jelly beans, and 10 orange jelly beans, that a jelly bean selected will <u>not</u> be red?

    Solution: There are 80 jelly beans totals, and 45 are <u>not</u> red.

    > **Answer: <u>45/80</u>** (or if reduced, **<u>9/16</u>**)

----

2. If a pair of dice are rolled, what are the odds that they will roll two 5's?

    Solution: Each dice (or "die") has 6 numbers on it, so there are <u>36</u> (6 · 6) different possible combinations. But there is only <u>1</u> way to roll "5" on each dice.

    > **Answer: <u>1/36</u>**

    (Alternate method: each dice has a 1/6 chance to roll a "5", so the probability that 2 dice will each roll a "5" is 1/6 · 1/6 = <u>1/36</u>)

----

3. If a number consists of <u>3</u> distinct digits each greater than 0, what is the probability that each digit will be prime? (Note: the prime single digits are 2, 3, 5 and 7)

    Solution: There are <u>9</u> possible digits (1-9), but only <u>4</u> are prime. So the odds that one digit will be prime is <u>4/9</u>. The odds the 2nd digit is prime is also 4/9, and same is true for the 3rd digit.

    > **Answer:** 4/9 · 4/9 · 4/9 = **<u>64/729</u>** (approximately .09)

26. LOGIC PROBLEMS

Many problems on the **SAT** Math section require a logical problem-solving approach: determining what is being asked and how to go about solving the problem; then solving the problem in the easiest and most logical manner; and finally, reviewing your answer to see that it makes sense.

Some questions rely more specifically on Logic and are excellent brain-teaser problems. They don't necessarily involve math, but they are analytical and therefore qualify as Math problems.

Here are a couple of sample **SAT** Logic problems:

1. Assumed Fact: If it is Tuesday, it is raining.
    Given the above statement, what can we definitively deduce?
    - **I. If it is not raining, it is not Tuesday.**
    - **II. If it is raining, it must be Tuesday.**
    - **III. In any consecutive ten-day period, it will rain at least two days.**

       A) I only

       B) I and II

       C) II only

       D) I and III

       E) I, II and III

    > **Answer: A**

    (**II** is not necessarily true: it may be raining on <u>any</u> day of the week; **III** is not necessarily true: if the ten-day period begins on a Wednesday, Thursday, Friday or Saturday there may possibly be only one day of rain.)

2. Two brothers walk to school only when it is sunny (on cloudy days, their mother drives them to school). Which of the following <u>must</u> be true:
    - **I. If their mother drives them to school, it is a cloudy day.**
    - **II. On sunny days, the two boys are not driven to school.**
    - **III. If, in a five-day school week, every other day is sunny, then the boys will walk to school at least two days.**

       A) I only

       B) I and II

       C) I and III

       D) III only

       E) none of the above

    > **Answer: E**

    (The information states that the *only* time the boys will walk to school is when it is sunny, but it does not say that they aren't sometimes driven to school on sunny days. Therefore, in any five-day school week they could be driven to school *every* day. The *only* definite conclusion that can be made regarding how they will go to school is that on cloudy days, the two boys will be driven.)

*(focusing on basic arithmetic skills frequently tested on the **SAT**)*

(circle your answer)
[answers on page 182]

1. $\frac{1}{3} + \frac{1}{4} =$

    A) $\frac{1}{6}$

    B) $\frac{1}{12}$

    C) $\frac{7}{12}$

    D) $\frac{2}{7}$

    E) $\frac{1}{7}$

2. $28 - 4 \cdot 6 + 9 \div 3 =$

    A) $^-8$

    B) 1

    C) 51

    D) 7

    E) 8

3. $2^4 =$

    A) 6

    B) 16

    C) 32

    D) 8

    E) 24

4. $^+24 \div {}^-3 =$

    A) $^+8$

    B) $^{-1}/_8$

    C) $^+21$

    D) $^-8$

    E) $^-21$

5. $\sqrt[3]{64} =$

    A) 4

    B) 8

    C) 16

    D) 32

    E) 192

6. $\frac{1}{8} =$ _____ %

    A) 18

    B) 80

    C) 8

    D) 12.5

    E) 1.8

7.   12.8
    x 7.4

    A) 94.72

    B) 936.6

    C) .9472

    D) 93.66

    E) 9.472

8. $8 : 2 =$

    A) $^{14}/_7$

    B) $^4/_1$

    C) $^{16}/_3$

    D) $^{36}/_8$

    E) $^8/_{10}$

9. The average (arithmetic mean) of 6, 8, 4, and $^-2$ is

    A) $6^2/_3$

    B) 2

    C) $^-4$

    D) 5

    E) 4

10. 15% of 6 is

    A) 9

    B) 25

    C) 40

    D) .9

    E) 4

11. -4^2 =

    A) ⁻8

    B) ⁻16

    C) $(4)^2$

    D) 16

    E) $(⁻4)^2$

12. ⁻5 − ⁻3 =

    A) ⁻15

    B) ⁺2

    C) ⁺8

    D) ⁻2

    E) ⁻8

13. The median of the set containing the numbers {5, 4, 3, 4, 5} is

    A) 3

    B) 3.5

    C) 4

    D) 4.2

    E) 5

14. 872% =

    A) 87.2

    B) .872

    C) 8.72

    D) .0872

    E) 872

15. 48 is not a multiple of

    A) 6

    B) 10

    C) 4

    D) 12

    E) 8

16. ⁻5 + 6(⁻2) + 4 − 5(⁺2) =

    A) 0

    B) ⁻23

    C) 10

    D) 21

    E) ⁻3

17. Rounded to the nearest tenth, 1.456 =

    A) 1.0

    B) 1.5

    C) 1.46

    D) 0

    E) 1.4

18. 3^3 <

    A) $⁻3^3$

    B) 4^2

    C) $(⁻5)^3$

    D) 27

    E) $(⁻6)^2$

19. 13.72 ÷ 1 =

    A) 13.72

    B) 1

    C) ⁻13.72

    D) 0

    E) 13.71

20. 18 − 1 · 6 ÷ 2 · 0 =

    A) 15

    B) 51

    C) 0

    D) 6

    E) 18

1. $(6 + 8)(8 + 2) =$
   A) 140
   B) 76
   C) 8
   D) 16
   E) 24

2. What is 50% of 14?
   A) 28
   B) 7
   C) 70
   D) 2.8
   E) 36

3. $^2/_9 - ^1/_7 =$
   A) $^1/_2$
   B) $^1/_{18}$
   C) 1
   D) $^5/_{63}$
   E) $^1/_{63}$

4. If a cup holds four ounces of liquid, how many full cups are needed to raise the level of a larger container from forty-two ounces to seventy-eight ounces?
   A) $10^1/_2$
   B) $19^1/_2$
   C) 24
   D) 9
   E) 16

5. $1 + 2 + 3 \cdot 4 + 5 \cdot 6 \div 3 =$
   A) 25
   B) 17
   C) 123
   D) 15
   E) 57

6. If a mountain which stands 8,231 feet above sea level also extends 6,221 feet below sea level, what is the total height from its uppermost point to its lowest level?
   A) 1,090 ft.
   B) 3, 010 ft.
   C) 15,452 ft.
   D) 2,010 ft.
   E) 14,452 ft.

7. In 45 games played, the Boston Beans won 25 and lost the remainder. What percentage of their total games played did the Beans lose?
   A) $44\,^4/_9\%$
   B) $66\,^2/_3\%$
   C) 20%
   D) $55^5/_9\%$
   E) $33\,^1/_3\%$

8. $.41 \div .2$, rounded to the nearest tenth, is
   A) 2.0
   B) 2.5
   C) .5
   D) 2.05
   E) 2.1

9. If set **Q** contains all positive even integers between 5 and 11, and set **R** contains all positive odd integers between 3 and 13, what is the maximum value of **Q** – **R**?
   A) 1
   B) 2
   C) 5
   D) 6
   E) 8

10. If there are twenty-four boys in a class of thirty-six boys and girls, the ratio between girls and boys can be expressed in all of the following *except*

   A) 1 : 2
   B) 5 : 10
   C) $^1/_3 : {^2/_3}$
   D) 12 : 24
   E) 2 : 3

11. Which of the following is *not* a multiple of 3?

   A) 9^9
   B) 12^{15}
   C) 3^3
   D) 6^4
   E) 10^6

12. **W** = {0, 1, 2, 3, 0}

   If   **T** is the mean of set **W**
        U is the median of set **W**
   and **V** is the mode of set **W**
   what is the value of $\dfrac{\mathbf{T} + \mathbf{V}}{\mathbf{U}}$?

   A) .6
   B) 1.2
   C) 2
   D) 2.2
   E) 3

Questions 13-16 refer to the following information.

   In a certain word-game, points are allotted to various letters. The total amount of points per word is determined as the product of the sum of the points by the number of letters in the word. For example, a 6-letter word whose letters total 27 points constitutes 6 · 27 = 162 points.

Point-values of selected letters are as follows:

A = 3 points	H = 6 points	N = 5 points	R = 3 points
B = 4 points	I = 1 point	O = 1 point	Y = 6 points
E = 2 points	L = 4 points	P = 4 points	Z = 10 points

13. What is the total-point-value of the word **BABY**?

   A) 52
   B) 68
   C) 44
   D) 17
   E) 51

14. How many more points would a player gain by changing the word **PLANE** to **AIRPLANE**?

   A) 18
   B) 35
   C) 56
   D) 110
   E) 200

15. Which of the following words has the *greatest* total-point-value?

   A) **PHONE**
   B) **ARRAY**
   C) **LAZY**
   D) **BROIL**
   E) **LINEN**

16. Which of the following words are of *different* total-point-value?

   A) **HAZY** and **ANNOY**
   B) **HAPPEN** and **ZIPPER**
   C) **ALONE** and **RIPEN**
   D) **OILY** and **YORE**
   E) **LILLY** and **ZANY**

17. If a banker originally had $100,000 but misplaced $101, how much money does he now have?

A) $99,989

B) $100,101

C) $90,899

D) $99,899

E) $100,099

18. $^-40 \div 4 + 6(^-8) =$

A) $^-58$

B) $^-12$

C) $^+480$

D) $^+38$

E) $^+32$

19. What symbol satisfies the relationship in the following: $^-3^2 + 4^2$ _____ $^-5^2 + 4^2$?

A) <

B) =

C) >

D) ||

E) The relationship cannot be determined from the information given.

20. What is 25% of $\dfrac{^1/_2}{.25}$?

A) $^1/_4$

B) 2

C) $^1/_2$

D) 1

E) 25

MASTERING **SAT** ALGEBRA SKILLS

Some mathematics problems encountered on the **SAT** require a minimum knowledge of basic algebra. A letter (usually "**x**" or "**y**") is used to indicate an unknown value. When a variable is used more than once within the same problem, it refers to the same number. For example, if **3x − 5 = 2x + 3**, the missing number ("**x**") must fit into both sides of the equation to create a balance. The answer **x = 8** satisfies the equation, since **3(8) − 5 = 2(8) + 3** (both have the same value, which in this problem is **19**).

If "**x**" and "**y**" are used together, they may or may not represent the same numerical value. Additionally, other letters may be used as variables, though **x** and **y** tend to be the most frequently encountered.

Examples are provided for each of the **WHAT YOU NEED TO KNOW** algebra-headings. If you are not sure how a problem was solved, ask a friend to clarify the concept. Because algebra utilizes several concepts simultaneously, it is important to shore up any weaknesses you may have here. One seemingly minute skill-gap can result in errors in several different problems, seriously eroding your overall **SAT** math score. Be sure you've got these basic algebra concepts under your belt – it will make a big difference in the long run!

27. SOLVING BASIC ALGEBRAIC EQUATIONS

$3x - 4 = 23$

$$\begin{array}{rl} 3x - 4 &= 23 \\ +4 \quad +4 & \\ \hline 3x &= 27 \end{array}$$

[Note: $3x = 27$ *is read as*
   "3 times <u>*what number* (**x**)</u> $= 27$"]

$1x = 9$
$x = \underline{\mathbf{9}}$

$4y + 6 = 18$

$$\begin{array}{rl} 4y + 6 &= 18 \\ -6 \quad -6 & \\ \hline 4y &= 12 \end{array}$$

[Note: $4y = 12$ *is read as*
   "4 times <u>*what number* (**y**)</u> $= 12$"]

$1y = 3$
$y = \underline{\mathbf{3}}$

$(2\,^1/_2)z + 3 = 18$

$(3\,^3/_8)w - 6 = 21$

[Note: Always change mixed numbers to improper fractions when solving algebraic equations.]

$$\begin{array}{rl} (^5/_2)z + 3 &= 18 \\ -3 \quad -3 & \\ \hline (^5/_2)z &= 15 \\ (^2/_5)\,(^5/_2)z &= {}^{15}/_1\,(^2/_5) \\ 1z &= {}^{30}/_5 \\ z &= \underline{\mathbf{6}} \end{array}$$

$$\begin{array}{rl} (^{27}/_8)w - 6 &= 21 \\ +6 \quad +6 & \\ \hline (^{27}/_8)w &= 27 \\ (^8/_{27})\,(^{27}/_8)w &= {}^{27}/_1\,(^8/_{27}) \\ 1w &= 8 \\ w &= \underline{\mathbf{8}} \end{array}$$

---

two equations: add or subtract both equations (whichever operation is appropriate), then solve:

if solving for **x**:
$$\begin{array}{rl} 3x + 2y &= 11 \\ + 2x - 2y &= 4 \\ \hline 5x &= 15 \\ x &= \mathbf{3} \end{array}$$

$[y = \underline{\mathbf{1}}]$

if solving for **y**:
$$\begin{array}{rl} 6x + 3y &= 39 \\ - 6x + 2y &= 32 \\ \hline y &= \underline{7} \end{array}$$

$[x = \underline{\mathbf{3}}]$

more than two equations:
add equations, then solve:

if solving for **x**:
$$\begin{array}{rl} x + y - z &= 6 \\ 2x - 3y + 2z &= 4 \\ + 5x + 2y - z &= 14 \\ \hline 8x &= 24 \\ x &= \underline{\mathbf{3}} \end{array}$$

[*The* **SAT** *will not usually seek solutions for* **y** *and* **z**.]

[Note: *Although, in high school math, algebraic solving may involve rather complicated problems, the* **SAT** *usually restricts itself to basic, simpler ones.*]

WORD-PROBLEMS USING BASIC ALGEBRA

1. If the product of a number and seven is four less than the sum of the number and ten, what is the number?

   Solution:

   $$7x = (x + 10) - 4$$
   $$7x = x + 6$$
   $$\underline{-x \quad -x}$$
   $$\frac{6x}{6} = \frac{6}{6}$$
   $$x = 1$$

   > **Answer:** The number is **1**

----

2. A number decreased by one-half the number is twenty-five less than the sum of the number and twice that number. What is the number?

   Solution:

   $$x - \frac{1x}{2} = (x + 2x) - 25$$
   $$\frac{1x}{2} = 3x - 25$$
   $$\underline{-3x \qquad -3x}$$
   $$-2\tfrac{1}{2}x = {}^{-}25$$
   $$\left(\tfrac{-2}{5}\right)\left(\tfrac{-5x}{2}\right) = \left(\tfrac{-25}{1}\right)\left(\tfrac{-2}{5}\right)$$
   $$x = 10$$

   > **Answer:** The number is **10**

CONSECUTIVE-INTEGER PROBLEMS USING BASIC ALGEBRA

1. If the sum of four **consecutive** integers is 38, what are the numbers?

   [Note: *Consecutive integers are set up as*

   $$x = 1^{st} \text{ integer}$$
   $$x+1 = 2^{nd} \text{ integer}$$
   $$x+2 = 3^{rd} \text{ integer, etc.}]$$

   Solution: $x + (x+1) + (x+2) + (x+3) = 38$
   $$4x + 6 = 38$$
   $$4x = 32$$
   $$x = 8$$

   Answer: The four numbers are **8, 9, 10 and 11**

2. If the average (arithmetic mean) of three **consecutive even** integers is six less than twice the smallest integer, what are the integers?

   [Note: *Consecutive even integers are set up as*

   $$x = 1^{st} \text{ integer}$$
   $$x+2 = 2^{nd} \text{ consecutive even integer}$$
   $$x+4 = 3^{rd} \text{ consecutive even integer, etc.}]$$

   Solution:
   $$\frac{x + (x+2) + (x+4)}{3} = 2x - 6$$

   $$\frac{3x + 6}{3} = 2x - 6$$

   $$3x + 6 = 3(2x - 6)$$

   $$3x + 6 = 6x - 18$$
   $$\underline{-3x + 18 \qquad\qquad -3x + 18}$$
   $$24 \div 3 = \qquad 3x \div 3$$
   $$8 = x$$

   Answer: The integers are **8, 10 and 12**

3. The product of the middle and largest of three **consecutive odd** integers is fifty more than the square of the smallest. What is the largest of the three integers?

   [Note: *Consecutive odd integers are set up the <u>same</u> as for consecutive even integers*:

   $$x = 1^{st} \text{ integer}$$
   $$x + 2 = \text{ the second consecutive odd integer}$$
   $$x + 4 = \text{ the third consecutive odd integer, etc.}]$$

   Solution: $* (x + 2)(x + 4) = x^2 + 50$

   $$x^2 + 6x + 8 = x^2 + 50$$
   $$\underline{-x^2 \qquad\quad - 8 \quad -x^2 - \quad 8}$$
   $$6x \div 6 = 42 \div 6$$
   $$x = 7$$

   Answer: The largest of the three integers $(x + 4)$ is **11**

   [*note: for discussion on expanding quadratics, see FACTORING AND EXPANDING QUADRATICS (page 89)]

RATIO-PROBLEMS USING BASIC ALGEBRA

1. If a 12-inch line is divided into two segments whose lengths are in the ratio 2 to 1, what is the length of the longer segment?

   Solution:
   $$2x = \text{longer segment}$$
   $$x = \text{shorter segment}$$

   $$2x + x = 12$$
   $$3x = 12$$
   $$x = 4$$
   (the shorter segment is 4 inches)

   > **Answer:** The longer segment ($2x$) is **8 inches**.

---

2. The measure of angles in a triangle is in the ratio 6 : 5 : 4. What is the degree measure of the middle angle?

   Solution:
   $$6x = \text{largest angle}$$
   $$5x = \text{middle angle}$$
   $$4x = \text{smallest angle}$$

   $$6x + 5x + 4x = 180\,*$$
   $$15x = 180$$
   $$x = 12$$

   > **Answer:** The middle angle ($5x$) is **60°**.
   > (the other two angles are 48° ($4x$) and 72° ($6x$))

[*note: for discussion on angles, see DEGREES IN A TRIANGLE (page 110)]

28. ABSOLUTE VALUE PROBLEMS

The absolute value of a number is its *positive* number equivalent. Here are several sample problems along with a couple of equations involving absolute values. Once you become familiar with them, these problems won't pose any further difficulty for you.

1. $|\,^-3\,|$ = ___

2. $|\,^+4\,|$ = ___

3. $|\,^+4 + ^+3\,|$ = ___

4. $|\,^-3 + ^+5\,|$ = ___

5. $|\,^-3 + ^-2\,| - |\,^+3 - ^-3\,|$ = ___

6. $|\,^-2\,| - |\,^-3\,|$ = ___

7. $|\,^-4 + ^-3\,| - |\,^-6 - 5\,|$ = ___

8. $|\,7 - 3\,| - |\,4 - 8\,|$ = ___

9. $|\,^-3\,| \cdot |\,^-2 + 3\,|$ = ___

10. $|\,^-6 \div 3\,| + |\,^-5 \cdot ^+2\,|$ = ___

Answers:

1. **3**

2. **4**

3. **7**

4. **2**

5. $5 - 6 =$ **$^-1$**

6. $2 - 3 =$ **$^-1$**

7. $7 - 11 =$ **$^-4$**

8. $4 - 4 =$ **0**

9. $3 \cdot 1 =$ **3**

10. $2 + 10 =$ **12**

Solve for **x**:

1. $|\,^-3 - 2\,| = \mathbf{x} + 1$

2. $|\,^-4 + 3\,| - \mathbf{x} = |\,^-6 + ^-3\,|$

3. $|\,\mathbf{x} - 1\,| = 7$

4. $|\,3\mathbf{x} + 2\,| = |\,^-4 - 3\,|$

Answers:

1. $5 = \mathbf{x} + 1; \underline{\mathbf{x} = 4}$

2. $1 - \mathbf{x} = 9; \underline{\mathbf{x} = ^-8}$

3. $\mathbf{x} - 1 = 7$ or $\mathbf{x} - 1 = ^-7;$

     $\underline{\mathbf{x} = 8}$ or $\underline{\mathbf{x} = ^-6}$

check to be sure the two answers each makes sense:

$|\underline{8} - 1| = 7$ (Yes) and $|\,\underline{^-6} - 1| = 7$ (Yes)

4. $|3\mathbf{x} + 2| = 7$

     $3\mathbf{x} + 2 = 7$ or $3\mathbf{x} + 2 = ^-7$

     $3\mathbf{x} \qquad = 5$ or $^-9$

     $\underline{\mathbf{x} = ^5/3}$ or $\underline{\mathbf{x} = ^-3}$

29. INTEGER FACTORS

An *integer factor* is an integer that can be divided evenly (i.e. without a remainder) into another number. For example, the positive integer factors of 48 are: 1, 2, 3, 4, 6, 8, 12, 16, 24, and 48. (The negative integer factors are ‾1, ‾2, ‾3, ‾4, ‾6, ‾8, ‾12, ‾16, ‾24, and ‾48.) Unless stated otherwise, "factors" are regarded as *positive integer factors*.

Factors of 100 are: 1, 2, 5, 10, 25, 50, 100

Factors of 49 are: 1, 7, 49

Here's an example, applying factors to more easily simplify:

$$\frac{27 \cdot 8 \cdot 9 \cdot 40}{72 \cdot 20} = \frac{27 \cdot \cancel{8} \cdot \cancel{9} \cdot \cancel{20} \cdot 2}{\cancel{8} \cdot \cancel{9} \cdot \cancel{20}} = 54$$

---

30. PRIME/COMPOSITE NUMBERS

A *prime number* is a positive integer greater than 1 which does not contain any positive factors other than 1 and itself. A *composite number* is a positive integer greater than 1 which is not prime.

(example)

Number	Positive Factors	Prime Or Composite?
2	1, 2	PRIME
7	1, 7	PRIME
9	1, 3, 9	COMPOSITE
26	1, 2, 13, 26	COMPOSITE
47	1, 47	PRIME

[Note: "1" is neither *prime* nor *composite*]

31. FACTORING, SIMPLIFYING AND ESTIMATING INTEGER SQUARE ROOTS

FACTORING and SIMPLIFYING

[Note: *The goal is to break the number down by factoring, then locate groups of 2 identical factors; for each couple circled, the number "breaks out" of the $\sqrt{}$ and goes outside! The remainder stays inside.*]

Examples, using two different methods:

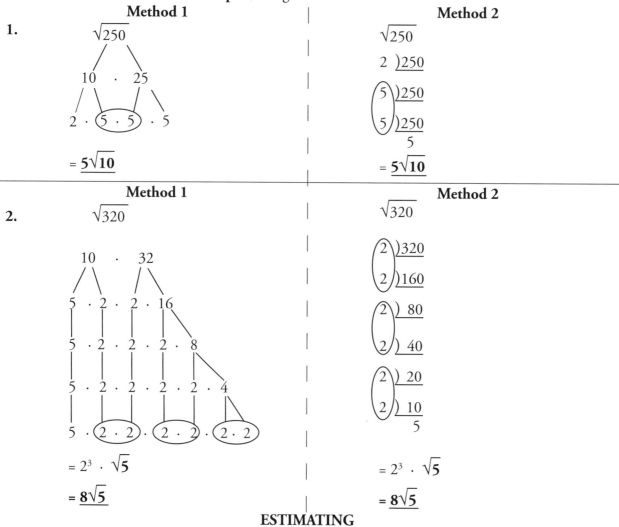

Method 1	Method 2
1.	

$\sqrt{250}$

$= 5\sqrt{10}$ $= 5\sqrt{10}$

Method 1   **Method 2**

2. $\sqrt{320}$

$= 2^3 \cdot \sqrt{5}$ $= 2^3 \cdot \sqrt{5}$

$= 8\sqrt{5}$ $= 8\sqrt{5}$

ESTIMATING

[Note: *Occasionally the **SAT** does not seek exact answers but merely those <u>estimated</u> to the nearest integer. To estimate, simply determine which two integers are the closest, then choose the nearer of the two.*]

Examples:

1. $\sqrt{70}$

$\sqrt{64}$ is 8; $\sqrt{81}$ is 9

$\sqrt{70}$ is therefore between 8 and 9, closer to **8**

2. $\sqrt{46}$

$\sqrt{36}$ is 6; $\sqrt{49}$ is 7

$\sqrt{46}$ is therefore between 6 and 7, closer to **7**

32. FACTORING SQUARE ROOTS INVOLVING VARIABLES

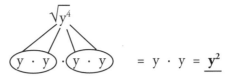

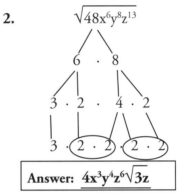

$= y \cdot y = \underline{\mathbf{y^2}}$

[Note: *To simplify square roots with variables, divide the exponent by 2, leaving any remainder inside the $\sqrt{}$*]

Example, using this simplified method: $\sqrt{w^5 x^{12} y^{24} z^{47}} = w^2 x^6 y^{12} z^{23} \sqrt{wz}$

Examples involving numbers and variables:

1. $\sqrt{64 m^5 n^4 p^3}$

Answer: $\mathbf{8 m^2 n^2 p \sqrt{mp}}$

2. $\sqrt{48 x^6 y^8 z^{13}}$

6 · 8

3 · 2 · 4 · 2

3 · 2 · 2 · 2 · 2

Answer: $\underline{\mathbf{4 x^3 y^4 z^6 \sqrt{3z}}}$

33. FACTORING AND EXPANDING QUADRATICS

[Note: *If you have difficulty following these examples, consult an algebra book for a more detailed explanation.*]

FACTORING

1. $x^2 + 3x - 10$

Answer: $\underline{\mathbf{(x + 5)(x - 2)}}$

2. $x^2 - 36$

Answer: $\underline{\mathbf{(x + 6)(x - 6)}}$

EXPANDING (Reverse-Operation of FACTORING)
(Using F.O.I.L. – <u>F</u>irst, <u>O</u>utside, <u>I</u>nside, <u>L</u>ast – Method)

3. $(x - 3)(x + 6)$

Solution: $x^2 + 6x - 3x - 18$

Answer: $\underline{\mathbf{x^2 + 3x - 18}}$

5. $(x - 5)(x + 5)$

Solution: $x^2 + 5x - 5x - 25$

Answer: $\underline{\mathbf{x^2 - 25}}$

4. $(x - 4)(x - 9)$

Solution: $x^2 - 9x - 4x + 36$

Answer: $\underline{\mathbf{x^2 - 13x + 36}}$

6. $(2\sqrt{x} - \sqrt{y})(\sqrt{x} - \sqrt{y})$

Solution: $2x - 2\sqrt{xy} - \sqrt{xy} + y$

Answer: $\underline{\mathbf{2x - 3\sqrt{xy} + y}}$

34. COMBINING TERMS AND FACTORS (examples for every occasion):

Example #1

$3x^4 + 8x^4 = 11x^4$

[Note: *To add variables, they <u>must</u> have the same exponent value.*]

Example #2

$4x^6 - x^6 = 3x^6$

[Note: *To subtract variables, they <u>must</u> have the same exponent value.*]

Example #3

$z^4 \cdot z^5 = z^9$

[Note: *When multiplying variables, simply <u>add</u> their exponents.*]

Example #4

$4w^5 \cdot 7w^3 = 28w^8$

Example #5

$3m^6 \cdot m = 3m^7$

Example #6:

$12t^8 \div 6t^3 = 2t^5$

[Note: *When dividing variables, simply <u>subtract</u> their exponents.*]

Example #7

$(y^6)^4 = y^{24}$

[Note: *When a variable's exponent is exponentialized, simply <u>multiply</u> the exponents.*]

Example #8:

$(3b^3)^4 = 81b^{12}$

[Note: *This is the same as* $(3b^3)(3b^3)(3b^3)(3b^3) = 3 \cdot 3 \cdot 3 \cdot 3 \cdot b^3 \cdot b^3 \cdot b^3 \cdot b^3 = 81b^{12}$]

Challenging Example:

$k^8 \div k^8 = k^0 = ?$

Answer: $\underline{k^0 = 1}$!

[Note: *This is true for <u>any</u> real number except 0:* $x^0 = 1$]

35. FUNCTIONS

Many **SAT** Function questions are simply problems that require **substitution**.

Here are a couple of sample problems:

1. If $f(x) = 3x^2 + 2$, what is $f(2)$?

Solution: $f(2) = 3(2)^2 + 2$

> **Answer:** $\underline{f(2) = 14}$

---

2. If $f(x) = x^2 - 2$, what is $f(f(3))$?

Solution: $f(3) = 3^2 - 2 = \underline{7}$;

$f(7) = 7^2 - 2 = \underline{47}$

> **Answer:** $\underline{f(f(3)) = 47}$

36. DIRECT AND INVERSE VARIATION

Although these terms sound complicated, they are merely another instance of problems involving substitution. The following examples should clarify how to solve such problems; the subsequent samples should then be very easy to answer.

[Remember: your object is to find the value of <u>k</u> (a constant) so you can substitute it into the second equation.]

DIRECT VARIATION FORMULA: $y = kx$

Example #1: If y varies directly as x, and $y = 5$ when $x = 10$, what is the value of y when x is 30?

Solution: $5 = k \cdot 10$, <u>**k** = ½</u>; therefore, the question is solved by substituting the "constant" **k** and the new value of the variable (x): $y = ½ \cdot 30$

$$\boxed{\textbf{Answer: } \underline{y = 15}}$$

Example #2: If y varies directly as x, and $y = 15$ when $x = 5$, what is the value of x when y is 8?

Solution: $15 = k \cdot 5$, <u>**k** = 3</u>; therefore $8 = 3 \cdot x$; $8 = 3x$

$$\boxed{\textbf{Answer: } \underline{x = {}^{8}/_{3}}}$$

INVERSE VARIATION FORMULA: $xy = k$ (also written as $y = {}^{k}/_{x}$)

Example #1: If x varies inversely as y, and $x = 2$ when $y = 6$, what is the value of x when y is 12?

Solution: $2 \cdot 6 = k$, <u>**k** = 12</u>; therefore $x \cdot 12 = 12$

$$\boxed{\textbf{Answer: } \underline{x = 1}}$$

Example #2: If x varies inversely as y, and $x = 5$ when $y = 1$, what is the value of y when x is 30?

Solution: $5 \cdot 1 = k$; <u>**k** = 5</u>; therefore $30 \cdot y = 5$; $y = {}^{5}/_{30} = {}^{1}/_{6}$

$$\boxed{\textbf{Answer: } \underline{y = {}^{1}/_{6}}}$$

DIRECT VARIATION

Problem #1

If y varies directly as x, and $y = {}^3/_4$ when $x = {}^1/_2$, what is the value of y when x is 6?

Solution:

$${}^3/_4 = k \cdot {}^1/_2, \underline{k = {}^6/_4 = {}^3/_2}; \quad y = {}^3/_2 \cdot 6 = {}^{18}/_2$$

Answer: $\underline{y = 9}$

Problem #2

If y varies directly as x, and $y = 12$ when $x = 2$, what is the value of x when $y = 2$?

Solution:

$$12 = k \cdot 2, \underline{k = 6}$$
$$2 = 6 \cdot x; \quad x = {}^2/_6$$

Answer: $\underline{x = {}^1/_3}$

INVERSE VARIATION

Problem #1   If x varies inversely as y, and x = .5 when y = 3.5, what is the value of x when y = 7.5?

Solution:

$$.5 \cdot 3.5 = k, \underline{k = 1.75}$$
$$x \cdot 7.5 = 1.75, \quad x = 1.75 \div 7.5$$

Answer: $\underline{x = .233}$ (or ${}^7/_{30}$)

Problem #2   If x varies inversely as y, and $x = 8$ when $y = 36$, what is the value of y when $x = 6$?

Solution:

$$8 \cdot 36 = k, \underline{k = 288}$$
$$6 \cdot y = 288; \quad y = 288 \div 6$$

Answer: $\underline{y = 48}$

37. COORDINATE AXIS

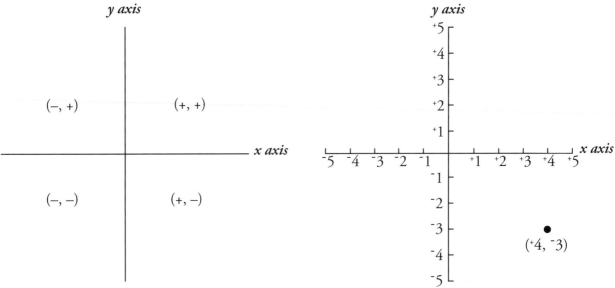

A point is plotted by determining its distance and direction on the **x**-axis (similar to the horizontal number line), then its distance and direction on the **y**-axis (similar to a vertical number line). For example, the point ($^+$4, $^-$3) is found by moving $^+$4 units on the **x**-axis, then going $^-$3 units on the **y**-axis. This point has been appropriately plotted in the above coordinate-axis drawing.

38. MIDPOINT FORMULA

The midpoint ("middle point") of the points (x_1, y_1) and (x_2, y_2) can be found as:$\left(\dfrac{x_1 + x_2}{2}, \dfrac{y_1 + y_2}{2} \right)$

Examples:

1. the midpoint of (3, 4) and (8, 12) is: $\dfrac{3 + 8}{2}$, $\dfrac{4 + 12}{2}$ = **(5.5, 8)**

2. the midpoint of ($^-$6, 0) and (4, 4) is: $\dfrac{^-6 + 4}{2}$, $\dfrac{0 + 4}{2}$ = **($^-$1, 2)**

39. DISTANCE FORMULA

The distance between two points can be found as: $\sqrt{(x_2 - x_1)^2 + (y_2 - y_1)^2}$

Examples:

1. the distance between points (3, 2) and (9, 8) is:
$$d = \sqrt{(9 - 3)^2 + (8 - 2)^2} = \sqrt{(6)2 + (6)2} = \sqrt{36+36}$$
$$= \sqrt{72} = \sqrt{36 \cdot 2} = \mathbf{6\sqrt{2}}$$

2. the distance between points ($^-$2, $^-$5) and (8, 3) is:
$$d = \sqrt{(8 - ^-2)^2 + (3 - ^-5)^2} = \sqrt{10^2 + 8^2} = \sqrt{164}$$
$$= \sqrt{41 \cdot 4} = \mathbf{2\sqrt{41}}$$

40. LINE SLOPE

To determine the slope of a line easily, apply the $\frac{\textbf{rise}}{\textbf{run}}$ formula.

Example:

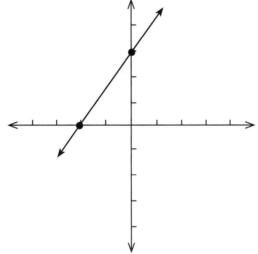

Two points are clearly identifiable: (⁻2, 0) and (0, 3). The line "rises" 3 units and "runs" 2 units to get from the first point to the second. The slope of the line is therefore ³/₂.

Slope Formula: slope ("**m**") = $\dfrac{y_2 - y_1}{x_2 - x_1}$

Example 1: A line containing the points (1, 2) and (4, 3) has slope of $\dfrac{3 - 2}{4 - 1} = $ ¹/₃.

Example 2: A line which passes through the origin* and contains the point (9, 6) has a slope of

$$\dfrac{6 - 0}{9 - 0} \; = \; ^{2}/_{3}.$$

[* Note: (0, 0) *is the coordinate pair denoting the origin.*]

SLOPE-EQUATION INCLUDING y-INTERCEPT

In the equation $y = mx + b$, you can immediately determine the slope of the line (the slope is "m") and the point at which the line will cross the **y-axis** (called the "**y-intercept**", which is determined as "**b**"). To find the **x-intercept**, simply set $y = 0$, then solve for **x**.

Here are a couple of examples:

    1. $y = {}^{-}5x - 4$
       slope is ${}^{-}5$; *y-intercept* is ${}^{-}4$
       (x-*intercept* is ${}^{-}4/5$)

    2. $y = {}^{1x}/_2 + 4$
       slope is ${}^{+}1/_2$; *y-intercept* is ${}^{+}4$
       (x-*intercept* is ${}^{-}8$)

Here are a few sample problems. Identify the *slope* and *y-intercept*
(Optional: determine the x-*intercept*):

    1. $y = 2x - 10$

> **Answer:** slope is ${}^{+}2$
>   y-intercept is ${}^{-}10$
>   x-intercept is ${}^{+}5$)

---

    2. $x - 9y = 15$

Solution: first, set up in *slope-intercept format*:
              $x = 15 + 9y$,
              $9y = x - 15$,
              $y = {}^{x}/_9 - {}^{15}/_9$
              $y = {}^{1x}/_9 - {}^{15}/_9$

> **Answer:** slope is ${}^{1}/_9$
>   y-intercept is ${}^{-15}/_9$ (or ${}^{-}1{}^{2}/_3$)
>   (x-intercept is 15)

Slope-specific question:

    3. If **m** = 3, what is the slope of a line
       whose equation is $y = 2m + 4$?

> **Answer:** slope is $2 \cdot 3 = \underline{\mathbf{6}}$
>   i.e., the slope of a line is determined as **m** <u>and any coefficient of **m**</u>.

SLOPES OF PARALLEL AND PERPENDICULAR LINES

*Parallel lines share the **same slope**; the slope of a perpendicular line is the **negative reciprocal** ($^-1/\mathbf{m}$) of the other line.*

Here are two examples:

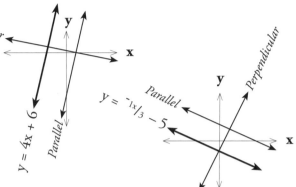

1. original line equation: $y = 4x + 6$

   slope of any line ***parallel*** to this line: <u>$^+4$</u>

   slope of any line ***perpendicular*** to this line: <u>$^-1/_4$</u>

2. original line equation: $y = {}^{-1x}/_3 - 5$

   slope of any line ***parallel*** to this line: <u>$^-1/_3$</u>

   slope of any line ***perpendicular*** to this line: <u>$^+3$</u>

Here are a few sample problems: Identify the slope of a line *parallel* and the slope of a line *perpendicular* to the following lines as determined by the given points or equations:

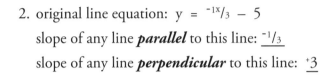

1. $y = {}^{3x}/_4 - {}^7/_8$

> **Answer:** *parallel* slope: $^{+3}/_4$
> *perpendicular* slope: $^{-4}/_3$

---

2. line containing the points (4, 3) and (2, $^-3$)

Solution: Find the slope using the slope formula on page 95: $\dfrac{3 - {}^-3}{4 - 2} = 6/2 = 3$ *

[* Note: To find the slope, you can use either point's **y**-coordinate, as long as you use the corresponding **x**-coordinate.

In this problem, $3 - {}^-3$ is easier than $^-3 - 3$, but remember to then use $4 - 2$, not $2 - 4$.]

> **Answer:** *parallel* slope: $^+\mathbf{3}$
> *perpendicular* slope: $^-1/_3$

---

3. $2x + 3y = 12$

Solution: $3y = {}^-2x + 12$, $y = {}^{-2x}/_3 + 4$

> **Answer:** *parallel* slope: $^-2/_3$
> *perpendicular* slope: $^{+3}/_2$

41. GRAPHS

LINEAR EQUATIONS

To graph a line, simply plot points and connect. Here are a few elementary examples:

1. $y = x$

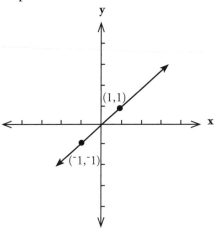

2. $y = x + 3$

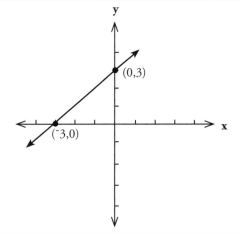

3. $y = 2x - 1$

x	y
⁻2	⁻5
⁻1	⁻3
0	⁻1
1	1
2	3

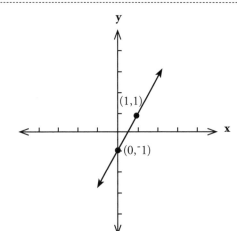

QUADRATIC EQUATIONS

To graph any quadratic equation, simply select points and then connect them. The more points you select, the more accurate the graph will be when points are joined. The following sample problems and explanations will help you see how easy it is to graph points, no matter how complex the problem may appear. (And don't let $f(x)$ or $g(x)$ etc. confuse you; that's just a mathematical way of saying "**y**". So if $f(x)$ = **x + 4**, that's the same as **y = x + 4**.)

Graph the following (answers with accompanying point-charts are on page 100)

1. $f(x) = x^3 - 2$

2. $g(x) = |2x + 3| - 3$

3. $f(x) = x^{2/3}$

MASTERING SAT ALGEBRA SKILLS

Answers:

1. *

x	f(x)
⁻3	⁻29
⁻2	⁻10
⁻1	⁻3
0	⁻2
1	⁻1
2	6
3	25

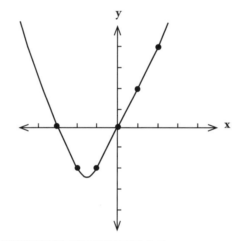

2. *

x	g(x)
⁻3	0
⁻2	⁻2
⁻1	⁻2
0	0
1	2
2	4
3	6

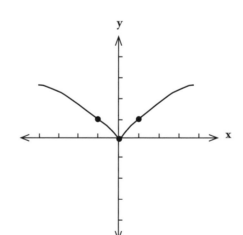

[note: $x^{2/3} = \sqrt[3]{x^2}$]

3. *

x	g(x)
8	4
⁻1	1
0	0
1	1
8	4

* (note: always try to use x-values that yield easy-to-graph integer values)

TRANSLATION OF GRAPHS ("shifting")

To make these problems easier to understand, use this helpful formula:

> Through TRANSLATION ("shifting"), $f(x)$ becomes $f(x - h) + k$;
> the graph is shifted **h** units on the **x**-axis and **k** units on the **y**-axis.

Sample:

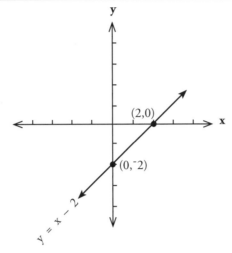

If **y** = $f(x)$ as shown in the drawing, what would the graphs of the following look like:

1. y = $f(x - 1)$
2. y = $f(x + 2)$
3. y = $f(x + 3) + 4$

Traditional Approach

To find the new graphs, we can plot the new points, being careful to recognize that in Sample 1., $f(x - 1)$ must equal the original value for **y**. In other words, because one of the original points is (2,0) [$f(2)$ = 0)], the $f(x - 1) = f(2)$, so x = **3** (3 − 1 = 2) in the new graph when y = 0. The new graph contains point (3,0), shifting the line one unit to the right (the slope does not change).

For Sample 2., because (2,0) was an original point [$f(2)$ = 0)], the newly-translated equation is $f(x + 2) = f(2)$, in which case the new x = **0** (0 + 2 = 2) when y = 0. This means that the line has shifted from (2,0) to (0,0), which is 2 units to the left (the slope is not changed).

Sample 3: Using our original point (2,0) [$f(2)$ = 0)], the new translation has $f(x + 3)$ = 0; and therefore to make is $f(x + 3) = f(2)$, x = ⁻**1**; the new x-coordinate is shifted 3 units to the left (the slope is not changed). However, **y** is now moved ⁺4 as well, which RAISES the line 4 units (the new point is (⁻1,4).)

● See next page for **easier method** ●

Here are pictures of the three translated ("shifted") lines described on page 101:

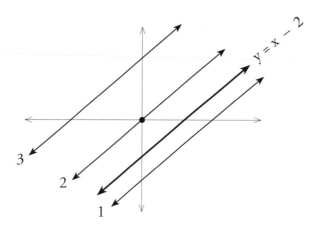

Easier method, *using* $y = f(x - h) + k$ *formula:*

Sample 1. $y = f(x - 1)$, so h = ⁺1 (line is shifted ⁺1 unit on the x-axis)

Sample 2. $y = f(x + 2)$, so h = ⁻2 (line is shifted ⁻2 units on the x-axis)

Sample 3. $y = f(x + 3) + 4$, so h = ⁻3 and k = ⁺4
(line is shifted ⁻3 units on the **x**-axis and ⁺4 on the **y**-axis)

It's so much easier to use the above formula for solving "translation" problems!
– follow whichever method works best for you! –

ALGEBRA QUIZ 1 (20 Questions – 15 Minutes)
*(focusing on basic algebra skills frequently tested on the **SAT**)*

[answers on page 182]

(circle your answer)

1. If $2x + 5 = 11$, $x =$

   A) 8

   B) 9

   C) 3

   D) 0

   E) 14

2. $\sqrt{27} \cdot \sqrt{3} =$

   A) $2\sqrt{6}$

   B) 81

   C) $\sqrt{30}$

   D) 9

   E) 3

3. $^-(3a)^2 =$

   A) $^-9a^2$

   B) $9a^2$

   C) $^-6a^2$

   D) $^-3a^2$

   E) $3a^2$

4. Which of the following is a prime number?

   A) 21

   B) 25

   C) 15

   D) 23

   E) 27

5. $\dfrac{18x^6 \cdot 27y^5 \cdot 36z^4}{9^3x^2y^5z} =$

   A) $2x^3z^3$

   B) $9^2x^4yz^3$

   C) $108x^4z^3$

   D) $24x^4z^3$

   E) $648x^3z^4$

6. $(2x^2)^4 =$

   A) $2x^6$

   B) $16x^8$

   C) $8x^6$

   D) $16x^6$

   E) $2x^8$

7. Three less than the product of **x** and 4 is 5.

   x =

   A) 2

   B) 4

   C) $^{17}/_4$

   D) $^2/_5$

   E) $^1/_2$

8. $\sqrt{72} =$

   A) 9

   B) $2\sqrt{23}$

   C) $8\sqrt{3}$

   D) $4\sqrt{3}$

   E) $6\sqrt{2}$

9. $(4a^2)^3 \div (2a)^3 =$

   A) $8a^2$

   B) $2a^3$

   C) $64a^2$

   D) $2a^2$

   E) $8a^3$

10. $4x^2 + (3x)^2 =$

   A) $13x^2$

   B) $25x^4$

   C) $49x^2$

   D) $10x^2$

   E) $25x^2$

Mathematical Reasoning

[answers on page 182]

11. To the nearest integer, $\sqrt{59}$ =
   A) 7.5
   B) 8
   C) 9
   D) 29
   E) 30

12. Six less than the product of **m** and **9** can be written as
   A) 6m – 9
   B) 9m – 6
   C) (m + 9) – 6
   D) 6 – 9m
   E) 6m + 9

13. If $(2\,^1/_3)d = 28$, d =
   A) 16
   B) 14 $^1/_3$
   C) 70
   D) 12
   E) 14

14. Which of the following is NOT a factor of 42?
   A) 3
   B) 6
   C) 7
   D) 9
   E) 21

15. $6c^6/2c^2$ =
   A) $3c^3$
   B) $4c^4$
   C) $3c^4$
   D) $8c^4$
   E) $4c^3$

16. The sum of three consecutive odd integers can be written as
   A) x + 3
   B) 3x + 3
   C) 3x + 5
   D) x + 5
   E) 3x + 6

17. $3r^4 \cdot 4r^3$ =
   A) $7r^7$
   B) $12r^7$
   C) $7r$
   D) $12r^{12}$
   E) $7r^{12}$

18. $\sqrt{8} + \sqrt{32}$ =
   A) $2\sqrt{6}$
   B) $6\sqrt{2}$
   C) $2\sqrt{10}$
   D) 2
   E) 6

19. $\sqrt{50} \div \sqrt{2}$ =
   A) 3
   B) 4
   C) 5
   D) $4\sqrt{3}$
   E) $2\sqrt{13}$

20. If 3e = 4f – 2, then f =
   A) $\dfrac{2 - 3e}{4}$
   B) $\dfrac{3e - 2}{2}$
   C) $^3/_4 e$
   D) $^3/_4 e + 2$
   E) $\dfrac{3e + 2}{4}$

(focusing on basic algebra skills frequently tested on the **SAT***)*

[answers on page 182]

(circle your answer)

1. $^-(5y)^2 - (5y)^2 =$
   A) $25y^2$
   B) $^-25y^4$
   C) 0
   D) $25y^4$
   E) $^-50y^2$

2. Rounded to the nearest tenth, the product of .7x and .8x is
   A) $.5x$
   B) $5.7x^2$
   C) $.6x^2$
   D) $.57x^2$
   E) $.56x^2$

3. $(^-4y)(^-3y) - 2y^2 =$
   A) ^-9y
   B) $10y^2$
   C) $14y^4$
   D) $^-24y^2$
   E) $9y$

4. If $6x - 3 = 2x + 9$, then $x =$
   A) $1^1/_2$
   B) 2
   C) $^1/_3$
   D) 4
   E) 3

5. $\sqrt{36} - \sqrt{8}$ is closer to which integer?
   A) 2
   B) 3
   C) 4
   D) 5
   E) 6

6. If $3x + 2y = 28$, and $5x - 2y = 20$, then $y =$
   A) $3^1/_2$
   B) 4
   C) 5
   D) 6
   E) 7

7. In its simplified form, $\sqrt{96x^8y^{11}z^{17}}$ is
   A) $4x^2y^3z^4\sqrt{6x^2y^2z}$
   B) $4x^4y^5z^8\sqrt{6yz}$
   C) $16x^7y^{10}z^{16}\sqrt{6xyz}$
   D) $16x^4y^5z^8\sqrt{6yz}$
   E) $2\sqrt{48x^8y^{11}z^{17}}$

8. The average (arithmetic mean) of 4, 9, 13, and y is 16. The value of y is
   A) 32
   B) $^-16$
   C) 40
   D) 38
   E) 24

9. Which of the following satisfies the inequality $^-.25 < x < .50$?
   A) $^1/_3$
   B) $^1/_2$
   C) $^2/_3$
   D) $^{-1}/_3$
   E) $^{-1}/_2$

10. If $x^2 + 3x - 6 = 2y$, and $x = 2$, then $y =$
    A) 2
    B) 1
    C) $^1/_2$
    D) 4
    E) $1^1/_2$

[**answers on page 182**]

11. $2\sqrt{21}$ is the same as which of the following?
   A) $\sqrt{23}$
   B) $\sqrt{84}$
   C) $\sqrt{882}$
   D) $\sqrt{42}$
   E) $21\sqrt{2}$

12. $\dfrac{x^2 + 3x + 2}{x^2 - 3x - 10}$ can be simplified as
   A) $^{-3}/_{11}$
   B) $^{-1}/_{5}$
   C) $\dfrac{x + 1}{x - 5}$
   D) $\dfrac{x + 2}{x - 10}$
   E) $^{+1}/_{5}$

13. In a bag containing only blue, green and red marbles, if the ratio of blue marbles to green marbles is 3 to 2, and the ratio of green marbles to red marbles is 4 to 3, how many red marbles are in a bag containing 30 blue marbles?
   A) 5
   B) 10
   C) 9
   D) 30
   E) 15

14. $y^2 + 8y + 7$ can be factored as
   A) $(y - 1)(y - 7)$
   B) $(y + 8)(y + 1)$
   C) $(y + 4)(y + 3)$
   D) $(y + 1)(y + 7)$
   E) $(y - 8)(y - 1)$

15. Eight less than twice a number is four more than three times the number. What is the number?
   A) $^-12$
   B) 12
   C) $^-4$
   D) $^-4/_5$
   E) $^4/_5$

16. Which of the following is NOT a factor of $68xy^2$?
   A) $17x$
   B) $34y^2$
   C) $2xy^2$
   D) $4x^2y$
   E) $68xy^2$

17. The product of $(\sqrt{x} + \sqrt{y})$ and $(\sqrt{x} - \sqrt{y})$ is
   A) $x - y$
   B) $2\sqrt{x}$
   C) $2\sqrt{y}$
   D) $x + y$
   E) $x^2 + 2\sqrt{xy} + y^2$

18. If $3x - 2 = 8$, then $8 - 12x =$
   A) $^-16$
   B) 32
   C) $^-32$
   D) $^-8$
   E) 16

19. $\dfrac{x^3 \cdot x^5 \cdot y^8}{(xy^2)^4}$
   A) x^2
   B) x^4y^2
   C) x^{11}
   D) $x^{15}y^8$
   E) x^4

20. Given two consecutive positive odd integers such that the smaller is four more than the square root of the larger, what is the larger number?
   A) 3
   B) 5
   C) 7
   D) 9
   E) 25

The **SAT** Math sections include an assortment of geometry problems. Fortunately, they are all basically quite easy and do not require extensive review. The few formulas that may be used are provided at the beginning of each **SAT** section, but it is advisable that you become familiar with them and not waste valuable time referring to them during the test. Examples are provided for each of the **WHAT YOU NEED TO KNOW** geometry-headings to help simplify each concept and avoid any need for lengthy theoretical explanations.

42. PERIMETER OF POLYGONS

To determine the perimeter of (distance around) any polygon (such as a rectangle, triangle, pentagon, etc.), simply add up the lengths of the sides.

Examples:

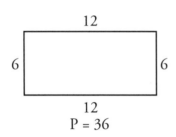

P = 36

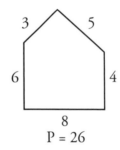

P = 26

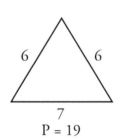

P = 19

43. AREA OF A SQUARE

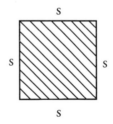

Area = s^2 (where s = length of a side)

Example:

Area = 7^2 = 7 · 7 = **49**

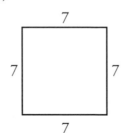

AREA OF A RECTANGLE

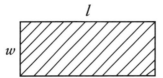

Area = **l** · **w** (where **l** = length
and **w** = width)

Example:

Area = 8 · 3 = **24**

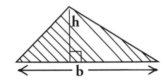

AREA OF A TRIANGLE

[Note: "**h**" *denotes height, found by drawing a line from the upper vertex point perpendicular to the base, which is denoted as "***b***"*]

Area = ¹/₂**bh**

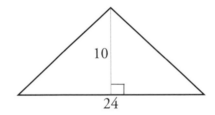

Example:

Area = ¹/₂ · 24 · 10 = **120**

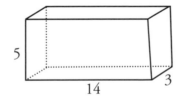

---

44. VOLUME OF RECTANGULAR SOLIDS

Volume = **l** · **w** · **h**

Examples:

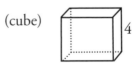

Volume = 14 · 3 · 5 = **210** cubic units

(cube)

Volume = 4 · 4 · 4 = **64** cubic units

45. CIRCLES

Radius (**r**)

Diameter

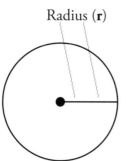

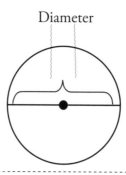

AREA OF A CIRCLE

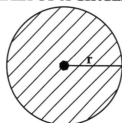

Area = $\pi \mathbf{r}^2$

[Note: *the value of* π *(pi) is approximately 3.14, or* $^{22}/_7$ *(fraction equivalent);* $\mathbf{r}^2$ *means* $\mathbf{r} \cdot \mathbf{r}$]

Example:

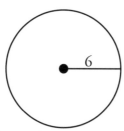

Area = $\pi \cdot 6^2$ = 36π
[or roughly 36 · 3.14 = **113**]

[Note: *the volume of a* <u>right circular cylinder</u> *(a soda can is this shape) can be found by determining the area of the circular base · the height:* $\mathbf{V} = \pi \mathbf{r}^2 \mathbf{h}$]

CIRCUMFERENCE (C) OF (distance around) A CIRCLE

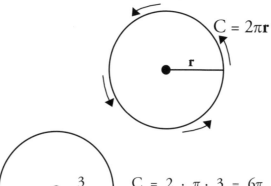

C = $2\pi \mathbf{r}$

Example:

C = 2 · π · 3 = 6π
[or roughly 6 · 3.14 = **19**]

46. DEGREES IN A TRIANGLE, CIRCLE, STRAIGHT LINE

Every triangle contains three angles whose total degree measurement is *always* 180°.

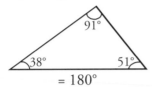
= 180°

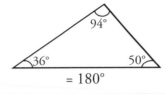
= 180°

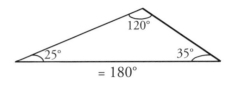
= 180°

The degree-measure of a circle is *always* 360°.

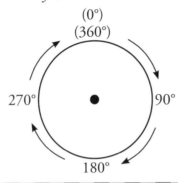

A straight-line angle is *always* 180°.

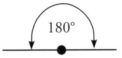

[Note: *two straight angles = a circle:* 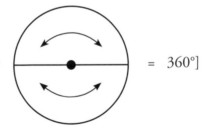 = 360°]

47. ANGLES AND ARC-MEASUREMENTS OF A CIRCLE

Example:

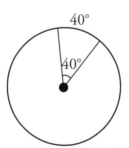

The measure of an arc intercepted by a central angle is **equal** to the measure of the central angle.

Example:

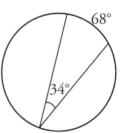

The measure of an arc intercepted by an angle whose vertex (end-point) lies on the circle is **twice** the measure of that angle.

48. PARALLEL LINES AND TRANSVERSALS

Two lines which are *parallel*

and are crossed by a third line [a "transversal"] will be divided into angles of corresponding measure,

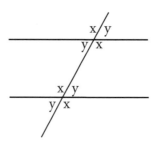

where all "x" are equal, and all "y" are equal.

Example 1: $l_1 \parallel l_2$ [line 1 is parallel to line 2]

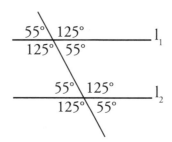

Example 2: $l_1 \parallel l_2$ [line 1 is parallel to line 2]

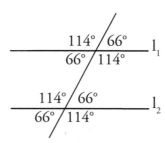

- -

[Note: *If the lines are not parallel, then this correspondence will not apply;*

however, <u>vertical angles</u> ———⊘——— will always be equal.]

49. SIDES AND ANGLES OF TRIANGLES

In any triangle, the side opposite a larger angle of a triangle is the larger side. This principle also applies to a side opposite a smaller angle. The converse statements apply as well.

Examples:

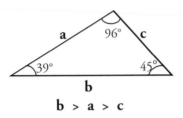

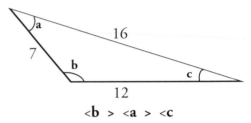

b > a > c

["*The measure of side* **b** *is greater than the measure of side* **a**, *which is greater than the measure of side* **c**".]

<b > <a > <c

["*The measure of angle* **b** *is greater than the measure of angle* **a**, *which is greater than the measure of angle* **c**".]

In any triangle, the sum of the measure of two sides is <u>always greater</u> than the measure of the third side.

Example 1:

8 + 10 > 17
10 + 17 > 8
8 + 17 > 10

[*this is therefore a valid drawing with valid measurements*]

Example 2:

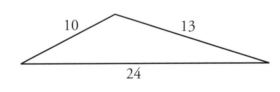

*10 + 13 ≯ 24
13 + 24 > 10
10 + 24 > 13

[**this is <u>not</u> a valid drawing (10 + 13 is <u>not</u> greater than 24); it is not possible to draw a triangle with these measurements because the rule is violated*]

Sample Problem:

In a triangle with two sides measuring 6 and 14, what range of lengths might the third side, **x**, be?

• (Hint: To find the range, simply **add** the two known lengths, then **subtract** the two known lengths: **x** must be **between** these two numbers!) •

Solution:
$$6 + 14 = \underline{20}$$
$$14 - 6 = \underline{8}$$

Answer: **8 < x < 20**

ISOSCELES TRIANGLE

If two sides of a triangle are equal (this type of triangle is called an *Isosceles Triangle*), then the angles opposite these two sides are equal to one another. The converse statement also applies.

Examples:

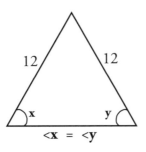

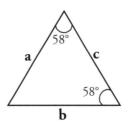

[*"The measure of angle **x** is equal to the measure of angle **y**"*]

side **a** = side **b**

[Note: *We don't know the specific measures of angles **x** and **y**, or of sides **a** and **b**; we only know that they are <u>equal</u>.*]

EQUILATERAL TRIANGLE

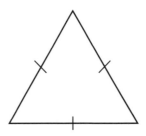

If all sides (or all angles) of a triangle are equal (an *Equilateral Triangle*), each angle measures 60°.

50. PYTHAGOREAN FORMULA

Given a right triangle (a triangle containing a 90° angle, as designated in the following example),

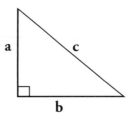

the square of the length of the hypotenuse (the side opposite the 90° angle) is equal to the sum of the squares of each of the legs (the other two sides): $c^2 = a^2 + b^2$ (more commonly written $a^2 + b^2 = c^2$)

Examples:

1.

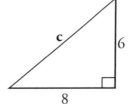

$$6^2 + 8^2 = c^2$$
$$36 + 64 = c^2$$
$$100 = c^2$$

$$\boxed{c = 10}$$

2.

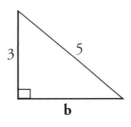

$$3^2 + b^2 = 5^2$$
$$9 + b^2 = 25$$
$$b^2 = 16$$

$$\boxed{b = 4}$$

[*Note: In this example, we are finding the length of a leg of the triangle.*]

3.

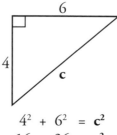

$$4^2 + 6^2 = c^2$$
$$16 + 36 = c^2$$
$$52 = c^2$$

$$\boxed{c = \sqrt{52}}$$

[*$\sqrt{52}$ is somewhere between $\sqrt{49}$ and $\sqrt{64}$ . . . in other words, between 7 and 8, closer indeed to 7. It is a good idea to be able to quickly estimate square-root values, since occasionally an estimated answer is sought. A calculator is helpful here.*]

51. SPECIAL TRIANGLES

Given the following angles, the ratio of measurements of the sides can be immediately determined. The ratios utilize the Pythagorean Formula, but knowing them can help eliminate a few steps and therefore save time.

30° - 60° - 90° TRIANGLE	45° - 45° - 90° TRIANGLE

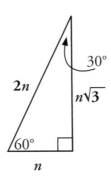

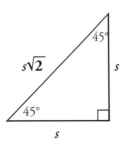

Example:

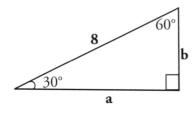

Example:

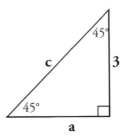

Solution:

$$a = 4\sqrt{3}$$
$$b = 4$$

Solution:

$$a = 3$$
$$c = 3\sqrt{2}$$

52. SPATIAL (VISUAL) RELATIONSHIPS

Many **SAT** Math problems do not offer drawings or other visual aids, yet sometimes require a visual understanding of the problem to successfully answer the question. The key to answering Spatial problems is to carefully comprehend what is being asked and, if helpful, to draw an accompanying illustration to facilitate solving the problem.

Here are a few Spatial problems. Remember that the **SAT** Math isn't merely a statistical exam – it has much visual content as well.

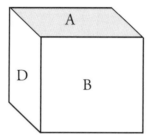

1. The cube above is marked with the letters A, B, C, D, E and F such that A and C (not shown) are on opposite sides.

    What can be definitely deduced from the cube above?
    I. B and E are adjacent sides
    II. E and F are adjacent sides
    III.C and E are adjacent sides

    A) I and II

    B) II only

    C) I and III

    D) II and III

    E) III only

Answer: **D**

2. What is the maximum number of total points of intersection involving a square and a circle?

    Solution:

    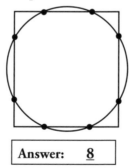

Answer: **8**

3. If an 8-sided regular polygon and a 14-sided regular polygon have the same perimeter, which has a greater area?

    (A "regular" polygon is a polygon with all sides and interior angles equal.)

    Solution: Whenever you are asked to compare, you may wish to exaggerate the data given. For instance, the first polygon has fewer sides than the second, so why not exaggerate the question by comparing a 4-sided polygon (square) with a multi-sided (almost approaching a circle) one and use numbers.

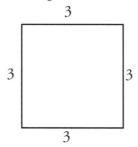
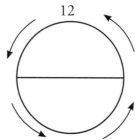

    [In our drawing, the square's perimeter is 12, so the circle's circumference
    (the circle's "perimeter") must also be 12]

    It's now easier to figure out the areas.

    The area of the above square is **9**. The area of the 14-sided regular polygon will be nearly as much as the area of the circle above.

    Since $2\pi r$ (circumference formula) = 12, r = $^6/\pi$, the area of the circle ($\pi r^2 = \pi \cdot {}^6/\pi \cdot {}^6/\pi$) is $^{36}/\pi$, which is a little more than **11**. The 14-sided regular polygon therefore has an area that is **very close to 11**, which is visibly greater than **9**.

    > **Answer:** the **14-sided polygon** has a greater area

    Without drawing with exaggeration, it's nearly impossible to be sure which has a larger area, unless of course your "spatial logic" is so good that you can actually visualize the two!

4. A pair of parallel lines is connected by two separate segments, **AB** and **CD**. The acute angle measurement formed by **AB** and the parallel lines is 38°, the acute angle measurement formed by **CD** is 39°. Which line-segment is longer?

    Solution: Why draw the picture as specified when all we need to know is that **AB** forms a *smaller angle* than does **CD**?!

    Here's a better (exaggerated) drawing which more clearly shows the **answer:**

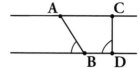

    > **Answer:** **AB** is longer than **CD**

    Spatial relationship problems can therefore be greatly simplified by drawing the problem (and sometimes by exaggerating it) or, if you have the knack, by mentally visualizing it. Either way, you'll find that many SAT Math problems rely on some sort of visual approach.

Clarification (to avoid confusion)

[Note: *Figure not drawn to scale*.]: WHAT DOES THIS MEAN?

In order to avoid being responsible for drawing "perfect" geometrical figures with "perfect" angles," the **SAT** oftentimes adds the "Figure not drawn to scale" label below an illustration. When you see this note you may assume that the figures are as shown, though the sizes and angle-measurements may not be exact.

For example, if you see a triangle inside a circle, you can assume that there is a triangle inside a circle; however, you cannot assume that the triangle contains a right angle or that it is equilateral, even if it looks as though it is.

What is considered "given" information and what is not? In the following mini-quiz, determine which *three* of the following illustrations correctly imply the information in parentheses, and which three do not necessarily lead to the assumption within the parentheses:

QUIZ (6 Questions – 2 Minutes)
[answers are explained on page 119]
(circle the 3 correctly-labeled problems)

1.

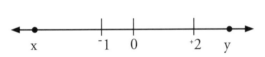

(**x** is less than ⁻1 and can probably be assumed to represent ⁻2.5; y is greater than 2 and probably represents the number ⁺2.5)**?**

2.

Circle Q

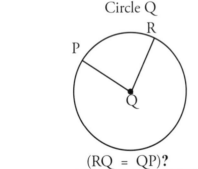

(RQ = QP)**?**

3.

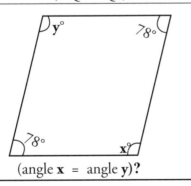

(angle **x** = angle **y**)**?**

4.

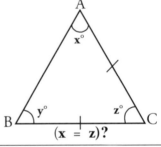

(**x** = **z**)**?**

5.

RS = ¹/₂RT

RT = TU

Point R, S, T and U lie on the same line

(RS = ST, ST = ¹/₂ TU)**?**

6.   Two circles, each with center T

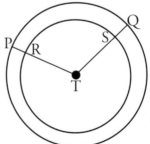

(length of minor arc **PQ** > length of minor arc **RS**)**?**

QUIZ ANSWERS

The first example is a portion of a *number line*, which is considered accurate as drawn. The information within the parentheses *is* accurately assumed.

The second illustration is designated as Circle Q, indicating that it is a circle with center at point Q. Since all radius segments are of equal length, the information in parentheses *is* accurately assumed.

The third drawing, a quadrilateral (4-sided figure) which appears to be a parallelogram, does *not* allow us to deduce that angle **x** = angle **y** in measurement. If the drawing were a parallelogram, then this would be correctly assumed. However, there is no mention that opposite sides are parallel or equal, and therefore all we can assume is that **x** + **y** = 204° (the sum of the angles of a quadrilateral = 360°). But we *cannot* assume that angle **x** and angle **y** are necessarily equal in degree measurement.

The fourth illustration denotes, using markings, that **BC** = **AC**. Using our knowledge of the rule assuming "opposite angles of sides of equal length," we can rightfully deduce that the degree measurement of angle **x** = angle **y**. However, we *cannot* deduce that the degree measurement of angle **x** = angle **z** because we do not know whether the side opposite angle **z** is equal to the other two sides. Not enough information is provided.

The fifth illustration is a straight line with information as given, the four points not placed in any specific order. Therefore, we can place the points in order of R-S-T-U with appropriate lengths to match the information given, or we can order the points S-R-T-U, still maintaining consistency with the information given. In the latter setup, however, RS would *not* be equal in length to ST, nor would ST = $^1/_2$ TU. The problem is ambiguous, and therefore the assumption is *not* necessarily valid.

The sixth illustration shows two circles, each with center T. Arc PQ lies on the outer circle and RS in the inner circle, as shown. The degree measure of each arc is equal, but we are being asked to determine which arc is *longer*. Clearly, outer arc PQ is longer, and therefore the information deduced *is* accurate.

GEOMETRY QUIZ 1 (20 Questions – 15 Minutes)
(focusing on basic geometry skills frequently tested on the SAT)
[answers on page 182]
(circle your answer)

1. Area of square units in the rectangle =
   A) 24
   B) 29
   C) 30
   D) 44
   E) 26

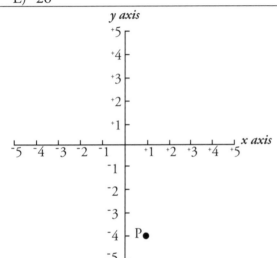

2. Coordinates of point P =
   A) (+, +)
   B) (‾, +)
   C) (+, ‾)
   D) (+, 0)
   E) (‾, ‾)

All sections have an equal area.

3. x =
   A) 30
   B) 72
   C) 60
   D) 12¹/₂
   E) 45

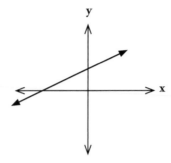

4. The above line contains the following points:
   (‾4, ‾1) and (‾1, 1).

   What is the slope of the line?

   A) ²/₃
   B) ²/₅
   C) 0
   D) ⁵/₂
   E) ‾³/₂

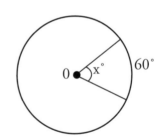

5. x =
   A) 15
   B) 60
   C) 90
   D) 30
   E) 120

6. Area of triangle (in square units) =
   A) 64
   B) 33
   C) 128
   D) 144
   E) 81

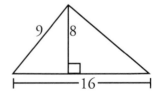

ABFG and DCEF are squares

C is the midpoint of BF

$\overline{AB}$ = 10

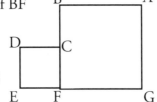

7. Area of ABCDEFG
   (in square units) =

   A) 45

   B) 75

   C) 125

   D) 115

   E) 50

8. **x** =

   A) 50

   B) 90

   C) 100

   D) 130

   E) 230

9. Perimeter of rectangle =

   A) 84

   B) 12

   C) 24

   D) 63

   E) 48

10. Area of circle =

    A) 6π

    B) 9π

    C) 36π

    D) 3π

    E) 12π

11. Length of $\overline{AB}$ =

    A) ⁻4

    B) 4

    C) ⁻6

    D) 6

    E) 2

    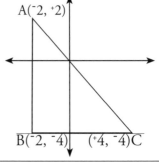

12. Area of square (in square units) =

    A) 3

    B) 12

    C) 81

    D) 27

    E) 9

13. **x** =

    A) 18

    B) 12

    C) 10

    D) 8

    E) 6

    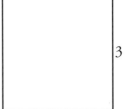

14. Length of $\overline{UV}$ =

    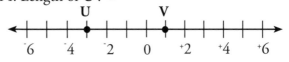

    A) ⁻4

    B) ⁻3

    C) 2

    D) 3

    E) 4

15. Circumference of circle =

A) 8π

B) 16π

C) 12π

D) 2π

E) 4π

18. **x** =

A) 75

B) 150

C) 285

D) 25

E) 105

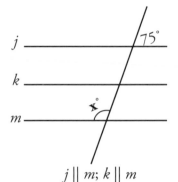

$j \parallel m; k \parallel m$

16. Length of side **c** =

A) $6\sqrt{2}$

B) $12\sqrt{3}$

C) 6

D) $6\sqrt{3}$

E) $3\sqrt{2}$

19. **x** =

A) 120

B) 280

C) 40

D) 80

E) 160

$80°$

$x°$

17. Perimeter of square =

A) $^{49}/_4$

B) 21

C) 14

D) 28

E) 49

7

20. **x** =

A) 68

B) 112

C) 56

D) 118

E) 124

$56°$ $x°$

GEOMETRY QUIZ 2 (20 Questions – 25 Minutes)
*(focusing on basic geometry skills frequently tested on the **SAT**)*
[answers on page 182]
(circle your answer)

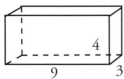

1. The volume of the rectangular solid is how many cubic units greater than that of the cube?
   A) 12
   B) 27
   C) 44
   D) 92
   E) 108

4. $10 - 2b =$
   A) ⁻2
   B) ⁻¹/₂
   C) 0
   D) ¹/₂
   E) 2¹/₄

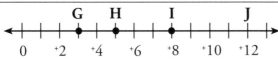

2. The ratio of the lengths of $\overline{GI}$ to $\overline{HJ}$ is
   A) 5 : 12
   B) 5 : 7
   C) 1 : 2
   D) 3 : 4
   E) 2 : 3

5. A circle with center **E** is divided into three equal parts, as shown below. What is the measure, in degrees, of arc **BC**?

   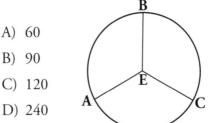

   A) 60
   B) 90
   C) 120
   D) 240
   E) It cannot be determined from the information given.

BCDE is a rectangle bordering the **x** and **y** axis as shown. BD and EC are diagonals, intersecting at point F.

$\overline{ED} = 5$
$\overline{CD} = 3$

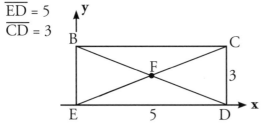

3. The coordinates of point F are
   A) (³/₂, ⁵/₂)
   B) (⁵/₂, ³/₂)
   C) (⁻³/₂, ⁻⁵/₂)
   D) (⁻⁵/₂, ³/₂)
   E) (⁻⁵/₂, ³/₂)

6. A car's tire tracks reveal that, while passing through a muddy road, the wheels have made four complete revolutions. If the radius of the wheel (including the tire) is twelve inches, how many feet through the mud has the vehicle traveled?
   A) 96π
   B) 36π
   C) 48π
   D) 6π
   E) 144π

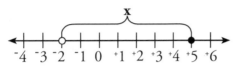

7. In the above graph for **x**, what are the possible solution values?

A) $2 < \mathbf{x} \le 5$

B) $5 \ge \mathbf{x} < 2$

C) $^-2 \le \mathbf{x} \le 5$

D) $^-2 < \mathbf{x} < 5$

E) $^-2 < \mathbf{x} \le 5$

8. If a cylindrical soda can has a circular base with radius 3 inches and a height of 8 inches, how many cubic inches does the volume contain?

A) 576π

B) 12π

C) 192π

D) 24π

E) 72π

(Volume of a cylinder: area-of-**b**ase · **h**eight)

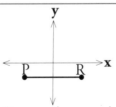

[Note: Figure not drawn to scale.]

9. What are the possible coordinates of the midpoint of **PR**?

   I. (0, ⁻3)

   II. (⁻8, +5)

   III. (⁻6, ⁻2)

A) I only

B) I and II

C) I and III

D) III only

E) neither I, II or III

ABC is an isosceles triangle, AB = AC

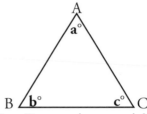

[Note: Figure not drawn to scale.]

10. If $<\mathbf{a} = 54°$, what is the measure, in degrees, of $<\mathbf{b}$?

A) 27

B) 54

C) 63

D) 72

E) 126

11. A rectangular sheet of paper measuring 8"x10" is folded in half, then folded in half again. What is the ratio of the area of one of the smaller rectangles the area of the original sheet?

A) $1 : 4$

B) $1 : 2$

C) $1 : 1$

D) $1 : 8$

E) $1 : 16$

12. In terms of x, **z** =

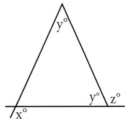

A) $180 - {}^x/_2$

B) $180 + x$

C) $90 - x$

D) $90 + x$

E) $180 + {}^x/_2$

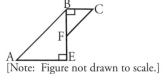

13. If the numerical measure of a circle's area is equivalent to the numerical measure of its circumference, the diameter of the circle is
    A) 1
    B) 2
    C) 3
    D) 4
    E) 8

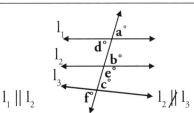

$l_1 \parallel l_2$ $l_2 \nparallel l_3$

14. What can we deduce from the figure above?
    I.   a = b = c
    II. d + e = 180
    III. b ≠ f
    A) I only
    B) I and II
    C) II only
    D) III only
    E) II and III

15. If a cube has a volume of 64 cubic units, how many square units is the total area of its faces?
    A) 64
    B) 32
    C) 16
    D) 128
    E) 96

16. A four-sided polygon may have which of the following?
    I.   three parallel sides
    II. four equal angle-measurements
    III. three sides of equal length
    A) I only
    B) I and II
    C) II only
    D) II and III
    E) III

$\overline{AB}$ = 20
$\overline{BC}$ = 8
$\overline{AE}$ = 16

[Note: Figure not drawn to scale.]

17. The length of $\overline{CE}$ (not drawn) is
    A) $3\sqrt{2}$
    B) $2\sqrt{77}$
    C) 10
    D) $4\sqrt{13}$
    E) $4\sqrt{5}$

18. What is the *maximum* number of points that intersect both two distinct circles and one triangle?
    A) 0
    B) 1
    C) 2
    D) 3
    E) 4

[Note: Figure not drawn to scale.]

19. Which of the following *must* be true regarding the triangle above?
    I.   2 < AC < 10
    II. CA < BA
    III. Area of triangle ABC < 12
    A) I only
    B) I and II
    C) I and III
    D) II and III
    E) I, II, and III

20. Participants in a marathon must run a circular route five full times to complete the 1540-meter competition. Approximately how many meters of land does the racetrack span from one side to the other? (use $^{22}/_7$ for π)
    A) 49
    B) 98
    C) 154
    D) 308
    E) 484

SAT MATH MULTIPLE-CHOICE: Word-Problems with 5 Possible Answers

There is nothing new or special about **SAT** Multiple-Choice Math problems. They need to be solved just like any other math problem, though there are a couple of distinct advantages.

1) You can always plug in the answer-choices to see which one works. This "guess and check" method is an effective way to answer many Multiple-Choice Math problems.

2) If you're not sure how to solve the problem but do understand the general question, you can always **eliminate** those choices that are obviously not correct and then use the "educated guess" (**elimination**) method.

No matter how you approach Multiple-Choice problems, the best advice once again is to <u>work slowly and carefully</u> and be sure you answer the question being asked. ***Avoid careless errors!***

MULTIPLE-CHOICE QUIZ 1 (10 Questions – 10 Minutes)
(focusing on basic-skills questions in **SAT** Multiple-Choice format)
[Note: *Figures not always drawn to scale.*]
[answers on page 182]
(circle your answer)

1. The average of 4.501, 6.02, and 5.37 is
   A) 6.201
   B) 2.357
   C) 3.991
   D) 5.297
   E) 15.892

2. After deducting a discount of 25%, the price of a stereo was $225.00. The regular price of the stereo was
   A) $1000.00
   B) $300.00
   C) $250.00
   D) $900.00
   E) $56.25

3. $^{11}/_{13}$ + $^{3}/_{4}$ =
   A) $^{14}/_{17}$
   B) $^{7}/_{8}$
   C) 2
   D) $1^{13}/_{15}$
   E) $1^{31}/_{52}$

4. All of the following fractions are equivalent to $^{40}/_{90}$ EXCEPT
   A) $^{2}/_{3}$
   B) $^{4}/_{9}$
   C) $^{12}/_{27}$
   D) $^{20}/_{45}$
   E) $^{8}/_{18}$

5. 32 is 50% of
   A) 16
   B) 160
   C) 64
   D) 96
   E) 32

6. If $\mathbf{x}$ = 65 and $\mathbf{y}$ = 35, then $(\mathbf{x} + \mathbf{y})(\mathbf{x} - \mathbf{y})$ =
   A) 2125
   B) 3000
   C) 400
   D) 900
   E) 2700

7. In the figure above, circle O is inscribed in square ABCD. Which geometric figure has a larger area?
   A) circle O
   B) square ABCD
   C) they are equal
   D) both
   E) The answer cannot be determined from the information given.

8. The average of $^{3}/_{5}$ and $^{5}/_{9}$ is
   A) $^{26}/_{45}$
   B) $^{2}/_{3}$
   C) $^{4}/_{7}$
   D) $^{16}/_{49}$
   E) 1

9. If W is a negative integer, W^{7} could equal
   A) W^{6} + W
   B) $^{+}128$
   C) $^{-}1$
   D) 0
   E) W^{12} – W^{5}

10. The number of cubic feet contained in a box 2 feet long, 6 inches wide, and 3 feet deep is
    A) 6
    B) 36
    C) 9
    D) 3
    E) 48

STRATEGIC APPROACH: Plug In The Choices

Occasionally, you might be better off using the five choices to help determine an answer. An example of such a problem might be multiplication involving two decimals in which all the choices contain the same numerals but with differing decimal-point placement. By reviewing the choices beforehand, you may notice that multiplication is *not* necessary; the only task needed is to properly place the decimal point. A quick review of the answers may therefore help save time and avoid needless work.

Many algebra problems on the **SAT** can also be solved more easily by previewing the choices given. In many of these instances, the choices can be "plugged" into the question to see which "fits." As with a jigsaw puzzle, if the choice satisfies the situation it is undoubtedly the correct answer.

Here is a strategy QUIZ to test your ability to *plug in the choices* and *discover which one fits*. In problem #1, for example, simply determine whether the problem makes sense if Gerry is 4 years old, 5 years old, 6 years old, 7 years old, or 8 years old – one choice will satisfy the question. The problem can be solved in "traditional" algebraic steps; however, for many this *plug in the choices* technique will prove faster and less confusing!

STRATEGY QUIZ 1 (10 Questions – 15 Minutes)
For **SAT** Multiple-Choice Math Problems
Strategy: *"Plug in" the choices (see what fits!)*
[answers on page 182]
(circle your answer)

1. Gerry is **c** years old, and his sister Jill is half his age. Two years ago, Gerry was three times as old as Jill. How many years old is Gerry now?
   A) 4
   B) 5
   C) 6
   D) 7
   E) 8

2. If **m**/5 is an even integer and **m**/4 is an odd integer, **m** could equal
   A) 50
   B) 80
   C) 30
   D) 40
   E) 20

$$\frac{x}{1 + \dfrac{x}{2 + \dfrac{x}{2}}} = 2 \quad [x > 0]$$

3. **x** =
   A) 1
   B) 2
   C) 3
   D) 4
   E) 6

4. If $(2 - \mathbf{r})^2 = (\mathbf{r} + 2)^2$, then **r** =
   A) 2
   B) 3
   C) $^-1$
   D) 0
   E) 1

5. If **a** < 0 and $(\mathbf{a} - 2)^2 = 49$, then **a** =
   A) $^-4$
   B) $^-5$
   C) $^-6$
   D) $^-7$
   E) $^+9$

$$\mathbf{x(x + 4)} = {}^-\mathbf{4}$$

6. **x** =
   A) $^-2$
   B) 0
   C) 4
   D) 2
   E) $^-4$

7. Which of the following values for **n** satisfies the equation $\mathbf{n}^2 + 5\mathbf{n} - 11 = 3\mathbf{n} + 4$?
   A) 5
   B) 3
   C) 2
   D) 1
   E) 0

8. If **x** > 0 and $2\mathbf{x} = \mathbf{x}^2$, **x** =
   A) 2
   B) 4
   C) 3
   D) 6
   E) 1

$$^1/_\mathbf{a} + {}^1/_\mathbf{b} = \mathbf{3}$$

9. Which of the following may be the values of **a** and **b**?
   A) a = 2; b = 1
   B) a = 3; b = 0
   C) a = $^1/_3$; b = 1
   D) a = 1; b = $^1/_2$
   E) a = 6; b = 6

$$\begin{array}{r} \mathbf{1B} \\ \times\, \mathbf{2B} \\ \hline \mathbf{2CC} \end{array}$$

10. If the product of the above two-digit numbers (each of which contains the same unit's digit) equals a three-digit number whose ten's and unit's digit are the same, which of the following is a possible value for **B**?
    A) 5
    B) 4
    C) 3
    D) 2
    E) 1

Mathematical Reasoning

STRATEGIC APPROACH: Number-Substitution

There is yet another time-saving, hassle-free strategy frequently employed on the **SAT**. In many problems it is the only method by which they can be solved in an affordable amount of time.

When variables dominate a problem, confusion often results; **substituting numbers for variables** often helps make the problem more intelligible.

If $6x = y^2$ and $y = 3z$, then $z/x =$

A) $\frac{1}{2}$

B) $2/y$

C) $y^2/3$

D) $3y/2$

E) $2y$

In such a problem, you are faced with a time-consuming ball-of-confusion involving three variables. But by substituting numbers for the variables, the problem becomes much easier to manage.

For instance, let $x = 24$; $y = 12$; and $z = 4$ so that the equations remain valid: $6(24) = 12^2$ and $12 = 3(4)$.

Now, to solve z/x is as simple as
- substituting the numbers ($4/24$)
- simplifying when necessary ($1/6$)
- and then replacing the numbers into each of the choices given:

A) $\frac{1}{2}$

B) $2/12$

C) $12(12)/3$

D) $3(12)/2$

E) $2(12)$

It is quite obvious now that $1/6 = 2/12$; the only choice that satisfies the problem is **B**.

Any algebra problem on the **SAT** can be solved using algebraic principles, but for many this is not a feasible or comfortable procedure. *Substituting numbers for variables* helps turn all the ambiguous "letters" into easy-to-understand "numbers"!

Here is a strategy-check QUIZ to test your ability to substitute numbers for variables and see what works! In problem #1, for example, try substituting "5" for "**P**" and "100" for "**n**," then solve the problem and substitute the appropriate values into each of the choices given. The answer will appear as if by magic!

STRATEGY QUIZ 2 (10 Questions – 20 Minutes)
For **SAT** Multiple-Choice Math Problems
Strategy: *Substitute numbers for variables (see what works!)*
[**answers on page 182**]
(**circle your answer**)

1. Jean pays **P**% sales tax for groceries. If the total purchase without tax is $**n**, how many dollars does Jean need to pay, including tax?

   A) $\dfrac{n + P}{100}$

   B) $n + {}^{P}/_{100}$

   C) $\dfrac{nP + P}{100}$

   D) $n + {}^{P}/_{n}$

   E) $n + {}^{Pn}/_{100}$

2. In terms of **b** and **c**, **a** =

   A) $\sqrt{c - b}$

   B) $\sqrt{c^2 - b^2}$

   C) $c^2 - b^2$

   D) $\sqrt{{}^{c}/_{b}}$

   E) $\sqrt{{}^{b}/_{c}}$

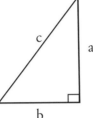

3. If **x** is a positive integer and **y** is a negative integer, which of the following is always true?

   A) ${}^{xy}/_{y}$ is negative

   B) ${}^{x^2y^2}/_{y}$ is positive

   C) $2x - 3y$ is positive

   D) $y - x$ is positive

   E) $y^2 + {}^{x}/_{y}$ is negative

4. On a number line points **E**, **F**, **G** and **H** are arranged in the order given. In units of measure, **FG** = **GH** and **EF** = $^{1}/_{2}$**FG**. What is the ratio of the lengths of **EG** : **FH**?

   A) 1:4

   B) 3:8

   C) 1:3

   D) 3:4

   E) 1:15

5. If $Q - R = 7$, then $R - Q =$

   A) $^{-}7$

   B) $^{-1}/_{7}$

   C) 0

   D) $^{1}/_{7}$

   E) 7

6. Let **x**, **y** and **z** represent positive integers such that **z** ÷ **y** = **x**. Which of the following must also be true?

   A) $^{1}/_{z} = {}^{y}/_{x}$

   B) $^{xy}/_{z} = 1$

   C) $xz = y$

   D) $z - y = x$

   E) $^{x}/_{y} = z$

7. If $2x/y = p$, then $^{1}/_{2}y =$

   A) $4px$

   B) $2x/p$

   C) $^{p}/_{4x}$

   D) $^{1}/_{2}px$

   E) px

8. Let **m** be any integer such that $\text{ⓜ} = {}^{3m}/_{2}$ and $\boxed{m} = {}^{m}/_{2}$. What is the result of $\text{ⓜ}/\boxed{m}$?

   A) 1

   B) 3

   C) m

   D) 3m

   E) $^{m}/_{2}$

$^{1}/_{4} \cdot L = 3S \quad [S \neq 0]$

9. $^{L}/_{S} =$

   A) $^{1}/_{7}$

   B) $^{3}/_{4}$

   C) $^{1}/_{12}$

   D) 7

   E) 12

10. If an employee must empty the complete contents of a can **x** times to fill up a larger container of **y** ounces, what fraction of the container will the person fill with the contents of one can?

    A) $^{1}/_{x}$

    B) $^{1}/_{y}$

    C) xy

    D) $^{x}/_{y}$

    E) $^{y}/_{x}$

ARTIFICIAL OPERATIONS

In most **SAT** Multiple-Choice problems, we have seen that an answer can be determined by:

1. Solving the Problem
2. Plugging In the Answer-Choices

or

3. Substituting Numbers for Variables

On occasion, however, an alien-looking **SAT** problem may emerge, daring you to skip it because it seems awesome and overwhelming. However, do not become intimidated by such problems; they are simply "made-up" operations testing your ability to follow directions, and they can be easily solved. For example, here is the type of problem one might encounter:

For any integer V, **V** is defined as V^2, and ***V*** is defined as $3V - 2$.

The following three questions refer to this operation.

1. If V = 4 then **V** − ***V*** =

   A) 9
   B) 6
   C) 5
   D) 3
   E) 0

2. **V** − ***V*** =

   A) $V^2 - 2$
   B) $4V^2 + 2$
   C) $V^2 - 3V + 2$
   D) $V^2 + V$
   E) $V^2 + 3V - 2$

3. **6** · ***2*** =

   A) ***6*** · **2**
   B) **8**
   C) **12**
   D) ***144***
   E) **4** · ***3***

In a series of problems with "made-up" operations, the first is usually the easiest, while the last usually takes a bit more time to solve. But these are not difficult and should be approached with confidence. Remember, these "strange-looking" problems are not from some advanced book; they are simple problems dressed up to look spooky!

Problem 1: <u>**B**</u> **V** = 16, ***V*** = 12 − 2 = 10; 16 − 10 = 6

Problem 2: <u>**C**</u> **V** = V^2, ***V*** = 3V − 2; $V^2 - (3V - 2) = V^2 - 3V + 2$

                                         Very simple problem!

Problem 3: <u>**C**</u> **6** = 6^2 = 36, ***2*** = (3 · 2) − 2 = 4; 36 · 4 = 144

      We must now sort through the answers to determine which one also equals 144

      12 = 12 · 12 = 144, so the answer that fits is **C**

SAT MATH MULTIPLE-CHOICE:
General Strategy Review

Not all **SAT** Math problems can be easily solved by one of the strategies presented: some are too complex, others simply too time-consuming. In these cases, you should resolve to select either of two options: *estimate* (eliminate choices that seem highly unlikely, then make an "educated guess" from what remains) or *skip* the problem. If you can understand what the problem is asking, you should be able to take an educated guess; if the problem seems unintelligible or is simply too lengthy to make sense out of in any nominal period of time, then it is best to "bail out." Selecting an "appropriate answer" is ideal, but wasting too much valuable time on "educated guessing" is self-defeating. Answer every math question that you understand, but if the problem is going to take several minutes to resolve, skip the problem and don't worry about it; <u>spend your time where it is most needed and least consumed</u>!

If one point is to be emphasized above all the rest, it should be that problems contained in the **SAT** Mathematics section are *relatively easy*. They do not require vocabulary training or memorization of extensive formulas. They simply require a commonsense approach, with careful reading a necessity. You may already have discovered that all **SAT** Math tests strongly resemble one another, logically so because they are attempting to test the same basic concepts. Feeling confident in your ability to manage the test will make a tremendous difference in how well you perform on the **SAT** Mathematics portion; the other ingredients that will ensure success are **practice** and **review**.

If any sample problem seems unusually complex, show it to a friend or instructor. The question may simply be camouflaged to appear more difficult than it really is. But if a problem is indeed unusually complicated and lengthy to solve, remember to <u>skip it</u> and move on so time can be spent more judiciously. Answer as many problems as possible, though the need to answer all of them is not as crucial as it is on the Critical Reading portion. The following QUIZ on Multiple Choice questions offers a variety of problems you are likely to encounter on the **SAT**. Remember to apply whatever strategy is appropriate for the problem at hand.

If a problem seems difficult
or
time-consuming,
skip it
(you can always come back
to it if time remains)

The following are typical **SAT** Math Multiple-Choice problems. Follow your game-plan: If you don't understand a problem, go on to the next one (return later if it is worthwhile); answer the ones you feel are easy; and work slowly/carefully. This may be a timed test, but when it comes to Math you've got all the time you need to complete whatever you can. There is absolutely no governing rule that says you should finish the test.

When you are done, look over your mistakes to see which were careless and avoidable. The **SAT** Math test is amazingly repetitive; therefore, once you catch your mistakes you are likely not to fall for the same type of error in the future. Try your best and you'll see your score (and your confidence) zoom!

[answers are explained on pages 136 – 139]
(circle your answer)

1. $18 - 5 + 3 \cdot 0 =$
   A) 0
   B) 10
   C) 13
   D) 16
   E) 18

2. How many positive integers between 21 and 50 are divisible by 6?
   A) 8
   B) 4
   C) 3
   D) 6
   E) 5

3. The product of two prime numbers can be which of the following?
   I. an even number
   II. an odd number
   III. a prime number
   A) I only
   B) I and II
   C) II only
   D) II and III
   E) I, II and III

4. The perimeter of a rectangle is 22 and its length is 2 more than twice the width. The area of the rectangle is
   A) 24
   B) 11
   C) 44
   D) 16
   E) 28

5. If **X** is a member of the set {2, 4, 6, 8} and **Y** is a member of the set {1, 3, 5, 7}, how many different values are there for **X** + **Y**?
   A) 4
   B) 7
   C) 9
   D) 12
   E) 16

Questions 6 and 7 refer to the following operation:
$$\triangle a = 2a - 3$$
$$\triangledown a = 3a - 2$$

6. What is the value of $\triangle 2 + \triangledown 3$?
   A) 22
   B) 20
   C) 13
   D) 8
   E) 5

7. Which of the following is equivalent to $\triangle 4 + 2(\triangledown 3)$?
   A) $\triangle 9 + \triangledown 3$
   B) $\triangle 18 - \triangledown 8$
   C) $\triangle 5 + \triangledown 3$
   D) $\triangle 16 - \triangledown 4$
   E) $\triangle 5 + \triangledown 5$

8. **T** represents the set of prime integers between 11 and 19. **R** represents the set of composite (non-prime) integers between 7 and 13. What is the *maximum* value of when a member of **R** is subtracted from a member of **T**?

    A) 4
    B) 5
    C) 9
    D) 10
    E) 12

9. If a blue and a green jacket each belongs to one different person in a group of three boys, what information would be sufficient to identify to whom each jacket belongs?

    I. if one boy admits he doesn't own either
    II. if one boy selects his jacket
    III. if one boy selects his jacket and one other boy admits he doesn't own either

    A) I only
    B) I and II
    C) I and III
    D) III only
    E) neither I, II or III

10. If $3^{2n-2} = 9^{18}$, then **n** =

    A) 7
    B) 8.5
    C) 19
    D) 21
    E) 22

11. Tom bowled four games and averaged 155. What does he need to average in the next two games for an overall average of 170?

    A) 160
    B) 180
    C) 185
    D) 190
    E) 200

$$2x - 3y + 2z = 4$$
$$5z + 4y - 3x = 7$$
$$2x - 7z - y = 9$$

12. Given the equations above, what is the value of 2**x**?

    A) 40
    B) 20
    C) 14
    D) 6
    E) 2

[Note: *Figure not drawn to scale.*]

13. If **p** is an integer, what is the *least* possible value for **p**?

    A) 10
    B) 8
    C) 6
    D) 3
    E) 2

14. If it takes **r** ounces to fill **s** bottles of perfume, how many bottles can be filled with **t** pounds of the fragrant liquid?

    A) $^{16st}/_r$
    B) $^{rst}/_{16}$
    C) $^{16r}/_{st}$
    D) $16t - {}^s/_r$
    E) $^{16t}/_{rs}$

15. In Bob's Ice Cream Parlor, pineapple sundaes are served with three scoops of ice cream. If his menu includes chocolate, strawberry, vanilla, and mint ice cream scoops, how many different types of pineapple ice cream sundaes can be made?

    [Note: A sundae may contain more than one scoop of the same flavor; the order of the ice cream flavors does not affect the type of sundae.]

    A) 12
    B) 15
    C) 18
    D) 19
    E) 20

Did you have enough time to do the ones you knew? You probably did, and what's more you probably got them correct. You may have also realized that a calculator helps only on occasion; at other times it is easier to simply work out a problem in your test booklet. Students often perform poorly when they rely too heavily on their calculators. Those who score best are those who understand each problem and use their calculators only when computation is needed. In general, **SAT** Math problems can be solved without the use of a calculator. A calculator can be helpful, but it can also impede the problem-solving process necessary to adequately comprehend and correctly answer the question.

1. **C** This problem requires proper order of operations. Multiply and divide first, then go back and add and subtract. The final step should read: $18 - 5 + 0 = 13$.

2. **E** As with almost all mathematics problems, this one should be worked out to avoid any potential careless error.
   The integers between 21 and 50 that are divisible by 6 are: 24, 30, 36, 42 and 48.

3. **B** The best way to approach this type of problem is to select a couple of prime numbers and multiply them. For example, $7 \cdot 7 = \underline{49}$ which is odd. Therefore II is possible, which eliminates **A**. 2 is a prime number, and $2 \cdot 7 = \underline{14}$ which is an even number. Thus, I is also possible. We can now eliminate **C** and **D**. The only question remaining is whether any of our products ($\underline{49}$ and $\underline{14}$) are prime numbers. They are not: **E** is therefore also eliminated.
   (As a reminder, 1 is neither a prime nor composite number.)

4. **A** In many instances a picture will prove to be quite helpful. This is one of those situations. Draw a rectangle and label the sides **x** and **2x + 2**.
   With a drawing it's easier to see that the perimeter is

   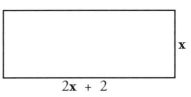

   $$2(x + 2x + 2) = 22$$
   $$6x + 4 = 22$$
   $$6x = 18$$
   $$x = 3$$

   Replacing the value for each variable yields dimensions of 3-by-8. The area is then easily found by multiplying the two numbers.

5. **B** Work this problem out carefully and you will get it correct. Select one number from the first set and add it to each of the numbers of the other set. Then take the next number from the first set and repeat this process. You will find your results to be:

   3, 5, 7, 9
     5, 7, 9, 11
       7, 9, 11, 13
         9, 11, 13, 15

   Always be sure to double-check that you have answered the question being asked before moving on to the next problem. In this problem there are 16 values, but only 7 *different* values.

6. **D** Questions 6 and 7 are much easier than they might at first appear to be. They simply contain made-up operations governed by a set of instructions; your job is to follow directions to solve the problem. In this specific problem, the answer is found by doing the following:

$$[2(2) - 3] + [3(3) - 2]$$
$$= (4 - 3) + (9 - 2)$$
$$= 1 + 7$$
$$= 8$$

7. **D** The second problem of a "made-up" set is usually more time-consuming, though not usually very difficult. In this problem you need to evaluate each choice until you come up with a result that matches the original problem. To save time, once you have a match you needn't work any further. However, as time is not the critical factor in this section (<u>getting the correct answer</u> is more important than being time-conscious), don't worry if you are forced to work out all the choices. It's worth the time if you can get it correct.

$$\underline{4} + 2(\underline{3}) =$$
$$[2(4) - 3] + 2 \cdot [3(3) - 2]$$
$$= 5 + (2 \cdot 7)$$
$$= 19$$

A) $= [2(9) - 3] + [3(3) - 2] = 15 + 7 = 22$
B) $= [2(18) - 3] - [3(8) - 2] = 33 - 22 = 11$
C) $= [2(5) - 3] + [3(3) - 2] = 7 + 7 = 14$
D) $= [2(16) - 3] - [3(4) - 2] = 29 - 10 = 19$
E) $= [2(5) - 3] + [3(5) - 2] = 7 + 13 = 20$

8. **C** To find a minimum or maximum value, you need to select the largest value of one and the smallest value of the other, or vice versa, when the operation involves subtraction; or the smallest or largest values of each, when the operation involves addition. In this problem, you need to determine the greatest value of **T** and the smallest value of **R** that satisfies the question. In this problem, **T** must be a prime integer between 11 and 19, and **R** must be a composite (non-prime) integer between 7 and 13. the solution-sets are:

T: {13, 17}

R: {8, 9, 10, 12}

The answer can now be easily obtained by determining which numbers to choose to get the maximum value. It's quite easy: 17 – 8. The answer is obvious once you've set the problem up correctly. For more practice on this type of problem, see MINIMUM / MAXIMUM discussion (page 65).

9. **D** A simple logic problem such as this one requires careful reading and clear thinking. Only III will ensure that we know who belongs to each of the two jackets.

10. **C**   This problem requires basic knowledge of exponents. The key here is know where to start: simplifying 9^{18} to the common base $\underline{3}$ is the best place. $9^{18} = (\underline{3^2})^{18} = \underline{3^{36}}$; therefore substituting 3^{36} into our original problem, you have $3^{2n-2} = 3^{36}$. (When solving for exponents, *the bases must be the same*.) Because the exponents must be equal, solving this problem is easy:

$$2n - 2 = 36$$
$$2n = 38$$
$$n = 19$$

11. **E**   Whenever a problem contains an "average," the first step is to multiply to see what the <u>total</u> is. In this problem, multiply 155 and 4 (total games bowled) to arrive at the total amount of pins scored: <u>620</u>.

Tom needs to average 170 for 6 games, which means he must hit down $170 \cdot 6 = \underline{1020}$ pins total. He needs to knock down <u>400</u> more pins and he has <u>two</u> games to do so. Divide 400 by 2 and you have the answer. This approach works with all problems containing "average" questions. (The technical term for this particular type of problem is a *weighted average* problem.)

12. **A**   Although this problem appears to resemble Algebra II, it is really much simpler. Whenever you see multiple equations, consider *adding* them together. In almost all cases the answer will appear as if by magic! In this problem, adding the three equations will yield the equation:

$$x = 20$$

Therefore, $2x = 40$

13. **D**   A simple construction-principle applies here: the sum of any two sides of a triangle must be greater than the third side. In this problem (which is not drawn to scale, so do not assume that you can measure side **p**; it may not be reliable) **p** $+$ 8 must be greater than 10. Because **p** is an integer, it must be an integer 3 or greater. (By the way, if the question were to ask for the greatest possible value for **p**, it would be found as follows:
8 $+$ 10 $>$ **p**; <u>18 $>$ **p**</u>; **p** is therefore less than 18. If **p** were restricted to integers, the greatest possible value for **p** would be 17.) For more practice on this type of problem, see SIDES AND ANGLES OF TRIANGLES (page 117).

14. **A** This type of problem is one of the most difficult to solve unless a strategic approach is taken. Then it becomes very easy, though nonetheless time-consuming. Unless you are a math-wizard and can figure out the problem algebraically, it behooves you to use numbers in place of the variables. For example, try replacing the following:

$r = 20$

$s = 5$

$t = 3$

The key is to understand the problem so you will select appropriate numbers (otherwise, you may find yourself working needlessly with fractions). Given these numbers, we are saying that it takes 20 ounces to fill 5 bottles of perfume. In other words, each bottle contains 4 ounces. With 3 lbs. (that's 48 ounces), you can fill 12 bottles. We now have our **answer:** 12.

All you need to do is replace the values in the choices and see which yields a result of 12:

A) $16st/r = (16)(5)(3) / 20 = \underline{12}$

B) $rst/16 = (20)(5)(3) / 16 = 300/16 = \underline{18.75}$

C) $16r/st = (16)(20) / (5)(3) = 320/15 = \underline{21.33}$

D) $16t - s/r = (16)(3) - 5/20 = \underline{47.75}$

E) $16t/rs = (16)(3) / (20)(5) = \underline{0.48}$

The answer can be arrived at with relative ease, but it takes time. For most students this problem isn't worth the time consumed; however, for those seeking an 800 it is important to realize that even the most difficult **SAT** Math problem can be readily solved if there is sufficient time.

15. **E** This is a tricky problem requiring time and careful work. The only way to be sure you won't miss this is to write out the various letter-combinations. For example, label the flavors C, S, V, and M. Chart out the flavors with these letters and write out the combinations. Be sure you first understand the problem: the order does not matter, but you can have more than one scoop of the same ice cream flavor. Here are the basic combinations: CSV; CSM; SVM; CVM; CCS; CCV; CCM; SSC; SSV; SSM; VVC; VVS; VVM; MMC; MMS; MMV; CCC; SSS; VVV; and MMM. This problem is simple to solve as long as you don't resort to confusing mathematical formulas. Often, the most difficult part of a problem is understanding it; in this case, answering it correctly is equally challenging!

Strategy: *Substitute numbers for variables (see what works!)*
[answers on page 182]
(circle your answer)

1. $^6/_{30}$ is equal to all of the following <u>except</u>
   A) $^2/_{15}$
   B) $^4/_{20}$
   C) $^8/_{40}$
   D) $^7/_{35}$
   E) $^9/_{45}$

2. If five times a number is twelve less than seven times that number, the number is
   A) 2
   B) 3
   C) 5
   D) 6
   E) 9

3. Which of the following results in a negative answer?
   A) $(^-2)^4$
   B) $(^-1/_2)^6$
   C) $(^-1)(^-2)(^-4)^2$
   D) $(^-3)^3(^-2)^3$
   E) $(^-4)^2(^-2)^3$

4. $2\mathbf{x} + 3\mathbf{y} = 5\mathbf{z}$. If $\mathbf{x} = 1$ and $\mathbf{y} = 6$, $\mathbf{z} =$
   A) 3
   B) 4
   C) 5
   D) 6
   E) 7

5. If $\mathbf{y}$ varies directly as $\mathbf{x}$ ($\mathbf{y} = \mathbf{kx}$, $\mathbf{k}$ is a constant) such that $\mathbf{y} = 5$ when $\mathbf{x} = 15$, what is the value of $\mathbf{y}$ when $\mathbf{x} = 27$?
   A) 3
   B) 5
   C) 7
   D) 9
   E) 11

6. Let Y be a digit such that $57Y = Y32 + 1YZ$.
   $\mathbf{Z} =$
   A) 2
   B) 4
   C) 6
   D) 8
   E) 9

7. If $\mathbf{m}$ is 20% of $\mathbf{n}$ and $\mathbf{n}$ is 40% of $\mathbf{p}$, what % of $\mathbf{p}$ is $\mathbf{m}$?
   A) 5%
   B) 8%
   C) 10%
   D) 20%
   E) 50%

8. If $\dfrac{2x + 1}{3}$ is an odd integer and $\dfrac{x - 3}{4}$ is an even integer, $\mathbf{x}$ can be
   A) 7
   B) 13
   C) 19
   D) 13
   E) 55

9. If $\mathbf{a} \sim \mathbf{b}$ is defined as a^2/b, what is the value of $\dfrac{\mathbf{x} \sim \mathbf{y}}{\mathbf{y} \sim \mathbf{x}}$?   [x ≠ 0], [y ≠ 0]
   A) 0
   B) 1
   C) $^x/_y$
   D) $^y/_x$
   E) x^3/y^3

10. Sandy has \$24, and Bill has $\mathbf{h}$ dollars less than Sandy. If Bill gives Sandy $^1/_2$ of his money, how many more dollars will Sandy have than Bill?
    A) $12 + h$
    B) $12 + ^h/_2$
    C) 24
    D) $48 + h$
    E) 48

11. If **r** is an odd integer, which of the following describes r^3?
    I. r^3 can be even or odd
    II. r^3 can be positive or negative
    III. r^3 must be greater than r
  A) I only
  B) I and II
  C) II only
  D) II and III
  E) neither I, II or III

12. The coordinates of the center of a circle are (‾3, ‾1) and the coordinates of point **X** on the circle are (4,‾7), what are the coordinates of point **Y** if **XY** is a diameter of the circle?
  A) (‾10, ⁺3)
  B) (‾10, ⁺5)
  C) (‾7, ‾8)
  D) (‾7, ‾6)
  E) (⁺1, ⁺4)

13. If $|x| + 3 < y$, what is the minimum integer value of **y**?
  A) 4
  B) 3
  C) 2
  D) 1
  E) 0

14. If $x^4 = 16y^8$, then $x =$
  A) $2y^2$
  B) $4y^2$
  C) $2y^4$
  D) $4y^4$
  E) $16y^4$

15. If $y = \sqrt[3]{2x}$, what is the value of **y** when $x/3 = 36$?
  A) $2\sqrt{3}$
  B) 6
  C) 18
  D) $6\sqrt{3}$
  E) 108

16. If the side of a cube is **x**, what is the ratio of the surface area to the total volume?
  A) 1 : x
  B) 1 : 2
  C) 1 : 1
  D) 6 : x
  E) 1 : 6x

17. Which of the following *may* be true?
    I.   x > z
    II. y > z
    III. x = y = z

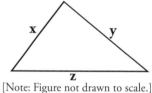
[Note: Figure not drawn to scale.]

  A) I only
  B) I and II
  C) I and III
  D) III only
  E) I, II and III

18. A board 48 feet long is cut into equal length pieces, each piece measuring 24 inches. Tom arrives at noon and purchases a quarter of those pieces. Two hours later, Josephine arrives and purchases a third of the available pieces. What can we deduce?
  A) Tom purchased more pieces than Josephine.
  B) Josephine purchased more pieces than Tom.
  C) Both Tom and Josephine purchased the same number of pieces.
  D) One or more of the smaller boards must be cut in order for the purchases to be made as stated.
  E) Not enough information is provided to arrive at a specific deduction.

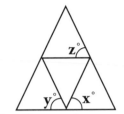

[Note: Figure not drawn to scale.]

19. The figure above shows two equilateral triangles, the smaller one inscribed within the larger. What do we know of **x**, **y** and **z**?

A) x + y = 90°

B) x + y = z

C) x = y = z

D) x + y + z = 180°

E) There is not enough information to determine any of the above.

20. The sum of the first **p** positive odd integers is **s**. In terms of **p** and **s**, what is the sum of the first **p** negative even integers?

A) $p^2 + s$

B) $s^2 - p$

C) $^-p^2 - s$

D) $^-p - s$

E) $s^2/^-p$

STUDENT-PRODUCED ANSWERS ("Grid-In" Math Problems)

In one **SAT** Math portion, you will find 10 questions that are *not* multiple-choice format but instead require bubbling in the numeric answers in the given Grids. But don't be intimidated by this section – the problems are really quite easy to solve. Just remember that, as with all math problems, you need to **read the question carefully and *solve* the problem**. Although you can't use the strategies available in the Multiple-Choice portion (including *elimination*), there are many commonsense ways to find answers to Grid-In problems because the questions are so simple to solve!

Unlike Multiple-Choice problems on the **SAT** – which have a small penalty assessed for incorrect answers – there is **no penalty for wrong answers on this portion**. However, this fact shouldn't affect your game-plan approach.

• •

SPORTS-ANALOGY (basketball):

If you shoot and miss or don't shoot at all, you won't ever score!

SOLUTION: Shoot with the intention of *scoring*!

• •

When you approach a Grid-In problem, your goal should be as it is with *any other* **SAT** Math problem: answer what you know and get it ***correct***. Getting at least half of the Grid-Ins correct will ensure a score of over 500 for this section; skipping them all will certainly lead to defeat. The problems are generally quite easy to understand and to answer. Work slowly and carefully with the goal of getting as many ***correct*** as possible and you'll do just fine on this portion of the **SAT**.

Practice and review are instrumental in maximizing Grid-In score increases, especially when you discover just how easy these problems can be to solve. For many, this section is the least difficult in terms of skills tested. All you need to do is become *familiar with* and *confident in* solving Grid-In problems.

The following quiz on Grid-Ins offers a variety of problems you are likely to encounter on the **SAT**. Remember to work carefully and be sure you are answering the question being asked. Of course, don't forget to bubble in your answer once you've solved a problem.

Grids for GRID-INS QUIZ 1 (on following page)

1.
2.
3.
4.
5.
6.
7.
8.
9.
10.

Directions: **Solve each problem, then bubble the appropriate answer in the grid on the previous page.**

No question has a negative answer.

[Note: *Some problems may have more than one possible correct answer; in such cases, enter only one answer.*]

[answers on page 182]

1. What is the total cost of two pounds of cashews which sell for $4.50 per pound plus 5% sales tax?
   (Disregard the $ sign when gridding your answer.)

2. In the above problem, what numerical value is represented by the digit D?

```
  A B C
x   B C
  C 6 D
B 4 6 0
B 8 B D
```

3.
```
AA . . . . . . . . . . row 1
AAA . . . . . . . . . row 2
AAAAA . . . . . . . row 3
AAAAAAA . . . . . . row 4
```
   In the diagram above, the number of A's in each row represents the prime integers in ascending order.

   If this pattern were repeated, how many total A's would be in rows 1 – 7?

4. The angle measurements of a triangle are in the ratio of 2 : 3: 4.

   How many degrees is the difference between the largest and smallest angles?

5. What is the slope of a line perpendicular to another line containing the points

   ($^-$2, 1) and (6, $^-$5)?

Set **A** = {3, 3, 4, 5, 6}

6. In a 4-digit number consisting of 4 of the 5 elements in Set **A**, how many different numbers beginning with 3 and ending with 6 can be formed?

x	$f(x)$
0	5
6	z
9	11

7. In the table above, if $f(x) = {^{2x}/_3} + 5$, what is the value of **z**?

8. If the product of the lengths of two equal sides of an isosceles triangle is 49, what is the maximum integer length of the third side?

9. Against a heavy wind, a man is pushed back two steps after taking five steps forward.

   At this rate, how many forward steps must he take to progress forty-five paces towards his destination?

10. If x and y are negative integers such that

    $^-8 < | x | < 3$ and $^-4 < | y | < 4$,

    what is the maximum value of x − y?

The following quiz contains more typical **SAT** Math Grid-Ins. Proceed carefully and be sure to work out each problem on the test booklet to avoid careless errors. If you don't understand what a problem is asking, even after a second read-through, skip it and move on.

Remember that <u>there is no penalty for wrong answers in this portion</u>, but also remember that your goal is to <u>get as many **correct** as you can</u>.

Grids for GRID-INS QUIZ 2 (on following page)

1.
2.
3.
4.
5.

6.
7.
8.
9.
10.

Directions: Solve each problem, then bubble the appropriate answer in the grid on the previous page.

No question has a negative answer.

[Note: *Some problems may have more than one possible correct answer; in such cases, enter only one answer.*]

[answers on pages 148 – 149]

1. What is the difference between the product of the first four positive integers and the sum of the first three positive odd integers?

2. After a team has won 30% of its first twenty games and then wins its next five games, what is its new percent of winning games?
   (In your answer, disregard the percent sign.)

3. If a 70-foot-long board is cut into three pieces such that the longest piece is twice the length of the middle piece, and the middle piece is three times as long as the shortest piece, how many feet long is the longest piece?

4. If Kalani and Marla each begin running along the same route at the same time but Kalani travels at a pace twice as fast, in how many *minutes* will Kalani be $8^3/_4$ miles ahead if Marla is running at an average pace of $3^1/_2$ miles per hour?

Questions 5-6 refer to the following chart:

Score	Number of Students
20	3
18	5
14	3
12	3
10	3
9	4

x represents the MEAN score of the students in the chart above, **y** represents the MEDIAN score, and **z** represents the score that is the MODE.

5. What is the value of **z – y**?

6. What is the value of **x – y**?

7. If the ratio of the sides of two cubes is 2 : 3 and a side of the larger cube is 6 inches, what is the volume of cubic inches of the smaller cube?

8. Aaron wants to buy some pencils and pens. If the cost each for pencils and pens is 8¢ and 17¢, respectively (tax included), how many total pencils and pens can he buy for exactly $2.06?

9. Sue has a collection of 32 scarves: 4 are green, 6 are blue, and the rest are yellow.

   If she gives away 4 of them, picked at random, and the first two given away are yellow, the third is green and the fourth is blue, what is the probability that the fifth scarf she picks at random will be blue?

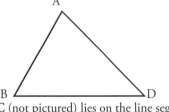

point **C** (not pictured) lies on the line segment between **B** and **D**

10. If the ratio of the area of △ **ABC** to the area of △ **ABD** is 4 : 7 and the length of **BC** is 9, what is the length of **CD**?

Were the problems easier than you expected? They tend to be, though for inexperienced test-takers understanding the *directions* can be the most difficult hurdle to surmount. It's a pity that a test that supposedly measures math-reasoning skills can be presented in such a way that some students don't even know what to do. But their disadvantage is your advantage, because now you know exactly what to do and how easy this portion of the **SAT** really is!

1. **15**   Grid-Ins are so easy if you just take your time to work out the problem. In this instance, the answer is found by computing as follows:

    $(1 \cdot 2 \cdot 3 \cdot 4) - (1 + 3 + 5) = 24 - 9 = \underline{15}$.

2. **44**   Grid-In problems (officially known as "Student-Produced Answers") require simple problem-solving. In this question you need to determine that the team has won 6 of its first 20 games (6 is 30% of 20). If the team wins its next 5 games, it will have won 11 total out of 25 games played, which is $\underline{44}$%.

3. **42**   In this simple ratio problem (ratios are very popular on the **SAT**), it is helpful to draw a picture and assign variables to each piece of the board. With **x** designating the shortest piece, the middle piece is 3**x** and the longest piece is $2 \cdot 3\mathbf{x} = 6\mathbf{x}$. You now have the three lengths: **x**, 3**x** and 6**x** (10**x** total). $10\mathbf{x} = 70, \mathbf{x} = 7$. The three boards therefore measure 7 feet, 21 feet and 42 feet. Be careful to answer the *question*; in this problem, they want the length of the *longest* board.

4. **150**   As with most word problems on the **SAT**, this one is easy to solve once you understand the question. Always take the time to determine how to go about solving the problem; it will make solving it a lot easier. In this question Marla is running at an average pace of $3^1/_2$ miles per hour and Kalani is running at 7 miles per hour. For every hour, Kalani will gain $3^1/_2$ miles distance. If you divide $8^3/_4$ by $3^1/_2$, you will find how many hours it will take to reach the desired distance:

    $^{35}/_4 \div {^7}/_2 = {^{35}}/_4 \cdot {^2}/_7 = {^5}/_2 = 2^1/_2$ hours, which is equivalent to $\underline{150 \text{ minutes}}$.

5. **4**   As with all multi-part **SAT** Math questions, it is well worth the time to try to understand what the chart or diagram is indicating. The terms MEAN, MEDIAN and MODE come into play here: the MEAN is the average (found by adding the scores and dividing by the number of students); the MEDIAN is determined by ordering the scores and then finding the one in the middle; the MODE is the score that appears the most often. Once you have these terms under your belt, you are ready to tackle the problem. The MODE (**z**) is clearly 18, because more students scored 18 than did any other score. To find the MEDIAN you need to write the scores out or else be aware that the 11th score is the middle one (there are 21 total student scores): 14 is the MEDIAN.

    The answer to #5 is now very simple: $18 - 14 = \underline{4}$.

6. **0**   This problem is not difficult but will take a minute or two to solve. You know that **y** is 14, but to find the MEAN you need to add up all the scores and divide by the number of students. In this problem the work is as follows: $20 \cdot 3 = 60; 18 \cdot 5 = 90; 14 \cdot 3 = 42; 12 \cdot 3 = 36; 10 \cdot 3 = 30; 9 \cdot 4 = 36$. The total points is 294, and there are 21 total students; the MEAN therefore is $294 \div 21 = 14$.

    The value of $\mathbf{x} - \mathbf{y} = 14 - 14 = \underline{0}$.

7. **64**   This is a simple teaser which requires clearheadedness. The first thing to realize is that the length of a side of the smaller square is 4 (which is $^2/_3$ the size of a side of larger cube).

    The volume of a cube is found by cubing the length of the side; therefore, the volume of the smaller cube is $4 \cdot 4 \cdot 4 = \underline{64}$.

8. **19**   This is another simple teaser requiring the proper time and thought to figure out what needs to be done. The question defies any word-problem setup and is moreso a commonsense problem than anything else. The best approach is to take the 17¢ figure and simply begin multiplying it until the remainder, when subtracted from 206, yields a number that is a multiple of 8, the price (in cents) of each pencil. It takes a while, but it's very solvable:

$1 \cdot 17 = 17;\ 206 - 17 = 189$ (not a multiple of 8)

$2 \cdot 17 = 34;\ 206 - 34 = 172$ (not a multiple of 8)

$3 \cdot 17 = 51;\ 206 - 51 = 155$ (not a multiple of 8)

$4 \cdot 17 = 68;\ 206 - 68 = 138$ (not a multiple of 8)

$5 \cdot 17 = 85;\ 206 - 85 = 121$ (not a multiple of 8)

$6 \cdot 17 = 102;\ 206 - 102 = 104$ (104 _is_ a multiple of 8)

Therefore, Aaron bought 6 17¢ pens and 13 8¢ pencils ($104 \div 8 = 13$) for a total of _19_ items.

9. **5/28** (or **.178** or **.179**)

In this ratio problem, some simple computing is necessary to arrive at the answer. To begin with, there are 4 green scarves, 6 blue scarves and 22 yellow scarves. After subtracting the scarves she has given away, Sue is left with 3 green scarves and 5 blue scarves and 20 yellow scarves, for a total of 28 remaining scarves. Now the problem is easy.

There are 5 remaining blue scarves out of a total of 28 scarves, so the probability (odds) she will select a blue scarf is _5/28_.

10. **27/4** (or **6.75**)

In this problem, it is advised that point C be drawn into the illustration for clarity. With the point clearly visible, it is easier to realize that both triangles in question have the same height. Given the formula of the area of a triangle ($\mathbf{A} = \frac{1}{2}\mathbf{bh}$) and the ratio of the two triangles, you have the equation:

$$\frac{\frac{1}{2} \cdot BC \cdot \mathbf{h}}{\frac{1}{2} \cdot BD \cdot \mathbf{h}} = \frac{4}{7}$$

Through simplification,

$$\frac{BC}{BD} = \frac{4}{7}$$

Because $BC = 9$ (information stated in the problem), through substitution and cross-multiplication you have:

$$\frac{9}{BD} = \frac{4}{7}$$

$$63 = 4 \cdot BD$$

$$BD = {}^{63}/_4 = 15^3/_4$$

The question, however, is asking for the length of CD, which is

$$BD - BC, \text{ or } 15^3/_4 - 9 = 6^3/_4$$

Be careful not to grid this in as 63/4; this would be read as $63 \div 4$, not $6^3/_4$.

The correct Grid-In form is either _27/4_ or _6.75_.

Reminder Rules For Gridding In Your Answer (be sure you understand them!)

OVAL-GRID FORMAT
(per problem)

General Directions:

Mark The Ovals In The Special Grid; Mark Only One Oval Per Column

Caution 1: 21/2 is read as $^{21}/_2$; to write $2^1/_2$ you must fill in either $^5/_2$ or 2.5.

Caution 2: To write $^2/_3$ as a decimal, you must enter either .666 or .667; an answer of .66- [which the computer reads as .660] will be marked as an incorrect answer.

Note 1: No question has a negative number.

Note 2: Some problems have more than one possible answer; in such cases, select only *one* answer.

[For example: "If $2 < x^2 < 48$, a possible positive integer value for **x** is ____." Several answers are possible; enter only *one*.]

Note 3: For answers that contain fewer than 4 characters, a blank oval may be used at the beginning or end.

[For example: "604" may be recorded as "-604" or "604-", the "-" indicating no oval has been filled in.]

Note 4: The computer scores <u>only what is filled in the ovals</u> [writing the answers in the boxes is optional; it is highly recommended, but it is **not** the part being scored]; <u>be sure you've filled in the correct ovals</u> (and be sure it is the Grid # that corresponds to the problem you are working on)!

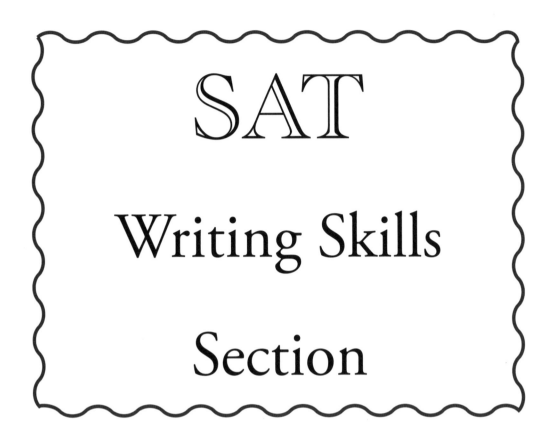

SAT

Writing Skills

Section

THE ESSAY: An Opportunity To Be Heard Loud & Clear

The **SAT** begins with a 25-minute essay which requires you to address a question or topic and present your views on it. Although much hullabaloo has been made over its significance, it is merely one component of the Writing Skills section. However, it is a golden opportunity to go beyond the multiple-choice limitations and really express yourself. An impacting essay can go a long way, because colleges can access it online to see how well you present your views in written format under test conditions.

The key to effective writing is to have something relevant to say. Don't worry about grammar and punctuation, nor whether your handwriting is below par. More important is whether you understand what the topic question is concerned with – and even more important, **<u>what you have to say about it</u>**.

If the topic "wakes you up," you'll probably do quite well. On the other hand, if you're more concerned about your sentence-structure and neatness, your "inner voice" probably won't have a chance to express itself. The key is to stick to the topic and ***have an opinion***. Approach this first section of the **SAT** with a passion – it's your only chance on the **SAT** to express how you feel!

If you have been told by teachers and counselors of the high value placed on writing proficiency, consider it as sound advice. After all, college essays (those required as part of the entrance application for many schools) are very important and may be the determining factor between acceptance and denial. Any essay submitted to a college should be carefully written and reviewed both for content and grammatical structure and, as with the **SAT** essay, it should be written from the *heart*, with your true feelings coming across.

The 25-minute **SAT** essay is therefore similar to a general college essay except that less emphasis is given to grammatical structure. Instead, the key to scoring well on the **SAT** essay is to be sincere and have something interesting to say when answering the question being asked, including well-developed examples that support your opinion. Don't try to "wow" the readers with your vocabulary. Instead, try to move them with your warmth and passionate feeling. The "personal inner voice" in an essay is that immeasurable golden touch that inevitably separates an excellent, impacting essay from the rest.

Here is a quick list of do's and don'ts to maximize your performance on the essay portion of the **SAT**:

DON'T use "you" in the essay (instead, select an **example** to support your claim)

DON'T sidetrack (instead, state your opinion and stick to it – don't waver from it)

DON'T use generalities such as "people often" … "there's a singer who" … "suppose a person were to …" (instead, select and develop **specific** examples)

DON'T preach or moralize with comments such as "we all need to …" or "our generation has fallen into …" (such editorial generalities stray from your main objective, which is to **defend your position**)

DON'T write in awkward prose with stilted phrases such as "It is my opinion that …" "As my introduction …" "Here is an example…" "My conclusion therefore is …" (instead, get to the point and state your case)

- -

DO use clearly defined paragraphs (for your introduction, body, and conclusion)

DO present a specific point of view in your introduction which is then developed in the body and reviewed in your conclusion

DO support your opinion with **specific examples**, the best of which are drawn either from literature (not from movies) or from historical events (literary characters/historical people are most effective); develop the examples and relate them to personal experiences for maximum success (but be sure to stick to the topic being discussed)

DO conclude with a decisive and supportive thought, one which drives home your point in a convincing manner

- -

In addition to the above DO's and DON'Ts, here are a few pitfalls to avoid:

- don't restate the question (instead, **state your opinion**)

- don't title the essay

- don't ask and answer your own questions (essays should not include digressive rhetoric)

With regard to the question "Does length matter?" the answer is "**Yes**": fully developed paragraphs necessitate some degree of length in any essay.

The following exemplifies a successful essay. Note how it follows the DO's and DON'Ts outlined in the previous page.

Eighteenth century Scottish historian and essayist Thomas Carlyle wrote "A man lives by believing something . . ." Is belief in one's cause the primary component for success in one's endeavors? Plan and write an essay in which you <u>develop your point of view</u> on this topic, <u>supporting it with relevant examples</u> from reading, observation or personal experience.

(sample essay)

Although it is critical to maintain deep convictions while pursuing one's goals, hard work is the primary component necessary for such goals to reach fruition. Without such follow-through, one's convictions will amount to little more than pipe-dreams.

Business mogul Donald Trump exemplifies the adage "keep on trying until you do succeed," having gone from riches to bankruptcy and then – through hard work and dedication – back on top. He surely believed in his cause, but that was not enough to stave off disaster due to factors some of which were beyond his control. It was instead his resolve to succeed that eventually helped him regain his supremacy.

Not all efforts, however, lead to success. Sisyphus has become the poster child for hard work gone unrewarded, for legend remembers him as the Corinthian king condemned to roll a heavy rock up a hill in Hades only to fail again and again just as it neared the top. Sisyphus is the embodiment of all of us who believe in our cause, doggedly pursue it, yet do not see success as a result. But this didn't stop Sisyphus, nor does it stop millions of hardworking Americans from pursuing their dreams despite the setbacks encountered.

Without belief in one's cause, there seems little reason to try one's hardest; but without the hard work that invariably accompanies all successful endeavors, success can never be achieved. Sisyphus' laborious sentence is legendary, but Donald Trump's success is current and real. What Sisyphus never achieved, Donald Trump accomplished twice. They both were believers, but Donald Trump apparently worked harder for success.

SAT ESSAY SCORING

The Essay is read very quickly (in less than a minute) by each of two scorers (most often by English/History teachers) and then is given a score of 0–6 by each person. The total score (0–12) is converted into a Scaled Score that usually has only a modest impact on the overall score of the Writing/Grammar Section. Here is a thumbnail sketch of what generally determines a score of 0–6 (scores of 0–2 are rarely given). Notice how the "personal inner voice" is of critical significance to obtaining the highest scores. Literary and historical examples also contribute greatly.

[Note: Essay is scored in terms of *content* and *organization*. Grammar and spelling play only a minor roll; neatness is *not* a factor in the scoring.]

Score Range	Grade Equivalent	Concise Score-Analysis
9 – 12	A⁻ – A⁺	Question has been addressed and position stated (in the introductory paragraph) and supported with two or three well-developed examples (literary, historical or personal) in the body. Writing style is polished and thoughts organized into distinct paragraphs. Conclusion reflects a well-thought-out argument.
7 – 8	C – B⁺	Question has been addressed and position supported with relevant examples. Paragraphing is evident, though writing style is not polished and examples not significantly developed.
5 – 6	D – C⁻	Although essay addresses the question, it is short and lacks specific examples. Paragraphing (inc. focused introduction and distinct conclusion) may be lacking.
0 – 4	F	Essay is either too brief to allow adequate discussion or else does not address the question being asked.

GRAMMAR: EVERYBODY USES IT (…so why not use it correctly?!)

Much has been said about the **SAT** Essay, but <u>it is the Grammar portion that comprises most of this section's points</u>. It is therefore imperative that you carefully review this chapter and learn the basic rules regarding word-usage, punctuation and sentence-structure. The best way to improve on this section is to *practice* and *review* **SAT** Grammar sample questions. Once you begin to see where you are weak, you will not only improve your Writing Skills section score but will also see noticeable improvement in your overall writing.

Of all the sections on the **SAT**, the Grammar portion is the one that will probably benefit you most in your college life. After all, success in college is determined by the degree to which one is able to express one's ideas, and at the heart of all communication – oral and written – is grammatical structure and organization. Therefore, consider this portion as one of immeasurable value well beyond the confines of the **SAT**!

• Most Frequent Grammar Errors •

*Can you identify the 10 most common errors found in the **SAT** multiple-choice Grammar section? They are contained in the following sentences! For answers, see next page.*

(The following advice will help your SAT Grammar score become higher than other students on the SAT.)

- Doing well on the SAT writing-skills multiple-choice questions require each test-taker to pay particular attention both to grammar correctness and to proper writing style.

  (Careful reading is essential for recognizing <u>errors</u> in sentences so that you can get it all correct.)

- Everyone should do their best on this section.

- If working too slowly, time will prevent you from answering the final problems.

- Allow adequate time to answer all questions, don't waste time on any one problem.

- Speed is not as critical as is being accurate.

  (Work carefully, eliminate selectively, and always be keeping an eye open for any obvious answer.)

- By following these rules, you can all become a winner on the SAT Writing Skills section!

  (With practice, you can even score higher than any person in your school!)

  (This advice applies to everyone, including you and I!)

  Because time and accuracy are precious,
  be sure to work quickly and carefully.

Answers to **10** Most Frequent Grammar Errors

(The following advice will help your **SAT** Grammar score become
1 higher than other **students' scores** on the SAT.)

- *2* <u>Doing well</u> on the SAT writing-skills multiple-choice questions **requires** each test-taker to pay particular attention both to grammar correctness and to proper writing style.

  3 (Careful reading is essential for recognizing <u>errors</u> in sentences so that you can get **them** all correct.)

- *4* <u>Everyone</u> should do **his** (or **her**) best on this section.

- *5* If working too slowly, **you will be prevented** from answering the final problems.

- *6* Allow adequate time to answer all questions; don't waste time on any one problem.

- *7* Speed is not as critical as is **accuracy**.
  (Work carefully, eliminate selectively, and always **keep an eye open** for any obvious answer.)

- *8* By following these rules, you can all become **winners** on the SAT Writing Skills section!

  9 (With practice, you can even score higher than any **other** person in your school!)
  10 (This advice applies to everyone, including you and **me**!)

> Because time and accuracy are precious,
> be sure to work quickly and carefully.

GENERAL GRAMMAR QUIZ (100 Questions – 35 Minutes)
to test your overall grammar proficiency (and to prepare you for this section!)

<u>Directions</u>: Circle the word, words or punctuation that is grammatically or structurally in error. Some sentences have no errors.
[answers on pages 163-167]

1. If two pounds of butter and one cup of sugar is mixed together, the result is a high-calorie sweet concoction.

2. I had not hardly begun my speech when hecklers in the audience emerged.

3. From the outset, I knew it would be Sarah and me going against a world of opposition.

4. Only one of the three flavors of ice cream were available.

5. In poorer third world countries, children roam the streets with no food and no shelter, too.

6. We were disappointed to find that, when it was our turn to order, only one of the five menu entrées was left.

7. In arithmetic, six and five are always eleven.

8. There is much to be saying about our globally precarious plight.

9. Having spilled the drink, the waiter knew he should of been more careful.

10. When the electricity failed, residents of the hotel were forced to ascend up the stairs to access their rooms.

11. To survive in the wild, animals must react fast to changing conditions.

12. As far as you and me are concerned, there is nothing more to be discussed on the issue.

13. Mother yelled at us, telling us to stay off of the floor.

14. My teacher would not condone tardiness nor laziness.

15. In the discussion, there were a lack of constructive suggestions presented.

16. If you can eliminate at least one of the five choices, one should attempt to answer the question.

17. One of our answers are wrong.

18. If one wants to and can succeed, he will find a way to do that.

19. After the lengthy illness, the patient did not look very well.

20. Having completed their first drafts, students were encouraged to be sure and check for spelling errors.

21. Susan B. Anthony was an early pioneer that paved the way for advancement of women's rights.

22. A union representative spoke out for the behalf of the many protesters at the meeting.

23. There was little evidence to prove whether it was indeed she who had perpetrated the prank.

24. Summer months are often spent frolicking at the beach, socializing at the mall, or aimlessly on the telephone.

25. On a gallon of gas, the compact car traveled further than the mid-sized one.

26. Each of the prizes awarded were valued at over one hundred dollars.

27. We go a long way back together, Sonny and I.

28. We looked everywhere for the missing bracelet, it had obviously been either stolen or misplaced.

29. The spelling bee finals came down to him and I.

30. Of the two trees mentioned, the redwood was by far the tallest.

31. Many Italian words are similar with Spanish words.

32. The problem had never arose before.

33. In some underdeveloped countries, one out of every two children do not know how to read.

34. Reading involves concentration, good eyesight, and knowing what the subject is about.

35. Unable to decide between the three travel destinations, the family eventually went nowhere.

36. When she turned eighteen, the girl set her sights to become a movie star.

37. As a result of the earthquake, every one of the houses on the block were destroyed.

38. Looking at my rear-view mirror, a car approached rapidly from behind.

39. I was surprised that, when the two stepped on the scale, her brother weighed more than her.

40. A brown house stands in the center of the block with a two-car garage.

41. After the piano recital, a large amount of audience members stood for an encore.

42. Geoffrey was the oldest of the twins, though only by two minutes.

43. We humans waste natural resources, as evidenced by automobiles.

44. Neither three bags of rice nor even one bag were delivered that evening.

45. Because it was raining, she could not go outside.

46. Between you and I, there is no way we can't surmount any obstacle.

47. Smoking habitually, lung cancer often is an irrevocable fate.

48. With only two pies remaining, she had difficulty choosing among them.

49. The gas line ruptured as the building was uninhabited.

50. The salesman was courteous, friendly, and he helped us with our shopping.

51. My young friend came to school accompanied with his mother.

52. A combination of the right colors make a painting come to life.

53. In Morse Code, every letter corresponds with a unique set of dots and dashes.

54. From the clues, the sleuth deduced that the guilty person was she.

55. As it turned out, none of the parole candidates were granted early release.

56. He became the only member of the group of twelve athletes who were able to cross the finish line in under two minutes.

57. Unable to eat another bite, the waiter removed the food from my table.

58. There are less people living in Japan than in China.

59. For Halloween, the youngster dressed up like a ghost.

60. I felt that I put in a greater effort than him.

61. Accidents occur when a motorist is least aware of traffic conditions around them.

62. Fraternal twins often look strikingly different than one another.

63. The meal was cold and the drinks watery.

64. In the marathon little league classic, both pitchers walked only one batter.

65. It is time to stand up for our freedom rather than letting others control us.

66. As the alarm began to sound, everyone dashed out of the classroom.

67. The traffic was heavy, and that is why he was late to work.

68. I looked anxiously at the team roster where I hoped my name would be found.

69. With regards to filing taxes, it is imperative that forms be sent in promptly.

70. Police weren't sure whether any of the passengers were injured in the mishap.

71. An ophthalmologist's specialty is eyes.

72. Due to an unexpectedly lengthy phone call, he found himself arriving home an hour later than the previous day.

73. The class was told to do exactly what the teacher instructed.

74. Prior to the performance, the orchestra tuned their instruments.

75. Cleopatra's beauty surpassed all others.

76. Until only recently, Roger Maris had hit more homeruns in a single season than any baseball player in the major leagues.

77. The language spoken in Austria is different from Germany.

78. Police were unable to determine who caused the accident.

79. To work carefully rather than rushing is the best way to approach an SAT math problem.

80. Between a penny, nickel and dime, the nickel is the largest.

81. With less than a week remaining, nobody seemed to know their lines at all.

82. My teacher insisted on me staying after school.

83. Neither the man nor his wife were suspects.

84. The couple was arguing over where to eat out.

85. The difficulty is not in earning money but saving it for a rainy day.

86. The teacher told everyone to take off their shoes before entering the gymnasium.

87. In golf, one's goal is to equal, if not better, the competition.

88. The cheetah is faster than any land animal in the world.

89. Hoisting a heavy object with a double-strand rope is inadvisable, for it may place undue strain on the rope.

90. To qualify for the spelling bee finals, no words can be missed.

91. Even though it may be a Saturday or Sunday, one should not consider those days time to lie idly around.

92. The odds of him winning the chess game were remote.

93. In the United States, temperatures in the North are typically cooler than the South.

94. A ride in a Rolls Royce is as comfortable or even more comfortable than a ride in any other car on the market.

95. When one gets older, one tends to walk slower.

96. Some mushrooms are edible, others are not.

97. Each of us will eventually be judged by the company we keep.

98. The two lads dreamed of one day becoming a rich and famous movie star.

99. In a triangle the hypotenuse is larger, and never equal to, either of the two legs.

100. No time has been as critical to maintaining peace as today.

GENERAL GRAMMAR QUIZ
ANSWERS

1. If two pounds of butter and one cup of sugar **are** mixed together, the result is a high-calorie sweet concoction.

2. I **had hardly** begun my speech when hecklers in the audience emerged.

3. From the outset, I knew it would be Sarah and **I** going against a world of opposition.

4. Only one of the three flavors of ice cream **was** available.

5. In poorer third world countries, children roam the streets with no food and no shelter, **either**.

6. *no error*

7. In arithmetic, six and five **is** always eleven.

8. There is much to be **said** about our globally precarious plight.

9. Having spilled the drink, the waiter knew he should **have** been more careful.

10. When the electricity failed, residents of the hotel were forced to **ascend the stairs** to access their rooms.

11. To survive in the wild, animals must react **quickly** to changing conditions.

12. As far as you and **I** are concerned, there is nothing more to be discussed on the issue.

13. Mother yelled at us, telling us to stay **off the floor**.

14. My teacher would not condone tardiness **or** laziness.

15. In the discussion, there **was** a lack of constructive suggestions presented.

16. If you can eliminate at least one of the five choices, **you** should attempt to answer the question.

17. One of our answers **is** wrong.

18. If one wants to and can succeed, he will find a way to do **so**.

19. After the lengthy illness, the patient did not look very **good**.

20. Having completed their first drafts, students were encouraged to be sure **to** check for spelling errors.

21. Susan B. Anthony was an early pioneer **who** paved the way for advancement of women's rights.

22. A union representative spoke out **on behalf** of the many protesters at the meeting.

23. *no error*

24. Summer months are often spent frolicking at the beach, socializing at the mall, or **chatting aimlessly** on the telephone.

25. On a gallon of gas, the compact car traveled **farther** than the mid-sized one.

26. Each of the prizes awarded **was** valued at over one hundred dollars.

27. *no error*

28. We looked everywhere for the missing bracelet**;** it had obviously been either stolen or misplaced.

29. The spelling bee finals came down to him and **me**.

30. Of the two trees mentioned, the redwood was by far the **taller**.

31. Many Italian words are similar **to** Spanish words.

32. The problem had never **arisen** before.

33. In some underdeveloped countries, one out of every two children **does** not know how to read.

34. Reading involves concentration, good eyesight, and **subject knowledge**.

35. Unable to decide **among** the three travel destinations, the family eventually went nowhere.

36. When she turned eighteen, the girl set her sights **on becoming** a movie star.

37. As a result of the earthquake, every one of the houses on the block **was** destroyed.

38. Looking at my rear-view mirror, **I could see a car approaching** rapidly from behind.

39. I was surprised that, when the two stepped on the scale, her brother weighed more than **she**.
    (her brother weighed more than she did)

40. A brown house **with a two-car garage** stands in the center of the block.

41. After the piano recital, a large **number** of audience members stood for an encore.

42. Geoffrey was the **older** of the twins, though only by two minutes.

43. We humans waste natural resources, as evidenced by **our excessive use of gasoline in automobiles**.

44. Neither three bags of rice nor even one bag **was** delivered that evening.

45. *no error*

46. Between you and **me**, there is no way we can't surmount any obstacle. (*note: it can also be written **Between me and you**, which is saying the same as **Between you and me***)

47. Smoking habitually, **one finds that** lung cancer is often an irrevocable fate.

48. With only two pies remaining, she had difficulty choosing **between** them.

49. The gas line ruptured **while** the building was uninhabited.

50. The salesman was courteous, friendly and **helpful**.

51. My young friend came to school accompanied **by** his mother.

52. A combination of the right colors **makes** a painting come to life.

53. In Morse Code, every letter corresponds **to** a unique set of dots and dashes.

54. *no error; (<u>she</u> was the guilty person)*

55. As it turned out, none of the parole candidates **was** granted early release.

56. He became the only member of the group of twelve athletes who **was** able to cross the finish line in under two minutes.

57. Unable to eat another bite, **I asked the waiter to remove** the food from my table.

58. There are **fewer** people living in Japan than in China.

59. For Halloween, the youngster dressed up **as** a ghost.

60. I felt that I put in a greater effort than **he**.

61. Accidents occur when a motorist is least aware of traffic conditions around **him**. (or **her**)

62. Fraternal twins often look strikingly different **from** one another.

63. The meal was cold and the drinks **were** watery.

64. In the marathon little league classic, **each pitcher** walked only one batter.

65. It is time to stand up for our freedom rather than **let** others control us.

66. **When** the alarm began to sound, everyone dashed out of the classroom.

67. The traffic was heavy, **which** is why he was late to work.

68. I looked anxiously at the team roster **on which** I hoped my name would be found.

69. With **regard** to filing taxes, it is imperative that forms be sent in promptly.

70. Police weren't sure whether any of the passengers **was** injured in the mishap.

71. An ophthalmologist's specialty is **in** eyes.

72. Due to an unexpectedly lengthy phone call, he found himself arriving home an hour later than **on** the previous day.

73. The class was told to do exactly **as** the teacher instructed.

74. *no error; (the orchestra represents the individual members)*

75. Cleopatra's beauty surpassed all **others' beauty**.

76. Until only recently, Roger Maris had hit more homeruns in a single season than any **other** baseball player in the major leagues.

77. The language spoken in Austria is different from **that spoken in** Germany.

78. Police were unable to determine who **had** caused the accident.

79. To work carefully rather than **to rush** is the best way to approach an SAT math problem.

80. **Among** a penny, nickel and dime, the nickel is the largest.

81. With less than a week remaining, nobody seemed to know **his** (or **her**) lines at all.

82. My teacher insisted on **my** staying after school.

83. Neither the man nor his wife **was a suspect**.

84. The couple **were** arguing over where to eat out.

85. The difficulty is not in earning money but **in** saving it for a rainy day.

86. The teacher told everyone to take off **his** (or **her**) shoes before entering the gymnasium.

87. In golf, one's goal is to equal, if not better, the **competition's score**.

88. The cheetah is faster than any **other** land animal in the world.

89. Hoisting a heavy object with a double-strand rope is inadvisable, for **doing so** may place undue strain on the rope.

90. To qualify for the spelling bee finals, **a person cannot miss any words**.

91. Even though it may be a Saturday or Sunday, one should not consider **such a day** time to lie idly around.

92. The odds of **his** winning the chess game were remote.

93. In the United States, temperatures in the North are typically cooler than **those in** the South.

94. A ride in a Rolls Royce is **as comfortable as** or even more comfortable than a ride in any other car on the market.

95. **As** one gets older, one tends to walk slower.

96. Some mushrooms are edible**;** others are not.

97. Each of us will eventually be judged by the company **you or I** keep.

98. The two lads dreamed of one day becoming **rich and famous movie stars**.

99. In a triangle the hypotenuse is larger **than**, and never equal to, either of the two legs.

100. No **other** time has been as critical to maintaining peace as today.

GRAMMAR (Multiple-Choice) SECTION: General Format

On the Grammar (Multiple-Choice) portion of the **SAT**, the first dozen or so sentences have part or all of the sentence underlined, followed by four rewrites of the underlined portion. In this section, you are asked to determine which of the choices is the *best* in terms of grammar and writing style. **A** is always the same as the original sentence; the other four are rewrites. One rule proves very helpful in this section: unless there is a grammatical discrepancy, the **shortest** of the choices is usually the best; the others are probably redundant or unnecessarily verbose. Put simply, if it's short and makes sense, it's probably the best answer.

The next part of the Grammar section contains sentences with four underlined words/ phrases. Your task is to identify which one of the underlined parts contains a grammatical error. **E** is the answer if all four underlined portions are grammatically sound. Errors may be found in improper tense-shift, lack of subject/verb agreement, misuse of a word, faulty punctuation, or any other grammatical faux pas the **SAT** test-makers can manufacture.

The final handful of questions relate to a short reading passage, but unlike in the Reading portion of the **SAT**, the questions here are structure- or grammar-oriented, not reading-comprehension oriented. Therefore, it is not as important to read the passage as it is to address the structural/grammatical questions associated with it; this is far different from our focus on reading in the **SAT** Critical Reading passages.

Despite the three different formats, the Grammar Multiple-Choice section is consistent throughout in its focus on *structure* and *grammar*. No questions concern spelling (though some emphasis is placed on misused words, including misuse of prepositions); in addition, there are no vocabulary questions or deeply analytical reading questions.

TIME: Because this section more closely resembles Reading than Math, it is important to move quickly rather than slowly-and-carefully on this section. In the first portion, quick elimination of two or three *incorrect* rewrites will help in locating the best answer; in the second part, any immediate identification of the error can help save time and effort; and on the last portion (containing the reading passage), a combination of skimming or quick reading and focusing on the questions will gain the best results with minimal time spent.

Similar to the Critical Reading Section, the Grammar portion does allow adequate time to complete all problems if you manage your time by maintaining a brisk pace. The last part (which contains the reading) is not as vital as are the Critical Reading passages and therefore does not usually demand much additional time allocated, but because this is considered by many to be the best-scoring part (i.e., the <u>easiest part</u>) of the Grammar test, be sure you have allocated sufficient time to address these questions.

All in all, questions on the Grammar section are easy to answer; after all, their primary concern is grammar, not content, making this section fast-paced and quite manageable.

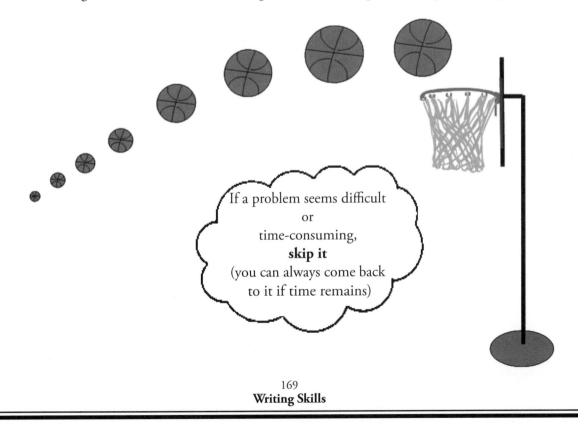

If a problem seems difficult
or
time-consuming,
skip it
(you can always come back
to it if time remains)

Because there are three different sub-sections in the Grammar section, you need to be aware of the different directions (as glossed over in the previous pages).

PART ONE: choosing the best (and most concise) answer.

Example: <u>When he arrived, all his friends came to meet him at the airport.</u>

A) When he arrived, all his friends came to meet him at the airport.
B) Arriving at the airport, all his friends came to meet him.
C) When all his friends came to meet him at the airport, he arrived.
D) Arriving at the airport, his friends had come to meet him.
E) All his friends came to meet him when he arrived at the airport.

The strategy for answering questions of this type is fast and simple:

1) Read the original sentence and ask yourself if it makes sense and is grammatically sound. If you think it is a good sentence, look quickly through and eliminate **B**, **C**, **D**, and **E**. Once you have indeed eliminated the other four choices, select **A** on your answer sheet and move on. (**A** is the same as the original sentence and is marked when the original sentence is the best.)

2) If the original sentence does not appear correct, look at the other choices and eliminate those that are obvious in error. After eliminating two or three choices, select the best answer from those that remain and move on.

(If the shortest sentence makes sense, choose it; the others obviously contain unnecessary words. A <u>concise</u> sentence is *always* preferred over a long-winded one.)

> The answer to the PART ONE sample sentence is **E**.

(The phrase "at the airport" needs to be placed together with "when he arrived"; only **E** addresses this structural requirement.)

PART TWO: choosing the incorrect answer

Example: <u>Walking</u> down <u>the street</u>, <u>my books</u> <u>fell</u>. <u>No error</u>
                   A   B   C   D   E

The strategy for answering questions of this type is fast and simple:

1) Read the sentence quickly to understand what is being said.

2) Look for any <u>obvious</u> grammatical error. If you see one, mark the appropriate bubble on your answer sheet and move on to the next question. Take advantage of time-saving easy problems.

3) If you don't notice any obvious error, reread the sentence to see if you may have missed something. If you see an error upon the second read-through, mark that answer and move on.

4) If you still don't see anything wrong, quickly eliminate the choices that seem correct. If you find them all grammatically and structurally sound, mark **E** ("no error") and move on.

> The answer to the PART TWO sample sentence is **C**.

(<u>My books</u> were not walking down the street!)

PART THREE: selecting the <u>best</u> answer to questions that relate to a given reading passage

In this portion of the Grammar section, you will need a minute or two to quickly skim the passage, gain a general understanding of the nature of the essay and its tone, and perhaps even notice where structural errors exist. Do not spend much time on this first reading because (as is true with Critical Reading), the key here is to **<u>answer the questions correctly</u>** (through *elimination*, of course!).

The strategy for answering Grammar Reading questions is quite elementary:

1) Skim the passage quickly to gain a general, superficial understanding of the nature and development of the passage.

2) Answer questions concerned with grammar and those referring to specific sentences. You may need to read around the lines (as is the case with Critical Reading questions) to gain a fuller context of the question, but you will find such questions easy to answer.

3) If you find an obvious answer, mark it on your answer sheet and move on. If the answer is not obvious, employ *elimination* to select the "best" choice.

4) Return to the more general questions. You may need to reread a part of the passage to address a question, but you needn't reread the entire passage (as might be the case when attempting to answer more-difficult Critical Reading questions). Eliminate two or three choices, then select the best answer from what remains. Don't spend much time on any one question; on the other hand, since this is the final part of the Grammar section, you may find that you have ample time to work slowly and carefully (time-management triumphs!).

◆ ◆

GENERAL ORGANIZATION

The Grammar section is organized such that the first problems on each portion are generally the easiest, the final ones the hardest. The reading portion tends to differ and follow the format of the **SAT** Critical Reading: the first questions tend to embody the earlier part of the essay, the final questions the latter part.

The following quiz will give you a good idea how proficient you are in the **SAT** Grammar section. Look over your mistakes so you don't repeat the same errors on the real **SAT**. Improving your grammar will invariably aid in developing better writing skills; the two are inextricably bound. If you can get at least two-thirds of the problems correct, you are doing quite well on **SAT** Grammar.

Directions: Select the letter of the choice that <u>best</u> and <u>most concisely</u> expresses the thought of the sentence. If the original sentence is the best, select **A**.

[answers are explained on pages 175 – 176]

(circle your answer)

1. <u>Entering the haunted house</u>, the sound of screams was most daunting.

   A) Entering the haunted house

   B) When entering the haunted house

   C) For those entering the haunted house

   D) While entering the house

   E) Upon the entrance of the house

2. There were many people <u>that visited the museum</u> to view the ancient dinosaur.

   A) that visited the museum

   B) which visiting the museum

   C) coming to visit the museum

   D) visiting upon

   E) who visited the museum

3. Pondering the many avenues of escape, <u>he chose eventually to flee on foot</u>.

   A) he chose eventually to flee on foot

   B) the best escape was on foot

   C) fleeing on foot was his choice

   D) by foot was how he chose to flee eventually

   E) his eventual choice was to flee on foot

4. <u>Diaries contain people's most intimate thoughts, which is why they are so popular.</u>

   A) Diaries contain people's most intimate thoughts, which is why they are so popular.

   B) Diaries contain people's most intimate thoughts, and that is why they are so popular.

   C) Because diaries contain people's most intimate thoughts, they are so popular.

   D) Containing people's most intimate thoughts makes diaries so popular.

   E) Diaries, containing people's most intimate thoughts, are so popular.

5. Babe Ruth was a better hitter <u>than any team today</u>.

   A) than any team today

   B) than anyone playing today

   C) than all teams today

   D) than anyone could do today

   E) than any other player today

Directions: Select the letter containing a grammatical error. If there is no error, select E.
[answers are explained on pages 175 – 176]
(circle your answer)

6. <u>Every</u> one of the houses <u>that</u> overlooked
    A   B

   the valley <u>were</u> destroyed in the <u>blazing</u>
               C   D

   inferno.   <u>No error</u>
                E

7. It has long been known that a daily exercise

   <u>regimen</u> is healthy for everyone, <u>even</u> those

   A B

   as physically <u>fit</u> as you and <u>I</u>. <u>No error</u>
                C   D   E

8. <u>Although</u> dogs and cats are popular
    A

   house pets, <u>many people</u> prefer cats
             B

   <u>because</u> of <u>their</u> independent nature.
    C   D

   <u>No error</u>
     E

9. Oftentimes, <u>during</u> chaotic and rampant
           A

   lawlessness <u>replete</u> <u>with</u> civil riots and
             B   C

   uncontrolled rebellions <u>come</u> widespread
                   D

   looting. <u>No error</u>
           E

10. Even after prices were reduced 10% on all

   merchandise, it soon became clear to the

   <u>wary</u> customers that none of the items
    A

   <u>were</u> <u>yet</u> <u>reasonably</u> priced. <u>No error</u>
    B C   D   E

Directions: Select the best answer to the questions based on content and construction of the following passage.

[answers are explained on pages 175 – 176]
(circle your answer)

(1) I've always wondered whether realists are pessimists or optimists. (2) To me, a realist is a person who does not place too much reliance on luck; he is aware of the nature of events and has no expectations that a bolt of lightning will come down and strike him with a Midas touch. (3) For him, luck is replaced with effort and resolute consistency. (4) Gamblers never win.

(5) To be an optimist, one must see the best in life and expect the best to occur. (6) But if this optimism is truly compatible with real expectations – not pipe dreams – it can only exist when your own efforts can generate positive results. (7) An optimist would therefore be as unlikely to expect to win a lottery as would a realist. (8) But while both have a solid grip on reality, the pessimist on the other hand looks upon the future as an impending doom. (9) He does not see any effort capable of generating positive gains. (10) His attitude is the opposite of the dreamer, not the optimist.

(11) The realist is simply an optimist who doesn't openly voice this optimism in the future. (12) Whereas the pessimist feels nothing will turn out for the better, the realist knows that any favorable outcome is dependent upon one's present actions – a view I feel surely is more positive than negative.

---

11. If this essay were written to stimulate discussion in an audience of college philosophy students, which of the following versions of Sentence **1** would most effectively introduce the point in question?
   A) I've always wondered whether results realists are pessimists or optimists.
   B) Realists may be pessimists or they may be optimists.
   C) Are realists pessimists or optimists?
   D) A discussion worthy of investigation is whether realists are pessimists or optimists.
   E) A realist: pessimist or optimist?

12. Which of the following words needs to be changed in Sentence **6** to maintain grammatical consistency?
   A) But
   B) this
   C) it
   D) your
   E) positive

13. In Sentence **8**, whom does "both" refer to?
   A) the pessimist and realist
   B) the realist and dreamer
   C) the pessimist and dreamer
   D) the pessimist and optimist
   E) the realist and optimist

14. Which sentence could be omitted from the essay without affecting its tenor?
   A) Sentence 1
   B) Sentence 4
   C) Sentence 7
   D) Sentence 10
   E) Sentence 11

15. Which two sentences contain contrasting subjects?
   A) Sentences 1 and 2
   B) Sentences 2 and 3
   C) Sentences 5 and 6
   D) Sentences 7 and 8
   E) Sentences 11 and 12

SAT GRAMMAR QUIZ

Answers With Detailed Explanation

1. **C** **A** implies that "the sound of screams" was "entering the haunted house."

   B is as similarly flawed as A.

   D suffers the same faulty structure.

   E is another way of repeating the above errors.

2. **E** People always receives a "who" (or "whom"), never a "that" or "which", eliminating **A** and **B.**

   C "coming to enter" is vague and grammatically poor (**E** is more direct and forceful).

   D uses "upon" in an unacceptable manner.

3. **A** **B**, **C** and **E** suffer from the dangling participle "Pondering." The subject of the sentence is the person who is "pondering the many avenues of escape," and that is not **B** ("the best escape"), **C** ("fleeing on foot"), or **E** ("his eventual choice").

   D is awkwardly written and grammatically unacceptable.

4. **C** **A** and **B** are too indirect and therefore needlessly lengthy. **D** and **E** don't relate the popularity of diaries clearly. Diaries are popular <u>because</u> they contain people's most intimate thoughts. (And to answer the question "Can a sentence begin with 'Because'?" the answer is <u>Yes</u>!)

5. **B** Babe Ruth was a better hitter than any <u>hitter</u> of today; one cannot compare an individual with a complete team. (eliminating **A** and **C**).

   D "could do" is ambiguous and does not specifically relate to any antecedent in the sentence.

   E is chronologically inaccurate: "was" is a clue that he is no longer playing, so to include him with today's players ("than any *other* player today") is erroneous.

6. **C** The subject of the sentence is "every one," which is a *singular* noun. ("Every one...**was** destroyed...")

7. **E** No error.

8. **D** "Their" is ambiguous; does it refer to "many people" or to "cats"?

9. **D** The subject of this sentence is *looting*. Phrased more succinctly, but not altering the grammatical format, "Looting **comes** oftentimes during lawlessness."

10. **B** Once again, the issue involves identifying the subject (of a clause) and relating it with its verb: "None **was** reasonably priced." ("*none*" <u>always</u> takes a singular verb)

SAT GRAMMAR QUIZ
ANSWERS continued

11. **C** The Reading portion of the Writing section asks questions relating to grammar, sentence structure, essay development, and content. This first question focuses on content and appropriate tone; *elimination* is always the best way to approach such questions. Here, the key is to determine what type of introductory sentence would be most appropriate for an audience of college philosophy students. It should be direct; it should be focused. **A** places undue emphasis on "I," **D** is too indirect and excessive in length, and **E** is simply not clear in its intent. The decision is between **B** and **C**. One needs to realize that the sentence should stimulate thought but also flow smoothly in transition with the following sentences. **C** is a more stimulating and provocative opening sentence than **B**, and therefore it is the best answer.

12. **D** Instead of "your," "one's" should be used.

13. **E** For this question, a quick review of relevant portions of the essay will clarify what is being discussed and said. Without reading the paragraph, one might think the two referred to are the realist and pessimist, but the previous sentence invalidates any such assumption. The two referred to are the optimist and realist, and both are contrasted in Sentence **8** with the attitudes of the pessimist. To avoid being duped by questions such as this one, you need to allot sufficient time to review specific parts of the passage when necessary.

14. **B** This type of question often looks to be difficult; in truth, it usually isn't. Of the five choices, one will most likely appear glaringly inappropriate. Don't spend too much time here; select the sentence that is of least importance and move on.

15. **D** Strictly a grammar issue, this question requires identification of the subjects in each of the five group of sentences. Here are the subjects:

Sentences **1** and **2**: "I" and "realist"

Sentences **2** and **3**: "realist" and "luck"

Sentences **5** and **6**: "one" and "it"

Sentences **7** and **8**: "optimist" and "pessimist"

Sentences **11** and **12**: "realist" and "realist"

Now the answer is obvious.

PUTTING IT ALL TOGETHER: THE SAT GAME-PLAN IN REVIEW

Now that you have prepared a game-plan for taking the **SAT**, let's review and highlight key points.

CRITICAL READING SECTION

Sentence Completions: Get the easy ones (the first half) correct. *Eliminate* to help narrow down your choices, and double-check the sentence to be sure it makes sense with the words you've selected. Don't waste time and energy on those final HARD sentences. (One suggestion is to skip the last half and return to them if you have time after completing the Reading portion.) If, in a hard sentence, (whether in a one-blank or two-blank question), you see a word that looks like it might fit, select that answer and move on. You can't score if you don't shoot, but just don't spend too much time doing it!

Critical Reading Passages: Be aware that your main goal here is to get the *questions* answered correctly. Therefore, you should keep one eye on the questions as you read through the passage one paragraph at a time. And because the questions generally go in order of the reading (i.e., in sequential order), it should be easy to spot where the answers are to be found. (Line-number references are also quite helpful, but be sure to read not only those lines but also before and after the lines, because the answer is usually found in the *vicinity* of the reference lines. That's why it's so important to read one *paragraph* at a time!) *Elimination* is a key strategy here; look for **wrong** answers to narrow down the number of remaining choices.

One thorough reading is oftentimes all you need, after which (especially if you are answering the questions as you read along) every question should be answered. (A second reading is an option only if you have enough time to do so.) Using the answer-as-you-read strategy, you won't need to go back and reread the passage or be forced to remember what you read while you go back to the questions. It's fast, it's easy…and it's an approach that really works!

MATH SECTION

Multiple-Choice Questions: Work carefully (and if you are using a calculator, use one you are familiar with). Double-check each answer to be sure it matches with what the question is asking. Don't rush – instead, be sure that whatever problems you do you get *correct*.

Unless you're very comfortable with Math, don't do the hard problems. Instead, save your time and energy to double-check the ones you've done. If you can get $^1/_2$ correct and avoid getting mired in the hard problems, you'll easily score over 500! (But if you've practiced and understood the various math problem-types, then there's really no reason why you can't score 700$^+$!)

Student-Produced Answers: Work just as you would on the Multiple-Choice problems: Read each question carefully and solve the problem by working it out. Don't rush, and be sure your answer matches what is being asked. Double-check that you've bubbled the answer in the Grid that corresponds with the problem you're working on (i.e., #15 answer goes on Grid marked #15, etc.).

◆ ◆

There are many different ways to solve **SAT** Math problems, ranging from a mathematical approach (e.g., setting up algebraic equations) to a commonsense approach (using logic or applying the "guess-and-check" method) to an arithmetic approach (e.g., substituting numbers for variables and solving, then – if in Multiple-Choice format – checking to see which answer matches).

SAT Math problems are ingeniously produced, offering any student an even chance to get them correct even if you may not be a math-wizard. Common sense can go a long way on this test! Just be careful that you don't make silly mistakes; this test is simply too important to make costly avoidable errors on.

WRITING SKILLS SECTION

Writing (the Essay): Stick to the topic, write using complete sentences, and say what you feel with words you feel comfortable using. As long as it reads in an organized and intelligible manner, you'll score just fine on this portion. Remember: Grammar, spelling and vocabulary are not as important as what you have to say and how effectively you get your feelings (your "inner voice") across! Examples (especially literary/historical and personal ones) will really help your essay too, even moreso when they are developed or expanded upon.

Grammar: Remember what you've practiced – the Grammar portion basically always covers the same material. Don't go into this section without having first practiced and corrected your errors; otherwise, you're likely to make those same errors again.

In the "best sentence" portion, eliminate sentence-choices that are glaringly wrong or awkward-sounding, then select from those that remain. *Elimination* is vital for ensuring a good score. And remember that, unless grammatically flawed, the shortest answer is the best.

On the "locate the error" portion, remember that there is only 1 error (or "no error"); so if you see an obvious error, select that answer and move on. Don't look for a 2nd error – you won't find one, and in the meanwhile you'll be wasting valuable time.

On the "paragraph" (Reading) portion of the Grammar section, be aware that the questions are generally grammar-related. It is NOT a Critical Reading passage, so avoid treating it as seriously. If you are a good reader, you may want to quickly skim the passage to get a general idea what it is about, but because it will most likely be filled with grammar and logic errors, don't try to make too much sense out of it. Be sure you spend most of your time on this portion focused on the *questions*; and if you're running short on time, go straight to the questions and avoid wasting valuable time in pre-skimming.

If you are able to complete the Critical Reading and the Writing Skills sections, and if you are able to answer (hopefully, **_correctly_**) at least half of the Math problems, you will have achieved your primary game-plan goal. Following this game-plan and remembering the best approach to take within each of the individual portions will ensure success in your college crusade.

All it takes is a carefully-laid-out plan of attack, and you will find

SAT

Victory!

QUIZ ANSWERS

SENTENCE COMPLETIONS QUIZ 1 (pages 15 – 16)	SENTENCE COMPLETIONS QUIZ 2 (pages 18 – 19)	CRITICAL READING QUIZ 2 (pages 34 – 36)	ARITHMETIC QUIZ 1 (pages 76 – 77)	ARITHMETIC QUIZ 2 (pages 78 – 80)
1. **C** 11. **A**	1. **C** 11. **B**	1. **A** 6. **A**	1. **C** 11. **B**	1. **A** 11. **E**
2. **A** 12. **C**	2. **C** 12. **E**	2. **C** 7. **D**	2. **D** 12. **D**	2. **B** 12. **B**
3. **C** 13. **B**	3. **B** 13. **A**	3. **C** 8. **E**	3. **B** 13. **C**	3. **D** 13. **B**
4. **D** 14. **A**	4. **A** 14. **E**	4. **E** 9. **C**	4. **D** 14. **C**	4. **D** 14. **D**
5. **E** 15. **B**	5. **D** 15. **A**	5. **D** 10. **D**	5. **A** 15. **B**	5. **A** 15. **C**
6. **B** 16. **E**	6. **B** 16. **A**		6. **D** 16. **B**	6. **E** 16. **E**
7. **A** 17. **E**	7. **D** 17. **A**		7. **A** 17. **B**	7. **A** 17. **D**
8. **E** 18. **D**	8. **D** 18. **E**		8. **B** 18. **E**	8. **E** 18. **A**
9. **D** 19. **C**	9. **E** 19. **B**		9. **E** 19. **A**	9. **C** 19. **C**
10. **B** 20. **B**	10. **C** 20. **C**		10. **D** 20. **E**	10. **E** 20. **C**

ALGEBRA QUIZ 1 (pages 103 – 104)	ALGEBRA QUIZ 2 (pages 105 – 106)	GEOMETRY QUIZ 1 (pages 120 – 122)	GEOMETRY QUIZ 2 (pages 123 – 125)	MULTIPLE-CHOICE QUIZ 1 (page 127)
1. **C** 11. **B**	1. **E** 11. **B**	1. **D** 11. **D**	1. **C** 11. **A**	1. **D** 6. **B**
2. **D** 12. **B**	2. **C** 12. **C**	2. **C** 12. **E**	2. **B** 12. **A**	2. **B** 7. **B**
3. **A** 13. **D**	3. **B** 13. **E**	3. **B** 13. **B**	3. **B** 13. **D**	3. **E** 8. **A**
4. **D** 14. **D**	4. **E** 14. **D**	4. **A** 14. **E**	4. **D** 14. **E**	4. **A** 9. **C**
5. **D** 15. **C**	5. **B** 15. **A**	5. **B** 15. **A**	5. **C** 15. **E**	5. **C** 10. **D**
6. **B** 16. **E**	6. **C** 16. **D**	6. **A** 16. **A**	6. **A** 16. **D**	
7. **A** 17. **B**	7. **B** 17. **A**	7. **C** 17. **D**	7. **E** 17. **D**	
8. **E** 18. **B**	8. **D** 18. **C**	8. **A** 18. **E**	8. **E** 18. **C**	
9. **E** 19. **C**	9. **A** 19. **E**	9. **E** 19. **C**	9. **C** 19. **A**	
10. **A** 20. **E**	10. **A** 20. **D**	10. **C** 20. **D**	10. **C** 20. **B**	

STRATEGY QUIZ 1 (pages 129)	STRATEGY QUIZ 2 (pages 131)	MULTIPLE-CHOICE QUIZ 3 (pages 140 – 142)	GRID-INS QUIZ 1 (pages 145)
1. **E** 6. **A**	1. **E** 6. **B**	1. **A** 11. **C**	1. **9.45** 6. **6**
2. **E** 7. **B**	2. **B** 7. **C**	2. **D** 12. **B**	2. **9** 7. **9**
3. **D** 8. **A**	3. **C** 8. **B**	3. **E** 13. **A**	3. **58** 8. **13**
4. **D** 9. **D**	4. **D** 9. **E**	4. **B** 14. **A**	4. **40** 9. **73**
5. **B** 10. **C**	5. **A** 10. **A**	5. **D** 15. **B**	5. $^4/_3$ 10. **2**
		6. **A** 16. **D**	(or **1.33**)
		7. **B** 17. **E**	
		8. **C** 18. **C**	
		9. **E** 19. **E**	
		10. **C** 20. **D**	

183

SAT

Full-Length

Examination

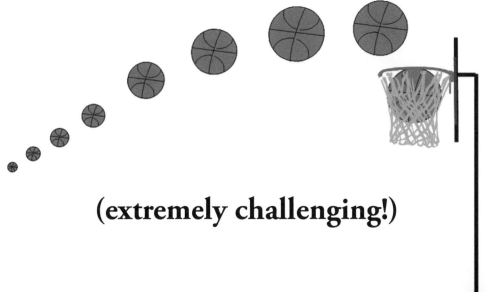

(extremely challenging!)

ANSWER SHEET – Full-Length **SAT**

Section 2 - Critical Reading 25 Minutes	Section 3 - Math 25 Minutes	Section 4 - Critical Reading 25 Minutes	Section 5 - Math 25 Minutes
1. (A) (B) (C) (D) (E)	1. (A) (B) (C) (D) (E)	1. (A) (B) (C) (D) (E)	1. (A) (B) (C) (D) (E)
2. (A) (B) (C) (D) (E)	2. (A) (B) (C) (D) (E)	2. (A) (B) (C) (D) (E)	2. (A) (B) (C) (D) (E)
3. (A) (B) (C) (D) (E)	3. (A) (B) (C) (D) (E)	3. (A) (B) (C) (D) (E)	3. (A) (B) (C) (D) (E)
4. (A) (B) (C) (D) (E)	4. (A) (B) (C) (D) (E)	4. (A) (B) (C) (D) (E)	4. (A) (B) (C) (D) (E)
5. (A) (B) (C) (D) (E)	5. (A) (B) (C) (D) (E)	5. (A) (B) (C) (D) (E)	5. (A) (B) (C) (D) (E)
6. (A) (B) (C) (D) (E)	6. (A) (B) (C) (D) (E)	6. (A) (B) (C) (D) (E)	6. (A) (B) (C) (D) (E)
7. (A) (B) (C) (D) (E)	7. (A) (B) (C) (D) (E)	7. (A) (B) (C) (D) (E)	7. (A) (B) (C) (D) (E)
8. (A) (B) (C) (D) (E)	8. (A) (B) (C) (D) (E)	8. (A) (B) (C) (D) (E)	8. (A) (B) (C) (D) (E)
9. (A) (B) (C) (D) (E)	9. (A) (B) (C) (D) (E)	9. (A) (B) (C) (D) (E)	9.
10. (A) (B) (C) (D) (E)	10. (A) (B) (C) (D) (E)	10. (A) (B) (C) (D) (E)	
11. (A) (B) (C) (D) (E)	11. (A) (B) (C) (D) (E)	11. (A) (B) (C) (D) (E)	
12. (A) (B) (C) (D) (E)	12. (A) (B) (C) (D) (E)	12. (A) (B) (C) (D) (E)	
13. (A) (B) (C) (D) (E)	13. (A) (B) (C) (D) (E)	13. (A) (B) (C) (D) (E)	
14. (A) (B) (C) (D) (E)	14. (A) (B) (C) (D) (E)	14. (A) (B) (C) (D) (E)	
15. (A) (B) (C) (D) (E)	15. (A) (B) (C) (D) (E)	15. (A) (B) (C) (D) (E)	
16. (A) (B) (C) (D) (E)	16. (A) (B) (C) (D) (E)	16. (A) (B) (C) (D) (E)	
17. (A) (B) (C) (D) (E)	17. (A) (B) (C) (D) (E)	17. (A) (B) (C) (D) (E)	
18. (A) (B) (C) (D) (E)	18. (A) (B) (C) (D) (E)	18. (A) (B) (C) (D) (E)	
19. (A) (B) (C) (D) (E)	19. (A) (B) (C) (D) (E)	19. (A) (B) (C) (D) (E)	
20. (A) (B) (C) (D) (E)	20. (A) (B) (C) (D) (E)	20. (A) (B) (C) (D) (E)	
21. (A) (B) (C) (D) (E)		21. (A) (B) (C) (D) (E)	
22. (A) (B) (C) (D) (E)		22. (A) (B) (C) (D) (E)	
23. (A) (B) (C) (D) (E)		23. (A) (B) (C) (D) (E)	
24. (A) (B) (C) (D) (E)		24. (A) (B) (C) (D) (E)	

Section 5 - Math Problems 10-18

10. 11. 12. 13.

14. 15. 16. 17. 18.

ANSWER SHEET – Full-Length **SAT**

Section 6 - Writing 25 Minutes	Section 7 - Critical Reading 20 Minutes	Section 8 - Math 20 Minutes	Section 9 - Writing 10 Minutes
1. Ⓐ Ⓑ Ⓒ Ⓓ Ⓔ	1. Ⓐ Ⓑ Ⓒ Ⓓ Ⓔ	1. Ⓐ Ⓑ Ⓒ Ⓓ Ⓔ	1. Ⓐ Ⓑ Ⓒ Ⓓ Ⓔ
2. Ⓐ Ⓑ Ⓒ Ⓓ Ⓔ	2. Ⓐ Ⓑ Ⓒ Ⓓ Ⓔ	2. Ⓐ Ⓑ Ⓒ Ⓓ Ⓔ	2. Ⓐ Ⓑ Ⓒ Ⓓ Ⓔ
3. Ⓐ Ⓑ Ⓒ Ⓓ Ⓔ	3. Ⓐ Ⓑ Ⓒ Ⓓ Ⓔ	3. Ⓐ Ⓑ Ⓒ Ⓓ Ⓔ	3. Ⓐ Ⓑ Ⓒ Ⓓ Ⓔ
4. Ⓐ Ⓑ Ⓒ Ⓓ Ⓔ	4. Ⓐ Ⓑ Ⓒ Ⓓ Ⓔ	4. Ⓐ Ⓑ Ⓒ Ⓓ Ⓔ	4. Ⓐ Ⓑ Ⓒ Ⓓ Ⓔ
5. Ⓐ Ⓑ Ⓒ Ⓓ Ⓔ	5. Ⓐ Ⓑ Ⓒ Ⓓ Ⓔ	5. Ⓐ Ⓑ Ⓒ Ⓓ Ⓔ	5. Ⓐ Ⓑ Ⓒ Ⓓ Ⓔ
6. Ⓐ Ⓑ Ⓒ Ⓓ Ⓔ	6. Ⓐ Ⓑ Ⓒ Ⓓ Ⓔ	6. Ⓐ Ⓑ Ⓒ Ⓓ Ⓔ	6. Ⓐ Ⓑ Ⓒ Ⓓ Ⓔ
7. Ⓐ Ⓑ Ⓒ Ⓓ Ⓔ	7. Ⓐ Ⓑ Ⓒ Ⓓ Ⓔ	7. Ⓐ Ⓑ Ⓒ Ⓓ Ⓔ	7. Ⓐ Ⓑ Ⓒ Ⓓ Ⓔ
8. Ⓐ Ⓑ Ⓒ Ⓓ Ⓔ	8. Ⓐ Ⓑ Ⓒ Ⓓ Ⓔ	8. Ⓐ Ⓑ Ⓒ Ⓓ Ⓔ	8. Ⓐ Ⓑ Ⓒ Ⓓ Ⓔ
9. Ⓐ Ⓑ Ⓒ Ⓓ Ⓔ	9. Ⓐ Ⓑ Ⓒ Ⓓ Ⓔ	9. Ⓐ Ⓑ Ⓒ Ⓓ Ⓔ	9. Ⓐ Ⓑ Ⓒ Ⓓ Ⓔ
10. Ⓐ Ⓑ Ⓒ Ⓓ Ⓔ	10. Ⓐ Ⓑ Ⓒ Ⓓ Ⓔ	10. Ⓐ Ⓑ Ⓒ Ⓓ Ⓔ	10. Ⓐ Ⓑ Ⓒ Ⓓ Ⓔ
11. Ⓐ Ⓑ Ⓒ Ⓓ Ⓔ	11. Ⓐ Ⓑ Ⓒ Ⓓ Ⓔ	11. Ⓐ Ⓑ Ⓒ Ⓓ Ⓔ	11. Ⓐ Ⓑ Ⓒ Ⓓ Ⓔ
12. Ⓐ Ⓑ Ⓒ Ⓓ Ⓔ	12. Ⓐ Ⓑ Ⓒ Ⓓ Ⓔ	12. Ⓐ Ⓑ Ⓒ Ⓓ Ⓔ	12. Ⓐ Ⓑ Ⓒ Ⓓ Ⓔ
13. Ⓐ Ⓑ Ⓒ Ⓓ Ⓔ	13. Ⓐ Ⓑ Ⓒ Ⓓ Ⓔ	13. Ⓐ Ⓑ Ⓒ Ⓓ Ⓔ	13. Ⓐ Ⓑ Ⓒ Ⓓ Ⓔ
14. Ⓐ Ⓑ Ⓒ Ⓓ Ⓔ	14. Ⓐ Ⓑ Ⓒ Ⓓ Ⓔ	14. Ⓐ Ⓑ Ⓒ Ⓓ Ⓔ	14. Ⓐ Ⓑ Ⓒ Ⓓ Ⓔ
15. Ⓐ Ⓑ Ⓒ Ⓓ Ⓔ	15. Ⓐ Ⓑ Ⓒ Ⓓ Ⓔ	15. Ⓐ Ⓑ Ⓒ Ⓓ Ⓔ	
16. Ⓐ Ⓑ Ⓒ Ⓓ Ⓔ	16. Ⓐ Ⓑ Ⓒ Ⓓ Ⓔ	16. Ⓐ Ⓑ Ⓒ Ⓓ Ⓔ	
17. Ⓐ Ⓑ Ⓒ Ⓓ Ⓔ	17. Ⓐ Ⓑ Ⓒ Ⓓ Ⓔ		
18. Ⓐ Ⓑ Ⓒ Ⓓ Ⓔ	18. Ⓐ Ⓑ Ⓒ Ⓓ Ⓔ		
19. Ⓐ Ⓑ Ⓒ Ⓓ Ⓔ	19. Ⓐ Ⓑ Ⓒ Ⓓ Ⓔ		
20. Ⓐ Ⓑ Ⓒ Ⓓ Ⓔ			
21. Ⓐ Ⓑ Ⓒ Ⓓ Ⓔ			
22. Ⓐ Ⓑ Ⓒ Ⓓ Ⓔ			
23. Ⓐ Ⓑ Ⓒ Ⓓ Ⓔ			
24. Ⓐ Ⓑ Ⓒ Ⓓ Ⓔ			
25. Ⓐ Ⓑ Ⓒ Ⓓ Ⓔ			
26. Ⓐ Ⓑ Ⓒ Ⓓ Ⓔ			
27. Ⓐ Ⓑ Ⓒ Ⓓ Ⓔ			
28. Ⓐ Ⓑ Ⓒ Ⓓ Ⓔ			
29. Ⓐ Ⓑ Ⓒ Ⓓ Ⓔ			
30. Ⓐ Ⓑ Ⓒ Ⓓ Ⓔ			
31. Ⓐ Ⓑ Ⓒ Ⓓ Ⓔ			
32. Ⓐ Ⓑ Ⓒ Ⓓ Ⓔ			
33. Ⓐ Ⓑ Ⓒ Ⓓ Ⓔ			
34. Ⓐ Ⓑ Ⓒ Ⓓ Ⓔ			
35. Ⓐ Ⓑ Ⓒ Ⓓ Ⓔ			

1   **1**   **1**   **1**   **1**   **1**   **1**

SECTION 1 (Essay – 25 Minutes)

Charles Dickens wrote, "It is well for a man to respect his own vocation whatever it is and to think himself bound to uphold it and to claim for it the respect it deserves."

Should a person's vocation be respected more for its financial or personal merit? Plan and write an essay in which you develop your point of view on this topic, supporting it with relevant examples from reading, observation, or personal experience.

_____

_____

_____

_____

_____

_____

_____

_____

_____

_____

_____

_____

_____

_____

_____

_____

_____

_____

_____

_____

_____

_____

_____

_____

_____

_____

_____

_____

_____

_____

_____

_____

_____

_____

_____

_____

_____

_____

_____

_____

_____

_____

_____

_____

_____

_____

_____

_____

_____

_____

_____

_____

SECTION 2 (25 Minutes – 24 Questions)
Sentence Completions *(Select the letter whose word(s) best complete the thought of the sentence.)*

1. The college graduate's credentials and qualifications made him _____ of nomination to the most _____ position available.

   A) notable...desirous

   B) available...indispensable

   C) worthy...superior

   D) capable...prominent

   E) loathsome...heinous

2. Although once content to pursue a life of a homemaker, Mari Ko eventually became one of the foremost _____ in the land, _____ herself in her commitment to justice.

   A) balladeers...accompanying

   B) housewives...belittling

   C) architects...representing

   D) villains...commending

   E) attorneys...distinguishing

3. A devout rebel, Billy was _____ when his friends agreed to _____ to the new school rules.

   A) disgruntled...conform

   B) introverted...transcend

   C) enfeebled...modulate

   D) enlightened...establish

   E) confused...condescend

4. The solution the clerk proposed was simply not _____ given the proprietor's lack of resources.

   A) variable

   B) luminous

   C) feasible

   D) endless

   E) diligent

5. _____ misuse of fluorocarbons will eventually destroy our troposphere and make us more _____ to the influences of radiation.

   A) Blatant...despicable

   B) Inadvertent...vulnerable

   C) Innocuous...susceptible

   D) Conscious...aware

   E) Carefree...blighted

6. Besides its _____ appeal, the ingenious artwork also served as a functional timepiece.

   A) constructive

   B) mundane

   C) resourceful

   D) aesthetic

   E) elementary

7. _____ is often necessary to prevent _____.

   A) Nicety...ruthlessness

   B) Demolition...sweltering

   C) Defensiveness...endurance

   D) Tolerance...indifference

   E) Surveillance...vandalism

8. The meal was an _____ display of epicurean delight.

   A) unseemly

   B) optimal

   C) outlandish

   D) ambrosial

   E) auspicious

Directions: *In the following section, answer the questions on the basis of what is* <u>stated</u> *or* <u>implied</u> *in the reading.*

Line

PASSAGE 1

High school athletics have often been criticized for detracting from academic and realistic personal aspirations, but empirical evidence attests to a high correlation of success on the gridiron with that in the classroom and in future endeavors. The goal-oriented nature of sports is truly compatible with our societal structure geared toward collaborative productivity

5   and marketplace success. To deny our youth the opportunity to demonstrate valor on the battlefield is to undermine the very principles of initiative and follow-through we espouse in all other facets of life. It is analogous to disallowing a person the opportunity to seek promotion through hard work and personal dedication.

PASSAGE 2

How can victory on the football field possibly translate to victory in the real world? Unless

10   one finds his (or her) talents worthy of that "next step," it is highly unlikely (at best) that a high school athlete will ever be able to realize monetary gain in the sport or achieve any degree of independence as a result of such talent. Instead, the person is more likely to pursue a deluded course spiraling downwards while more sober peers develop skills apropos to the life experience. When is the last time you ever saw a high school athlete successfully utilize

15   his talents as a team player in the dog-eat-dog business world? The very juxtaposition of "team player" and "business world" is in itself an oxymoron, and those who subscribe to the correlation, dupes.

9. What does the author of Passage **1** see as an attribute of high school sports that the author in Passage **2** disregards?
   A) emphasis on perseverance
   B) the value of teamwork
   C) the opportunity to excel
   D) a realistically goal-oriented springboard
   E) focus on the need to succeed

10. Which one of the following rebuttals might most closely match a response of the author of Passage **1** to comments made in Passage **2**?
    A) Money isn't everyone's goal in life.
    B) Unless one has played in high school sports, one cannot be a valid judge of its worth.
    C) Many high school athletes find successful professional careers in sports.
    D) The economic marketplace is indeed team-oriented.
    E) People with delusions often find happiness despite overwhelming odds.

11. What has the author of Passage **2** employed that Passage **1** lacks?
    I.   a rhetorical question
    II.   an analogy
    III. definition of a term

    A) I only
    B) I and II
    C) I and III
    D) II only
    E) none

12. In Passage **2**, which phrase, as used in context, parallels the reference in Passage **1** of "societal structure" (line 4)?
    A) "team player" (line 15)
    B) "deluded course" (line 13)
    C) "life experience" (line 14)
    D) "an oxymoron" (line 16)
    E) "dog-eat-dog business world" (line 15)

The following passage outlines the events and attitudes leading up to
colonial America's revolution against its motherland.

Line

During the latter part of the 18th century, the relationship between Britain and those living in its American colonies had become increasingly tense. The colonists had a long list of "taxing" problems with the Crown. The Sugar Act of 1764 had raised the duty on refined sugar imported into the colonies, and duties had also been placed on wines, coffee, and various textiles that
5   bypassed English ports. These measures severely curtailed commercial relationships with other lands, including the lucrative trade with the Azores and the French West Indies. The Currency Act of 1764 was meant to make it impossible to circumvent these unpopular laws; it prohibited colonists from issuing their own paper currency. By passing such laws, the British had established a monopoly on trade with the colonies, but they had done so at the cost of deep
10 resentment among the colonists.

The British inflamed American tempers yet again when they imposed the Stamp Act of 1765. Under this measure, legal documents, licenses, newspapers, pamphlets and even playing cards were required to carry a stamp that reflected a tax ranging from a halfpenny to as much as ten pounds per item. The move angered some of the loudest voices in the new land; newspaper
15 criticism of the Stamp Act was intense. Even the Massachusetts assembly issued a formal protest.

Speaking out against the oppressive Stamp Act were such now-legendary figures as Patrick Henry, Samuel Adams and James Otis. Otis railed against taxation without representation, which he considered "tyranny," and spoke in no uncertain terms of a citizen's God-given right
20 to resist those who would seek to deny him his liberty. Words quickly turned to deeds, as colonial merchants demonstrated a near-universal refusal to abide by the edicts of the Stamp Act. British exports to America plummeted as well, and the proponents of the Stamp Act and its sister law, the Sugar Act, were forced to repeal them in March, 1766, to regain trade relations.

25 Whatever goodwill among the colonists such a move may have earned, it did not last long. In 1767 the British passed the Townshend Acts, which levied new duties on glass, lead, paper and tea. American anger reached new levels, and confrontations in Manhattan and Boston in 1770 and 1771 between British forces and colonists took lives on both sides. The clashes foreshadowed the greater conflict to come.

30 In April of 1773, the British passed a Tea Act that laid heavy taxes on all tea imported from countries other than Britain. In December of that year, a band of sixty colonists snuck aboard three British cargo ships as they lay in anchor in Boston Harbor. The men threw 342 chests of tea overboard to protest the Act, destroying property worth about eighteen thousand pounds. The British Parliament, infuriated, passed laws forbidding any trade in or out of Boston until
35 the tea was paid for, additionally increasing the power of the royal governor, strengthening the Crown's authority to seize private property, and empowering British authorities to relocate trials if they wished. The laws became known as the Intolerable Acts, and even though they were aimed primarily at residents of Massachusetts, they infuriated Americans from other colonies as well.

40 Support among the colonists for the economically blacklisted residents of Massachusetts was swift and strong. Calls for a Continental Congress suddenly became louder and more insistent. The battle lines for the American Revolution were drawn.

Directions: Select the letter of the choice that best answers the question, based on what is stated or implied in the previous passage.

13. Which of the following titles best summarizes the contents of this passage?
    A) The Azores and the West Indies: Important Trading Partners
    B) The Boston Tea Party: One Step Towards Freedom
    C) Taxing the Colonies
    D) The Declaratory Acts and Colonial Retaliation
    E) Growing Discontent Between England and Her Colonists

14. Besides the literal meaning of "taxing" (line 2), what other definition is best implied from the context?
    A) oppressive
    B) confusing
    C) stimulating
    D) unwelcome
    E) revengeful

15. Which group is most likely referred to as the "loudest voices" in the new land (line 14)?
    A) town mayors
    B) merchants and vendors
    C) farmers
    D) members of the church
    E) newspaper editors

16. Patrick Henry, James Otis and Samuel Adams are three examples of
    A) British renegades
    B) national heroes
    C) colonial martyrs
    D) international loudmouths
    E) American hypocrites

17. Which of the following examples best exemplifies the phrase "words quickly turned to deeds" (line 20)?
    A) A sailor embarks upon a hazardous expedition to prove his courage, though the fierce nature of the seas cuts his mission short.
    B) A young girl tells her friends she plans to go to school wearing a polka-dot hat; the next day she arrives in school sporting a polka-dot hat.
    C) A teenager defiantly disregards his parents' wishes to hang up the telephone and converses, instead, until his parents disconnect the phone line.
    D) A doctor writes a paper in defense of the recent calls for increased financial support to fund research in the area of nuclear medicine.
    E) The school principal offers a special prize for the class that best beautifies the campus through creative decorations and a litter-collection campaign.

18. According to the passage, why did the British eventually rescind the Sugar Act and Stamp Act?
    A) Their revenues had fallen sharply as a result.
    B) The acts angered the colonists.
    C) They had proven their power over their colonial subjects.
    D) A new monarchy heralded changes in policy.
    E) They realized that oppression was not the answer.

19. In line 27, "confrontations" most nearly means
    A) bitter physical battles
    B) stubborn resistance
    C) name-calling attacks
    D) peaceful protests
    E) covert resentment

20. What words best describe how the British and colonists, respectively, felt regarding the Act of 1773?
    A) relieved; confused
    B) embittered; infringed upon
    C) patronized; deceived
    D) insistent; taken advantage of
    E) emancipated; invigorated

21. It can be inferred from the passage that the American colonists and British government both were
    A) determined to gain their freedom.
    B) seeking retaliation against the other.
    C) stubborn in their efforts.
    D) willing to compromise.
    E) engaged in monopolistic activities.

22. Given the tone of the colonists' discontent after the Boston Tea Act protest, which of the following might the British government have done to alleviate the tempers and avert a strong reaction?
    A) Prohibit the use of firearms by either side.
    B) Allow the colonists to produce their own currency with which to pay taxes.
    C) Let the colonists regulate their own tax system.
    D) Reduce the tax on British-shipped tea to America.
    E) Formally present all demands to the colonists.

23. According to the passage, why was the incident at Boston Harbor so important to the future revolutionary movement?
    A) It showed the colonists how easy victory could be achieved.
    B) It reflected the British lack of interest in enforcing their laws abroad.
    C) It convinced many British soldiers that taxation without representation was undemocratic.
    D) It helped fuel the fire for American independence.
    E) It ensured the colonies that they would no longer need to pay taxes to England.

24. The author's attitude towards the British can best be described as which of the following?
    A) Sympathy for their efforts but disapproval of their methods.
    B) Disapproval of their ideologies and their methods of maintaining the trans-Atlantic foothold.
    C) Disdain for their efforts in promoting imperialism and derision for their inefficiency in managing their own economic affairs.
    D) Admiration for their tenacity but disappointment with their inability to realize their goals.
    E) Support of their intentions but irritation by their lack of follow-through.

SECTION 3 (25 Minutes - 20 Questions)

The following information is for your reference – **it is provided on every SAT**

A circle measures 360°

A straight line measures 180°

The sum of the angles of a triangle is always 180°

Definition of symbols:

= *equal to*

≠ *not equal to*

< *less than*

> *more than*

≤ *less than or equal to*

≥ *more than or equal to*

‖ *parallel to*

⊥ *perpendicular to*

All numbers used are real numbers

FORMULAS

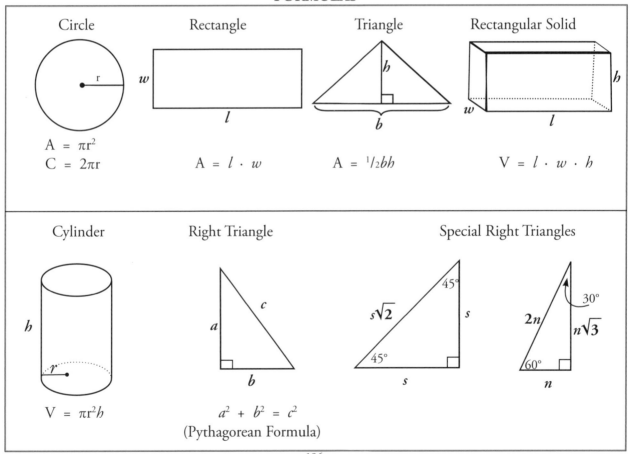

Multiple-Choice Problems

1. If on a number-line, the point labeled X corresponds to the number ⁻8, and the point corresponding to the number ⁻3 is labeled Y, what is the distance of segment **XY**?

   A) ⁻11

   B) ⁻5

   C) 0

   D) 3

   E) 5

2. If ¹/₃ of 45 = ¹/₄ of x, then x − 10 =

   A) 30

   B) 60

   C) 75

   D) 40

   E) 50

Questions 3-4 refer to the following information.

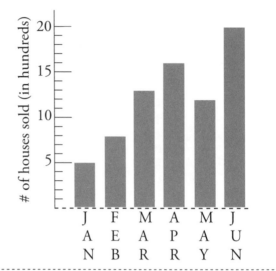

3. How many more houses were sold in April than in May?

   A) 4

   B) 120

   C) 160

   D) 400

   E) 1600

4. What was the approximate difference between the number of houses sold in the best month and the sum of those sold in the two worst months listed?

   A) 5

   B) 13

   C) 700

   D) 1300

   E) 1500

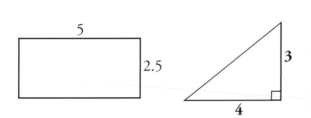

5. The ratio of the perimeter of the rectangle to that of the triangle is

    A) 5 : 4
    B) 25 : 24
    C) 25 : 12
    D) 15 : 14
    E) 5 : 8

Test Results

Test Score	Number of Students
20	4
19	4
18	6
17	4
14	1
9	1
8	1

6. If **H** represents the mode and **J** represents the median of test scores based on the above chart, what is the value of **H** − **J**?

    A) 17
    B) 9
    C) 0
    D) 1
    E) 15

7. In the following graph, for how many values of **x** does **f(x)** = ½?

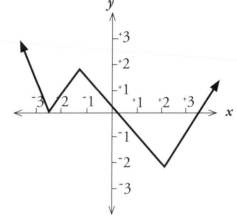

    A) 0
    B) 1
    C) 2
    D) 3
    E) 4

8. If the sun sets at 6:55 p.m., exactly eleven-and-one-half hours after sunrise, what time did the sun rise?

    A) 4:45 a.m.
    B) 4:55 a.m.
    C) 6:25 a.m.
    D) 7:05 a.m.
    E) 7:25 a.m.

9. If $|x - 1| = |x + 2|$, what is the value of **x**?

    A) $^-1\frac{1}{2}$
    B) $^-\frac{1}{2}$
    C) 0
    D) $^+\frac{1}{2}$
    E) $^+3$

Questions 10-11 refer to the following definition.

The operation $\triangle$ is defined as the sum of the largest prime number factor of **c** and the square of **c**.

For example,

$\overline{/20\backslash} = 5 + 20^2 = 405$

10. $\overline{/13\backslash} - \overline{/12\backslash} =$

    A) 1

    B) 12

    C) 13

    D) 25

    E) 35

- -

11. $(\overline{/6\backslash} - \overline{/5\backslash})^{\overline{/3\backslash}} / \overline{/2\backslash} =$

    A) $\overline{/8\backslash} - \overline{/3\backslash}$

    B) $\overline{/3\backslash} + \overline{/5\backslash} + \overline{/6\backslash}$

    C) $\overline{/6\backslash} + \overline{/5\backslash} - \overline{/3\backslash}$

    D) $\overline{/9\backslash} - \overline{/5\backslash}$

    E) $\overline{/18\backslash} - \overline{/10\backslash}$

12. In the xy-coordinate plane, if a line is perpendicular to another line that contains point ($^-$2, 6) and passes through the origin, intersecting at a point whose coordinates are (**x**, 4), what is the value of **x**?

    A) $^-$8

    B) $^{-4}/_3$

    C) 0

    D) $^{+1}/_2$

    E) $^+$4

13. If **x** varies directly as **y** and inversely as **z** such that **x** = **ky** and $\mathbf{x} = \dfrac{\mathbf{k}}{\mathbf{z}}$, **k** being a constant; and if **x** is **8** as **y** is **2**, when **x** is **36**, **z** =

    A) $^1/_9$

    B) $^1/_4$

    C) 0

    D) 9

    E) 144

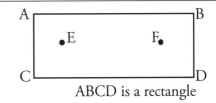

ABCD is a rectangle

14. In the figure above, what do we know regarding the total length of $\overline{CE} + \overline{EB} + \overline{DF} + \overline{FA}$?

    A) It must be less than or equal to $\overline{AD} + \overline{CB}$.

    B) It must be less than $\overline{AD} + \overline{CB}$.

    C) It must be greater than or equal to $\overline{AD} + \overline{CB}$.

    D) It must be greater than $\overline{AD} + \overline{CB}$.

    E) None of the above is necessarily correct.

15. In Zottstown, rain falls precisely every 25th day. If it has just rained on a Tuesday, what day of the week did it last rain?

    A) Friday

    B) Saturday

    C) Sunday

    D) Monday

    E) Wednesday

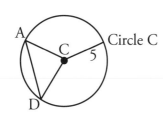

[Note: Figure not drawn to scale]

16. What can we determine regarding the perimeter of **Δ ACD**?

    I. The precise perimeter cannot be determined.

    II. The perimeter may be greater than 15.

    III. The perimeter may be less than 10.

  A) I only

  B) I and II

  C) II only

  D) II and III

  E) III only

17. Mr. Xavier always goes to the supermarket only on Thursdays and Saturdays. Mrs. Bennett always goes to the same supermarket only on Fridays and Saturdays. Which of the following is NOT true?

  A) If Mr. Xavier meets Mrs. Bennett at the supermarket, it must be Saturday.

  B) If it is Thursday, Mr. Xavier will not meet Mrs. Bennett at the supermarket.

  C) If Mr. Xavier and Mrs. Bennett do not meet at the supermarket, it must be Thursday.

  D) If it is not Saturday, Mr. Xavier will not meet Mrs. Bennett at the supermarket.

  E) There is an equal chance that Mr. Xavier will meet Mrs. Bennett at the supermarket on Thursday as on Friday.

18. In the graph below, $y = |x - 1|$. Which of the following would be the most accurate graph of the equation $y - 3 = |x - 1|$?

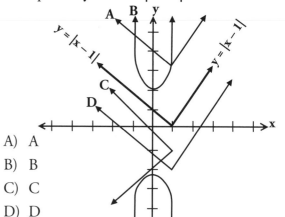

  A) A

  B) B

  C) C

  D) D

  E) E

19. If $(2^6 - 2^5)(2^5 - 2^4) = 2^b$, then $b =$

  A) 2

  B) 4

  C) 6

  D) 9

  E) 12

20. If the output of the toys **O(t)** per hour is defined as $O(t) = k(p + m)$ in which **k** is a constant, **p** denotes the number of people scheduled, and **m** represents the number of machines in operation, which of the following would reflect the decrease in the number of toys produced per hour if the number of people scheduled was reduced by 4?

  A) $4(k + m)$

  B) $4k + m$

  C) $4k$

  D) $k(p - 4)$

  E) $4k/m$

SECTION 4 (25 Minutes - 24 Questions)

Sentence Completions *(Select the letter whose word(s) <u>best</u> complete the thought of the sentence.)*

1. When the dog was ____, it bolted across the street in a ___ rage.

   A) unsettled...predictable

   B) unleashed...fierce

   C) removed...mild

   D) disturbed...placid

   E) relaxed...headstrong

2. Although the concept of relativity is considered one of the most global discoveries of the twentieth century, initially it wasn't highly _____.

   A) perceived

   B) taunted

   C) debated

   D) publicized

   E) disliked

3. After six years of ___, the couple realized they were truly ___.

   A) hardihood...pathetic

   B) complacency...deadlocked

   C) antagonism...incompatible

   D) amnesty...irreparable

   E) wrangling...euphonious

4. Helen Keller's successes were ___ and reflected her indomitable spirit.

   A) manifold

   B) implicit

   C) brash

   D) restricted

   E) qualified

5. Such a ____ attitude only serves to ___ greater ignorance upon the young audience.

   A) puritanical...endeavor

   B) listless...incite

   C) sedentary...presuppose

   D) philanthropic...engender

   E) chauvinistic...instill

Directions: *In the following section, answer the questions on the basis of what is* _stated_ *or* _implied_ *in the reading.*

Line

One of the most popular of the martial arts, karate employs many elements borrowed from other cultural sources and melds them into an art all its own. Many of its moves are similar to an older form of self-defense: jujitsu. In addition, breath-control techniques as well as philosophical attitudes, such as the necessity of being mentally calm, have been taken from

5   Zen Buddhism.

Although the aim in karate is to focus the body's total muscular power toward one moment's action (such as in wooden block-breaking), the actual matches themselves last two or three minutes and do not stress contact or submission. In fact, blows are stopped short before impact and points awarded instead to technique.

6. According to this passage, jujitsu

   A) borrowed from Zen Buddhism

   B) is more violent than karate

   C) is less popular than karate

   D) predates karate

   E) lacks elements predominant in karate

7. In the passage, what is the relationship between the two paragraphs?

   A) Paragraph one provides a general description; paragraph two provides specific examples.

   B) Paragraph one presents a religious perspective; paragraph two, a social perspective.

   C) Paragraph one offers historical relevance; paragraph two, technical relevance.

   D) An aspect mentioned in paragraph one is contradicted in paragraph two.

   E) Paragraph one reviews past significance; paragraph two offers future relevance.

Line

The method of producing a stereoscopic image without using a camera is called holography. Using a single beam from a laser that is then split into two beams, a hologram film is formed. To reconstruct the three-dimensional picture, light of the same wavelength is shone onto the hologram, which in turn produces the lifelike image. Although originally suggested in theory in

5   1947, it would take another sixteen years before technology allowed it to be put into practice.

8. According to this passage, what does a hologram offer that camera photographs don't?

   A) realistic color

   B) true-to-life images

   C) technological superiority

   D) cost savings

   E) ease of production

9. From the passage, it can be inferred that which of the following might not have existed in 1947?

   A) color photography

   B) seminal concepts regarding holography

   C) three-dimensional images

   D) the laser

   E) stereo sound capabilities

Directions: *In the following section, answer the questions on the basis of what is <u>stated</u> or <u>implied</u> in the reading.*

Lemmings possess one of the most inexplicable drives, described in the following passage.

Line

No rodent has baffled man more than that belonging to the family Cricetidae, tribe Lemmini. Known throughout Europe and North America as lemmings, these small mice-like creatures have taken upon themselves, for reason unbeknownst to any but perhaps themselves, a migratory trail whose final steps are self-destruction. Far from a fairy-tale journey, their
<u>5</u>   mission does not end "happily ever after," for their chosen destination – their Mecca* – is the ocean, a refuge for fish but not for land-loving rodents.

The farmlands of Norway and Sweden are the most common sites for inundations of lemmings, heading instinctively towards the Atlantic Ocean or the Gulf of Bothnia. Down from the highlands they advance – "falling out of the sky," Norwegian lore accounts – steadily but
<u>10</u> slowly increasing in numbers as they approach the shorelines. Stray packs join the onrush, and the ensuing stampede assumes an almost-maniacal nature crossing streams and lakes several miles wide, trampling anything in their path. As if driven to their destination by an obsessive compulsion, these individually harmless balls of fluff become a formidable adversary for all that stand in their way and a machine of devastation for the grassy fields and farmlands which
<u>15</u> provide the ravenous herd with life-sustaining nutrients.

The unorthodox lemming migration is not a safe travel for many of the rodents themselves. Farm animals attack the lemmings, whose presence threatens their very food supply. Wild animals and birds of prey relish the lemmings' arrival as a welcome meal. Meanwhile, man represents one of the greatest threats, seeking to exterminate them for much the same reason
<u>20</u> as do the farm animals. The lemmings' diurnal feeding comes at a time when competition for food is most fierce and farmers are most vigilant. All in all, the lemming migration, lasting in total from one to two years, resembles that of the early American pioneer settlers: long, dangerous and "no turning back."

Lemmings are a restless, courageously uncompromising lot whose pugnacious spirit
<u>25</u> propels them onwards, undaunted by geographical and predatorial obstacles. Paradoxically, all their efforts lead them not to a paradise – or, as some authorities have proposed, to a land which once offered abundant food supplies before being covered by oceans of water – but to their demise. What may once have been an exodus from overcrowded, underfed conditions to vast grasslands has now become much the opposite: a journey to destruction.

* The religious capital of Saudi Arabia and spiritual center of Islam;
in general, any desired destination of a pilgrimage.

Directions: *Select the letter of the choice the best answers the question, based on what is* <u>stated</u> *or* <u>implied</u> *in the previous passage.*

10. In the context of the passage, "inundations" (line 7) most nearly means
    A) feeding cycles
    B) destruction
    C) attacks
    D) migrations
    E) swarms

11. Why might some Norwegians believe that lemmings come "out of the sky" (line 9)?
    A) The rodents' ability to jump makes it appear that they are descending from the clouds.
    B) The vast swarm descends from the hills towards the seas almost as if a lemming "flood" has occurred.
    C) Lemmings have a limited ability to fly during migrations.
    D) Many lemmings are found crushed to death, explained only by having suffered a sudden descent.
    E) During the migration, there are no birds to be found.

12. According to the passage, what is the primary difference in the reasons man and wild animals pursue the lemming?
    A) Lemmings compete with man for food; they provide food for wild animals.
    B) Lemmings threaten man's food supply; they interfere with the feeding habits of wild animals.
    C) Lemmings bring diseases to man; they feed off the young of wild animals.
    D) Man pursues lemmings for sport; wild animals pursue them for survival.
    E) Lemmings threaten man's existence; they threaten the food supply of wild animals.

13. Which of the following scenes would most likely reflect the nature of the lemming during their ocean-bound migration?
    A) scurrying to safety to avoid an unexpected gust of wind
    B) fighting amongst themselves for leadership on the migration
    C) casually feasting on the farmland vegetation
    D) hurrying without regard to safety to cover as much territory possible
    E) carefully watching over their offspring

14. According to the passage, which of the following is/are true?
    I.   Lemmings eat during the day.
    II. The lemming migration lasts up to a couple of years.
    III. Humans safeguard lemming migrations towards the ocean.
    A) I only
    B) II only
    C) III only
    D) I and II only
    E) II and III only

15. It can be inferred from the passage that the lemmings' journey shares no fairy-tale ending because
    A) many lemmings die along the way.
    B) their trek is rooted in fact, not fiction.
    C) they meet a tragic fate.
    D) they must compete with fish for continued survival.
    E) the food supplies are not as abundant as in eons earlier.

16. The best title for this passage would be
    A) The Lemmings' Fight For Food
    B) Lemmings: Survival Through Migration
    C) Land Of The Lemmings
    D) The Indomitably Courageous Lemming
    E) The Mystery Of The Lemming Migration

The following passage is an excerpt from a story about a teenager's road to self-discovery.

I presented the ring to Janet in a most unusual way, asking her to hand me the ketchup and then intercepting her delivery. "You have the softest skin of anyone I have ever met," I added as her eyes met mine. "But I know what would make it even more attractive."

Janet was confused for a moment, but only a moment as I moved the golden band from my
5 finger onto hers. She flinched initially, uncertain of my intention, but then surrendered herself to my amorous display. "Do you want to go somewhere tonight?" I continued cautiously.

With the aplomb of a cheerleader, Janet replied "Why not? Tomorrow's Saturday and the drive-in movie is open late. You have anything particular in mind?"

A thousand juvenile thoughts raced through my mind as I contemplated the mischief we
10 had masterminded in the seventh grade, Janet and I building a reputation as the havoc-wreakers of Johnson Intermediate. The incident at Jerry's Deli earned us both the respect from our peers and fear from the establishment, an enemy we had conspired to overthrow together. Few remembered for long just what it was we had cleverly concocted, but the aura of our triumph over a world of puritanism and traditional values continued to encircle us for the remainder
15 of the schoolyear. We were saviors, we were the chosen duo – Batman and Batgirl – whose mission it was to rid Gotham City of adult tyranny and herald a new youthful leadership in the land. True, our approach wasn't very mature; in fact, it was downright sophomoric. But in one single act of mutual bravado, Janet and I let Philadelphia know we would not be silenced.

We had accomplished so much in the seventh grade, but one inescapable obstacle came
20 crashing down on me in the course of two years' passing. No, it was not the law, nor was it any single person. The culprit was time, and I was its most unsuspecting victim. Janet was not just "another guy" anymore; she had blossomed to full radiance. She was a gem whom I had once known as a marble; she was an angel with whom I had once committed deviltry.

So much had come between us – her sports, my academic involvement – but I never wanted
25 the bond between us to end. Ever. But things *had* changed. My interests lay elsewhere, though deep inside I yearned for the companion I once knew. The words that came forth were from my alter ego, my adult self endeavoring to readjust to life as a young man.

"Maybe we can sneak into the second show," I began searchingly, "and then ask someone if we can sit in the back of their van." I took a deep, silent breath, wondering if she comprehended
30 my innuendo. And yet, I myself wondered what it was I truly wanted.

"Van?" Janet replied politely, as if setting me up for a punch line. "Do you really think we can accomplish anything stuck in the back of somebody's van?"

I was taken aback. Janet wasn't interested in my adult attempts to express feelings I wasn't yet ready for. She knew me for who I was, and probably who I always will be. There was
35 magic in the air for the first time since Jerry's; we were still on the same wavelength.

<u>Directions</u>: *Select the letter of the choice the best answers the question, based on what is <u>stated</u> or <u>implied</u> in the previous passage.*

17. What can be assumed regarding the speaker and Janet?
   A) They have met only recently.
   B) They have been going steady for at least one year.
   C) Janet was not expecting to receive a ring from the speaker.
   D) Janet is more shy and amorous than the speaker.
   E) They are both enrolled in the same classes.

18. In the context of the passage, "aplomb" (line 7) most nearly means
   A) poise
   B) cautiousness
   C) attractiveness
   D) explosiveness
   E) eloquence

19. The setting of this passage would most likely be
   A) in a hallway between classes
   B) in Johnson Intermediate
   C) at a drive-in movie
   D) in Gotham City
   E) in a high school cafeteria

20. What information is given concerning the incident Janet and the narrator hatched in the seventh grade?
   A) no details are presented
   B) Jerry was also involved
   C) no one was injured
   D) they were never caught
   E) they wore masks

21. What is the narrator's intent in calling Janet "a marble" (line 23)?
   A) to maintain that she was never a real person
   B) to show how she was before she changed with time
   C) to admit frankly that he never fully understood who she really was
   D) to reveal that she was once less than perfect
   E) to recall how she was a childhood companion

22. How do the speaker and Janet envision the van (line 29)?
   A) The speaker envisions it in an amorous light, but Janet has other ideas.
   B) Both see it as an opportunity to get to know one another better.
   C) Both view it as the perfect place from which to watch the drive-in movie.
   D) The speaker sees it as a source for mischief, but Janet sees it as trouble brewing.
   E) Both are ambivalent towards the van.

23. Which of the following best sums up the series of events as seen by the speaker?
   A) shocking with an ironic undertone
   B) unexpectedly satisfying
   C) juvenile and frustrating
   D) sadly anticipated
   E) romantic but discouraging

24. Which question is answered for the speaker in the passage?
   A) Am I really in love?
   B) Is there a way to express how I feel?
   C) Has time changed our friendship?
   D) Will we ever understand ourselves?
   E) Will a drive-in movie really satisfy my desires?

SECTION 5 (25 Minutes – 18 Questions)
The following information is for your reference – **it is provided on every SAT**

A circle measures 360°
A straight line measures 180°
The sum of the angles of a triangle is always 180°

Definition of symbols:
- = *equal to*
- ≠ *not equal to*
- < *less than*
- > *more than*
- ≤ *less than or equal to*
- ≥ *more than or equal to*
- || *parallel to*
- ⊥ *perpendicular to*

All numbers used are real numbers

FORMULAS

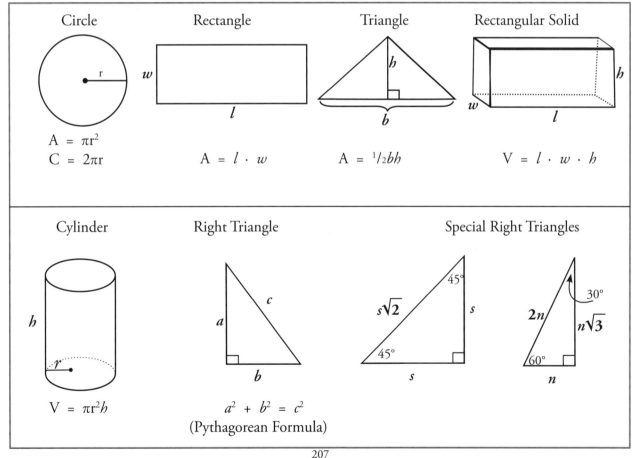

Circle
$A = \pi r^2$
$C = 2\pi r$

Rectangle
$A = l \cdot w$

Triangle
$A = \frac{1}{2}bh$

Rectangular Solid
$V = l \cdot w \cdot h$

Cylinder
$V = \pi r^2 h$

Right Triangle
$a^2 + b^2 = c^2$
(Pythagorean Formula)

Special Right Triangles

Multiple-Choice Problems

1. $\sqrt{3}$ is what percent of $4\sqrt{3}$?

   A) 20

   B) 25

   C) 30

   D) $33^{1}/_{3}$

   E) 50

2. $(^{-}1)^{42} + (^{+}1)^{42} =$

   A) $^{-}84$

   B) 0

   C) 1

   D) 2

   E) 84

Questions 3-4 refer to the following information.

	B	C	D
B		20	50
C	20		?
D	50	?	

Total distances (in units) between
points **B**, **C** and **D**

3. How much farther is the distance of
   B to **D** than **C** to **B**?

   A) 70 units

   B) 50 units

   C) 30 units

   D) 20 units

   E) 10 units

4. If **B, C**, and **D** represent three vertices of
   a triangle, what is the maximum possible
   length in units of **CD**, rounded to the nearest
   integer?

   A) 30

   B) 50

   C) 69

   D) 70

   E) It cannot be determined from the
      information given.

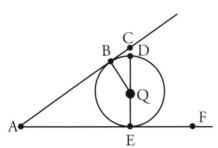

[Note: Figure not drawn to scale]

$\overline{AC}$ is tangent to circle **Q** at **B**

$\overline{AF}$ is tangent to circle **Q** at **E**

< **BAE** = 40°

5. What fraction of the circle's total boundary does arc **BD** represent?

A) $1/9$

B) $1/6$

C) $1/4$

D) $2/5$

E) $1/12$

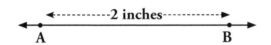

scale: $1/2$ inch = 25 miles

6. If point **C** is located on the same line as **AB**, and **BC** measures **1.5 inches** on the map, what is the actual distance from **A to C**?

A) .5 miles

B) 25 miles

C) 75 miles

D) 175 miles

E) It cannot be determined from the information given.

7. Three years ago, Tom was half Sam's age, and three years before that Tom was one-third Sam's age. How old is Sam now?

A) 24 years

B) 18 years

C) 15 years

D) 12 years

E) 9 years

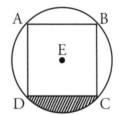

ABCD is a square inscribed in circle of center **E**.

AE = 6

8. What is the area of the shaded region?

A) $27\pi/4$

B) $9\pi - 18$

C) $12\pi - 9$

D) $9\pi - 1$

E) $36\pi - 72$

Directions: *Solve each problem, then mark the appropriate ovals in the special grid corresponding with your answer.*
Mark only one oval per column. No question has a negative answer.
[**Note:** **Some problems may have more than one possible correct answer; in such cases, grid only one answer.**]

9. It takes Mary three days to travel 18 miles. How many days would it take her, at the same average rate of speed, to travel 24 miles?

10. When Mrs. Johansen was selected to run the 120-year-old company, she became the 6th chief officer of the firm. What was the average number of years that each of her predecessors ran the company?

11. If four times a number, decreased by three, is 21, what is twice that number?

12. If in the series defined as $y = 2^x$, in which x represents consecutive odd integers greater than 0, what is the fourth term of the series if the first term is 2?

$\overline{AE}$ **is a diameter of Circle O**
<AOD = 90°
<BOC = 25°

13. In the circle above, segment **CO** bisects **<BOD**.
What is the degree measure of arc **BAE**?

14. If the distance between point **(2, 6)** and **(9, y)** is **8**, what is one positive value of **y**, rounded to the nearest integer?

15. In a mixture of assorted marbles – each of which is the same size and weight as the others – a pound of red marbles is mixed with a pound that has an equal number of blue, green, orange and red marbles. What fraction of the entire mixture consists of red marbles?

16. If **y** satisfies the equation $|y + 2| = |x + 1|$ for ⁻3, what would the positive value of **z** be when $|3z - 2| = |3 - x|$?

17. If $y = f(x)$, then what is the minimum value of **y** for which $f(x) = |4x - ^1/_2| + 5$?

18. In a local arm-wrestling tournament, every contestant has a match against each of the other participants. If there are 12 people entered in the tournament, how many total matches will take place?

SECTION 6 (25 Minutes - 35 Questions)

Directions: *Select the letter of the choice that best and most concisely expresses the thought of the sentence. If the original sentence is the best, select* **A**.

1. Surfing is a sport which is very enjoyable for him on weekends.
   A) Surfing is a sport which is very enjoyable for him on weekends.
   B) On weekends, surfing for him is a very enjoyable sport.
   C) He enjoys surfing on weekends.
   D) For him on weekends, surfing is a very enjoyable sport.
   E) On weekends, surfing is enjoyed by him.

2. If a person cannot accept criticism, you won't ever learn from it.
   A) you won't ever learn from it
   B) nothing will be learned from it
   C) he won't ever learn from it
   D) it won't teach him anything
   E) they won't ever learn from it

3. The club treasurer refused to be giving out funds unless it was for a good cause.
   A) to be giving out funds unless it was
   B) to give out funds unless
   C) giving out funds unless being
   D) funds to be given out unless
   E) unless it was giving funds out

4. Election results were questioned as soon as it became clear that not all ballots were counted.
   A) as soon as it became clear
   B) as it was becoming clear
   C) as everyone saw clearly
   D) when clearly it had become known
   E) when it became clear

5. Unlike his younger cousin who had brown eyes, he had blue ones.
   A) eyes, he had blue ones
   B) eyes, the ones he had were blue
   C) eyes and he, blue
   D) eyes while his were blue
   E) eyes, blue eyes are what he had

6. The patients were not happy with their food, a few demanding a hearing with the superintendent.
   A) food, a few demanding
   B) food and a few were demanding
   C) food because a few demanded
   D) food who demanded
   E) food and as a result were demanding

7. On the family vacation, the children enjoyed <u>swimming and being able to spend long evenings</u> <u>playing games</u>.

 A) swimming and being able to spend long evenings playing games

 B) swimming and to be spending long evenings to play games

 C) to swim and spend long evenings playing games

 D) swimming, spending long evenings, playing games

 E) swimming and spending long evenings playing games

8. The inveterate gambler had several <u>vices, among them being</u> women and alcohol.

 A) vices; among them being

 B) vices, their including

 C) vices, being

 D) vices, among them

 E) vices, including which were

9. Many dinosaurs were <u>heavier than a truck and ate a lot, too</u>.

 A) heavier than a truck and ate a lot, too

 B) heavier than a truck and had large appetites

 C) heavier and ate more than a truck

 D) heavier, with larger appetites, than a truck

 E) heavier than a truck and had a larger appetite than one

10. <u>Looking both ways, no cars could be seen in either direction.</u>

 A) Looking both ways, no cars could be seen in either direction.

 B) No cars could be seen looking in either direction.

 C) After looking both ways, no cars could be seen in either direction.

 D) Looking both ways, she could see no cars in either direction.

 E) In either direction, no cars could be seen by her.

11. The team <u>performed its roles in perfect harmony</u>.

 A) performed its roles in perfect harmony

 B) performed their roles in perfect harmony

 C) performed in perfect harmony its roles

 D) in perfect harmony their roles performed

 E) being in perfect harmony performed its roles

Directions: *Select the letter containing a grammatical error. If there is no error, select* **E**.

12. <u>With</u> his nose totally clogged, he <u>found</u> it <u>most</u> difficult to breathe <u>good</u>. <u>No error</u>
    A   B   C   D   E

13. <u>Them</u> protesters <u>were</u> <u>both</u> rowdy and <u>characteristically</u> belligerent. <u>No error</u>
    A   B   C   D   E

14. Awarded a medal <u>for</u> bravery, the fireman instead <u>lauded</u> all those <u>that</u> helped <u>in</u> the dramatic
                  A   B   C   D

    rescue. <u>No error</u>
            E

15. There <u>is</u> a number of <u>different</u> theories <u>regarding</u> the origin <u>of</u> life. <u>No error</u>
        A   B   C   D   E

16. The witness could not <u>maintain</u> consistency <u>in</u> her account, <u>which</u> strayed <u>away</u> from the
                      A   B   C   D

    truth. <u>No error</u>
        E

17. At the conference, one of the <u>more senior</u> representatives <u>was</u> asked to try <u>and</u> explain
                             A   B   C

    the <u>sales shortfall</u>. <u>No error</u>
          D   E

18. <u>Between</u> you <u>or me</u>, I think I am the <u>stronger.</u> <u>No error</u>
    A   B C   D   E

19. <u>Either</u> his wife or <u>he</u> would <u>have to stay</u> home to babysit the <u>ailing</u> tot. <u>No error</u>
    A   B   C   D   E

20. The Greek legendary hero Hercules, who could lift <u>as much</u> if not <u>more than</u> ten ordinary men,
                                        A   B

    <u>was said</u> to have even done battle <u>against</u> the Grim Reaper himself. <u>No error</u>
    C   D   E

21. Reading a book requires <u>committed</u> concentration, ample lighting, <u>and</u> <u>making sure of</u>
                       A   B   C

    <u>absolute silence</u>. <u>No error</u>
        D   E

22. Never <u>were</u> there more <u>dissenting</u> voices <u>than</u> at the town meeting <u>that</u> afternoon. <u>No error</u>
         A   B   C   D   E

23. The test <u>covered</u> both early folklore <u>as well as</u> <u>more</u> modern stories of legendary <u>proportion</u>.
            A   B   C   D

    <u>No error</u>
      E

24. The candidate <u>refused to budge</u> an inch <u>on</u> his opinions <u>nor</u> even listen to <u>opposing</u> viewpoints.
                  A   B   C   D

    <u>No error</u>
      E

25. <u>As</u> the bell rang, students quickly <u>jumped</u> to <u>their</u> feet and ran <u>out of</u> the classroom.
    A   B   C   D

    <u>No error</u>
      E

26. At the hot dog <u>eating</u> competition, the smallest person <u>there</u> <u>consumed</u> more hot dogs than
                A   B   C

    <u>anyone</u>. <u>No error</u>
      D   E

27. <u>Of</u> the two plants, the <u>one</u> exposed <u>to</u> sunlight grew the <u>best</u>. <u>No error</u>
    A   B   C   D   E

28. After a week out <u>of</u> the hospital, <u>the doctor</u> remarked how <u>good</u> she <u>looked</u>. <u>No error</u>
               A   B   C   D   E

29. <u>Given</u> the limited resources <u>afforded</u>, us, <u>it</u> is now more important than <u>ever</u> to protect our
      A   B   C   D

    environment. <u>No error</u>
             E

(1) Waikiki Beach is a landmark in the Hawaiian Islands. (2) Tourists come from far and wide to bask in the sun, chat with fellow visitors, and perhaps even be surfing in one of the most famous spots on the planet.

(3) A tourist is known as a "malihini," whereas "kamaainas" are the local residents. (4) I wonder if there are such distinctions between native Alaskans, for example, and visitors there. (5) Many tourists wish they could become kamaainas; on the other hand, they often also realize that sitting on the beach day after day is not a rather productive lifestyle. (6) There comes a time when even the laziest of us wants to get back to the daily grind: going to school or work, shopping, and doing other mundane activities.

(7) Maybe paradise has its limitations. (8) The exception, however, is if you can call paradise "home."

Directions: *Select the best answer based on content and construction of the previous passage.*

30. What phrase in Sentence **2** is grammatically inconsistent with the remainder of the sentence?
    A) far and wide
    B) bask in the sun
    C) even be surfing
    D) one of the most famous
    E) on the planet

31. Which of the following sentences would best restate the contrast between "malihini" and "kamaaina" mentioned in Sentence **3**?
    A) Whereas a tourist is known as a "malihini," "kamaainas" are the local residents.
    B) Although tourists are "malihinis," local residents are "kamaainas."
    C) "Malihini" is a tourist and "kamaaina" is a local resident.
    D) A tourist is known as a "malihini"; "kamaaina" is a local resident.
    E) A tourist is known as a "malihini"; a local resident is a "kamaaina."

32. To maintain the continuity of the essay, where should Sentence **4** be placed?
    A) It should remain where it is.
    B) It should be omitted.
    C) after Sentence **2**
    D) after Sentence **5**
    E) after Sentence **8**

33. What rather silly assumption has been made in Sentence **6** that lends a humorous overtone to the essay?
    A) Local residents spend all their days sitting on the beach.
    B) People come to Waikiki Beach to talk with others.
    C) Lazy people enjoy the daily grind.
    D) Tourists and local residents are not noticeably different.
    E) Paradise can actually be someone's home.

34. Which of the following is/are presented in the essay?
    I. a comparison
    II. a term
    III. a specific reference
    A) I only
    B) II only
    C) I and II
    D) II and III
    E) I, II and III

35. Which of the following would best revise the conclusion of Sentence **8** (reproduced below) to more clearly explain the inferred concept of "home"?
    The exception, however, is if you can call paradise "home."
    A) if you can call paradise "home," which of course is where the heart is.
    B) if you can call paradise "home," in which case you are already lazy.
    C) if you can call paradise "home," in which instance work is already enjoyable.
    D) if you can call paradise "home," in which case you will always be living like a tourist.
    E) if you can call paradise "home," which offers the best of both worlds.

SECTION 7 (20 Minutes - 19 Questions)

Sentence Completions *(Select the letter whose word(s) best complete the thought of the sentence.)*

1. Pollutants invariably disturb wildlife and _____ destroy the _____.
   A) summarily...authenticity
   B) subtly...hospitality
   C) inconsequentially...ozone
   D) inevitably...environment
   E) spontaneously...habitat

2. Claims that medicines and vitamin supplements produce _____ strength and herculean _____ ought to be regarded as nothing short of overt misrepresentations.
   A) fortified...exhaustion
   B) complex...physique
   C) supernatural...brawn
   D) unqualified...placidity
   E) temporary...results

3. The early American pioneers were generally not especially _____; on the contrary, they were usually rather _____.
   A) poignant...ornate
   B) predatory...palatable
   C) demanding...ominous
   D) nomadic...sedentary
   E) volatile...unpredictable

4. Rather than tackle the various issues _____, the committee pursued the problems _____.
   A) voraciously...heatedly
   B) individually...hastily
   C) headlong...extravagantly
   D) thoroughly...comprehensively
   E) simultaneously...piecemeal

5. The double-agent was afforded great _____ in conducting what critics claimed were _____ activities.
   A) exposure...superfluous
   B) latitude...subversive
   C) hostility...hospitable
   D) luxury...menial
   E) respect...laudable

6. The _____ were later _____ by the very deeds they had committed.
   A) marauders...harried
   B) villagers...chastised
   C) antagonists...fettered
   D) benefactors...confronted
   E) outlaws...avenged

<u>Directions</u>: *In the following section, answer the questions on the basis of what is <u>stated</u> or <u>implied</u> in the reading.*

The Loch Ness monster has long been the subject of endless debate. In the following two passages, the existence of this legendary creature is pondered by writers with contrasting perspectives.

PASSAGE 1

Line

The so-called "monster" at Loch Ness represents more than what many term an "unresolved mystery"; it symbolizes man's need to search for answers to unknowns, even if these answers do not exist. In the murky depths of Scotland's Lake Ness, little can be clearly discerned below fifty feet. This visual limitation is the fodder for countless "confirmed" sightings by

5   hundreds of passersby and townsfolk alike who have nestled safely together to proclaim the existence of the creature 754 feet below, a secret that has never been confirmed, yet never wholly refuted. The defenders of this mystery of the deep cling to the credo "true until proven otherwise"; Nessie does in fact exist unless proven that she doesn't.

If our monster-of-the-deep has been so elusive, why has there been a plethora of sightings

10   since the 1933 newspaper report brought the creature to the public forefront? More peculiar, in the midst of the "confirmed" sightings why has there been no clean photographic evidence to substantiate what the human eye has witnessed? Could it be the human eye can penetrate these murky depths, or is it more likely that man's imagination can penetrate the depths of the unknown? Are the sightings the result of an objective, systematic analysis or are they man's

15   undying loyalty to myths and legends that give grace and mystery to an otherwise-mundane existence?

Conducting an investigation into the authenticity of the sightings of the Loch Ness monster, scientist William Akins weighed seven factors: the nature of the people who reported having seen the spectacle; where the monster was seen; the distance involved; the date and hour of

20   the sighting; duration of the event; climatic conditions; and the specificity of detail of the object viewed. For a report to be considered "viable" and worthy of follow-up, the sighting must have been for at least ten minutes, with greater attention placed on sightings during clear days. Not surprisingly, many new sightings were reported during clear days and for a longer period than ten minutes. But details varied on the number of bumps the beast had, the nature

25   of its swimming apparatus, the animal's color, and even its shape. Had Akins clarified the details he required, there is little doubt that reportings would have been consistent.

Man will forever reach beyond to maintain that the Loch Ness monster is alive and well in the largest body of fresh water in the United Kingdom. Proving whether or not the monster exists may not be of paramount importance for supporters of the legend; even if the lake were

30   drained – a feat of impossibility in itself – the stories would never be put to rest. As with ghost sightings and UFO sightings, Nessie would probably be relegated to the position of the "ghost of the Loch Ness monster," a sighting even more difficult to disprove.

PASSAGE **2**

The twentieth century has documented sightings previously considered no more than superstitious hearsay. The phenomenal legend of the monster in Scotland's Loch Ness is
35 one of the twentieth-century fiction-to-fact marvels. Hundreds of years of "tall-tales" and testimonials, passed from generation to generation by word of mouth, collided with the age of technology, and the results have been far from what debunkers might have expected. Rather than a dearth of evidence to support the sightings – or evidence proven to be false – a barrage of photographs and even a four-minute video have emerged showing actual evidence that
40 something of great size is frequenting the waters of the massive lake.

On May 2, 1933, the *Inverness Courier* reported the account of John McKay and his wife, who saw a huge creature rise out from the lake as they drove by. It resubmerged, but not without having given the two a show they would never forget. Reports in the *Daily Express* in Glasgow followed every couple of weeks – the McKays were obviously not alone in their
45 sighting. By year-end, over twenty different people reported having seen the monster, setting the rest of the world on a search for more evidence.

Although there have been more than 10,000 reported sightings of the Loch Ness monster since the earliest account in 565 A.D., only within the past century have devices such as cameras and sonar detectors been able to add credence to the claims. Pictures have been the
50 primary means of documenting the creature's rise to the surface, while sonar scanners have been used to detect the movements of these animals in the murky depths of their sanctuary. Sonar charts have confirmed the existence of several large objects moving as fast as seventeen miles per hour on or near the bottom of the loch.

Skeptics claim that no monster exists within the waters of Loch Ness. For them, proof can
55 be no less than the actual living body – or dead carcass – of the animal. Fortunately, modern man has learned that not all creatures on earth need to be captured or killed to indicate "proof" of a discovery. More sophisticated means of detecting the animals' presence have confirmed what were only folk-tales of the past; what is needed still is a photographic instrument that can scan the innermost depths of the loch to capture the daily movements of the most revered
60 family. Not only will we have confirmed for even the most dubious that the oldest living family in Europe resides seven hundred feet under water, but we will have established for mankind the largest aquarium of its kind, a natural habitat exhibition to provide observers an inside-glimpse into the world of this sole surviving family of the prehistoric age.

The creative inventiveness of the twentieth century will afford us the opportunity to live
65 in harmony with the creatures of the deep – rather than kill them to satisfy the curiosity of unbelievers – to watch them live undisturbed and to witness the latest mystery only now being unveiled for all on Earth to appreciate.

Directions: *Select the letter of the choice that best answers the question, based on what is <u>stated</u> or <u>implied</u> in the previous passage.*

7. In Passage **1**, what does the use of the word "so-called" (line 1) best reflect regarding the author towards the subject?
   A) naiveté
   B) anger
   C) satisfaction
   D) deference
   E) incredulity

8. In Passage **1**, to what do the "murky depths" (line 3) specifically refer?
   A) man's imagination
   B) the lake
   C) man's limitations
   D) recent sightings
   E) newspaper reports

9. Which of the following words best defines the implied use of "fodder" (line 4) in Passage **1**?
   A) concern
   B) security
   C) confusion
   D) stimulus
   E) mystery

10. In the context of Passage **1**, which of the following best rephrases what the author has written in line 8 ("Nessie does in fact exist unless proven that she doesn't")?
    A) There is no evidence that Nessie exists.
    B) There is ample proof that Nessie exists.
    C) If Nessie exists, the lake is deeper than 754 feet.
    D) Nessie represents man's search for answers.
    E) Nessie has been seen by hundreds of observers.

11. According to Passage **1**, which of the following would *not* be a factor for determining the credibility of a monster-sighting?
    A) size of the creature
    B) length of the time of sighting
    C) weather
    D) month of the year
    E) tide

12. Passage **1**, lines 23-24, what is implied in the sentence "Not surprisingly, many new sightings were reported during clear days and for a longer period that ten minutes"?
    A) More sightings are made when clearer information is presented to the public.
    B) There is an entire family of Loch Ness monsters within the lake.
    C) People will say anything to sustain the story of the animal's existence.
    D) The creature emerges more frequently during clear days.
    E) Weather is the most critical factor for successful long-term sightings of the Loch Ness monster.

13. Passage **2**, line 38, the word "dearth" most nearly means
    A) demise
    B) scarcity
    C) worldliness
    D) dispute
    E) surplus

14. In Passage **2**, upon what does the author rely to support his thesis regarding the truth to the Loch Ness monster?

    I.   **actual sightings**

    II. **animal remains**

    III. **findings from sophisticated equipment**

A) I only

B) II only

C) III only

D) I and II only

E) I and III only

15. In Passage **2**, what word does the author use which best describes the group to which the author of Passage **1** might belong?

A) "marvels" (line 35)

B) "debunkers" (line 37)

C) "skeptics" (line 54)

D) "observers" (line 62)

E) "detectors" (line 49)

16. Which of the following does the author of Passage **2** imply would convince the author of Passage **1** that the monster does exist?

    I.   **capturing the animal**

    II. **killing the animal**

    III. **taking a full-length film of the animal**

A) I only

B) II only

C) I and II only

D) I and III only

E) I, II and III

17. Although the author of Passage **2** calls the lake a "natural habitat exhibition" (line 62), how would the author of Passage 1 most likely refer to it?

A) as a "garden of dreams"

B) as a "land of surprise"

C) as an "ocean of monsters"

D) as a "twentieth-century aquarium"

E) as a "vision of despair"

18. What word best reflects the tone of the authors' conclusions in Passage **1** and Passage **2**, respectively?

A) perturbed; concerned

B) sarcastic; anticipative

C) solemn; enchanted

D) skeptical; disaffected

E) convinced; dubious

19. Assuming the posture of the author of Passage **1**, what finding would most likely shake the beliefs of the author of Passage **2** regarding the existence of the creature in Loch Ness?

A) The sonar devices are inconclusive in their claims.

B) At least 905 of the sightings are fraudulent.

C) The pollution of Loch Ness will render all life forms extinct within one thousand years.

D) The mud-content in the lake cannot support any life-forms.

E) During the Ice Age, the entire surface of the lake was frozen.

SECTION 8 (20 Minutes - 16 Questions)
The following information is for your reference – **it is provided on every SAT**

A circle measures 360°
A straight line measures 180°
The sum of the angles of a triangle is always 180°

Definition of symbols:
- = *equal to*
- ≠ *not equal to*
- < *less than*
- > *more than*
- ≤ *less than or equal to*
- ≥ *more than or equal to*
- || *parallel to*
- ⊥ *perpendicular to*

All numbers used are real numbers

FORMULAS

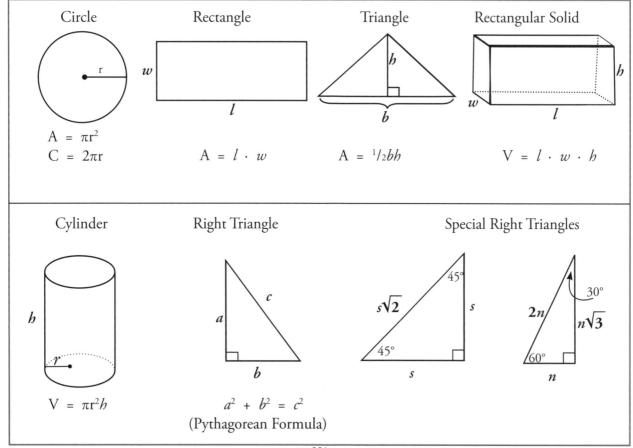

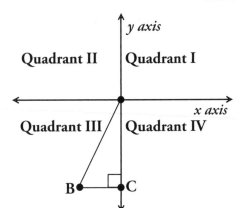

3. Which of the following is the most accurate graph of $2y = x^2 + 1$?

A)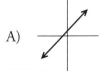

B)

C)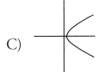

D)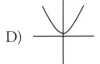

E)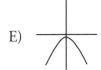

1. What are possible coordinates for **C**?

   A) $(^-4, 0)$

   B) $(0, 4)$

   C) $(3, ^-3)$

   D) $(^-3, ^-5)$

   E) $(0, ^-4)$

2. In the number 14.96, if the unit's digit and tenth's digit are switched, what is the change in the value of the number?

   A) $^-5.5$

   B) $^+4.5$

   C) $^+5.5$

   D) $^+27.0$

   E) $^+79.2$

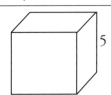

4. If the cube pictured above is cut into three equal pieces, what is the ratio of the volume of one of these pieces to the sum of the volumes of the other two?

   A) $1 : 2$

   B) $1 : 3$

   C) $1 : 8$

   D) $1 : 9$

   E) $1 : 27$

$$F = 9/5 \; C + 32$$

$$C = 5/9 \; (F + 32)$$

Consult this chart for Questions 5 – 6

5. Given the above temperature-conversion formula for Fahrenheit and Celsius, what would **50°C** be in **F°**?

A) 172

B) 122

C) 100

D) 60

E) 10

6. What temperature in **C°** corresponds with a reading of **0° F**?

A) ⁻32°

B) ⁻17⁷/₉°

C) 0°

D) 24⁵/₉°

E) 32°

7. For which value of **a** is $\dfrac{a^2 \cdot a^8}{a^5} = a^3$?

     I. ⁻1

     II. 0

     III. 1

A) none

B) III only

C) I and III

D) II and III

E) I, II and III

8. The results of a vote were in the ratio **6 : 5 : 2** for candidates **A**, **B**, and **C**, respectively.

What was the margin of difference between candidates **A** and **C** in a community of 910 voters?

A) 70 votes

B) 110 votes

C) 210 votes

D) 280 votes

E) 630 votes

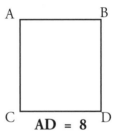

AD = 8

9. If the midpoints (not shown) of each of the sides of square **ABCD** are connected, what will be the area of the newly constructed inner square?

A) 16

B) $16\sqrt{2}$

C) 32

D) $64 - 16\sqrt{2}$

E) 48

10. Team A has 4 players whose average height is 5 ft. 8 in. How tall would a new teammate need to be to bring the team's average height up to exactly 6 feet?

A) 7 ft. 4 in.

B) 6 ft. 8 in.

C) 6 ft. 6 in.

D) 6 ft. 4 in.

E) 6 ft. 2 in.

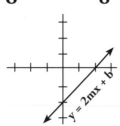

11. The figure above shows the graph of the line **y = 2mx + b,** where m and b are constants. Which of the following best represents the graph of the line **y = ¯4mx + b**?

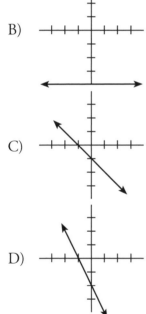

A)

B)

C)

D)

E)

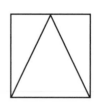

12. An isosceles triangle is placed inside a square so that the two share one side, and the vertex of the triangle bisects the opposite side. If the perimeter of the square is 28 units, what is the ratio of the area of the triangle to that of the square?

A) 3 : 2

B) 2 : 3

C) 4 : 7

D) 1 : 2

E) $\sqrt{3}$: 3

13. Stanley has $17 more than Mary and $13 more than Bert. If Stanley has $45 but wants everyone to have an equal amount of money, how much total money will he need to give to the other two?

A) $3

B) $5

C) $7

D) $10

E) $20

14. If it takes 4 globs and 3 flobs to build one clob, what is the maximum number of complete clobs Henry can build for $20 if the cost of the ingredients is as follows:

> **3 globs for $1**
>
> **4 flobs for $1**

[Note: globs and flobs can only be purchased in multiples listed; tax is included in the above prices]

A) 7

B) 8

C) 9

D) 10

E) 11

15. 7521 is an odd 4-digit number whose digits appear in descending order. How many odd 4-digit numbers between 8500 and 9000 contain digits that appear in descending order?

A) 14

B) 17

C) 19

D) 45

E) 250

16. Concentric circles are drawn so that each larger circle has a radius 50% greater than the previous, smaller circle. If the innermost circle has a radius of **x**, what is the area of the 3rd circle from the center?

A) $\dfrac{81\pi}{16}\mathbf{x}^2$

B) $\dfrac{9\pi}{16}\mathbf{x}^2$

C) $\dfrac{9\pi}{4}\mathbf{x}^2$

D) $16\pi\mathbf{x}^2$

E) $\dfrac{36\pi}{16}\mathbf{x}^2$

*Directions: Select the letter of the choice that best and most concisely expresses the thought of the sentence. If the original sentence is the best, select **A**.*

1. The car sped quickly away with the damaged headlight.

   A) The car sped quickly away with the damaged headlight.

   B) With the damaged headlight, the car sped quickly away.

   C) Speeding quickly away with the damaged headlight was the car.

   D) The car with the damaged headlight sped quickly away.

   E) The damaged headlight car sped quickly away.

2. Between us teens, there's nothing we can't do.

   A) Between us teens, there's nothing we can't do.

   B) There's nothing we can't do between us teens.

   C) As teens, we can't do nothing between us.

   D) Nothing between we teens can we not do.

   E) We as teens, there's nothing we can't do.

3. My children's needs are increasing faster than my bank account.

   A) faster than my bank account

   B) faster than is my bank account

   C) more quickly than my bank account can do

   D) faster than my bank account can handle

   E) faster than my bank account's

4. His constant complaining was not being well received at the dinner table.

   A) complaining was not being well received at the dinner table

   B) complaining at the dinner table was not well received

   C) complaining, not well received at the dinner table

   D) complaining was not being receiving well at the dinner table

   E) complaining, at the dinner table, was not being well received

5. At the movies, a good time was had by all.

   A) a good time was had by all

   B) by all was a good time was had

   C) all had a good time

   D) a good time was being had by all

   E) a good time was all that was had

6. Answers don't always come easily, oftentimes, they don't come at all.

   A) Answers don't always come easily, oftentimes, they don't come at all.

   B) Although they don't always come easily, oftentimes they don't come at all.

   C) Answers don't always come easily; oftentimes, they don't come at all.

   D) Not coming often, answers may not always come easily.

   E) Not coming often are answers that come easily.

7. <u>Because he was the youngest</u>, he was not asked to carry in the luggage.

A) Because he was the youngest

B) Being that he was the youngest

C) Because that he was the youngest

D) As a result of being the youngest

E) Youngest being that he was

8. My cousin had his coin collection appraised, <u>and it wasn't much</u>.

A) and it wasn't much

B) having little worth

C) unfortunately, it had little worth

D) it wasn't worth much

E) and it wasn't worth much

9. Our garage sale took in more money <u>than had last week's rummage sale</u>.

A) than had last week's rummage sale

B) than last week's rummage sale had

C) than the rummage sale of the prior week had

D) than did last week's rummage sale

E) than the week of the last rummage sale

10. <u>If everyone pursued their dreams</u>, the world would be a more cheerful place.

A) If everyone pursued their dreams

B) If everyone pursued her dreams

C) If dreams were pursued

D) Pursuing dreams

E) Their dreams pursued

11. Not surprisingly, <u>both siblings aspired to become a doctor</u>.

A) both siblings aspired to become a doctor

B) each sibling aspired to be doctors

C) both siblings aspired to be like a doctor

D) each sibling aspired to be as doctors

E) both siblings aspired to become doctors

12. Given but two choices, <u>mowing the lawn seemed the better</u>.

A) mowing the lawn seemed the better

B) mowing the lawn seemed the best

C) the better was in mowing the lawn

D) the best for me was mowing the lawn

E) to me mowing the lawn seemed the better

13. The youngster's height <u>was that of a mature adult</u>.

A) was that of a mature adult

B) equaled that of a mature adult

C) was, compared to a mature adult, that of one

D) was that of a mature adult's

E) was a mature adult's

14. <u>Were I to be a critic</u>, I could not have praised the movie less.

A) Were I to be a critic

B) Being a critic

C) As a possible critic

D) Were a critic me

E) A critic though I am not

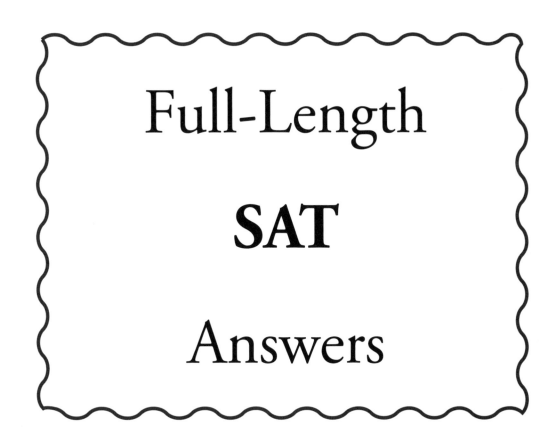

Full-Length

SAT

Answers

Full-Length SAT

Answers (Level)

Critical Reading

Section 2	Section 4	Section 7
1. C (1)	1. B (1)	1. D (1)
2. E (1)	2. D (2)	2. C (2)
3. A (2)	3. C (3)	3. D (3)
4. C (3)	4. A (4)	4. E (3)
5. B (3)	5. E (5)	5. B (4)
6. D (4)	6. D (2)	6. A (5)
7. E (4)	7. C (4)	7. E (4)
8. D (5)	8. B (2)	8. B (1)
9. C (4)	9. D (3)	9. D (3)
10. D (3)	10. E (4)	10. A (3)
11. A (3)	11. B (2)	11. E (2)
12. E (4)	12. A (3)	12. C (3)
13. E (2)	13. D (3)	13. B (4)
14. A (2)	14. D (5)	14. E (3)
15. E (1)	15. C (2)	15. C (2)
16. B (2)	16. E (3)	16. C (2)
17. B (3)	17. C (2)	17. A (3)
18. A (3)	18. A (4)	18. B (5)
19. A (4)	19. E (2)	19. D (3)
20. D (3)	20. A (3)	
21. C (3)	21. B (3)	
22. C (3)	22. A (4)	
23. D (3)	23. B (4)	
24. B (4)	24. C (3)	

Math

Section 3	Section 5	Section 8
1. E (1)	1. B (1)	1. E (1)
2. E (2)	2. D (1)	2. B (1)
3. D (1)	3. C (1)	3. D (3)
4. C (3)	4. D (5)	4. A (3)
5. A (3)	5. A (4)	5. B (2)
6. C (3)	6. E (4)	6. B (3)
7. E (3)	7. C (5)	7. C (4)
8. E (3)	8. B (5)	8. D (3)
9. B (4)	9. 4 (1)	9. C (4)
10. E (2)	10. 24 (2)	10. A (5)
11. B (5)	11. 12 (2)	11. D (4)
12. B (4)	12. 128 (3)	12. D (4)
13. A (4)	13. 220 (3)	13. D (4)
14. D (4)	14. 2 or 10 (4)	14. C (5)
15. A (4)	15. 5/8 or .625 (3)	15. C (5)
16. B (4)	16. 5/3 or 1.66 or 1.67 (4)	16. A (5)
17. C (4)	17. 5 (4)	
18. A (5)	18. 66 (5)	
19. D (5)		
20. C (5)		

Writing(Grammar)

Section 6	Section 9
1. C (1)	1. D (1)
2. C (1)	2. A (2)
3. B (2)	3. D (3)
4. E (3)	4. B (2)
5. A (3)	5. C (2)
6. A (3)	6. C (3)
7. E (2)	7. A (3)
8. D (3)	8. E (3)
9. B (3)	9. D (4)
10. D (4)	10. B (4)
11. B (5)	11. E (4)
12. D (1)	12. E (5)
13. A (1)	13. D (5)
14. C (2)	14. A (5)
15. A (2)	
16. D (3)	
17. C (3)	
18. B (4)	
19. E (4)	
20. A (4)	
21. C (4)	
22. E (3)	
23. B (4)	
24. C (3)	
25. A (4)	
26. D (5)	
27. D (4)	
28. B (5)	
29. D (5)	
30. C (2)	
31. E (3)	
32. B (3)	
33. A (3)	
34. E (3)	
35. E (4)	

SCORING

To score your test, simply count up the total amount of correct answers, then total the amount answered incorrectly (except for the Math Grid-In problems, which do not incur a penalty if they are answered incorrectly) and follow the directions below.

Critical Reading: _____ Number Correct
(Sections 2, 4, 7)

                                                  Number Incorrect: _____ ÷ 4 = *_____

                     − _____: * Subtract this number from the Number Correct

                         _____ This is your Raw Score

[Note: *If your Raw Score contains a fraction, round off to nearest integer*]

- -

Math: _____ Number Correct
(Sections 3, 5, 8)

                     Number Incorrect: _____ ÷ 4 = *_____
                     (Do Not include Grid-In problems that were incorrect)

                     − _____: * Subtract this number from the Number Correct

                         _____ This is your Raw Score

[Note: *If your Raw Score contains a fraction, round off to nearest integer*]

- -

Writing: _____ Number Correct
(exc. Essay)
(Sections 6, 9)

                     Number Incorrect: _____ ÷ 4 = *_____

                     − _____: * Subtract this number from the Number Correct

                         _____ This is your Raw Score

[Note: *If your Raw Score contains a fraction, round off to nearest integer*]

- -

To convert your Raw Score into Scaled Score (200 – 800), consult the appropriate Score Chart on page 232.

Full-Length SAT
Score Conversion Chart

Critical Reading						Mathematics						Writing (Grammar)*					
Raw Score	Scaled Score	Raw Score	Scaled Score	Raw Score	Scaled Score	Raw Score	Scaled Score	Raw Score	Scaled Score	Raw Score	Scaled Score	Raw Score	Scaled Score	Raw Score	Scaled Score	Raw Score	Scaled Score
67	800	42	580	17	420	54	800	29	530	4	320	49	800	24	530	-1	270
66	800	41	570	16	410	53	780	28	520	3	310	48	780	23	520	-2	250
65	780	40	560	15	410	52	760	27	520	2	290	47	760	22	510	-3	240
64	760	39	560	14	400	51	740	26	510	1	280	46	740	21	510		
63	750	38	550	13	390	50	730	25	500	0	260	45	730	20	500		
62	740	37	540	12	380	49	710	24	490	-1	250	44	710	19	490		
61	720	36	540	11	380	48	700	23	490	-2	240	43	700	18	480		
60	710	35	530	10	370	47	690	22	480	-3	220	42	690	17	470		
59	700	34	530	9	360	46	670	21	470			41	670	16	460		
58	690	33	520	8	350	45	660	20	460			40	660	15	450		
57	680	32	510	7	340	44	650	19	460			39	650	14	440		
56	670	31	510	6	330	43	650	18	450			38	650	13	430		
55	670	30	500	5	320	42	640	17	440			37	640	12	420		
54	660	29	500	4	310	41	630	16	430			36	630	11	410		
53	650	28	490	3	300	40	620	15	430			35	620	10	400		
52	640	27	480	2	280	39	610	14	420			34	610	9	390		
51	640	26	480	1	270	38	600	13	410			33	600	8	380		
50	630	25	470	0	250	37	590	12	400			32	590	7	370		
49	620	24	470	-1	240	36	590	11	390			31	590	6	360		
48	610	23	460	-2	230	35	580	10	380			30	580	5	350		
47	610	22	450	-3	220	34	570	9	380			29	570	4	340		
46	600	21	450			33	560	8	370			28	560	3	330		
45	590	20	440			32	560	7	360			27	560	2	320		
44	590	19	430			31	550	6	340			26	550	1	300		
43	580	18	430			30	540	5	330			25	540	0	290		

*Because the essay has only a nominal impact on the Writing Section Score (it usually does not affect the overall Writing Section Score by more than 50 points) and because it is somewhat subjective, we've chosen to put an objective score-equivalent for the remainder of the section. Remember: The multiple-choice "grammar" questions comprise most of this section's score; they are far more critical to the overall score than is the essay.

SO-AZP-438

CALIFORNIA EDITION

HOUGHTON MIFFLIN

Math

Steps

HOUGHTON MIFFLIN

Boston • Atlanta • Dallas • Denver • Geneva, Illinois • Palo Alto • Princeton

Grateful acknowledgment is given for the contributions of

Student Book

Rosemary Theresa Barry
Karen R. Boyle
Barbara Brozman
Gary S. Bush
John E. Cassidy
Dorothy Kirk

Sharon Ann Kovalcik
Bernice Kubek
Donna Marie Kvasnok
Ann Cherney Markunas
Joanne Marie Mascha
Kathleen Mary Ogrin

Judith Ostrowski
Jeanette Mishic Polomsky
Patricia Stenger
Annabelle L. Higgins Svete

Teacher Book
Contributing Writers

Dr. Judy Curran Buck
  Assistant Professor of Mathematics
  Plymouth State College
  Plymouth, New Hampshire

Dr. Richard Evans
  Professor of Mathematics
  Plymouth State College
  Plymouth, New Hampshire

Dr. Mary K. Porter
  Professor of Mathematics
  St. Mary's College
  Notre Dame, Indiana

Dr. Anne M. Raymond
  Assistant Professor of Mathematics
  Keene State College
  Keene, New Hampshire

Stuart P. Robertson, Jr.
  Education Consultant
  Pelham, New Hampshire

Dr. David Rock
  Associate Professor,
  Mathematics Education
  University of Mississippi
  Oxford, Mississippi

Michelle Lynn Rock
  Elementary Teacher
  Oxford School District
  Oxford, Mississippi

Dr. Jean M. Shaw
  Professor of Elementary Education
  University of Mississippi
  Oxford, Mississippi

Contents

UNIT 1 • TABLE OF CONTENTS

Place Value

Dear Family,

During the next few weeks, our math class will be learning and practicing place value.

You can expect to see homework that provides practice with rounding. Here is a sample you may want to keep handy to give help if needed.

Rounding to the Nearest Hundred

To round a number such as **4,175** to the nearest hundred, first find the digit in the hundreds place.

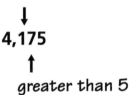

Hundreds Place

4,175

greater than 5

Next, look at the digit in the place to the right (**7**). If the digit in the place to the right is less than **5**, round down. If it is greater than or equal to **5**, round up.

Since the digit to the right of the hundreds place is greater than **5**, round **4,175** up to **4,200**, the nearest hundred.

During this unit, students will need to continue practicing rounding and other skills related to place value, such as comparing numbers.

Sincerely,

Write each number in standard form.

1. three thousand, five hundred thirty-nine _____

2. seventy-two thousand, one hundred four _____

3. six hundred fifty-three thousand, twenty _____

4. nine million, four hundred thousand, two _____

5. two hundred sixty million, twenty-five thousand, four hundred sixteen _____

6. thirty-one million, one hundred six thousand, seven hundred fifty-three _____

Write <, >, or =.

7.   567 ◯ 547   8.   3,209 ◯ 3,290   9.   9,900 ◯ 9,899

10. 13,000 ◯ 13,100   11. 89,745 ◯ 89,745   12. 750,221 ◯ 705,221

Round to the nearest hundred.

13. 449 _____   14. 850 _____   15. 44,061 _____   16. 178,888 _____

Round to the nearest ten thousand.

17. 75,503 _____   18. 549,840 _____   19. 1,427,607 _____

Round to the nearest hundred thousand.

20. 1,750,621 _____   21. 7,247,063 _____

The bar graph shows the number of hours a figure skater practices each day. Use the graph to solve each problem.

22. Look for a pattern in the number of hours the skater practices each day. Describe the pattern.

   _____

23. Use the pattern to predict the number of hours the skater will practice on Saturday. _____

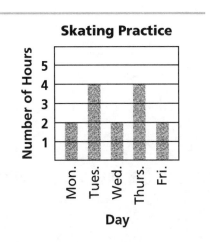

Skating Practice

1 A teacher has 42 sheets of paper for 7 students. If he divides the sheets of paper equally, how many sheets of paper will each student get?

A 9   C 7

B 8   D 6

2 The chart shows the population of four California cities.

California Cities	Population
Laguna Beach	23,170
Montclair	28,434
San Marcos	38,974
Monterey	31,954

Which shows the cities in order of population size, from *greatest* to *least*?

F San Marcos, Monterey, Laguna Beach, Montclair

G Laguna Beach, Monterey, San Marcos, Montclair

H Laguna Beach, Montclair, Monterey, San Marcos

J San Marcos, Monterey, Montclair, Laguna Beach

3 Which group of number sentences belong to the same family of facts as $8 \times 9 = 72$?

A $3 \times 3 = 9; 4 \times 2 = 8; 9 \div 3 = 3$

B $9 \times 8 = 72, 72 \div 8 = 9; 72 \div 9 = 8$

C $8 \times 8 = 64; 64 \div 8 = 8$

D $9 \times 6 = 63; 63 \div 9 = 6; 63 \div 6 = 9$

4 Linda's horse weighs 1,234 pounds. What is the number rounded to the nearest hundred?

F 1,200   H 1,300   K NH

G 1,240   J 1,400

5 Mrs. Mulligan pays 4 friends $9 each to work in her yard. How much money does she pay them in all?

A $18   C $32

B $27   D $36

6 Which group of number sentences belong to the same family of facts as $63 \div 9 = 7$?

F $9 \times 7 = 63; 7 \times 9 = 63; 63 \div 7 = 9$

G $3 \times 3 = 9; 7 \times 1 = 7; 9 \div 3 = 3$

H $7 \times 9 = 56; 56 \div 7 = 9; 9 \times 7 = 56$

J $63 \div 3 = 21; 21 \times 3 = 63$

7 A candy company gave away 70,065 samples of its new chocolate bar. What words mean 70,065?

A seventy-six thousand, sixty-five

B seventy thousand, six hundred fifty

C seventy thousand, six hundred five

D seventy thousand, sixty-five

Addition and Subtraction of Whole Numbers

Dear Family,

During the next few weeks, our math class will be learning and practicing addition and subtraction of whole numbers.

You can expect to see homework that provides practice with estimating sums. Here is a sample you may want to keep handy to give help if needed.

Estimating Sums

An estimate is a way to check an exact answer; it can be compared to an exact answer to help decide if that answer is reasonable.

Add:
$$\begin{array}{r} 6{,}379 \\ +\ 1{,}658 \\ \hline 8{,}057 \end{array}$$

To decide if this answer is reasonable, estimate by rounding each number to its greatest place. The greatest place in both **6,379** and **1,658** is thousands.

Estimate by rounding each number:

$$\begin{array}{rcr} 6{,}379 & \rightarrow & 6{,}000 \\ +\ 1{,}658 & \rightarrow & +\ 2{,}000 \\ \hline & & 8{,}000 \end{array}$$

An estimate of the exact answer is **8,000**. If the exact answer is close to **8,000**, it is a reasonable answer. If the exact answer is not close to **8,000**, the problem should be worked a second time.

During this unit, students will need to continue practicing addition and subtraction facts.

Sincerely,

The number line shows:

    4 + 3 = 7
    7 − 3 = 4

The number line also shows:

Subtraction is the **inverse,** or opposite, of addition.
Addition is the **inverse,** or opposite, of subtraction.

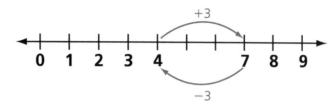

Since addition and subtraction are inverse operations, you can write a **fact family** using **4, 3,** and **7.**

    4 + 3 = 7   3 + 4 = 7

    7 − 3 = 4   7 − 4 = 3

Find each sum or difference. Write the number sentence that shows the inverse operation.

1. 7 + 3 = ___10___   8 − 3 = _____   9 + 3 = _____

    10 − 3 = ___7___   _____   _____

2. 17 − 9 = _____   10 − 1 = _____   2 + 3 = _____

    _____   _____   _____

Write a fact family for each group of numbers.

3.   3, 7, 10   2, 11, 9

    _____   _____

    _____   _____

Make each number sentence true. Write + or −. Then write a number sentence you could use to check your answer.

4. 15 $\bigcirc$ 5 = 10   5 $\bigcirc$ 9 = 14   13 $\bigcirc$ 9 = 4

    _____   _____   _____

5. 9 $\bigcirc$ 9 = 18   9 $\bigcirc$ 8 = 1   8 $\bigcirc$ 5 = 13

    _____   _____   _____

Complete each table.

6.

□	□ + 4
8	
7	
2	
6	
5	
9	
3	
4	

□	□ − 10
18	
23	
46	
35	
14	
29	
10	
47	

□	□ − 1
24	
	18
33	
	29
13	
	42
	17
25	

□	□ + 6
	22
17	
	36
11	
	19
10	
23	
	15

□	□ + 11
17	
12	
	11
26	
	49
	20
47	
28	

Problem Solving
Reasoning

7. Write the numbers **2** and **3** in the table so that the sum of each row, column, and diagonal is the same. (**6, 5,** and **4** are on a diagonal.)

8		4
1	5	9
6	7	

8. Write the numbers **2, 5,** and **9** in the table so that the sum of each row, column, and diagonal is the same.

3	8	7
10	6	
	4	

Test Prep ★ Mixed Review

9 What number is equal to 2,000,000 + 30,000 + 7,000?

A 2,037,000

B 2,003,700

C 2,000,370

D 2,000,037

10 In one month, 702,650 cars used a single exit off the interstate highway. What words mean 702,650?

F Seven hundred twenty thousand, six hundred fifty

G Seven hundred two thousand, six hundred fifty

H Seven hundred two thousand, six hundred five

J Seventy-two thousand, six hundred fifty

STANDARD

Number sentences contain numbers operations, and an equal sign.

Examples: $3 + 2 = 5$
$5 - 2 = 3$

$1 + 7 = 8$
$8 - 7 = 1$

$6 + 4 = 10$
$10 - 4 = 6$

In algebra, letters called **variables** are used to represent unknown numbers.

Examples: $n + 3 = 5$
$5 - 3 = n$

$x + 7 = 8$
$8 - 7 = x$

$n + 4 = 10$
$10 - 4 = n$

Number sentences with variables are called **open sentences**.

You can use a related number sentence to make an open number sentence true.

Find *n* in the number sentence $n + 5 = 11$.

1. Use a related number sentence.

   $n + 5 = 11$ Think: $11 - 5 = 6$, so $n = 6$.

2. Check your work. Replace *n* with **6** in the open sentence!

   Decide if the number sentence is true.

   $n + 5 = 11$
   $\downarrow$
   $6 + 5 = 11$ True

$7 + 3 = 10$ is a **True Sentence.**

$n + 3 = 10$ is an **Open Sentence.**

$7 + 3 = 12$ is a **False Sentence.**

Label each number sentence True, False, or Open.

1. $7 - 3 = 4$ $12 + 2 = 10$ $x - 1 = 5$ $11 + 4 = 15$

_____   _____   _____   _____

Use a related number sentence to find the value of *n*.

2. $n + 2 = 7$ $n + 9 = 15$ $n + 8 = 10$ $n + 3 = 6$

$n =$ _____ $n =$ _____ $n =$ _____ $n =$ _____

3. $n + 6 = 8$ $n + 1 = 5$ $n + 7 = 11$ $n + 5 = 5$

$n =$ _____ $n =$ _____ $n =$ _____ $n =$ _____

4. $n + 3 = 10$ $n + 4 = 9$ $n + 9 = 17$ $n + 8 = 15$

$n =$ _____ $n =$ _____ $n =$ _____ $n =$ _____

Subtraction rules can sometimes be used to find the value of a variable in an open sentence.

What is the value of n in the number sentence $n - 0 = 9$?

Rule: When you subtract zero from a number, the answer is that number.

So: If $n - 0 = 9$, then $n = 9$.

What is the value of x in the number sentence $5 - 5 = x$?

Rule: Any number subtracted from itself equals **0**.

So: If $5 - 5 = x$, then $x = 0$.

Write the value of x.

5. $8 - 8 = x$ $\qquad$ $4 - 0 = x$ $\qquad$ $7 - 2 = x$ $\qquad$ $10 - 0 = x$

$x =$ _____ $\qquad$ $x =$ _____ $\qquad$ $x =$ _____ $\qquad$ $x =$ _____

6. $3 - 3 = x$ $\qquad$ $12 - 5 = x$ $\qquad$ $16 - 7 = x$ $\qquad$ $11 - 11 = x$

$x =$ _____ $\qquad$ $x =$ _____ $\qquad$ $x =$ _____ $\qquad$ $x =$ _____

| Problem Solving |
| Reasoning |

Each number sentence below is false. Change one number in each sentence to make it a true number sentence.

7. $10 - 5 = 12 - 9$ $\qquad$ $15 - 8 = 7 - 6$ $\qquad$ $4 - 4 = 9 - 3$

✔ Quick Check

Solve.

8. $9 + 6 = 6 + \boxed{}$ $\qquad$ **9.** $(3 + 4) + 1 = 3 + (4 + \boxed{})$

10. $7 + 6 = (3 + \boxed{}) + 6$

Write the number sentence that shows the inverse operation.

11. $13 - 6 = 7$ $\qquad$ **12.** $18 + 6 = 24$ $\qquad$ **13.** $17 - 6 = 11$

_____ $\qquad$ _____ $\qquad$ _____

Use related number sentences to find the value of n.

14. $8 + n = 17$ $n =$ _____ $\qquad$ **15.** $5 + n = 13$ $n =$ _____

16. $n - 12 = 7$ $n =$ _____ $\qquad$ **17.** $15 - n = 4$ $n =$ _____

Work Space.

In this lesson, you will write number sentences to help you solve addition and subtraction problems.

You can use **addition** to find a total. You can use **subtraction** to find out how many are left, to compare two numbers, or to find a missing addend.

Problem

Paola bought a fleece jacket for $29. She also bought a pair of gloves. She spent a total of $41. How much did the gloves cost?

❶ Understand   As you reread, ask yourself questions.

• What facts are you given in the problem?

  The fleece jacket costs **$29**.
  The jacket and gloves together cost **$41**.

• What do you need to find out?

  _____

❷ Decide   Choose a method for solving.

Try the strategy Write a Number Sentence.

• Draw a circle around the number sentence that could be used to represent the problem.

  $(29 + n = 41)$ $29 + 41 = n$

❸ Solve   Find *n* in the number sentence $29 + n = 41$.

• Use a related number sentence.

  If **$29 + n = 41$**, then **$41 -$** _____ $= n$, or $n =$ _____.

• Check.   **$29 + n = 41$**

  $29 +$ _____ $= 41$ True.

❹ Look back   Write the answer to the problem below.

Answer _____

Read the problem again. Check your answer.

• Why is it important to go back and read the problem again to check your answer?

_____

Solve. Use the Write a Number Sentence strategy or any other strategy you have learned.

1. There are **18** girls and **13** boys in Mr. Hooper's class. How many students are in Mr. Hooper's class?

Think: What number sentence can be used to solve the problem?

Circle the correct sentence.

$18 + 13 = n$ or $13 + n = 18$

Answer: _____

2. Jasmine wants to buy a skateboard that costs **$39**. She has saved **$15**. How much more money does she need?

Think: What number sentence can be used to solve the problem?

Circle the correct sentence.

$15 + n = 39$ or $15 + 39 = n$

Answer: _____

3. Sally and Sean have the same birthday. Sean is **16** and Sally is **7**. How much older is Sean than Sally?

_____

4. Loralee and Susan bought balloons for a party. They used **32** balloons in all. Loralee used **14**. How many did Susan use?

_____

5. The town library subscribes to **53** monthly magazines and **34** weekly magazines. How many magazine subscriptions do they have?

_____

6. Denisha had **54** baseball cards. She gave **9** to her brother Aaron. How many baseball cards did Denisha have left?

_____

7. Write the next number in this sequence.

6, 11, 17, 24, 32, _____

8. Write the missing number in this sequence.

_____, **8, 10, 12, 14, 16**

9. Mr. Cohen is driving his family to visit their cousins who live **97** miles away. Mr. Cohen has driven **29** miles so far. How many more miles will he have to drive?

_____

10. Mrs. Sullivan is staying on the third floor of a hotel. There are **42** stairs from the lobby level to the third floor. She climbed up the stairs and then climbed back down. How many stairs did she climb?

_____

Estimating Sums and Differences

One way to estimate a sum or difference is to round each number to its greatest place value. The greatest place value of any number is the place farthest to the left.

Estimate the sum. *Tens* is the greatest place value of the addends.

$$\begin{array}{rl}
58 & \text{Round to nearest } 10 \rightarrow 60 \\
+\,29 & \text{Round to nearest } 10 \rightarrow +\,30 \\
\hline
& 90
\end{array}$$

A good estimate of the sum is 58 + 29 is **90**.

Estimate the difference. *Hundreds* is the greatest place value of the addends.

$$\begin{array}{rl}
742 & \text{Round to nearest } 100 \rightarrow 700 \\
-388 & \text{Round to nearest } 100 \rightarrow -400 \\
\hline
& 300
\end{array}$$

A good estimate of the difference is 742 − 388 is **300**.

Estimate each sum or difference by rounding to the greatest place value.

1.
$$\begin{array}{rl}
62 & \rightarrow 60 \\
+\,39 & \rightarrow +\,40 \\
\hline
\end{array}$$

$$\begin{array}{rl}
87 & \rightarrow \\
+\,46 & \rightarrow +\,\_\_\_ \\
\hline
\end{array}$$

$$\begin{array}{rl}
42 & \rightarrow \\
+\,37 & \rightarrow +\,\_\_\_ \\
\hline
\end{array}$$

$$\begin{array}{rl}
45 & \rightarrow \\
+\,35 & \rightarrow +\,\_\_\_ \\
\hline
\end{array}$$

2.
$$\begin{array}{rl}
64 & \rightarrow \\
-\,27 & \rightarrow -\,\_\_\_ \\
\hline
\end{array}$$

$$\begin{array}{rl}
51 & \rightarrow \\
-\,39 & \rightarrow -\,\_\_\_ \\
\hline
\end{array}$$

$$\begin{array}{rl}
83 & \rightarrow \\
-\,74 & \rightarrow -\,\_\_\_ \\
\hline
\end{array}$$

$$\begin{array}{rl}
94 & \rightarrow \\
-\,68 & \rightarrow -\,\_\_\_ \\
\hline
\end{array}$$

3.
$$\begin{array}{rl}
184 & \rightarrow \\
+\,453 & \rightarrow +\,\_\_\_ \\
\hline
\end{array}$$

$$\begin{array}{rl}
671 & \rightarrow \\
-\,305 & \rightarrow -\,\_\_\_ \\
\hline
\end{array}$$

$$\begin{array}{rl}
465 & \rightarrow \\
+\,275 & \rightarrow +\,\_\_\_ \\
\hline
\end{array}$$

$$\begin{array}{rl}
555 & \rightarrow \\
-\,250 & \rightarrow -\,\_\_\_ \\
\hline
\end{array}$$

4.
$$\begin{array}{rl}
776 & \rightarrow \\
-\,519 & \rightarrow -\,\_\_\_ \\
\hline
\end{array}$$

$$\begin{array}{rl}
168 & \rightarrow \\
+\,384 & \rightarrow +\,\_\_\_ \\
\hline
\end{array}$$

$$\begin{array}{rl}
627 & \rightarrow \\
-\,179 & \rightarrow -\,\_\_\_ \\
\hline
\end{array}$$

$$\begin{array}{rl}
814 & \rightarrow \\
-\,116 & \rightarrow -\,\_\_\_ \\
\hline
\end{array}$$

5.
$$\begin{array}{rl}
5{,}368 & \rightarrow \\
-\,2{,}154 & \rightarrow -\,\_\_\_ \\
\hline
\end{array}$$

$$\begin{array}{rl}
4{,}543 & \rightarrow \\
+\,3{,}568 & \rightarrow +\,\_\_\_ \\
\hline
\end{array}$$

$$\begin{array}{rl}
7{,}538 & \rightarrow \\
+\,1{,}524 & \rightarrow +\,\_\_\_ \\
\hline
\end{array}$$

6.
$$\begin{array}{rl}
4{,}762 & \rightarrow \\
-\,2{,}813 & \rightarrow -\,\_\_\_ \\
\hline
\end{array}$$

$$\begin{array}{rl}
6{,}151 & \rightarrow \\
+\,2{,}183 & \rightarrow +\,\_\_\_ \\
\hline
\end{array}$$

$$\begin{array}{rl}
1{,}805 & \rightarrow \\
-\,1{,}372 & \rightarrow -\,\_\_\_ \\
\hline
\end{array}$$

Solve.

Read each situation. Round the numbers to the greatest place value. Then use those numbers to write an estimated answer.

7. On their trip through Canada, Tom's family drove **206** kilometers one day and **98** the next. About how many kilometers did they drive in two days?

_____

8. In the auditorium, **735** chairs were set up. The audience used only **568**. About how many chairs were not used?

_____

9. A school parking lot has enough space for **275** cars. During the school play, **157** cars were parked in the parking lot. About how many spaces were not used?

_____

10. In Jane's school there are **917** pupils. There are **489** boys. About how many girls are there?

_____

11. Suppose you were asked this question: "How many people live in the city or town where you live?" To answer the question, would you give an estimate or an exact answer? Tell why.

_____

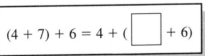

Test Prep ★ Mixed Review

12 What number should go in the ☐ to make the number sentence true?

$$(4 + 7) + 6 = 4 + (\boxed{} + 6)$$

A 4

B 6

C 7

D 9

13 The zoo had 127,678 visitors in July and August. What is this number rounded to the nearest ten thousand?

F 120,000

G 125,000

H 130,000

J 135,000

Adding Whole Numbers

Sometimes you may need to regroup when you add.

Add: **315 + 607.**

1. Add ones. Regroup **10** ones as **1** ten.

H	T	O
	¹	
3	1	5
+ 6	0	7
		2

2. Add tens.

H	T	O
	¹	
3	1	5
+ 6	0	7
	2	2

3. Add hundreds.

H	T	O
	¹	
3	1	5
+ 6	0	7
9	2	2

Add.

1.

H	T	O
	5	1
+	4	3

H	T	O
	1	7
+	8	9

H	T	O
	7	3
+	2	6

H	T	O
	6	4
+	9	6

H	T	O
	8	8
+	4	7

2.

H	T	O
5	4	8
+ 3	8	9

H	T	O
2	7	5
+ 1	9	9

H	T	O
7	4	6
+ 1	5	9

H	T	O
7	6	7
+ 1	5	3

H	T	O
2	3	9
+ 1	7	8

3.

```
  27        43        72        81        93        65
+ 31      + 19      + 36      + 14      + 50      + 25
```

4.

```
  12        26        70        34        51        48
+ 39      + 124     + 46      + 202     + 41      + 396
```

5.

```
 543       648       456       564       249       376
+ 189     + 275     + 266     + 268     + 395     + 487
```

6.

```
 543       716       324       327       186       561
+ 178     + 97      + 397     + 198     + 89      + 239
```

To find each sum, begin with the ones place. Regroup when necessary.

Add: **4,678 + 4,783.**	Add: **20,413 + 31,750.**	Add: **671 + 280 + 206.**
$\overset{1\ 1\ 1}{4{,}678}$	$\overset{1}{20{,}413}$	$\overset{1}{671}$
$+\ 4{,}783$	$+\ 31{,}750$	280
$9{,}461$	$52{,}163$	$+\ 206$
		$1{,}157$

Add.

7.
$$
\begin{array}{r} 2{,}639 \\ +\ 3{,}574 \end{array}
\qquad
\begin{array}{r} 6{,}181 \\ +\ 1{,}498 \end{array}
\qquad
\begin{array}{r} 4{,}107 \\ +\ 3{,}895 \end{array}
\qquad
\begin{array}{r} 5{,}728 \\ +\ 2{,}748 \end{array}
\qquad
\begin{array}{r} 57{,}240 \\ +\ 31{,}175 \end{array}
$$

8.
$$
\begin{array}{r} 12{,}743 \\ +\ 56{,}155 \end{array}
\qquad
\begin{array}{r} 26{,}604 \\ +\ 22{,}581 \end{array}
\qquad
\begin{array}{r} 46{,}367 \\ +\ 19{,}066 \end{array}
\qquad
\begin{array}{r} 948 \\ 160 \\ +\ 788 \end{array}
\qquad
\begin{array}{r} 646 \\ 129 \\ +\ 936 \end{array}
$$

Problem Solving Reasoning Solve.

9. Find the greatest possible sum of two **3**-digit numbers that use the digits **1, 2, 3, 4, 5, 6** only once.

10. Find the least possible sum of two **3**-digit numbers that use the digits **1, 2, 3, 4, 5, 6** only once.

✓ Quick Check

Estimate the sum or difference. Then find the exact answer.

11. $543 + 167$ **12.** $927 - 465$ **13.** $4{,}657 - 2{,}453$

Work Space.

Add.

14.
$$
\begin{array}{r} 3{,}479 \\ +\ 4{,}319 \end{array}
$$
15.
$$
\begin{array}{r} 5{,}587 \\ +\ 3{,}291 \end{array}
$$
16.
$$
\begin{array}{r} 2{,}477 \\ +\ 2{,}396 \end{array}
$$

17.
$$
\begin{array}{r} 177 \\ 564 \\ +\ 196 \end{array}
$$
18.
$$
\begin{array}{r} 477 \\ 673 \\ +\ 826 \end{array}
$$
19.
$$
\begin{array}{r} 369 \\ 208 \\ +\ 184 \end{array}
$$

Subtracting Whole Numbers

Sometimes when you subtract you must regroup.

Subtract: **832 − 478.**

1. Not enough ones. Regroup **1** ten as **10** ones. Subtract ones.

H	T	O
8	$\overset{2}{\cancel{3}}$	$\overset{12}{\cancel{2}}$
− 4	7	8

2. Not enough tens. Regroup **1** hundred as **10** tens. Subtract tens.

H	T	O
$\overset{7}{\cancel{8}}$	$\overset{12}{\cancel{3}}$	$\overset{12}{\cancel{2}}$
− 4	7	8
	5	4

3. Subtract hundreds.

H	T	O
$\overset{7}{\cancel{8}}$	$\overset{12}{\cancel{3}}$	$\overset{12}{\cancel{2}}$
− 4	7	8
3	5	4

Subtract.

1.

T	O
2	8
− 1	5

T	O
5	1
− 3	9

T	O
7	7
− 4	8

T	O
6	2
− 3	0

T	O
5	6
− 1	8

2.

H	T	O
3	1	4
− 2	0	3

H	T	O
6	7	5
− 4	8	1

H	T	O
5	2	6
− 1	1	9

H	T	O
9	4	2
− 8	5	2

H	T	O
7	2	1
− 4	6	5

3.

617	592	474	819	726	531
− 11	− 136	− 90	− 356	− 88	− 34

4.

432	384	452	925	824	341
− 235	− 198	− 378	− 257	− 267	− 162

5.

521	258	179	932	879	623
− 198	− 187	− 96	− 876	− 159	− 197

To find each difference, begin with the ones place
and regroup when necessary. Then subtract.

Subtract: **6,431 − 5,117**

$$\begin{array}{r} 6,4\overset{2\ 11}{\cancel{3}\cancel{1}} \\ -5,117 \\ \hline 1,314 \end{array}$$

Subtract: **94,727 − 36,180**

$$\begin{array}{r} \overset{8\ 14\ \ \ 6\ 12}{\cancel{9}\cancel{4},\cancel{7}\cancel{2}7} \\ -36,180 \\ \hline 58,547 \end{array}$$

Subtract.

6.

4,715	9,411	7,332	3,625	5,282
− 3,602	− 4,103	− 2,721	− 1,014	− 2,550

7.

82,613	71,195	24,381	39,837	54,923
− 41,501	− 28,040	− 15,129	− 33,225	− 36,044

Problem Solving
Reasoning

Solve.

8. Each time you subtract two numbers, you find a
difference. Is there a way to check if the
difference you find is correct? Explain.

_____

_____

9. Find the least possible difference
of two **2**-digit numbers that use
the digits **2, 4, 6,** and **8** only once
in each number.

_____

10. Find the greatest possible
difference of two **3**-digit numbers
that use the digits **3, 5, 7,** and **9**
only once in each number.

_____

Test Prep ★ Mixed Review

11. What number should go in the ☐ to
make the number sentence true?

$$8 + (9 + 4) = \boxed{} + (8 + 9)$$

A 9

B 8

C 4

D 2

12. Jason's parents bought him a bicycle
for $127 and a helmet for $25,
including tax. How much money did
they spend all together?

F $102

H $142

G $132

J $152

Subtracting Across Zeros

In some subtraction exercises, there may not be enough ones and tens to regroup. When this happens, you must regroup hundreds.

Subtract: **500 − 264.**

1. Not enough ones. Not enough tens. Regroup **1** hundred as **10** tens. You now have **4** hundreds and **10** tens.

$$\begin{array}{r} ^{4}\cancel{5}\,^{10}\cancel{0}\ 0 \\ -\ 2\ 6\ 4 \\ \hline \end{array}$$

2. Not enough ones. Regroup **1** ten as **10** ones. You now have **9** tens and **10** ones.

$$\begin{array}{r} ^{4}\cancel{5}\,^{9}\cancel{10}\,^{10}\cancel{0} \\ -\ 2\ 6\ 4 \\ \hline \end{array}$$

3. Subtract. Remember: Always start with the ones.

$$\begin{array}{r} ^{4}\cancel{5}\,^{9}\cancel{10}\,^{10}\cancel{0} \\ -\ 2\ 6\ 4 \\ \hline 2\ 3\ 6 \end{array}$$

Subtract: **308 − 189.**

1. Not enough ones. Not enough tens. Regroup **1** hundred as **10** tens. You now have **2** hundreds and **10** tens.

$$\begin{array}{r} ^{2}\cancel{3}\,^{10}\cancel{0}\ 8 \\ -\ 1\ 8\ 9 \\ \hline \end{array}$$

2. Not enough ones. Regroup **1** ten as **10** ones. You now have **9** tens and **18** ones.

$$\begin{array}{r} ^{2}\cancel{3}\,^{9}\cancel{10}\,^{18}\cancel{8} \\ -\ 1\ 8\ 9 \\ \hline \end{array}$$

3. Subtract. Remember: Always start with the ones.

$$\begin{array}{r} ^{2}\cancel{3}\,^{9}\cancel{0}\,^{18}\cancel{8} \\ -\ 1\ 8\ 9 \\ \hline 1\ 1\ 9 \end{array}$$

Subtract.

1.
800	500	400	600	900
− 132	− 348	− 334	− 412	− 406

2.
800	300	200	500	800
− 354	− 276	− 121	− 347	− 89

3.
801	502	603	904	705
− 692	− 147	− 259	− 236	− 287

4.
908	704	508	801	608
− 362	− 488	− 179	− 655	− 599

Sometimes you need to regroup across zeros when you subtract with greater numbers.

Subtract: **6,012 − 2,356**

```
      0 12                5 10 0 12             5  9 10
  6,0 1̸ 2̸           6̸,0̸ 1̸ 2̸            6̸,0̸ 1̸ 2̸
 − 2,3 5 6           − 2, 3 5 6           − 2, 3 5 6
─────────           ─────────           ─────────
        6                     6            3, 6 5 6
```

Subtract: **13,000 − 8,441**

```
   2  10                 2  9 10                2  9  9 10                0 12  9  9 10
 1 3̸,0̸ 0 0          1 3̸,0̸ 0̸ 0          1 3̸,0̸ 0̸ 0̸           1̸ 3̸,0̸ 0̸ 0̸
 − 8,4 4 1            − 8, 4 4 1            − 8, 4 4 1             − 8, 4 4 1
─────────            ─────────            ─────────             ─────────
                                                5 5 9             4, 5 5 9
```

Subtract.

5.
```
   4,105        8,800        7,040        5,000
 − 1,621      − 3,990      − 2,516      − 4,327
```

6.
```
  21,500       48,300       73,000       60,000
− 14,750     − 37,605     − 27,303     − 54,226
```

✔ Quick Check

Solve.   Work Space.

7. 573   **8.** 817   **9.** 4,726
      − 249   − 546   − 3,572

10. 7,647   **11.** 34,743   **12.** 61,794
       − 4,824   − 21,454   − 34,972

13. 805   **14.** 600   **15.** 5,705
       − 327   − 387   − 1,259

16. 7,000   **17.** 41,004   **18.** 67,074
       − 5,680   − 20,645   − 34,197

Name _____

These are some coins and bills we use.

twenty-dollar bill	ten-dollar bill	five-dollar bill

$20 or $20.00	$10 or $10.00	$5 or $5.00

one-dollar bill	half-dollar	quarter

$1 or $1.00	50¢ or $.50	25¢ or $.25

dime	nickel	penny

10¢ or $.10	5¢ or $.05	1¢ or $.01

Write the amounts. Then circle the amount that is greater.

1.

_____   _____

Write the amounts. Then circle the amount that is less.

2.

_____

_____

3.

_____

_____

Problem Solving Reasoning | **Complete each sentence.**

4. One dollar is the same as _____ pennies, _____ half-dollars, or _____ quarters.

5. Fifty cents is the same as_____ nickels, _____ quarters, or_____ dimes.

Test Prep ★ Mixed Review

6 What number should go in the ☐ to make the number sentence true?

$$(3 + 8) + 9 = \boxed{} + (8 + 9)$$

A 9   **C** 3

B 7   **D** 0

7 Melissa bought a jacket for **$64.79** and a pair of shoes for **$32.54**. How much more money did she spend on the jacket than on the shoes?

F $31.25   **H** $32.54

G $32.25   **J** $33.54

Cashiers use a cash register to find the total cost of your purchases. The cash register then subtracts the total from the amount of money that you give the cashier.
The cashier "counts out" the change to you.
Here is a way to check the amount of change you receive.

Thomas bought a yo-yo for **$1.39**.
He gave the clerk a **5-dollar bill**.
Thomas' change was **$3.61**.

The clerk gave Thomas his change by counting this way:

Draw your change. Use the fewest coins and bills.

	You have	You spend	
1.	$10.00	$6.25	
2.	$6.00	$5.19	
3.	$20.00	$4.39	
4.	$1.00	$.43	

Except for a dollar sign and a decimal point, adding and subtracting money is like adding and subtracting whole numbers.

Add: **$1.25 + $3.80**

Line up the decimal points. Then add as you would with whole numbers.

$$\begin{array}{r} \overset{1}{\$1.25} \\ + \ \$3.80 \\ \hline \$5.05 \end{array}$$

Subtract: **$2.94 − $1.78**

Line up the decimal points. Then subtract as you would with whole numbers.

$$\begin{array}{r} \$2.\overset{8\ 14}{\cancel{9}\cancel{4}} \\ - \ \$1.78 \\ \hline \$1.16 \end{array}$$

Remember to use a decimal point and a dollar sign when you write your sum or difference.

Add or subtract.

5.
$$\begin{array}{r} \$2.00 \\ + \ \$7.00 \end{array} \qquad \begin{array}{r} \$6.50 \\ - \ \$1.50 \end{array} \qquad \begin{array}{r} \$3.10 \\ - \ \$2.00 \end{array} \qquad \begin{array}{r} \$8.45 \\ - \ \$6.10 \end{array} \qquad \begin{array}{r} \$4.45 \\ - \ \$1.25 \end{array}$$

6.
$$\begin{array}{r} \$8.00 \\ - \ \$5.00 \end{array} \qquad \begin{array}{r} \$9.30 \\ + \ \$\ .20 \end{array} \qquad \begin{array}{r} \$7.12 \\ + \ \$3.55 \end{array} \qquad \begin{array}{r} \$4.10 \\ - \ \$\ .05 \end{array} \qquad \begin{array}{r} \$1.19 \\ + \ \$2.49 \end{array}$$

 Quick Check

Write the amount of money.

7. 4 dollar bills, 1 quarter, 2 dimes, 1 nickel, 3 pennies _____

8. 1 ten dollar bill, 1 five dollar bill, 2 quarters, 3 pennies _____

Work Space.

Compare. Write > or <.

9. 3 quarters ◯ 7 nickels

10. 2 quarters ◯ 6 dimes

Write the amount you would receive in change.

11. Cost: $2.28
Cash given: $5.00
_____

12. Cost: $6.65
Cash given: $10.00
_____

13. Cost: $13.47
Cash given: $20.00
_____

14. Cost: $19.25
Cash given: $20.00
_____

Problem Solving Application: Multiple-Step Problems

Sometimes you need to use both addition and subtraction in order to solve a problem.

Try to break these problems into smaller parts. Deciding when to add and when to subtract can help you break the problem into smaller parts.

Then find the sum or difference in each part. Use these answers to solve the whole problem.

> **Tips to Remember:**
>
> | 1. Understand | 2. Decide | 3. Solve | 4. Look back |
> |---|---|---|---|
>
> • Think about what the problem is asking you to do. What information does the problem give you? What do you need to find out?
> • Try to break the problem into parts.
> • Do you need both addition and subtraction to show what is happening? Which should you use first?

Solve.

1. Aurelia bought a burger for **$2.98**, fries for **$1.75**, a carton of juice for **$1.45**, and a cookie. She gave the cashier the exact amount, **$6.93**. How much did the cookie cost?

Think: What would you need to do first? Second?

_____

_____

Answer _____

2. Travis bought a hot dog for **$1.98**, fries for **$1.75**, and milk for **$1.50**. He gave the cashier **4** dollar bills, **3** quarters, and **5** dimes. How much change should he get?

Think: What two amounts do you need to know first?

_____

_____

Answer _____

3. Paula spent **$6.31** for a book and candy including tax. The book cost **$5.50**. The candy cost **$.45**. How much was the tax?

_____

4. Perry must read **128** pages in **3** days. The first day he read **63** pages. The second day he read **48** pages. How many pages must he read the third day?

_____

Solve.

5. Mrs. Ortiz bought two shirts at **$10.99** each and a sweater for **$15.98**. Was the total more or less than **$40**? How much more or less?

_____

6. Lauren bought a pencil for **$.25**, a pen for **$.79**, and a notebook for **$1.79**. How much change did she get back from **$3.00**?

_____

7. The school library has **178** history books. The librarian buys **99** more history books. If she would like to have a total of **400** history books, how many more books should she get?

_____

8. An adult's ticket to Aqualand costs **$10.50** and a child's ticket costs **$8.75**. Tom's mother has discount coupons that will allow her to save **$3.50** on each ticket. What is the total amount she will have to pay for **1** adult's ticket and **1** child's ticket?

_____

9. Two boys want to buy a plant for their mother. One boy has **2** quarters and **1** dime. The other boy has **3** quarters, **4** dimes, and **3** nickels. The plant costs **$3.59**. How much more money do they need?

_____

10. There were **29** people on a bus. At the first stop, **6** people got on and **4** got off. At the second stop, **7** people got on and **4** people got off. How many people were on the bus when the driver arrived at the third stop?

_____

11. What two numbers have a sum of **77** and a difference of **29**?

_____

12. If you count by 2's, what is the fiftieth number you will say?

_____

Extend Your Thinking

13. Explain how you solved problem **7**. Describe each step and the order in which you did the steps.

_____

_____

_____

14. Describe a different method you could have used to solve problem **7**.

_____

_____

_____

_____

Complete.

1. $2 + 9 = 9 +$ _____   **2.** $7 + 6 =$ _____ $+ 7$ **3.** _____ $+ 4 = 4 + 8$

4. $0 + 12 =$ _____   **5.** $9 + 0 =$ _____   **6.** $0 + 0 =$ _____

7. $(5 + 3) + 7 =$ _____ $+$ _____ $=$ _____

8. $5 + (3 + 7) =$ _____ $+$ _____ $=$ _____

Find each sum or difference. Write the number sentence that shows the inverse operation.

9. $7 + 3 =$ _____

_____

10. $12 - 3 =$ _____

_____

11. $15 - 9 =$ _____

_____

Estimate each sum or difference by rounding to the greatest place value.

12. $37 \rightarrow$ _____
      $+ 19 \rightarrow +$ _____

      _____

13. $723 \rightarrow$ _____
       $- 199 \rightarrow -$ _____

       _____

14. $6,555 \rightarrow$ _____
       $+ 8,299 \rightarrow +$ _____

       _____

Add or subtract.

15. 572
       $+ 635$

16. $\$36.04$
        $- \$4.75$

17. $34,570$
        $+ 5,299$

18. $29,400$
        $- 7,566$

Write each amount. Then draw your change. Use the fewest coins and bills.

19. You have   You spend   Your change

_____   _____   _____

Solve.

20. Michelle bought a book for **$4.50** and a magazine for **$1.95**. Write a number sentence that shows how much she spent.

_____

21. Roger wants to buy a hat for **$8.99** and a shirt for **$9.99**. How much change will he get back if he pays with a **$20** bill?

Name _____

1 The population of San Diego is shown in the box.

Population of San Diego	1,148,851

What words mean 1,148,851?

A one hundred forty-eight thousand, eight hundred fifty-one

B one million, forty-eight thousand, eight hundred fifty-one

C one million, one hundred forty-eight thousand, eight hundred fifty-one

D one hundred forty-eight million, eight hundred fifty-one thousand

2 Look at the box in question 1. What is the population of San Diego rounded to the nearest hundred thousand?

F 1,000,000   H 1,150,000   K NH

G 1,100,000   J 1,200,000

3 On Saturday, three groups toured the exhibits at the zoo. The table shows the number of people in each group.

Zoo Tours on Saturday	
Morning	62
Afternoon	127
Evening	68

How many people were in these groups in all?

A 121   C 227   E NH

B 211   D 257

4 Ms. Richards drove from McFarland to Cambria and then to San Jose along the road shown.

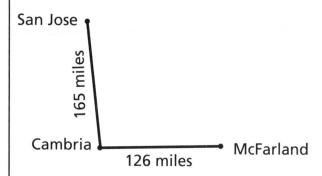

About how many miles did he drive?

F 200   H 400

G 300   J 600

5 The table below shows four items and their prices at a local store.

Item	Price
ice cream	$3.29
dog food	$9.67
flowers	$6.97
cereal	$2.75

Which shows the items in order of price from *least* to *greatest*?

A ice cream, cereal, flowers, dog food

B cereal, dog food, ice cream, flowers

C dog food, flowers, ice cream, cereal

D cereal, ice cream, flowers, dog food

UNIT 3 • TABLE OF CONTENTS

Multiplication of Whole Numbers

Dear Family,

During the next few weeks, our math class will be learning and practicing multiplication of whole numbers.

You can expect to see homework that provides practice with multiplying 4-digit numbers by 1-digit numbers. Here is a sample you may want to keep handy to give help if needed.

Multiplying 4-Digit Numbers by 1-Digit Numbers

To multiply **2,734** by **3**, first write the numbers in vertical form. Then multiply the digits in each place.

1. Multiply ones. Regroup to tens.	2. Multiply tens. Add the regrouped tens. Regroup to hundreds.	3. Multiply hundreds. Add the regrouped hundreds. Regroup to thousands.	4. Multiply thousands. Add the regrouped thousands.
$\begin{array}{r} 1 \\ 2{,}734 \\ \times\ \ 3 \\ \hline 2 \end{array}$	$\begin{array}{r} 1\ 1 \\ 2{,}734 \\ \times\ \ 3 \\ \hline 02 \end{array}$	$\begin{array}{r} 2\ 1\ 1 \\ 2{,}734 \\ \times\ \ 3 \\ \hline 202 \end{array}$	$\begin{array}{r} 2\ 1\ 1 \\ 2{,}734 \\ \times\ \ 3 \\ \hline 8{,}202 \end{array}$

Here is a short way to record multiplication.

$$\begin{array}{r} 2\ 2 \\ 8{,}165 \\ \times\ \ 4 \\ \hline 32{,}660 \end{array}$$

During this unit, students will need to continue practicing multiplication and addition facts.

Sincerely,

Multiplication has special properties or rules. Use these properties to find products.

- **Commutative Property of Multiplication**

  Changing the order of the factors does not change the product.

  $a \times b = b \times a$ $2 \times 3 = 3 \times 2$

  $$\begin{array}{r} 3 \\ \times\,2 \\ \hline 6 \end{array}$$

  $$\begin{array}{rl} 2 & \rightarrow \text{factor} \\ \times\,3 & \rightarrow \text{factor} \\ \hline 6 & \rightarrow \text{product} \end{array}$$

- **Property of Zero for Multiplication**

  The product of any number and zero is zero.

  $n \times 0 = 0$ $3 \times 0 = 0$ $0 \times 4 = 0$

- **Property of One for Multiplication**

  The product of any number and one is that number.

  $n \times 1 = n$ $5 \times 1 = 5$ $1 \times 3 = 3$

- **Associative Property of Multiplication**

  Changing the grouping of the factors does not change the product.

  $a \times (b \times c) = (a \times b) \times c$

  $3 \times (2 \times 4) = 24$ $(3 \times 2) \times 4 = 24$

Multiply. Use the Property of Zero or the Property of One when possible.

1.
$$\begin{array}{r} 6 \\ \times\,0 \\ \hline \end{array} \qquad \begin{array}{r} 5 \\ \times\,1 \\ \hline \end{array} \qquad \begin{array}{r} 2 \\ \times\,5 \\ \hline \end{array} \qquad \begin{array}{r} 5 \\ \times\,2 \\ \hline \end{array} \qquad \begin{array}{r} 0 \\ \times\,5 \\ \hline \end{array} \qquad \begin{array}{r} 1 \\ \times\,8 \\ \hline \end{array} \qquad \begin{array}{r} 8 \\ \times\,0 \\ \hline \end{array} \qquad \begin{array}{r} 1 \\ \times\,3 \\ \hline \end{array}$$

2.
$$\begin{array}{r} 2 \\ \times\,1 \\ \hline \end{array} \qquad \begin{array}{r} 0 \\ \times\,6 \\ \hline \end{array} \qquad \begin{array}{r} 7 \\ \times\,5 \\ \hline \end{array} \qquad \begin{array}{r} 9 \\ \times\,1 \\ \hline \end{array} \qquad \begin{array}{r} 5 \\ \times\,7 \\ \hline \end{array} \qquad \begin{array}{r} 4 \\ \times\,5 \\ \hline \end{array} \qquad \begin{array}{r} 3 \\ \times\,0 \\ \hline \end{array} \qquad \begin{array}{r} 5 \\ \times\,4 \\ \hline \end{array}$$

3.
$$\begin{array}{r} 0 \\ \times\,7 \\ \hline \end{array} \qquad \begin{array}{r} 3 \\ \times\,9 \\ \hline \end{array} \qquad \begin{array}{r} 8 \\ \times\,1 \\ \hline \end{array} \qquad \begin{array}{r} 7 \\ \times\,6 \\ \hline \end{array} \qquad \begin{array}{r} 6 \\ \times\,7 \\ \hline \end{array} \qquad \begin{array}{r} 9 \\ \times\,0 \\ \hline \end{array} \qquad \begin{array}{r} 7 \\ \times\,1 \\ \hline \end{array} \qquad \begin{array}{r} 1 \\ \times\,7 \\ \hline \end{array}$$

Multiply. Use the Associative Property.

4. $2 \times (3 \times 2) = 12$ $5 \times (1 \times 3) = 15$ $(2 \times 4) \times 5 = 40$

$(2 \times \underline{\hspace{1cm}}) \times 2 = 12$ $(5 \times \underline{\hspace{1cm}}) \times 3 = 15$ $2 \times (\underline{\hspace{1cm}} \times 5) = 40$

5. $(2 \times 4) \times 9 = \underline{\hspace{1cm}}$ $3 \times (\underline{\hspace{1cm}} \times 5) = 30$ $(4 \times \underline{\hspace{1cm}}) \times 7 = 56$

$2 \times (4 \times \underline{\hspace{1cm}}) = 72$ $(\underline{\hspace{1cm}} \times 2) \times 5 = 30$ $4 \times (2 \times \underline{\hspace{1cm}}) = 56$

Multiply. Use the properties of multiplication.

6. $3 \times 7 = \underline{\hspace{1cm}}$ $6 \times 2 = \underline{\hspace{1cm}}$ $9 \times 8 = \underline{\hspace{1cm}}$ $6 \times 7 = \underline{\hspace{1cm}}$

$7 \times 3 = \underline{\hspace{1cm}}$ $2 \times 6 = \underline{\hspace{1cm}}$ $8 \times 9 = \underline{\hspace{1cm}}$ $7 \times 6 = \underline{\hspace{1cm}}$

7.
4	9	8	5	3	6	3	0
$\times 9$	$\times 4$	$\times 5$	$\times 8$	$\times 6$	$\times 3$	$\times 0$	$\times 3$

8.
7	0	9	6	7	4	7	5
$\times 7$	$\times 4$	$\times 9$	$\times 1$	$\times 0$	$\times 5$	$\times 2$	$\times 5$

9.
9	8	4	8	5	7	9	6
$\times 3$	$\times 8$	$\times 8$	$\times 4$	$\times 5$	$\times 4$	$\times 6$	$\times 6$

10.
7	8	2	5	9	1	4	6
$\times 9$	$\times 7$	$\times 5$	$\times 2$	$\times 7$	$\times 1$	$\times 0$	$\times 8$

Problem Solving Reasoning

Use properties to find the value of *n*.

11. $2 \times 12 = n \times 2$ $n = \underline{\hspace{1cm}}$ $(2 \times 3) \times 6 = 2 \times (n \times 6)$ $n = \underline{\hspace{1cm}}$

12. $5 \times 9 = 9 \times n$ $n = \underline{\hspace{1cm}}$ $6 \times (1 \times 5) = (6 \times n) \times 5$ $n = \underline{\hspace{1cm}}$

Test Prep ★ Mixed Review

13 What number should go in the ☐ to make the number sentence true?

$(5 + 6) + \boxed{} = 5 + 6$

A 0

B 1

C 4

D 7

14 What number shows seventy-three thousand, sixty four in standard form?

F 703,640

G 73,640

H 73,604

J 73,064

Multiplying with Regrouping

To find the total number of blocks you can multiply.

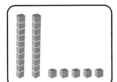 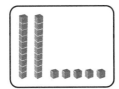 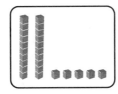

$$\begin{array}{r} 25 \\ \times\ 3 \\ \hline ? \end{array}$$

← blocks in each group
← number of groups
← total number of blocks

1. Multiply the ones.

2. Regroup ones as tens and ones. Write the ones digit.

3. Multiply the tens. Then add the regrouped tens. Write the tens digit.

3×5 ones = **15** ones

15 ones = **1** ten and **5** ones

$3 \times 2 = 6$ tens

6 tens + **1** ten = **7** tens

$$\begin{array}{r} 25 \\ \times\ 3 \\ \hline \end{array}$$

$$\begin{array}{r} {}^{1}\ \\ 25 \\ \times\ 3 \\ \hline 5 \end{array}$$

$$\begin{array}{r} {}^{1}\ \\ 25 \\ \times\ 3 \\ \hline 75 \end{array}$$

Multiply.

1.
$$\begin{array}{r}11\\ \times\ 5\\ \hline\end{array}\qquad \begin{array}{r}21\\ \times\ 3\\ \hline\end{array}\qquad \begin{array}{r}33\\ \times\ 2\\ \hline\end{array}\qquad \begin{array}{r}42\\ \times\ 2\\ \hline\end{array}\qquad \begin{array}{r}32\\ \times\ 3\\ \hline\end{array}\qquad \begin{array}{r}22\\ \times\ 4\\ \hline\end{array}\qquad \begin{array}{r}11\\ \times\ 7\\ \hline\end{array}$$

2.
$$\begin{array}{r}20\\ \times\ 6\\ \hline\end{array}\qquad \begin{array}{r}54\\ \times\ 2\\ \hline\end{array}\qquad \begin{array}{r}74\\ \times\ 2\\ \hline\end{array}\qquad \begin{array}{r}41\\ \times\ 4\\ \hline\end{array}\qquad \begin{array}{r}81\\ \times\ 3\\ \hline\end{array}\qquad \begin{array}{r}63\\ \times\ 3\\ \hline\end{array}\qquad \begin{array}{r}73\\ \times\ 2\\ \hline\end{array}$$

3.
$$\begin{array}{r}16\\ \times\ 5\\ \hline\end{array}\qquad \begin{array}{r}13\\ \times\ 7\\ \hline\end{array}\qquad \begin{array}{r}26\\ \times\ 3\\ \hline\end{array}\qquad \begin{array}{r}12\\ \times\ 6\\ \hline\end{array}\qquad \begin{array}{r}17\\ \times\ 2\\ \hline\end{array}\qquad \begin{array}{r}15\\ \times\ 6\\ \hline\end{array}\qquad \begin{array}{r}36\\ \times\ 2\\ \hline\end{array}$$

4.
$$\begin{array}{r}16\\ \times\ 4\\ \hline\end{array}\qquad \begin{array}{r}18\\ \times\ 3\\ \hline\end{array}\qquad \begin{array}{r}26\\ \times\ 2\\ \hline\end{array}\qquad \begin{array}{r}16\\ \times\ 3\\ \hline\end{array}\qquad \begin{array}{r}19\\ \times\ 2\\ \hline\end{array}\qquad \begin{array}{r}27\\ \times\ 3\\ \hline\end{array}\qquad \begin{array}{r}12\\ \times\ 7\\ \hline\end{array}$$

5.
$$\begin{array}{r}14\\ \times\ 6\\ \hline\end{array}\qquad \begin{array}{r}19\\ \times\ 3\\ \hline\end{array}\qquad \begin{array}{r}16\\ \times\ 2\\ \hline\end{array}\qquad \begin{array}{r}37\\ \times\ 2\\ \hline\end{array}\qquad \begin{array}{r}13\\ \times\ 4\\ \hline\end{array}\qquad \begin{array}{r}47\\ \times\ 2\\ \hline\end{array}\qquad \begin{array}{r}14\\ \times\ 3\\ \hline\end{array}$$

6.
$$\begin{array}{r}15\\ \times\ 4\\ \hline\end{array}\qquad \begin{array}{r}17\\ \times\ 4\\ \hline\end{array}\qquad \begin{array}{r}46\\ \times\ 2\\ \hline\end{array}\qquad \begin{array}{r}15\\ \times\ 3\\ \hline\end{array}\qquad \begin{array}{r}25\\ \times\ 3\\ \hline\end{array}\qquad \begin{array}{r}18\\ \times\ 5\\ \hline\end{array}\qquad \begin{array}{r}24\\ \times\ 4\\ \hline\end{array}$$

Multiply with **3**-digit numbers as you would with **2**-digit numbers.

1. Multiply the ones. Write the ones digit.

561
× 8
──
8

| 8 × 1 one = 8 |

2. Multiply the tens. Regroup **48** tens as **4** hundred **8** tens. Write the tens digit.

⁴
561
× 8
──
88

| 8 × 6 tens = 48 tens |

3. Multiply the hundreds. Then add the regrouped hundreds.

⁴
561
× 8
──
4,488

| 8 × 5 hundreds = 40 hundreds |

Multiply.

7.

124	247	132	113	151	121
× 3	× 2	× 4	× 5	× 6	× 8

8.

112	109	123	112	201	102
× 7	× 6	× 4	× 8	× 9	× 7

Problem Solving Reasoning Solve. Check that your answer is reasonable.

9. Jason can swim **350** feet per minute. If he keeps up that pace, how many feet will he swim in **5** minutes?

_____

10. Ruby works **8** hours a week at a part time job. How many hours will she work in a year? (Hint: There are **52** weeks in a year.)

_____

Test Prep ★ Mixed Review

11 What number should go in the ☐ to make the number sentence true?

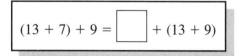

$(13 + 7) + 9 = \boxed{} + (13 + 9)$

A 7   **C** 13

B 9   **D** 22

12 What number shows three hundred two thousand, four hundred eighty in standard form?

F 302,408   **H** 320,480

G 302,480   **J** 324,080

Multiplying with Regrouping Twice

Sometimes when you multiply **3**-digit numbers,
you need to regroup twice.

Find: 5 × 156

1. Multiply ones. Regroup
30 ones as **3** tens.
Write the ones digit.

$$\begin{array}{r} \overset{3}{156} \\ \times\ \ 5 \\ \hline 0 \end{array}$$

5 × 6 tens = 30

2. Multiply tens. Add the
regrouped tens.
Regroup **28** tens as
2 hundreds **8** tens.

$$\begin{array}{r} \overset{23}{156} \\ \times\ \ 5 \\ \hline 80 \end{array}$$

5 × 5 tens = 25 tens

3. Multiply hundreds.
Add the regrouped
hundreds.

$$\begin{array}{r} \overset{23}{156} \\ \times\ \ 5 \\ \hline 780 \end{array}$$

5 × 1 hundred
= 5 hundreds

Multiply.

1.
$$\begin{array}{r} 145 \\ \times\ 4 \\ \hline \end{array} \qquad \begin{array}{r} 298 \\ \times\ 3 \\ \hline \end{array} \qquad \begin{array}{r} 378 \\ \times\ 4 \\ \hline \end{array} \qquad \begin{array}{r} 609 \\ \times\ 2 \\ \hline \end{array} \qquad \begin{array}{r} 453 \\ \times\ 5 \\ \hline \end{array} \qquad \begin{array}{r} 666 \\ \times\ 7 \\ \hline \end{array}$$

2.
$$\begin{array}{r} 893 \\ \times\ 3 \\ \hline \end{array} \qquad \begin{array}{r} 604 \\ \times\ 3 \\ \hline \end{array} \qquad \begin{array}{r} 708 \\ \times\ 5 \\ \hline \end{array} \qquad \begin{array}{r} 800 \\ \times\ 4 \\ \hline \end{array} \qquad \begin{array}{r} 403 \\ \times\ 6 \\ \hline \end{array} \qquad \begin{array}{r} 508 \\ \times\ 7 \\ \hline \end{array}$$

3.
$$\begin{array}{r} \$165 \\ \times\ 5 \\ \hline \end{array} \qquad \begin{array}{r} \$198 \\ \times\ 4 \\ \hline \end{array} \qquad \begin{array}{r} \$237 \\ \times\ 3 \\ \hline \end{array} \qquad \begin{array}{r} \$358 \\ \times\ 2 \\ \hline \end{array} \qquad \begin{array}{r} \$621 \\ \times\ 6 \\ \hline \end{array} \qquad \begin{array}{r} \$892 \\ \times\ 7 \\ \hline \end{array}$$

4.
$$\begin{array}{r} 490 \\ \times\ 2 \\ \hline \end{array} \qquad \begin{array}{r} 103 \\ \times\ 6 \\ \hline \end{array} \qquad \begin{array}{r} 130 \\ \times\ 5 \\ \hline \end{array} \qquad \begin{array}{r} 280 \\ \times\ 3 \\ \hline \end{array} \qquad \begin{array}{r} 303 \\ \times\ 9 \\ \hline \end{array} \qquad \begin{array}{r} 101 \\ \times\ 9 \\ \hline \end{array}$$

5.
$$\begin{array}{r} 485 \\ \times\ 6 \\ \hline \end{array} \qquad \begin{array}{r} 537 \\ \times\ 2 \\ \hline \end{array} \qquad \begin{array}{r} 479 \\ \times\ 4 \\ \hline \end{array} \qquad \begin{array}{r} 243 \\ \times\ 5 \\ \hline \end{array} \qquad \begin{array}{r} 570 \\ \times\ 7 \\ \hline \end{array} \qquad \begin{array}{r} 385 \\ \times\ 8 \\ \hline \end{array}$$

6.
$$\begin{array}{r} 604 \\ \times\ 7 \\ \hline \end{array} \qquad \begin{array}{r} 369 \\ \times\ 4 \\ \hline \end{array} \qquad \begin{array}{r} 984 \\ \times\ 6 \\ \hline \end{array} \qquad \begin{array}{r} 706 \\ \times\ 9 \\ \hline \end{array} \qquad \begin{array}{r} 736 \\ \times\ 5 \\ \hline \end{array} \qquad \begin{array}{r} 387 \\ \times\ 6 \\ \hline \end{array}$$

7.
$$\begin{array}{r} 399 \\ \times\ 3 \\ \hline \end{array} \qquad \begin{array}{r} 657 \\ \times\ 4 \\ \hline \end{array} \qquad \begin{array}{r} 478 \\ \times\ 2 \\ \hline \end{array} \qquad \begin{array}{r} 963 \\ \times\ 4 \\ \hline \end{array} \qquad \begin{array}{r} 783 \\ \times\ 5 \\ \hline \end{array} \qquad \begin{array}{r} 418 \\ \times\ 6 \\ \hline \end{array}$$

Multiply.

8.
999	894	971	406	670	550
× 2	× 4	× 4	× 5	× 3	× 6

9.
745	968	914	870	695	783
× 3	× 4	× 4	× 5	× 4	× 9

Problem Solving Reasoning   Solve.

10. The student price for a ticket to the museum is **$4**. How much will it cost for **234** students to go to the museum?

_____

11. By noon, **598** spaces in a parking lot were filled. By **5** P.M., **3** times as many spaces were filled. How many spaces were filled by **5** P.M.?

_____

12. There are **137** strawberry plants in one row of a farm. If there are **8** rows, how many plants are there in all?

_____

13. Jason sold **175** raffle tickets. Mary Beth sold twice as many. How many tickets did they sell together?

_____

✓ Quick Check

Complete to make the sentence true.

14. $7 \times 8 = \boxed{} \times 7$ **15.** $9 = 1 \times (3 \times \boxed{})$

16. $(7 \times 12) \times 3 = \boxed{} \times (12 \times 3)$

Work Space.

Multiply.

17.
223
× 3

18.
103
× 7

19.
218
× 4

20.
256
× 3

21.
304
× 6

22.
516
× 4

Multiplying Money

You multiply with money the same way you multiply whole numbers.

17¢	$.17	83	$.83	156	$1.56
× 2	× 2	× 2	× 2	× 2	× 3
34¢	$.34	166	$1.66	312	$3.12

Always remember to write your answer as cents or dollars and cents.

Write the $ and . in the answer.

1.

$.75	$.89	$.09	$.55	$.36
× 3	× 4	× 8	× 8	× 7
2 2 5	3 5 6	7 2	4 4 0	2 5 2

Multiply. Remember to write the dollar sign and decimal point in the product.

2.

$.24	$.02	$.45	$.09	$.73
× 6	× 5	× 3	× 4	× 8

3.

$.31	$.65	$.08	$.83	$.06
× 2	× 6	× 7	× 5	× 9

4.

$5.67	$8.19	$8.41	$1.29	$6.58
× 2	× 5	× 6	× 3	× 8

5.

$7.01	$8.02	$6.05	$8.19	$1.11
× 3	× 5	× 3	× 4	× 8

6.

$6.32	$2.19	$3.50	$8.22	$1.25
× 2	× 8	× 7	× 6	× 3

7.

$1.89	$6.79	$2.55	$7.23	$1.01
× 3	× 4	× 6	× 9	× 9

Solve. The tax is included in all the prices.

8. Peter bought **2** pairs of gloves that cost **$2.79** each. He also bought a tie for **$5.55**. How much did he spend?

_____

9. James had **$10.75**. He bought **4** pens for **$1.16** each and a notebook for **$5.79**. Did he spend all of his money.

_____

10. Mrs. Lee bought **2** dresses for Doreen. One dress cost **$11.35** and the other dress cost **$8.95**. Did Mrs. Lee spend more than **$20.00**?

_____

11. Melody bought **6** embroidered animal patches for **$3.55** each. How much did she spend?

_____

12. Matthew is buying **4** pairs of socks. Each pair costs **$1.19**. How much change does he receive from **$10.00**?

_____

13. Jenny bought roller blades for **$39.00**. Then she bought safety pads at **2** pieces for **$4.00**. She bought **6** safety pads. How much did she spend?

_____

14. Mr. Jackson is buying **3** plants. Each plant costs **$5.75**. He gives the clerk **$20.25**. How much change will he receive?

_____

15. Keisha wants to buy **8** pens for her family as gifts. Each pen costs **$1.99**. She has **$16.00**. Does she have enough money?

_____

Test Prep ★ Mixed Review

16 What number should go in the ☐ to make the number sentence true?

$$9 \times \boxed{} = 0$$

A 9   **C** 1

B 3   **D** 0

17 Each day a farmer harvested the amount of oranges shown. *About* how many pounds did he harvest in all?

Day	Oranges Harvested
Monday	256 pounds
Tuesday	220 pounds
Wednesday	373 pounds

F 700   **H** 1,000

G 900   **J** 1,100

Multiplying with 4-Digit Numbers

You can use what you know about multiplying with **3**-digit numbers to multiply with **4**-digit numbers.

1. Multiply ones. Regroup to tens.	**2.** Multiply tens. Add regrouped tens. Then regroup to hundreds.	**3.** Multiply hundreds. Add regrouped hundreds. Regroup to thousands.	**4.** Multiply thousands. Add regrouped thousands.
$\overset{4}{7{,}3}18$ $\times\quad 6$ _____ 8	$\overset{1\ 4}{7{,}3}18$ $\times\quad 6$ _____ 08	$\overset{1\ 1\ 4}{7{,}3}18$ $\times\quad 6$ _____ 908	$\overset{1\ 1\ 4}{7{,}3}18$ $\times\quad 6$ _____ 43,908

Multiply.

1.
$$3{,}421 \times 5 \qquad 7{,}614 \times 3 \qquad 2{,}835 \times 6 \qquad 6{,}024 \times 4 \qquad 5{,}106 \times 2$$

2.
$$4{,}425 \times 5 \qquad 3{,}781 \times 3 \qquad 9{,}065 \times 2 \qquad 4{,}235 \times 5 \qquad 9{,}142 \times 4$$

3.
$$4{,}126 \times 6 \qquad 4{,}562 \times 7 \qquad 8{,}395 \times 2 \qquad 9{,}517 \times 8 \qquad 3{,}084 \times 3$$

4.
$$\$61.25 \times 4 \qquad \$45.37 \times 7 \qquad \$37.86 \times 6 \qquad \$16.04 \times 5 \qquad \$80.31 \times 8$$

5.
$$\$71.36 \times 7 \qquad \$53.47 \times 3 \qquad \$90.06 \times 8 \qquad \$67.16 \times 4 \qquad \$13.95 \times 9$$

6.
$$\$21.15 \times 3 \qquad \$44.18 \times 5 \qquad \$82.13 \times 9 \qquad \$75.16 \times 8 \qquad \$13.25 \times 4$$

7.
$$5{,}623 \times 7 \qquad 3{,}412 \times 9 \qquad 6{,}222 \times 8 \qquad 1{,}919 \times 5 \qquad 2{,}617 \times 8$$

When you multiply with zero, you may need to write zeros in the product.

1. Multiply ones. Regroup to tens.

$$\begin{array}{r} \overset{4}{7{,}009} \\ \times\quad 5 \\ \hline 5 \end{array}$$

| 5 × 9 ones = 45 ones |

2. Multiply tens. Add regrouped tens.

$$\begin{array}{r} \overset{4}{7{,}009} \\ \times\quad 5 \\ \hline 45 \end{array}$$

| 5 × 0 tens = 0 tens |
| 0 tens + 4 tens = 4 tens |

3. Multiply hundreds. There are no regrouped tens. Write 0 in the hundreds place.

$$\begin{array}{r} \overset{4}{7{,}009} \\ \times\quad 5 \\ \hline 045 \end{array}$$

| 5 × 0 hundreds = 0 hundreds |

4. Multiply thousands.

$$\begin{array}{r} \overset{4}{7{,}009} \\ \times\quad 5 \\ \hline 35{,}045 \end{array}$$

| 5 × 7 thousands = 35 thousands |

Multiply.

8.

$$\begin{array}{r} 602 \\ \times\ 3 \\ \hline \end{array} \qquad \begin{array}{r} 801 \\ \times\ 6 \\ \hline \end{array} \qquad \begin{array}{r} 603 \\ \times\ 2 \\ \hline \end{array} \qquad \begin{array}{r} 510 \\ \times\ 4 \\ \hline \end{array} \qquad \begin{array}{r} 304 \\ \times\ 2 \\ \hline \end{array}$$

9.

$$\begin{array}{r} 5{,}113 \\ \times\ 3 \\ \hline \end{array} \qquad \begin{array}{r} 8{,}014 \\ \times\ 2 \\ \hline \end{array} \qquad \begin{array}{r} 9{,}001 \\ \times\ 6 \\ \hline \end{array} \qquad \begin{array}{r} 8{,}100 \\ \times\ 7 \\ \hline \end{array} \qquad \begin{array}{r} 8{,}011 \\ \times\ 6 \\ \hline \end{array}$$

10. $511 \times 9 =$ _____ $901 \times 8 =$ _____ $610 \times 7 =$ _____

11. $6{,}102 \times 4 =$ _____ $5{,}001 \times 9 =$ _____ $9{,}111 \times 6 =$ _____

Problem Solving Reasoning Solve.

12. There are **1,250** pushpins in each box. How many pushpins are in **5** boxes?

_____

13. There are **3,435** visitors to a web site every day. How many visitors are there each week?

_____

Test Prep ★ Mixed Review

14 What words mean 520,335?

A five hundred thousand, two hundred thirty-five

B five hundred two thousand, three hundred thirty-five

C five hundred twenty thousand, three hundred thirty-five

D five hundred thirty thousand, two hundred thirty-five

15 What number is equal to $6{,}000 + 400 + 70$?

F 647

G 6,407

H 6,470

J 6,740

To solve a problem, you may need to begin with a **conjecture** about the answer.

When you make a conjecture, you make a "first guess" about the answer. Then you **verify** or check to see if it is correct.

Problem

The school store sells erasers and pencils. Zoe bought one of each. The total cost was **$.36**. The pencil cost twice as much as the eraser. What was the cost of each?

---

1 Understand As you reread, ask yourself questions.

- What do you know about the cost of the items?

  The total cost is **$.36**. The cost of the pencil is **2** times the cost of the eraser.

- What do you need to find out?

  _____

---

2 Decide Choose a method for solving.

Try the strategy Conjecture and Verify.

- What will your first guess be?

  Eraser: **$.10**   Pencil: **$.20**

- Is the cost of the pencil twice as much as the

  cost of the eraser? _____

---

3 Solve Verify your conjecture. Try again if you need to.

First guess	Try Again	Try Again
Eraser: **$.10**	_____	_____
Pencil: **$.20**	_____	_____
Total: **$.30**	_____	_____

---

4 Look back Check your answer. Write the answer below.

Answer _____

- How did your first guess help you try again?

  _____

Solve. Use the Conjecture and Verify strategy or any other strategy you have learned.

PEANUT BUTTER

$1.99

WHOLE WHEAT BREAD
$2.39

COTTAGE CHEESE
$1.79

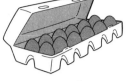
EGGS $1.49

YOGURT LEMON
$.99

APPLE PIE
$3.59

1. Lorinda bought **2** items. She spent **$4.18**. Which items did she buy?

Think: Can one apple pie be paired with any item to equal **$4.18**?

_____

Answer _____

2. Carley bought **2** items. She spent **$5.98**. Which items did she buy?

Think: Do you need to find an exact answer or estimate to answer the question?

_____

Answer _____

3. Jake bought **3** items. He spent **$4.77**. Which items did he buy?

_____

_____

4. Christopher bought **3** items. He spent **$7.97**. Which items did he buy?

_____

_____

5. As part of their grand opening, a new store is giving out prizes. The prizes will be given out according to a pattern. The store gives the **9th, 18th, 27th,** and **36th** customers each a prize. Which customer will get the next prize?

_____

6. Yosemite National Park in California covers **761,236** acres. Crater Lake National Park in Oregon covers **183,224** acres. How much larger is Yosemite National Park than Crater Lake National Park?

_____

7. Benjamin says "I am thinking of a number. If you triple my number and add **18**, you get **438**." What number is Benjamin thinking of?

_____

8. Samina has some dimes and quarters in her pocket. She has **7** coins in all and the total amount is **$1.15**. How many quarters does she have? How many dimes does she have?

_____

When you multiply a number by **10** or by **100**, the number of
zeros in both the factors is equal to the number of zeros in
the product.

25	35
× **10** ← one zero	× **100** ← two zeros
250 ← one zero	3,500 ← two zeros

When a multiple of **10** is multiplied by **10** or **100**, the number
of zeros in the product is equal to the total number of zeros
in the factors.

40 ← one zero	60 ← one zero
× **10** ← one zero	× **100** ← two zeros
400 ← two zeros	6,000 ← three zeros

Write the number of zeros in each product.

1. 12 × 10 _____   40 × 10 _____   10 × 100 _____

2. 650 × 10 _____   85 × 10 _____   720 × 100 _____

3. 80 × 10 _____   20 × 100 _____   24 × 10 _____

4. 99 × 10 _____   140 × 10 _____   50 × 10 _____

5. 30 × 100 _____   270 × 100 _____   810 × 10 _____

Multiply.

6.	462	691	57	83	739
	× **10**	× **10**	× **10**	× **10**	× **10**

7.	94	804	530	60	400
	× **100**	× **100**	× **100**	× **100**	× **100**

8. 10 × 72 = _____   100 × 72 = _____

9. 10 × 84 = _____   100 × 84 = _____

10. 10 × 59 = _____   100 × 59 = _____

11. 10 × 65 = _____   100 × 65 = _____

Multiply.

12. $10 \times 319 =$ _____ $100 \times 319 =$ _____

13. $10 \times 783 =$ _____ $100 \times 783 =$ _____

14. $10 \times 561 =$ _____ $100 \times 561 =$ _____

| Problem Solving |
| Reasoning |

Solve.

15. There are **12** months in a year. How many months are there in **10** years? In **100** years?

_____

16. Suppose your heart beats **72** times in **1** minute. How many times will it beat in **10** minutes? In **100** minutes?

_____

_____

17. Elliott weighed **80** pounds last year. He gained **10** pounds. How much does he weigh now?

_____

18. Gerry walks to and from school **23** times a month. How many times does she walk to and from school in **10** months?

_____

_____

✔ Quick Check

Multiply.

19. $.34
         $\times$ 2

20. $1.43
         $\times$ 3

21. $3.61
         $\times$ 5

22.   2,313
         $\times$ 3

23.   4,142
         $\times$ 4

24.   3,305
         $\times$ 5

25.   29
         $\times$ 10

26.   33
         $\times$ 100

27.   210
         $\times$ 100

Work Space.

Name _____

Estimating Products

STANDARD

You can estimate products. Round the factors.
Then multiply.

$$\begin{array}{r}62\\ \times\,45\end{array}\ \xrightarrow[\text{round up}]{\text{round down}}\ \begin{array}{r}60\\ \times\,50\\ \hline 3{,}000\end{array}$$

$$\begin{array}{r}97\\ \times\,76\end{array}\ \xrightarrow[\text{round up}]{\text{round up}}\ \begin{array}{r}100\\ \times\,80\\ \hline 8{,}000\end{array}$$

Rounding to the Nearest Ten

- If the ones digit is **5** or greater, round up to the next higher multiple of **10**.

- If the ones digit is less than **5**, round down to the next lower multiple of **10**.

Round to the nearest ten.

1. 62 → ____   **2.** 39 → ____   **3.** 45 → ____   **4.** 75 → ____

58 → ____   21 → ____   83 → ____   99 → ____

Round each of the factors to the nearest ten. Find the estimated product by multiplying the rounded factors.

5. 32 → 30   48 → ____   26 → ____
× 44 → × 40   × 89 → × ____   × 72 → × ____

6. 75 → ____   56 → ____   35 → ____
× 38 → × ____   × 63 → × ____   × 65 → × ____

7. 17 → ____   46 → ____   30 → ____
× 80 → × ____   × 83 → × ____   × 92 → × ____

8. 36 → ____   67 → ____   81 → ____
× 24 → × ____   × 31 → × ____   × 55 → × ____

9. 45 → ____   33 → ____   46 → ____
× 65 → × ____   × 75 → × ____   × 42 → × ____

Copyright © Houghton Mifflin Company. All rights reserved.

Unit 3 Lesson 8 61

Estimate each product. Round each of the factors to the nearest ten.

10.

63	75	38	44	55	23
× 25	× 35	× 71	× 12	× 55	× 36

11.

13	61	80	15	25	95
× 29	× 36	× 45	× 15	× 30	× 10

12.

18	64	67	78	92	10
× 41	× 81	× 40	× 52	× 56	× 87

Problem Solving
Reasoning

Decide whether you need an exact answer or an estimated answer. Then solve the problem.

13. Mr. Mason bought **30** boxes of pencils for the office. There are **12** pencils in each box. Does he have more than **400** pencils?

_____

14. Emily bought **2** notebooks for school. They each cost **$3.79**. How much change did she receive from a ten-dollar bill?

_____

15. Mrs. Benson bought **36** bags of apples for the school fair. Each bag holds **18** apples. If she sells each apple for **5¢**, about how much money could she make from the fair?

_____

16. Hassan made **15** quarts of lemonade. Each quart contains **4** cups of lemonade. Will he be able to sell at least **50** cups of lemonade?

_____

Test Prep ★ Mixed Review

17 Which problem has the same product as $13 \times (17 \times 19)$?

A 221×247

B $3 \times 7 \times 9$

C $13 \times (17 \times 19) \times 0$

D $(13 \times 17) \times 19$

18 Marla filled 57 bags with apples. She put 8 apples in each bag. How many apples did she use in all?

F 406

G 456

H 469

J 496

Patterns can help you multiply. Look at the number sentences below. Count the number of zeros in both the factors. Then count the number of zeros in the product. You will see a pattern.

$8 \times 3 = 24$ $80 \times 30 = 2,400$

$8 \times 30 = 240$ $80 \times 300 = 24,000$

$8 \times 300 = 2,400$ $800 \times 30 = 24,000$

$80 \times 3 = 240$ $800 \times 300 = 240,000$

Multiply. Look for a pattern.

1. $6 \times 9 =$ _____   **2.** $7 \times 4 =$ _____

$6 \times 90 =$ _____ $7 \times 40 =$ _____

$6 \times 900 =$ _____ $7 \times 400 =$ _____

$60 \times 9 =$ _____ $70 \times 4 =$ _____

$60 \times 90 =$ _____ $70 \times 40 =$ _____

$60 \times 900 =$ _____ $70 \times 400 =$ _____

$600 \times 900 =$ _____ $700 \times 400 =$ _____

Use a pattern to find the products.

3. $7 \times 4 =$ _____   **4.** $8 \times 5 =$ _____   **5.** $6 \times 7 =$ _____   **6.** $9 \times 6 =$ _____

$70 \times 4 =$ _____ $80 \times 5 =$ _____ $60 \times 7 =$ _____ $90 \times 6 =$ _____

$70 \times 40 =$ _____ $80 \times 50 =$ _____ $60 \times 70 =$ _____ $90 \times 60 =$ _____

7.
60	70	40	80	50	30
$\times\,90$	$\times\,80$	$\times\,50$	$\times\,40$	$\times\,30$	$\times\,80$

8.
20	70	30	90	40	20
$\times\,20$	$\times\,60$	$\times\,90$	$\times\,60$	$\times\,30$	$\times\,80$

9.
30	50	10	30	70	50
$\times\,30$	$\times\,20$	$\times\,70$	$\times\,60$	$\times\,20$	$\times\,50$

10.
40	60	20	80	10	80
$\times\,90$	$\times\,80$	$\times\,50$	$\times\,40$	$\times\,90$	$\times\,90$

You can use the associative property to multiply by multiples of **10**.

$$25 \times 30 = 25 \times (3 \times 10)$$
$$= (25 \times 3) \times 10$$
$$= 75 \times 10$$
$$= 750$$

Associative Property

Changing the grouping of the factors does not change the product.

$$(3 \times 2) \times 4 = 3 \times (2 \times 4)$$

Complete. Use the associative property.

11. $32 \times 40 = 32 \times ($ _____ $\times 10)$

$= ($ _____ $\times 4) \times$ _____

$=$ _____ $\times$ _____

$=$ _____

$47 \times 60 =$ _____ $\times ($ _____ $\times 10)$

$= ($ _____ $\times$ _____ $) \times$ _____

$=$ _____ $\times$ _____

$=$ _____

Multiply. Use the associative property.

12.

67	92	48	37	73
$\times 40$	$\times 70$	$\times 60$	$\times 20$	$\times 50$

13.

28	75	64	91	87
$\times 80$	$\times 30$	$\times 70$	$\times 60$	$\times 40$

✓ Quick Check

Round to the nearest ten. Then estimate.

Work Space.

14. $38 \times 27 = \boxed{}$ **15.** $73 \times 72 = \boxed{}$

16. $14 \times 89 = \boxed{}$ **17.** $47 \times 68 = \boxed{}$

Solve.

18.

53
$\times 20$

19.

32
$\times 30$

20.

35
$\times 80$

You know how to multiply by **1**-digit numbers.
Now you can multiply by **2**-digit numbers.

Find: 36 × 24.

1. Multiply **24** by **6** ones.

$$\begin{array}{r} \overset{2}{24} \\ \times\,36 \\ \hline 6 \times 24 \rightarrow \quad 144 \end{array}$$

2. Multiply **24** by **3** tens.

$$\begin{array}{r} \overset{\overset{1}{2}}{24} \\ \times\,36 \\ \hline 144 \\ 30 \times 24 \rightarrow \quad 720 \end{array}$$

3. Add the products.

$$\begin{array}{r} 24 \\ \times\,36 \\ \hline 144 \\ +\,720 \\ \hline 864 \end{array}$$

4. Estimate to decide if the product is reasonable.
You can see that **864** is close to **800**. So the
product is reasonable.

$$\begin{array}{rr} 24 \rightarrow & 20 \\ \times\,36 & \times\,40 \\ \hline & 800 \end{array}$$

**Multiply. Estimate to decide if the product
is reasonable.**

1.
$$\begin{array}{r} 24 \\ \times\,15 \\ \hline \end{array} \qquad \begin{array}{r} 36 \\ \times\,21 \\ \hline \end{array} \qquad \begin{array}{r} 48 \\ \times\,34 \\ \hline \end{array} \qquad \begin{array}{r} 18 \\ \times\,56 \\ \hline \end{array} \qquad \begin{array}{r} 75 \\ \times\,67 \\ \hline \end{array}$$

2.
$$\begin{array}{r} 27 \\ \times\,28 \\ \hline \end{array} \qquad \begin{array}{r} 76 \\ \times\,34 \\ \hline \end{array} \qquad \begin{array}{r} \$.42 \\ \times\;\;\;36 \\ \hline \end{array} \qquad \begin{array}{r} \$.94 \\ \times\;\;\;22 \\ \hline \end{array} \qquad \begin{array}{r} 32 \\ \times\,47 \\ \hline \end{array}$$

3.
$$\begin{array}{r} 52 \\ \times\,23 \\ \hline \end{array} \qquad \begin{array}{r} 57 \\ \times\,34 \\ \hline \end{array} \qquad \begin{array}{r} 43 \\ \times\,58 \\ \hline \end{array} \qquad \begin{array}{r} 68 \\ \times\,36 \\ \hline \end{array} \qquad \begin{array}{r} \$.69 \\ \times\;\;\;76 \\ \hline \end{array}$$

4.
$$\begin{array}{r} 26 \\ \times\,89 \\ \hline \end{array} \qquad \begin{array}{r} 89 \\ \times\,26 \\ \hline \end{array} \qquad \begin{array}{r} 75 \\ \times\,92 \\ \hline \end{array} \qquad \begin{array}{r} 92 \\ \times\,75 \\ \hline \end{array} \qquad \begin{array}{r} \$.83 \\ \times\;\;\;43 \\ \hline \end{array}$$

Multiply.

5.

47	39	56	32	56
× 19	× 54	× 77	× 24	× 38

6.

40	83	29	98	59
× 29	× 43	× 62	× 27	× 56

Problem Solving Reasoning **Solve.**

7. There are **24** stamps on each page of Lester's stamp album. There are **18** pages in his album. How many stamps are in Lester's collection?

_____

8. Sue Lynn collects coins. There are **52** coins in each of **15** boxes. Does Sue Lynn have more than **1,000** coins? Explain.

_____

_____

9. Mrs. Washington has **35** each of **22** different beads. How many beads does she have?

_____

10. Leonard has **10** times as many sports trading cards as his sister. His sister has **84**. How many does Leonard have?

_____

Test Prep ★ Mixed Review

11 What number could go in the ▢ to make the number sentence true?

$$5 \times \boxed{} < 25$$

A 7

B 6

C 5

D 4

12 What number should go in the ▢ to make the number sentence true?

$$3 \times \boxed{} = 3$$

F 0

G 1

H 3

J 6

Name _____

You can multiply with **3**-digit numbers the same way you multiply with **2**-digit numbers.

Find: 86×347.

1. Multiply **347** by **6** ones.

$$
\begin{array}{r}
347 \\
\times\ 86 \\
\hline
\end{array}
$$

$6 \times 347 \rightarrow 2{,}082$

2. Multiply **347** by **8** tens.

$$
\begin{array}{r}
347 \\
\times\ 86 \\
\hline
2{,}082 \\
\end{array}
$$

$80 \times 347 \rightarrow 27{,}760$

3. Add the products.

$$
\begin{array}{r}
347 \\
\times\ 86 \\
\hline
2\ 082 \\
+\ 27\ 76 \\
\hline
29{,}842 \\
\end{array}
$$

4. Estimate to decide if your answer is reasonable.

$$90 \times 300 = 27{,}000$$

$$
\begin{array}{r}
347 \rightarrow\quad 300 \\
\times\ 86 \rightarrow\quad \times\ 90 \\
\hline
27{,}000 \\
\end{array}
$$

You can see that **29,842** is close to **27,000**. So the product is reasonable.

Multiply. Estimate to decide if your answer is reasonable.

1.

$$
\begin{array}{r}
396 \\
\times\ 38 \\
\hline
\end{array}
\qquad
\begin{array}{r}
197 \\
\times\ 29 \\
\hline
\end{array}
\qquad
\begin{array}{r}
418 \\
\times\ 67 \\
\hline
\end{array}
\qquad
\begin{array}{r}
269 \\
\times\ 46 \\
\hline
\end{array}
\qquad
\begin{array}{r}
375 \\
\times\ 57 \\
\hline
\end{array}
$$

2.

$$
\begin{array}{r}
656 \\
\times\ 23 \\
\hline
\end{array}
\qquad
\begin{array}{r}
390 \\
\times\ 48 \\
\hline
\end{array}
\qquad
\begin{array}{r}
507 \\
\times\ 54 \\
\hline
\end{array}
\qquad
\begin{array}{r}
378 \\
\times\ 76 \\
\hline
\end{array}
\qquad
\begin{array}{r}
476 \\
\times\ 93 \\
\hline
\end{array}
$$

3.

$$
\begin{array}{r}
547 \\
\times\ 73 \\
\hline
\end{array}
\qquad
\begin{array}{r}
406 \\
\times\ 32 \\
\hline
\end{array}
\qquad
\begin{array}{r}
327 \\
\times\ 44 \\
\hline
\end{array}
\qquad
\begin{array}{r}
215 \\
\times\ 58 \\
\hline
\end{array}
\qquad
\begin{array}{r}
108 \\
\times\ 92 \\
\hline
\end{array}
$$

STANDARD

4.

48	109	55	212	498	290
× 13	× 24	× 55	× 29	× 84	× 30

5.

239	87	523	860	753	47
× 19	× 24	× 17	× 62	× 71	× 30

Problem Solving Reasoning Solve.

6. a. Teachers bought **6** pizzas for students who are on a field trip. Each pizza has **8** slices. If each student gets one slice, how many students will be served?

_____

b. Each pizza costs **$6.95**. How much did **6** cost? _____

7. a. The pizza restaurant sells single slices of pizza. Each slice is **$.95**. If **48** students each bought one slice, how much would they pay altogether?

_____

b. Is it cheaper to buy **6** pizzas or **48** single slices? What is the difference in cost?

_____

✓ **Quick Check**

Multiply.

Work Space.

8.
67
× 25

9.
32
× 46

10.
83
× 62

11.
417
× 22

12.
208
× 37

13.
457
× 43

A **pictograph** uses pictures or symbols to represent a number. The **key** shows the number that each picture or symbol represents.

The pictograph on this page shows information about the books Emily read during the summer. It shows the kind of books and the number of each kind.

You will use pictographs to solve the problems in this lesson.

EMILY'S SUMMER READING

Mystery	
Science Fiction	
Historical Fiction	
Nonfiction	

KEY: Each [book] stands for **4** books.

Tips to Remember:

1. Understand	2. Decide	3. Solve	4. Look back

- Reread the problem. Circle important words and numbers.
- When using a pictograph, remember to use the key.
- Think about the strategies you have already learned. Try using one of them to solve the problem.

Solve. Use the pictograph above.

1. How many science fiction books did Emily read?

Think: Why is it important to look at the key before answering the question?

_____

_____

_____

Answer _____

2. How many nonfiction books did Emily read?

Think: How can you figure out how many books [book] stands for?

_____

_____

_____

Answer _____

3. How many more mystery books than historical fiction books did Emily read?

_____

4. How many books did Emily read in all this summer?

_____

COLLECTIONS FOR UNICEF

Kindergarten	s	s	s	s	s			
Grade 1	s	s	s	s	s	s	s	
Grade 2	s	s	s	s	s	s	s	
Grade 3	s	s	s					
Grade 4	s	s	s	s	s	s	s	s
Grade 5	s	s	s	s	s			

KEY: Each ⬚ s stands for **$50**.

Solve. Use the pictograph above.

5. Which grade collected the most? How much did they collect?

_____

6. How much more did Grade **1** collect than Grade **2**?

_____

7. Grade **3** set a goal of **$200**. Did they meet their goal? How much more or less than their goal did they collect?

_____

8. Suppose Grade **4** had collected **$550**. How many symbols would show that amount on the graph above?

_____

9. What was the total amount collected by all grades?

_____

10. The school goal was **$2,000**. Did they reach their goal?

_____

Extend Your Thinking

11. Tell how you solved problem 6.

_____

_____

_____

12. Go back to problem 8. If each symbol in the graph stood for **$20**, how many symbols would be needed to show **$550**?

_____

_____

Name _____

Use properties to solve.

1. $(3 \times$ _____$) \times 2 = 24$ **2.** $4 \times 0 =$ _____   **3.** $1 \times 9 =$ _____

Multiply.

4. $\begin{array}{r} 53 \\ \times\ 7 \\ \hline \end{array}$ **5.** $\begin{array}{r} 81 \\ \times\ 5 \\ \hline \end{array}$ **6.** $\begin{array}{r} 301 \\ \times\ 9 \\ \hline \end{array}$ **7.** $\begin{array}{r} 7{,}326 \\ \times\ 6 \\ \hline \end{array}$ **8.** $\begin{array}{r} 1{,}205 \\ \times\ 2 \\ \hline \end{array}$

9. 15×10 **10.** 290×100 **11.** 60×40 **12.** 70×70

13. $\begin{array}{r} \$2.76 \\ \times\ 4 \\ \hline \end{array}$ **14.** $\begin{array}{r} \$17.25 \\ \times\ 5 \\ \hline \end{array}$ **15.** $\begin{array}{r} 26 \\ \times\ 16 \\ \hline \end{array}$ **16.** $\begin{array}{r} 66 \\ \times\ 34 \\ \hline \end{array}$ **17.** $\begin{array}{r} 125 \\ \times\ 28 \\ \hline \end{array}$

Use rounding to estimate the product.

18. $\begin{array}{r} 65 \rightarrow \underline{\quad} \\ \times\ 4 \rightarrow \times \\ \hline \end{array}$ **19.** $\begin{array}{r} 71 \rightarrow \underline{\quad} \\ \times\ 17 \rightarrow \times \\ \hline \end{array}$ **20.** $\begin{array}{r} \$6.29 \rightarrow \underline{\quad} \\ \times\ 32 \rightarrow \times \\ \hline \end{array}$

Solve.

21. Jennifer bought **2** notebooks and a pencil. One notebook cost twice as much as the other. The pencil cost **$.30**. She spent **$6.75**. How much did each notebook cost?

_____

22. Which school has the most runners? How many runners in total are at all three schools?

_____

_____

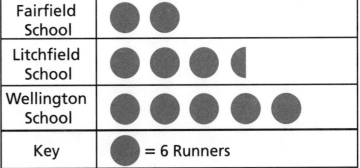

Number of Runners at Three Schools

Fairfield School	
Litchfield School	
Wellington School	
Key	= 6 Runners

1 On one day of their vacation, the Rodríquez family spent $26 for breakfast, $38 for lunch, and $79 for dinner. How much did they spend in all for these meals?

A $133

B $143

C $152

D $1223

E NH

2 A machine uses 27 gallons to paint the lines on 1 mile of highway. How many gallons will the machine need to paint the lines on 35 miles of highway?

F 655

G 745

H 945

J 965

K NH

3 A window washer finishes 1 window in 4 minutes. There are 76 windows on the building. *About* how many minutes will it take him to wash all the windows?

A 240

B 280

C 320

D 3200

E NH

4 A plane is flying from San Diego, California, to Seattle, Washington. The distance between these cities is 1,270 miles. If the plane has flown 396 miles, how many more miles are left?

F 1666   J 874

G 984   K NH

H 884

5 A total of 15,472 runners entered a road race. What is this number rounded to the nearest hundred?

A 15,000   D 16,500

B 15,400   E NH

C 16,000

6 What number is four hundred seventy thousand, nine in standard form?

F 47,009

G 407,009

H 470,009

J 470,090

7 Which problem has the same product as 217×3?

A $(200 \times 3) + (10 \times 3) + (7 \times 3)$

B $(200 \times 17) + (10 \times 17) + (3 \times 17)$

C $(200 \times 3) + (10 \times 3)$

D $(200 \times 19) + (10 \times 7) + (7 \times 3)$

E NH

UNIT 4 • TABLE OF CONTENTS

Division with 1-Digit Divisors

We will be using this vocabulary:

dividend in a division problem, the number that is divided

divisor the number that divides the dividend

quotient the number of groups or the number in each group

prime number a counting number greater than 1 that has exactly two different factors, itself and 1

composite number a counting number greater than 1 that has more than two different factors

remainder the number left over after the quotient is found

Dear Family,

During the next few weeks, our math class will be learning and practicing division of whole numbers.

You can expect to see homework that provides practice with finding averages. Here is a sample you may want to keep handy to give help if needed.

Finding an Average

During the first **5** soccer games of the year, the Parkside Elementary School soccer team scored **3, 0, 1, 6,** and **0** goals.

To find the average number of goals the team scored in each game, first add to find the total number of goals scored.

$$3 + 0 + 1 + 6 + 0 = 10$$ The team scored a total of **10** goals.

Then divide the total number of goals scored by the number of games the team played.

$$
\begin{array}{r}
2 \\
5{\overline{\smash{)}10}} \\
-10 \\
\hline
0
\end{array}
$$

During the first five games, the team scored an average of **2** goals per game.

During this unit, students will need to continue practicing addition, subtraction, multiplication, and division facts.

Sincerely,

Missing Factors and Division

Multiplication and division are **inverse operations**. You can use a related division fact to find a missing factor.

Inverse means opposite.

factor × factor = product

$? \times 6 = 48$

$48 \div 6 = ?$

$48 \div 6 = 8$, so $8 \times 6 = 48$

You can use a related number sentence to find the value of *n*.

Find *n* in the number sentence *n* × 5 = 30.

1. Use a related number sentence.

    $n \times 5 = 30$
    Think: $n = 30 \div 5$
    $n = 6$

Division is the inverse of multiplication. **Think: 30** divided by **5** is what number?

2. Check your work.

    Is the number sentence $n \times 5 = 30$ **true** when $n = 6$?

    $n \times 5 = 30$
    ↓
    $6 \times 5 = 30$ **Yes, it is true.**

Use related number sentences to find the value of *n*.

1. $n \times 2 = 18$ $n \times 9 = 63$ $n \times 8 = 64$

Think: $n = 18 \div$ _____   Think: $n = 63 \div$ _____   Think: $n =$ _____ $\div 8$

$n =$ _____ $n =$ _____ $n =$ _____

2. $n \times 6 = 36$ $n \times 1 = 40$ $n \times 7 = 28$

Think: $n = 36 \div$ _____   Think: $n =$ _____ $\div 1$ Think: $n =$ _____ $\div 7$

$n =$ _____ $n =$ _____ $n =$ _____

3. $4 \times n = 28$ $6 \times n = 54$ $7 \times n = 56$

Think: $n =$ _____ $\div 4$ Think: $n =$ _____ $\div 6$ Think: $n = 56 \div$ _____

$n =$ _____ $n =$ _____ $n =$ _____

Division rules can sometimes be used to find the value of a variable.

What is the value of *n* in the number sentence 0 ÷ 5 = *n*?

When you divide zero by any number, the answer is zero.

If **0 ÷ 5 = *n***, then ***n* = 0**.

Remember, you can never divide by zero.

What is the value of *n* in the number sentence 5 ÷ 5 = *n*?

Any number divided by itself equals **1**.

If **5 ÷ 5 = *n***, then ***n* = 1**.

What is the value of *n* in the number sentence 5 ÷ 1 = *n*?

Any number divided by **1** is that number.

If **5 ÷ 1 = *n***, then ***n* = 5**.

Find the value of *n*.

4. 8 ÷ 8 = *n*

n = _____

0 ÷ 4 = *n*

n = _____

18 ÷ 2 = *n*

n = _____

1 × 5 = *n*

n = _____

Problem Solving Reasoning

Complete each table. Think about multiplication facts to help you divide.

5.

Divide by 4	
16	
36	
24	
12	

6.

Divide by 7	
21	
56	
49	
28	

7.

Divide by 9	
45	
27	
63	
81	

Test Prep ★ Mixed Review

8 What number should go in the ☐ to make the number sentence true?

$(11 + 21) + 8 = \boxed{} + (11 + 8)$

A 21   C 8

B 11   D 7

9 What number should go in the ☐ to make the number sentence true?

$(3 \times 2) \times 10 = 3 \times \boxed{}$

F 20   H 3

G 10   J 2

Name _____

Order of Operations

STANDARD

A mathematical **expression** contains one or more numbers. It may also contain operation signs and letters that stand for numbers. These are all expressions:

$$2 \times 3 \qquad n + 1 \qquad 3 \div n \qquad 9 + 4$$

Sometimes an expression contains more than one operation. The **order of operations** is a set of rules that tells you which operation to do first.

$4 + 6 \times 2$ Multiply first, then add.

↓

$4 + \ \ 12$

↓

16

There is only one correct value for this expression.

Order of Operations

1. Do the operation in the parentheses first.

2. Multiply and divide from left to right.

3. Add and subtract from left to right.

Parentheses are grouping symbols that tell you what to do first. When an expression contains parentheses, do the operation inside the parentheses first.

$12 \div (6 - 2)$

↓

$12 \div \ \ 4$

↓

3

$(12 \div 6) - 2$

↓

$2 - 2$

↓

0

The values of the expressions are different.

Use the order of operations. Find the value of each expression.

1. $3 + 6 \times 2$ $\qquad$ $14 \div 2 + 3$ $\qquad$ $4 \div 2 \times 3$

2. $5 - 4 \div 2$ $\qquad$ $7 \times 3 - 3$ $\qquad$ $14 - 6 + 11$

3. $16 + 8 \div 4$ $\qquad$ $4 \times 3 - 2$ $\qquad$ $11 + 9 \div 3$

4. $8 + 6 \times 3$ $\qquad$ $16 - 10 \div 2$ $\qquad$ $16 \div 4 \times 8$

5. $24 \div 3 + 3$ $\qquad$ $30 - 5 \times 4$ $\qquad$ $21 - 3 \times 7$

6. $36 - 9 \times 4$ $\qquad$ $27 \div 3 + 6$ $\qquad$ $64 - 18 + 4$

7. $12 \times 3 - 1$ $\qquad$ $9 \div 9 \times 9$ $\qquad$ $64 + 16 \times 4$

8. $22 \times 4 - 1$ $\qquad$ $29 - 13 \times 2$ $\qquad$ $18 \div 6 \times 3$

9. $16 + 8 \div 4$ $\qquad$ $50 \times 4 \div 2$ $\qquad$ $27 - 9 \div 3$

10. $42 \div 6 \times 7$ $\qquad$ $30 + 5 - 4$ $\qquad$ $36 \div 3 \times 3$

Use the order of operations. Find the value of each expression.

11. $(56 - 6) \div 5$ _____ $(48 \div 6) \times 3$ _____ $(32 \div 8) + 5$ _____

12. $5 \times (4 + 7)$ _____ $4 \times (8 - 2)$ _____ $6 \times (9 \div 3)$ _____

13. $(4 \times 7) + 3$ _____ $(5 \times 6) \div 10$ _____ $(7 \times 7) \div 7$ _____

Draw parentheses to make each number sentence true.

14. $9 + 3 \times 2 = 24$ $4 \times 9 - 4 = 32$

15. $42 \div 2 \times 3 = 7$ $5 \times 3 + 3 = 30$

16. $7 - 28 \div 4 = 0$ $5 + 2 \times 4 = 13$

17. $15 - 4 \times 3 = 33$ $9 + 9 \div 6 = 3$

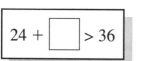

Problem Solving Reasoning

Use parentheses and the numbers 2, 3, and 4 to make each number sentence true.

18. ☐ × ☐ − ☐ = 5   ☐ + ☐ ÷ ☐ = 5

19. ☐ + ☐ × ☐ = 10   ☐ × ☐ ÷ ☐ = 6

20. ☐ ÷ ☐ + ☐ = 5   ☐ + ☐ × ☐ = 14

Test Prep ★ Mixed Review

21 Which number could go in the ☐ to make the number sentence true?

$$24 + \boxed{} > 36$$

   A 13

   B 12

   C 10

   D 9

22 Anthony practices golf at a driving range. He goes to the range 15 times and hits exactly 55 balls each time. How many balls does he hit in all?

   F 575

   G 805

   H 825

   J 3,075

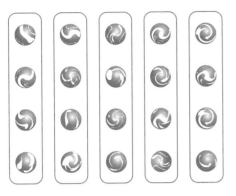

You have **5** groups of **4** with **1** marble left over.

Suppose you had **21** marbles and wanted to put **4** marbles in each group. How many groups would you have?

You can show this with division:

$$\begin{array}{r} 5 \leftarrow \textbf{quotient} \\ \textbf{divisor} \rightarrow 4\overline{)21} \leftarrow \textbf{dividend} \\ -20 \\ \hline 1 \leftarrow \textbf{remainder} \end{array}$$

The **1** left over is called the remainder. You write the answer as **5 R1**.

Other Examples:

$$\begin{array}{r} 6\ R2 \\ 4\overline{)26} \\ -24 \\ \hline 2 \end{array} \qquad \begin{array}{r} 4\ R5 \\ 7\overline{)33} \\ -28 \\ \hline 5 \end{array} \qquad \begin{array}{r} 8\ R8 \\ 9\overline{)80} \\ -72 \\ \hline 8 \end{array}$$

The remainder is always less than the divisor!

Complete. Make groups if you need to.

1.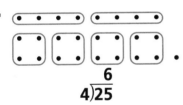

$$\begin{array}{r} 6 \\ 4\overline{)25} \end{array}$$

2.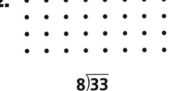

$$8\overline{)33}$$

3.

$$5\overline{)17}$$

4.

$$6\overline{)13}$$

5.

$$7\overline{)44}$$

6.

$$3\overline{)26}$$

Divide.

7. $4\overline{)17}$ $5\overline{)19}$ $8\overline{)41}$ $3\overline{)29}$ $7\overline{)38}$ $4\overline{)31}$

8. $3\overline{)26}$ $9\overline{)20}$ $6\overline{)52}$ $5\overline{)47}$ $9\overline{)73}$ $6\overline{)22}$

| Problem Solving Reasoning | **Solve.** |

9. $(6 \times 7) + 2 =$ _____ $36 = ($ _____ $\times 5) + 1$ $42 = (8 \times 5) +$ _____

10. $($ _____ $\times 5) + 3 = 23$ _____ $= (4 \times 5) + 1$ $(7 \times 6) + 3 =$ _____

11. $(7 \times$ _____ $) + 0 = 56$ _____ $= (4 \times 8) + 2$ $(6 \times 8) + 7 =$ _____

 ## Quick Check

Write the number that completes the number sentence.   Work Space.

12. $7 \times \boxed{} = 56$ **13.** $8 \times \boxed{} = 72$ **14.** $27 \div \boxed{} = 1$

Use the order of operations to find the value of each expression.

15. $4 + (17 - 2)$ **16.** $(2 \times 6) \div 3$ **17.** $(3 \times 5) + 2$

_____   _____   _____

Divide. Write the remainder if there is one.

18. $8\overline{)37}$ **19.** $4\overline{)27}$ **20.** $7\overline{)54}$

So far with your work in division, you have found one-digit quotients. Sometimes when you divide, the quotient has more digits.

Divide 48 blocks into 4 groups.

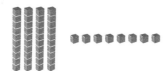

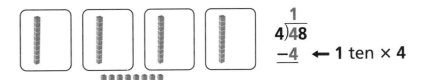

blocks in
each group
groups → 4)48 ← blocks in all

1. Divide the tens. Put **1** ten in each group.

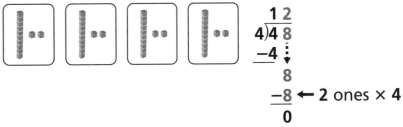

$$\frac{1}{4)48}$$
−4 ← **1** ten × **4**

2. Divide the ones. Put **2** ones in each group.

1 2
4)4 8
−4
8
−8 ← **2** ones × **4**
0

Answer: **12** blocks in each group

Divide.

1.

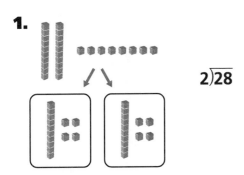

2)28

2.

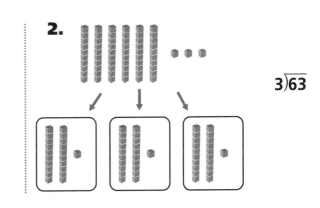

3)63

Divide.

3. 2)84   5)55   3)39   4)88   3)96   6)66   2)68

Sometimes you need to regroup.

Divide **53** blocks into **4** groups.

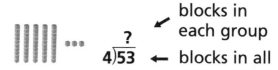

blocks in each group

← blocks in all

$$\frac{?}{4)\overline{53}}$$

1. Divide the tens.

Put **1** ten in each group.

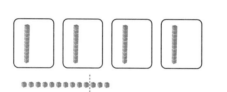

$$4)\overline{53}$$ with 1 above 5

$$-4$$ ← **1** ten × **4**

1

2. Regroup **1** ten as **10** ones.
1 ten + **3** ones = **13** ones

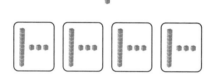

1
$$4)\overline{5\ 3}$$
$$-4\downarrow$$
1 3

3. Divide the ones.
Put **3** ones in each group.
13 ones ÷ **4** = **3** ones **R1**

Answer: **13 R1**

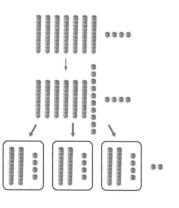

13 R1
$$4)\overline{53}$$
$$-4$$
13
$$-12$$ ← **3** ones × **4**
1

Divide.

4.

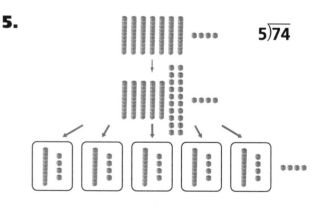

$$3)\overline{74}$$

5.

$$5)\overline{74}$$

Divide.

6. $8)\overline{97}$ $3)\overline{77}$ $4)\overline{93}$ $7)\overline{88}$ $5)\overline{84}$

Name _____

Follow these steps to divide without blocks.

Find $3\overline{)79}^{?}$

| **1. Divide tens.** | **2. Multiply and subtract.** | **3. Bring down the next digit. Regroup.** | **4. Divide ones.** | **5. Multiply and subtract.** |

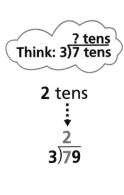

Think: $3\overline{)7 \text{ tens}}^{\text{? tens}}$

2 tens

$3\overline{)79}^{\ 2}$

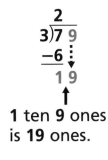

$\begin{array}{r} 2 \\ 3\overline{)79} \\ -6 \\ \hline 1 \end{array}$ ← 2 tens × 3

$\begin{array}{r} 2 \\ 3\overline{)7\ 9} \\ -6 \\ \hline 1\ 9 \end{array}$

1 ten 9 ones is 19 ones.

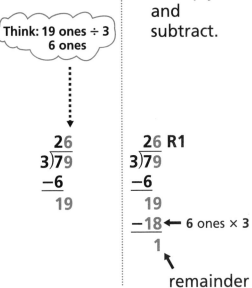

Think: 19 ones ÷ 3
6 ones

$\begin{array}{r} 26 \\ 3\overline{)79} \\ -6 \\ \hline 19 \end{array}$

$\begin{array}{r} 26 \text{ R1} \\ 3\overline{)79} \\ -6 \\ \hline 19 \\ -18 \\ \hline 1 \end{array}$ ← 6 ones × 3

remainder

6. Check your work.

Multiply the quotient by the divisor. Then add the remainder.

26 × 3 + 1 = 78 + 1 or 79

The result is the dividend, so this answer is correct.

Complete each division.

7.
$\begin{array}{r} 1 \\ 3\overline{)4\ 7} \\ -3 \\ \hline 1\ 7 \end{array}$
$\begin{array}{r} 1 \\ 6\overline{)8\ 4} \\ -6 \\ \hline 2\ 4 \end{array}$
$\begin{array}{r} 2 \\ 4\overline{)93} \\ -8 \\ \hline 13 \end{array}$
$\begin{array}{r} 3 \\ 2\overline{)71} \\ -6 \\ \hline 11 \end{array}$
$\begin{array}{r} 1 \\ 7\overline{)92} \\ -7 \\ \hline 22 \end{array}$

8.
$5\overline{)85}^{\ 1}$
$2\overline{)47}^{\ 2}$
$3\overline{)82}$
$7\overline{)95}$
$8\overline{)95}$

Divide.

9. $6\overline{)87}$ $2\overline{)93}$ $4\overline{)78}$ $5\overline{)78}$ $3\overline{)92}$

10. $3\overline{)55}$ $6\overline{)78}$ $4\overline{)67}$ $7\overline{)73}$ $2\overline{)91}$

11. $3\overline{)97}$ $4\overline{)84}$ $6\overline{)61}$ $4\overline{)87}$ $7\overline{)90}$

12. $2\overline{)59}$ $8\overline{)84}$ $5\overline{)67}$ $6\overline{)67}$ $3\overline{)65}$

Problem Solving Reasoning **Solve.**

13. Three boys divided **84** pennies equally among themselves. How many pennies did each boy get?

_____

14. Four girls played a game with **52** number cards. They divided the whole deck equally. How many cards did each girl get?

_____

Test Prep ★ Mixed Review

15 The population of the town of Carmichael, California, is 48,702. The population of the town of Fair Oaks is 26,867. What is the combined population of these two towns?

A 741,569

B 75,669

C 75,569

D 65,569

E NH

16 The store sold 67 T-shirts each hour. *About* how many T-shirts did it sell in 12 hours?

F 800

G 700

H 600

J 500

Working with 3-digit quotients is like working with 2-digit quotients.

Example: 3)875‾

1. Divide hundreds.

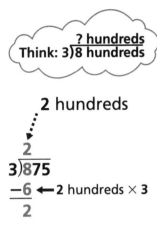

Think: 3)8 hundreds‾ **? hundreds**

2 hundreds

```
    2
3)875
 −6  ←2 hundreds × 3
────
    2
```

2. Bring down the next digit.

```
    2
3)8 7 5
 −6
────
  2 7
```

2 hundreds 7 tens is 27 tens

3. Divide tens.

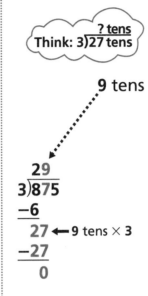

Think: 3)27 tens‾ **? tens**

9 tens

```
   29
3)875
 −6
────
  27  ←9 tens × 3
 −27
────
   0
```

4. Bring down the next digit. Divide ones.

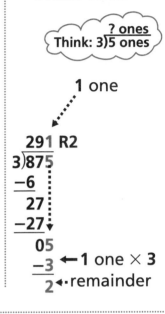

Think: 3)5 ones‾ **? ones**

1 one

```
  291 R2
3)875
 −6
────
  27
 −27
────
  05
  −3  ←1 one × 3
────
   2  ←remainder
```

5. Check your work.

Multiply the quotient by the divisor. Then add the remainder.

291 × 3 = 873 + 2 or 875

The result is the dividend, so the answer is correct.

Divide.

1.
```
    1
4)759
 −4
───
 35
```
```
    2
4)923
 −8
───
 12
```
```
    1
6)824
 −6
───
 22
```
```
    4
2)971
 −8
───
 17
```
```
    1
5)814
 −5
───
 31
```

2.
```
    2
3)762
```
```
    1
5)913
```
```
    2
4)882
```
```
    2
3)806
```
```
    1
7)932
```

Divide. Then check your work.

3. 6)718   Check:

4)805   Check:

2)953   Check:

4. 3)517   Check:

5)891   Check:

6)903   Check:

5. 7)856   Check:

4)735   Check:

3)572   Check:

Problem Solving
Reasoning   Solve.

6. Eric has **532** marbles and **5** marble bags. He wants each bag to contain the same number of marbles. How many marbles should he put in each bag?

_____

7. How many marbles does Eric need to add to his collection in order to have exactly **110** marbles in each of his **5** bags?

_____

Test Prep ★ Mixed Review

8 Andrea's heart beat 93 times a minute while she was running. She ran for 15 minutes. How many times did her heart beat during this run?

A   558

B 1,385

C 1,395

D 5,445

9 Eight friends share $96.00 equally. How much money does each friend get?

F $10.00

G $11.00

H $12.00

J $13.00

Sometimes, when you divide with a 3-digit dividend, the quotient has 2 digits.

Find: 237 ÷ 5.

1. Divide hundreds.

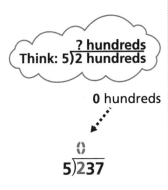

Think: 5)2 hundreds **? hundreds**

0 hundreds

0
5)237

Not enough hundreds. Regroup as tens.

2. Divide tens.

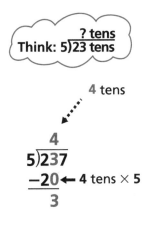

Think: 5)23 tens **? tens**

4 tens

4
5)237
−20 ← 4 tens × 5
3

3. Regroup as ones. Then divide ones.

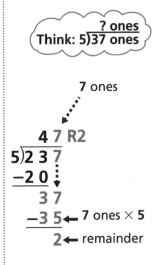

Think: 5)37 ones **? ones**

7 ones

4 7 R2
5)2 3 7
−2 0
3 7
−3 5 ← 7 ones × 5
2 ← remainder

Be sure to write the remainder.

4. Check.

```
    47
 ×   5
   235
 +   2
   237
```

The result, **237**, checks with the dividend, so the answer is correct.

Complete each division.

1.
```
      6
 3)194
  −18
   14
```
```
      3
 4)147
  −12
   27
```
```
      7
 5)381
  −35
   31
```
```
      4
 6)297
  −24
   57
```

2.
```
      4
 5)237
  −20
```
```
      4
 3)128
  −12
```
```
      8
 6)492
  −48
```
```
      7
 7)539
  −49
```

Divide.

3. 4)315   6)416   8)592   7)394

Divide.

4. 6)178   8)196   5)185   7)196

5. 5)283   4)195   5)387   6)389

Problem Solving Reasoning

Solve.

6. Tony needs **252** tiles to cover a wall. He needs the same number of red, green, and yellow tiles. How many of each color should he buy?

7. Ann put **365** tokens in **5** equal groups. How many tokens are in each group?

✔ Quick Check

Solve.

Work Space.

8. 4)95   **9.** 7)87   **10.** 2)73

11. 6)773   **12.** 4)523   **13.** 8)899

14. 8)733   **15.** 6)469   **16.** 5)407

STANDARD

Sometimes a quotient contains one or more zeros.

Example: 4)825 ?

1. Divide hundreds.	**2.** Bring down the **2**. Divide tens.	**3.** Bring down the **5**. Divide ones.	**4.** Check.

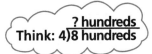

Think: 4)8 hundreds → ? hundreds

```
   2
4)825
 -8
 ──
  0
```

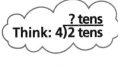

Think: 4)2 tens → ? tens

```
  20
4)825
 -8
 ──
  02
```

Not enough tens. Write a **0** in the tens place in the quotient.

Think: 4)25 ones → ? ones

```
  206 R1
4)825
 -8
 ──
  25
 -24
 ──
   1
```

```
   206
  ×  4
 ─────
   824
  +  1
 ─────
   825
```

The result, **825**, is the dividend. So the answer is correct.

Divide. Then check.

1. 6)645   2)609   3)302

2. 2)815   8)565   2)613

3. 4)438   7)761   6)364

4. 3)721   4)827   9)919

Write the greatest multiple of 100 that will make each sentence true.

5. $3 \times \underline{\ \ 300\ \ } < 945$ $5 \times \underline{\hspace{2cm}} < 800$ $\underline{\hspace{2cm}} \times 9 < 1{,}900$

6. $2 \times \underline{\hspace{2cm}} < 530$ $6 \times \underline{\hspace{2cm}} < 1{,}300$ $\underline{\hspace{2cm}} \times 6 < 2{,}300$

Circle the greatest number that makes the sentence true.

7. $5 \times \square < 98$ $8 \times \square < 769$ $2 \times \square < 721$

        1   2   10   20   80   90   800   900   30   40   300   400

Write the first digit of each quotient. Use your answers in Row 7 to help you.

8. $5\overline{)98}$ $8\overline{)769}$ $2\overline{)721}$

Divide and check.

9. $5\overline{)98}$ $8\overline{)769}$ $2\overline{)721}$

Problem Solving Reasoning   Solve.

10. Does a zero in the ones place of a quotient mean there is never a remainder? Explain.

_____

_____

Test Prep ★ Mixed Review

11 What number should go in the ☐ to make the number sentence true?

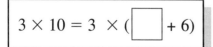

$$3 \times 10 = 3 \times (\square + 6)$$

A 2

B 4

C 6

D 8

12 Six friends divide 22 tennis balls evenly. How many balls are left over?

F 6

G 4

H 3

J 2

You can divide money just as you would divide whole numbers.

Example: 4)$5.40

1. Divide as if you were dividing whole numbers.

```
     1 35
4)$5.40
  −4
   14
  −12
    20
   −20
     0
```

2. Write the dollar sign and decimal point in the quotient.

```
    $1.35
4)$5.40
  −4
   14
  −12
    20
   −20
     0
```

Align the decimal point in the quotient with the decimal point in the dividend.

Divide. Remember to write the dollar sign and decimal point in the quotient when you need to.

1.   7)84¢   7)$.84   9)$6.48   8)$6.48

2.   2)$6.24   3)$4.26   3)$2.76   4)$.88

3.   8)$5.76   9)$8.10   3)$9.03   5)$9.75

4.   9)$3.78   6)$.84   7)91¢   6)$8.64

You can buy **6** balloons for **$10.20**. How much does **1** balloon cost?

To find out how much one item costs when all the items cost the same, divide the total amount by the number in the group.

```
         $ 1.70
    6)$10.20
      −6
       42
      −42
        0
```

Always remember to include the dollar sign and decimal point in your answer.

Find the cost of one item.

5. Two burgers cost **$7.80**.

One burger costs _____ .

6. Four cups of jello cost **$3.00**.

One jello costs _____ .

7. Five glasses of juice cost **$6.75**.

One juice costs _____ .

8. Six small salads cost **$9.00**.

One salad costs _____ .

Problem Solving Reasoning

Decide whether you need an exact answer or an estimated answer. Then solve the problem.

9. At the fair, Mrs. Washington gave her **4** children **$30.00**. She said they should share the money equally. How much did each child get?

_____

10. The school pageant had an attendance of **126** people on Monday and **214** people on Tuesday. It cost **$1.00** to attend. Did the school collect at least **$400.00**?

_____

Test Prep ★ Mixed Review

11. One pad of colored paper has 85 sheets of paper. How many sheets of paper do 12 pads have?

A 245

B 255

C 1,010

D 1,020

12. Howard is placing photographs in an album. He can fit 4 photographs on a page. How many pages will he need for 172 photographs?

F 40

G 43

H 430

J 688

Problem Solving Application: Choose the Operation

To solve problems, you need to decide whether to add, subtract, multiply, or divide. To choose the correct operation, think about how each operation can be used.

- Both **addition** and **multiplication** can be used to find a total.

- **Subtraction** can be used to find out how many are left, to compare two numbers, or to find a missing addend.

- **Division** can be used to find the number in each group or the number of groups.

Tips to Remember:

1. Understand	2. Decide	3. Solve	4. Look back

- Read the problem carefully. Ask yourself questions about any part that does not make sense. Reread to find answers.
- Find the action in the problem. Which operation shows the action best: addition, subtraction, multiplication, or division?
- Predict the answer. Then solve the problem. Compare your answer with your prediction.

Solve.

1. There are **108** students in the fourth grade at Eastbrook School. There are **4** fourth grade classes. Each class is the same size. How many students are in each class?

Think: How does the question help you decide what operation to use?

_____

_____

_____

Answer _____

2. Mrs. Chang bought a flannel shirt for each of her sons, Mike and Russell. Each shirt cost **$16.98**. What was the total cost?

Think: What operations can you use to find a total? What two methods could you use to solve this problem?

_____

_____

_____

Answer _____

Solve.

3. A total of **72** girls signed up to play in a soccer league. The league organized them into **6** teams, all with the same number of players. How many girls were on each team?

_____

4. On Wednesday, **288** students in a school ordered pizza for lunch. Nine students ordered fish. How many more students ordered pizza than ordered fish?

_____

5. Chairs were set up in the gym for a school play. There were **24** rows with **12** chairs in each row. How many chairs were there in all?

_____

6. Andrew saw a pair of rollerblades for **$69.95** in one store. He saw the same rollerblades in another store for **$57.99**. What was the difference in price?

_____

7. Alexandra earns money babysitting. During one weekend, she earned a total of **$36**. She earned **$15.50** of this total on Friday and **$10.50** on Saturday. How much did she earn on Sunday?

_____

8. Three brothers shared the cost of flowers for their mother. The flowers cost **$12.42**. If each boy paid the same amount, how much did each pay?

_____

9. There were **56** people on a bus—both students and teachers. There are **3** times as many students as teachers. How many teachers are on the bus?

_____

10. Everytime Jenna loses a tooth, **50¢** is added to her piggy bank. How many teeth does Jenna need to lose to make **$5.00**?

_____

Extend Your Thinking

11. Go back to problem 4. Compare the two numbers in a different way. Find the missing number in this sentence: The number of students who ordered pizza was __?__ times the number of students who ordered fish.

_____

12. Explain the method you used to solve problem 7. Did you use more than one operation?

_____

_____

_____

Divisibility

A number is divisible by another whole number when it can be divided by that number and there is no remainder.

Example: **21** is divisible by **3** but not by **5**.

$$21 \div 3 = 7 \text{ (no remainder)}$$
$$21 \div 5 = 4 \text{ R1}$$

Use these rules to help you decide if a number is divisible by **2, 5,** or **10.**

A number is divisible by **2** if the ones digit is **0, 2, 4, 6, 8.**	A number is divisible by **5** if the ones digit is **0** or **5.**	A number is divisible by **10** if the ones digit is **0.**
Examples: 30, 42, 54, 86, 128, 508, 724	Examples: 20, 35, 15, 100, 240, 365, 890	Examples: 30, 80, 90, 120, 230, 350, 810

Numbers that are **divisible by 2** are called **even** numbers.

> **Even Numbers**
> 2, 4, 6, 8, 10, 12, 14, 16 . . .

Numbers that are **not divisible by 2** are called **odd** numbers.

> **Odd Numbers**
> 1, 3, 5, 7, 9, 11, 13, 15 . . .

Circle the numbers that are divisible by 2. Use the rule shown above.

1. 30	42	27	63	74	92	140	271
2. 225	306	708	232	473	891	726	982

Circle the numbers that are divisible by 5. Use the rule shown above.

3. 20	37	65	42	55	74	125	102
4. 615	431	336	510	705	600	345	924

Circle the numbers that are divisible by 10. Use the rule shown above.

5. 36	47	60	52	76	40	130	408
6. 330	501	216	460	607	728	930	825

Use these rules to help you decide if a number is divisible by **3** or **9**.

A number is divisible by **3** if the sum of its digits is divisible by **3**. **27** is divisible by **3** since **2 + 7**, or **9**, is divisible by **3**.

Examples: **30, 42, 54, 87, 138, 507, 735**

A number is divisible by **9** if the sum of its digits is divisible by **9**. **36** is divisible by **9** since **3 + 6**, or **9**, is divisible by **9**.

Examples: **18, 72, 99, 108, 216, 594, 864**

Circle the numbers that are divisible by 3.
Use the rule shown above.

7. 15   24   36   45   90   122   35   606

8. 28   447   813   40   69   72   55   33

Circle the numbers that are divisible by 9.
Use the rule shown above.

9. 15   24   36   45   90   22   435   603

10. 28   147   81   240   69   72   855   33

Circle all the even numbers that are divisible by 3.

11. 18   27   36   42   45   54   63   75

 Quick Check

Solve.

Work Space.

12. $2\overline{)615}$

13. $5\overline{)533}$

14. $4\overline{)818}$

15. $9\overline{)\$2.16}$

16. $5\overline{)\$6.75}$

17. $7\overline{)\$9.31}$

18. Circle the numbers that are divisible by both 3 and 2.

    9   12   15   18   21   24

19. Circle all the odd numbers that are divisible by 9.

    27   36   54   63   81   99

Name _____

Factors: Prime and Composite Numbers

A number is a **factor** of another number if it divides that number with no remainder.

factors of 24

1, 2, 3, 4, 6, 8, 12, 24

A factor of a number is also a **divisor** of that number.

24 = 3 × 8
24 ÷ 8 = 3
24 ÷ 3 = 8
3 and **8** are divisors of **24**.

> If a number greater than **1** has **exactly two factors**, **1** and the number itself, it is called a **prime number**. A number having **more than two factors** is called a **composite number**.

The number 1 is neither a prime number nor a composite number. It has only one factor, itself.

Complete by writing each product with as many different pairs of factors as possible. Circle the prime numbers.

1.

1	2	3	4	5
1 × 1				

2.

6	7	8	9	10
1 × 6				
2 × 3				

3.

11	12	13	14	15

4.

16	17	18	19	20

Copyright © Houghton Mifflin Company. All rights reserved.

Unit 4 Lesson 11   97

STANDARD

Finding all the factors of a number is called factoring the number.

Example: Factor **36**.

Write all the pairs of factors.

1 × 36
2 × 18
3 × 12
4 × 9   When a factor repeats, you have
6 × 6 ← found all the factors.

Write the factors in order from least to greatest.

The factors of **36** are **1, 2, 3, 4, 6, 9, 12, 18,** and **36**.

Which list shows all the factors of the number?

5. 24 _____
A 2, 3, 4, 6, 8, 12
B 1, 2, 4, 6, 12,
C 1, 2, 3, 4, 6, 8, 12, 24

6. 21 _____
A 1, 3, 7, 21
B 3, 7
C 1, 21

7. 12 _____
A 1, 3, 4, 12
B 1, 2, 3, 4, 6, 12
C 1, 2, 6, 12

Factor the number.

8. 18

9. 15

10. 25

Problem Solving Reasoning Solve.

11. Are all prime numbers odd numbers? Explain. _____

Test Prep ★ Mixed Review

12 What number should go in the ☐ to make the number sentence true?

$5 \times 36 = 5 \times (30 + \boxed{})$

A 180   C 6
B 30   D 5

13 A school fair has a throwing contest. Each student throws 3 balls to hit a target. If 167 students play, how many balls are thrown in all?

F 321   H 501
G 381   J 521

98 Unit 4 Lesson 11

Copyright © Houghton Mifflin Company. All rights reserved.

When you divide with a **4**-digit number, use the same steps you use for dividing **3**-digit numbers.

Example: $6\overline{)3,587}$

1. Decide if there are enough thousands to divide. If not, regroup and divide hundreds.

   Continue dividing, following the steps you have learned.

   ```
        597 R5
   6)3,587
     -3 0
       58
      -54
       47
      -42
        5
   ```

2. With greater numbers, it is important to check your answer.

   Check: 597
   ```
     ×   6
   3,582
   +   5
   3,587  ← This is the dividend. So
              the answer is correct.
   ```

Divide. Then check.

1. $7\overline{)1,492}$ $6\overline{)4,985}$ $6\overline{)1,305}$

2. $8\overline{)2,870}$ $7\overline{)5,672}$ $7\overline{)6,390}$

Divide and check.

3. 8)5,892   9)8,489   8)5,049

4. 7)2,960   4)2,601   2)1,634

**Problem Solving
Reasoning** | Solve.

5. Leslie has **547** tomato plants. She wants to plant them in **5** equal rows. How many plants can she put in each row? How many plants will be left over?

6. A poultry farm produced **2,364** eggs. The eggs are put in packages of **6**. How many packages can they fill? How many eggs will be left over?

 Quick Check

Solve.   **Work Space.**

7. Find all the factors of 12. _____

8. Find all the factors of 16. _____

9. Circle the prime numbers.

   13   24   33   41   45

10. Circle all the composite numbers that are also odd numbers.

   7   15   21   29   35   41

11. 8)3,752   **12.** 4)2,902   **13.** 6)4,285

Some problems can be solved by working backward.

When working backward, you can often use opposite, or inverse, operations.

Adding and subtracting are inverse operations. Multiplying and dividing are inverse operations.

Problem

On Tuesday, Lauren rode her bike **3 miles** more than on Monday. On Wednesday, she rode **4 miles** less than on Tuesday. On Thursday, she rode twice as far as on the day before. On Friday, she rode **27 miles**. This was **5 miles** more than on Thursday. How far did she ride on Monday?

1 **Understand**   As you reread, organize the information.

Miles Lauren Rode

Mon.	Tues.	Wed.	Thurs.	Fri.
?	3 miles more than Mon.	_____ miles less than Tues.	2 times as many miles as Wed.	_____ miles more than Thurs. or 27

2 **Decide**   Choose a method for solving.

Try the strategy Work Backward.

• Show the operations in the order they are given in the problem.

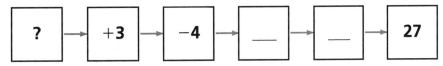

3 **Solve**   Work backward, using inverse operations.

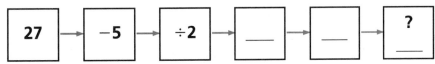

4 **Look back**   Check your answer. Write the answer below.

Answer _____

• Why is it important to go back to the problem to check your answer?

_____

Solve. Use the Work Backward strategy or any other strategy you have learned.

1. A class had a can drive. Cara collected **6** more cans than Diane. Cam collected **8** more cans than Cara. Maria collected twice as many cans as Cam. If Maria collected **76** cans, how many cans did Diane collect?

Think: What information will you start with? Explain.

_____

_____

Answer _____

2. Christina opened a savings account by depositing a check from her aunt. Ten days later, she put in **$12** more. A week later, she took out **$7**. She then had **$45** in her account. What was the amount of the check from Christina's aunt?

Think: What information will you start with? Explain.

_____

_____

Answer _____

3. Draw the missing figure in this sequence.

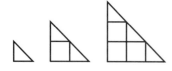

_____

4. Akil is thinking of a mystery number. If he divides his number by **4** and then multiplies it by **5**, the result is **135**. What is Akil's mystery number?

_____

5. On Monday, Mr. Riccio filled up his tank with gasoline. He then used up **6** gallons. On Tuesday, he used up **3** more gallons. On Wednesday, he put in **7** gallons. He then had **10** gallons of gasoline in the tank. How many gallons does the tank hold?

_____

6. A store owner had a large supply of purple shoes. The owner made the price **$5** less. There were still many pairs left. The store then sold them for half of the lower price. The new price was **$14**. What was the original price of the shoes?

_____

7. Look at the numbers in this sequence. What is the next number?

8,000, 4,000, 2,000, 1,000

_____

8. Lucy buys jeans and a shirt. The shirt costs half as much as the jeans. The total cost is **$36**. How much do the jeans cost?

_____

Suppose you went on a three-day hike. You walked **15** miles the first day, **21** miles the second day, and **12** miles the third day. You want to know the average number of miles you walked each day.

An **average** is a special way of describing a group of numbers. Here's one way to think about it.

1. Make **3** stacks of counters to show the number of miles you walked each of **3** days.

2. Put the stacks of counters together in one group.

3. Divide the group of counters into **3** equal stacks—one stack for each day.

Record the number of counters in each stack.

15, 21, 12

Find the total number of counters.

15 + 21 + 12 = 48

Find the number in each stack.

48 ÷ 3 = 16

You walked an average of **16** miles each day.

To find an average:

1. Add the given numbers.

2. Count the addends.

3. Divide the sum by the number of addends.

Write the number you divide by to find the average. Then find the average.

1. **2, 5, 4, 12, 7**

Divide by _____ Average _____

2. **25, 38, 42**

Divide by _____ Average _____

Write the number you divide by to find the average. Then find the average.

3. 76, 125, 117, 86

Divide by _____. Average _____

4. 132, 129, 138

Divide by _____. Average _____

Find the average.

5. 10, 8, 6

6. 9, 14, 7

7. 15, 10, 11

8. 68¢ 82¢, 96¢

9. 68, 93, 46

10. 98, 85, 75

| Problem Solving |
| Reasoning |

Solve.

11. Mario's class collected cans for recycling. They collected **76** cans the first day, **64** cans the second day, **116** cans the third day, and **92** cans the fourth day. What was the average number of cans they collected a day?

_____

12. Diane bowled **3** games. She knocked down **93** pins in the first game, **84** pins in the second, and **114** in the third. What was the average number of pins she knocked down in each game?

_____

13. Do you need to add and divide to find the average of these numbers: **45, 45, 45**? Explain.

_____

_____

14. List three numbers that have an average of **125**. Explain how you chose the three numbers.

_____

_____

Test Prep ★ Mixed Review

15 Which of the following is a prime number?

A 15

B 28

C 37

D 42

16 Which group of numbers shows all the factors of 15?

F 1, 3, 5, 15

G 1, 2, 3, 7, 15

H 1, 5, 15

J 15, 30, 45

Sometimes, when you divide greater numbers, the quotient will have four digits.

Long Division	Short Division	Long Division	Short Division

```
   1, 0 9 5
8)8, 7 6 0
 −8
   7 6
  −7 2
     4 0
    −4 0
       0
```

```
   1, 0 9 5
8) 8, 7⁷6⁴0
```

Think: Regoup 7 hundred 6 tens as 76 tens

```
    8,701 R1
2)17,403
 −16
   1 4
  −1 4
     03
    − 2
      1
```

```
   8, 701 R1
2)17,¹403
```

Think:
17 thousands − 16 thousands = 1 thousand.
Regroup 1 thousand 4 hundred as 14 hundreds.

Divide. Use long division.

1.
```
   3,
2)7,395
```

```
   4,
3)14,276
```

```
   1,
4)7,053
```

```
   2,
5)12,607
```

2. 6)19,490   6)7,156   7)52,613   7)9,273

3. 3)7,164   3)23,075   9)26,183   2)7,161

4. 6)10,538   3)1,538   5)3,932   4)9,387

Divide. Use short division. Check your work.

5. 8)8,402   5)4,407   7)5,675   7)756

6. 4)8,023   6)6,125   5)5,042   2)3,873

Problem Solving
Reasoning

Solve.

7. A total of **5,130** fans watched the first **6** soccer games of the season. What was the average number of fans for each game?

_____

8. Lisa's family is driving **2,569** miles in **7** days. If they want to drive the same distance every day, how many miles should they drive each day?

_____

 Quick Check

Find the average for each set of numbers.   **Work Space.**

9. 12, 13, 14   **10.** 17, 28, 36   **11.** 65, 68, 69, 74

_____   _____   _____

Divide.

12. 6)7,759   **13.** 8)9,606   **14.** 4)18,238

Use the order of operations to find the value of each expression.

1. $4 \times (6 + 3)$ **2.** $30 - 5 \times 5$ **3.** $4 + 9 \div 3$ **4.** $8 \times (4 \div 2)$

Divide.

5. $9\overline{)39}$ **6.** $3\overline{)262}$ **7.** $6\overline{)\$6.24}$ **8.** $7\overline{)2,447}$

Use divisiblity rule to solve.

9. Circle the numbers that are divisible by both **5** and **2**.

25   40   55   70   80   95

10. Circle the numbers that are divisible by both **2** and **3**.

20   36   42   45   50   78

Complete by writing the products with as many different pairs of factors as possible. Circle the prime numbers.

11. 24   **12.** 28   **13.** 67   **14.** 42

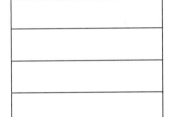 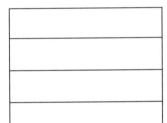 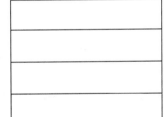 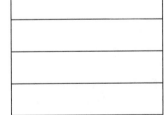

Find the average of each set of numbers.

15. 3, 7, 2, 8, 10   **16.** 21, 34, 53   **17.** 49¢, 18¢, 27¢, 14¢

Solve.

18. The clerk gave Tanya **$4.50** in change when she bought **3** notebooks for **$3.50** each, including tax. How much money did Tanya give the clerk?

_____

19. Terry paid **$1.35**, including tax, for **3** pens. Each pen was the same price. What was the price of each pen?

_____

Name _____

1 The Levitt family drove from San Francisco to Kansas City, Missouri. They drove the distances shown.

Cities	Distances
From San Francisco, California to Reno, Nevada	**215** miles
From Reno, Nevada to Aspen, Colorado	**940** miles
From Aspen, Colorado to Kansas City, Missouri	**804** miles

How far did they drive in all?

A 1,959 miles   D 1,859 miles

B 1,949 miles   E NH

C 1,895 miles

2 Angela is counting telephone poles from the window of a moving train. She counts 12 poles in 1 minute. *About* how many will she count in 1 hour?

F 500   H 5,000   K NH

G 600   J 6,000

3 Which group of numbers shows all the factors of 16?

A 1, 2, 3, 6, 16   C 1, 3, 9, 15, 16

B 1, 2, 4, 8, 16   D 1, 7, 8, 16

4 An airplane trip from Los Angeles to San Francisco and back again is **688** miles. Ms. Lee flies this distance 21 times in a year. How many miles has she flown all together?

F 17,248   H 14,248   K NH

G 14,448   J 2,354

5 Mr. Ivanson drove from Stockton, California, to Portland, Oregon, along the road shown.

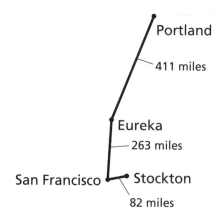

About how many miles did he drive?

A 400   C 800

B 600   D 1,000

6 The chart shows the number of students in 4 different schools.

School	Number of Students
School A	705
School B	457
School C	962
School D	926

Which shows the number of students in order from *greatest* to *least*?

F School D, School C, School A, School B

G School C, School A, School D, School B

H School C, School D, School A, School B

J School B, School A, School D, School C

Fractions and Mixed Numbers

Dear Family,

During the next few weeks, our math class will be learning about fractions and mixed numbers.

You can expect to see homework that provides practice with writing equivalent fractions. Here is a sample you may want to keep handy to give help if needed.

Writing Equivalent Fractions

For any given fraction, you can use multiplication or division to write equivalent fractions.

Example: Write three equivalent fractions for $\frac{3}{4}$.

Multiply the numerator (top number) and denominator (bottom number) of the fraction $\frac{3}{4}$ by the same number.

$$\frac{3 \times 2}{4 \times 2} = \frac{6}{8} \qquad \frac{3 \times 5}{4 \times 5} = \frac{15}{20} \qquad \frac{3 \times 10}{4 \times 10} = \frac{30}{40}$$

The fractions $\frac{6}{8}$, $\frac{15}{20}$, and $\frac{30}{40}$ are equivalent fractions for $\frac{3}{4}$.

Example: Write three equivalent fractions for $\frac{32}{48}$.

Divide the numerator (top number) and denominator (bottom number) of the fraction $\frac{32}{48}$ by the same number.

$$\frac{32 \div 2}{48 \div 2} = \frac{16}{24} \qquad \frac{32 \div 4}{48 \div 4} = \frac{8}{12} \qquad \frac{32 \div 16}{48 \div 16} = \frac{2}{3}$$

The fractions $\frac{16}{24}$, $\frac{8}{12}$, and $\frac{2}{3}$ are equivalent fractions for $\frac{32}{48}$.

During this unit, students will need to continue practicing multiplication and division facts.

Sincerely,

A **multiple** is the product of a number and another whole number. The number line shows some multiples of **3**.

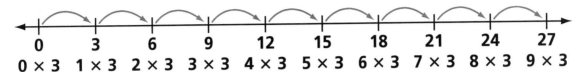

0	3	6	9	12	15	18	21	24	27
0 × 3	1 × 3	2 × 3	3 × 3	4 × 3	5 × 3	6 × 3	7 × 3	8 × 3	9 × 3

> A number that is a multiple of another number is also divisible by the first number.

21 is a multiple of **3**.
21 is also divisible by **3** and the remainder is **0**.

$$\overset{\textbf{7 R 0}}{3\overline{)21}}$$

16 is *not* a multiple of **3**.
16 is also *not* divisible by **3**.

$$\overset{\textbf{5 R 1}}{3\overline{)16}} \leftarrow$$ The remainder is not zero.

Complete the list of all the multiples shown on each number line.

1. Multiples of **4**

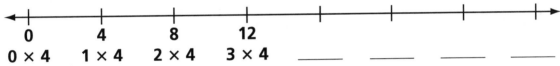

0	4	8	12
0 × 4	1 × 4	2 × 4	3 × 4	____	____	____	____

2. Multiples of **7**

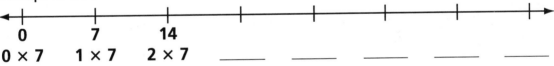

0	7	14
0 × 7	1 × 7	2 × 7	____	____	____	____

3. Multiples of **8**

0	8	16
0 × 8	1 × 8	2 × 8	____	____	____	____

4. Multiples of **9**

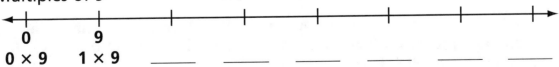

0	9
0 × 9	1 × 9	____	____	____	____	____

5. Multiples of **5**

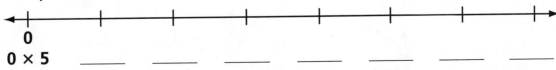

0
0 × 5	____	____	____	____	____	____

A multiple that is the same for two or more numbers is called a **common multiple**.

To find some common multiples of **3** and **5**, first list some of the multiples of each number. Then circle the multiples that are the same in both lists.

Multiples of 3: 3, 6, 9, 12, (15,) 18, 21, 24, 27, (30,) . . .
Multiples of 5: 5, 10, (15,) 20, 25, (30,) 35, 40, 45, . . .

So, **15** and **30** are common multiples of both **3** and **5**.

Complete the lists of multiples. Circle the common multiples.

6. Multiples of 2: 26, 28, ——, ——, ——, ——, 38, ——

Multiples of 5: 25, ——, ——, ——, 45

7. Multiples of 3: 30, 33, ——, ——, ——, ——, 48, ——, ——

Multiples of 4: 28, ——, 36, ——, ——, ——, ——, ——

8. Multiples of 6: ——, ——, ——, 54, ——, ——, ——, 78, ——, ——

Multiples of 9: ——, ——, 45, ——, ——, ——, ——, ——, 99

Problem Solving Reasoning Find multiples and common multiples to solve each problem.

9. Are all multiples of **9** also multiples of **3**? Explain.

_____

10. What are the first three common multiples of **5** and **6**?

_____

Test Prep ★ Mixed Review

11 An athlete runs around a track. Each complete trip around is 422 yards. He runs around the track 4 times. About how many yards does he run?

A 1,200   C 1,800
B 1,600   D 2,400

12 Which group of numbers shows all the factors of 36?

F 1, 2, 3, 4, 6, 9, 12, 18, 36
G 1, 3, 8, 10, 21, 36
H 1, 2, 5, 7, 13, 36
J 1, 2, 4, 8, 16, 36

Equivalent Fractions

Fractions that name the same number are called **equivalent fractions**. You can use number lines to find equivalent fractions.

The fraction $\frac{1}{2}$ is halfway between **0** and **1**.

The fractions $\frac{2}{4}$ and $\frac{4}{8}$ are also halfway between **0** and **1**.

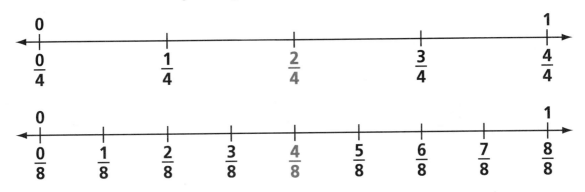

So, $\frac{1}{2}$, $\frac{2}{4}$, and $\frac{4}{8}$ are equivalent fractions.

Complete using the number lines above.

1. Write one equivalent fraction for $\frac{3}{4}$. _____

2. Write one equivalent fraction for $\frac{1}{4}$. _____

3. Write two equivalent fractions for $\frac{8}{8}$. _____, _____

4. Write two equivalent fractions for $\frac{1}{2}$. _____, _____

5. Write three equivalent fractions for **0**. _____, _____, _____

6. Write three equivalent fractions for **1**. _____, _____, _____

You can also use fraction models to find equivalent fractions.

$\frac{1}{4} = \frac{2}{8}$ or $\frac{1}{4} = \frac{3}{12}$ $\frac{3}{4} = \frac{6}{8}$ or $\frac{3}{4} = \frac{9}{12}$

Write a pair of equivalent fractions for each picture.

7.
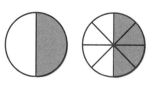

_____

8.

_____

9.
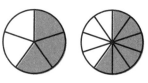

_____

10.
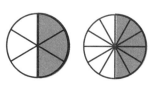

_____

11.
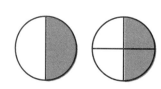

_____

12.
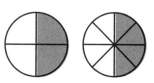

_____

Problem Solving Reasoning — Solve. Which fraction comes next in the pattern?

13. $\frac{1}{2}, \frac{1}{4}, \frac{1}{6}, \frac{1}{8}, \frac{1}{10},$ _____

14. $\frac{1}{3}, \frac{3}{9}, \frac{9}{27}, \frac{27}{81},$ _____

Test Prep ★ Mixed Review

15 What number should go in the ☐ to make the number sentence true?

$(5 \times 2) \times 4 = \boxed{} \times (2 \times 4)$

A 5

B 4

C 2

D 1

16 A factory makes and ships 1,120 model airplane kits in one day. One shipping carton holds 8 model kits. How many shipping cartons does the factory use in one day?

F 139

G 140

H 141

J 142

Equivalent Fractions and Simplest Form

You can use multiplication or division to find equivalent fractions.

Use **multiplication** to find equivalent fractions for $\frac{3}{4}$. Multiply the numerator and denominator by the same number.

$$\frac{3 \times 2}{4 \times 2} = \frac{6}{8} \qquad \frac{3 \times 3}{4 \times 3} = \frac{9}{12}$$

So, $\frac{3}{4}$, $\frac{6}{8}$, and $\frac{9}{12}$ are equivalent fractions.

Use **division** to find equivalent fractions for $\frac{8}{12}$. Divide the numerator and denominator by the same number.

$$\frac{8 \div 2}{12 \div 2} = \frac{4}{6} \qquad \frac{4 \div 2}{6 \div 2} = \frac{2}{3}$$

So, $\frac{8}{12}$, $\frac{4}{6}$, and $\frac{2}{3}$ are equivalent fractions.

A fraction is in **simplest form** when **1** is the only number that will divide both the numerator and denominator evenly.

These fractions are in simplest form.

$$\frac{2}{3} \quad \frac{3}{4} \quad \frac{1}{6} \quad \frac{7}{8}$$

These fractions are not in simplest form.

$$\frac{2}{4} \quad \frac{4}{6} \quad \frac{6}{8} \quad \frac{4}{10}$$

Complete to find equivalent fractions.

1. $\dfrac{3 \times 4}{4 \times} = \underline{}$ $\qquad$ $\dfrac{2 \times}{3 \times 3} = \dfrac{6}{}$ $\qquad$ $\dfrac{1 \times}{5 \times} = \dfrac{5}{}$ $\qquad$ $\dfrac{1 \times 2}{8 \times 2} = \underline{}$

2. $\dfrac{1 \times}{8 \times} = \dfrac{2}{}$ $\qquad$ $\dfrac{2 \times 6}{5 \times} = \underline{}$ $\qquad$ $\dfrac{5 \times}{8 \times} = \dfrac{20}{}$ $\qquad$ $\dfrac{1 \times}{5 \times} = \underline{}$

Write the equivalent fraction.

3. $\dfrac{2}{3} = \dfrac{}{6}$ $\qquad$ $\dfrac{1}{4} = \dfrac{}{12}$ $\qquad$ $\dfrac{3}{8} = \dfrac{}{16}$ $\qquad$ $\dfrac{2}{9} = \dfrac{}{27}$

4. $\dfrac{2}{5} = \dfrac{}{15}$ $\qquad$ $\dfrac{1}{6} = \dfrac{}{24}$ $\qquad$ $\dfrac{2}{7} = \dfrac{}{14}$ $\qquad$ $\dfrac{4}{5} = \dfrac{}{25}$

Divide to find the equivalent fraction.

5. $\dfrac{3 \div}{6 \div} = \underline{}$ $\qquad$ $\dfrac{3 \div}{12 \div} = \underline{}$ $\qquad$ $\dfrac{5 \div}{25 \div} = \underline{}$

6. $\dfrac{9 \div}{12 \div} = \underline{}$ $\qquad$ $\dfrac{18 \div}{20 \div} = \underline{}$ $\qquad$ $\dfrac{14 \div}{16 \div} = \underline{}$

Write each fraction in simplest form.

7. $\frac{4}{6}$ _____ $\frac{6}{8}$ _____ $\frac{3}{15}$ _____ $\frac{6}{9}$ _____ $\frac{8}{10}$ _____ $\frac{4}{16}$ _____

8. $\frac{9}{12}$ _____ $\frac{5}{10}$ _____ $\frac{12}{16}$ _____ $\frac{10}{12}$ _____ $\frac{2}{12}$ _____ $\frac{7}{14}$ _____

9. $\frac{4}{8}$ _____ $\frac{6}{10}$ _____ $\frac{8}{12}$ _____ $\frac{2}{6}$ _____ $\frac{2}{8}$ _____ $\frac{6}{12}$ _____

Is each fraction in simplest form? Write *yes* or *no*.

10. $\frac{4}{8}$ _____ $\frac{2}{3}$ _____ $\frac{4}{5}$ _____ $\frac{7}{12}$ _____ $\frac{3}{12}$ _____

11. $\frac{5}{15}$ _____ $\frac{2}{16}$ _____ $\frac{1}{6}$ _____ $\frac{5}{8}$ _____ $\frac{12}{15}$ _____

✓ Quick Check

Write the common multiples of each pair of numbers up to 50.

Work Space.

12. 3 and 5 _____   **13.** 4 and 6 _____

14. 3 and 7 _____

Write three equivalent fractions for each fraction model.

15. $\frac{3}{4}$ _____   **16.** $\frac{2}{3}$ _____   **17.** $\frac{4}{5}$ _____

Write each fraction in simplest form.

18. $\frac{4}{12}$ _____   **19.** $\frac{6}{10}$ _____   **20.** $\frac{4}{8}$ _____

Name _____

STANDARD

You can use a number line to compare and order fractions.

Compare $\frac{3}{4}$? $\frac{2}{4}$.

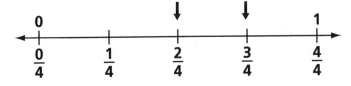

Find each fraction on the number line.

$\frac{3}{4}$ is to the right of $\frac{2}{4}$ $\frac{3}{4}$ is greater than $\frac{2}{4}$ $\frac{3}{4}$ > $\frac{2}{4}$

Order $\frac{2}{8}$, $\frac{7}{8}$, and $\frac{5}{8}$ from least to greatest.

Find each fraction on the number line.

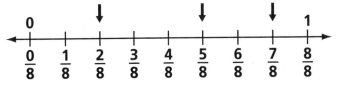

• $\frac{2}{8}$ is to the left of both $\frac{7}{8}$ and $\frac{5}{8}$.

$\frac{2}{8}$ is the least fraction.

• $\frac{7}{8}$ is to the right of both $\frac{2}{8}$ and $\frac{5}{8}$.

$\frac{7}{8}$ is the greatest fraction.

Ordered from least to greatest: $\frac{2}{8}$ $\frac{5}{8}$ $\frac{7}{8}$

If two fractions have like denominators, you can compare the number of equal parts or numerators.

Compare $\frac{5}{12}$? $\frac{7}{12}$.

$\frac{5}{12}$ and $\frac{7}{12}$ have the same denominator.

Since **7** is greater than **5**, then:

$\frac{7}{12}$ > $\frac{5}{12}$

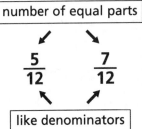

Use the number lines to compare the fractions. Write <, >, or =.

1. $\frac{1}{4} \bigcirc \frac{3}{4}$ $\frac{2}{4} \bigcirc \frac{1}{4}$ $\frac{7}{8} \bigcirc \frac{5}{8}$ $\frac{3}{8} \bigcirc \frac{7}{8}$

Write the following in order from the least to the greatest.

2. $\frac{1}{8}, \frac{3}{8}, \frac{5}{8}, \frac{4}{8}, \frac{0}{8}, \frac{7}{8}$ ____, ____, ____, ____, ____, ____

You can also compare and order fractions that have unlike denominators.

Compare $\frac{3}{5}$ (?) $\frac{7}{10}$.

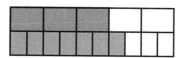

1. Write both fractions with like denominators. Find an equivalent fraction.

$$\frac{3 \times 2}{5 \times 2} = \frac{6}{10} \rightarrow \frac{6}{10} \, (?) \, \frac{7}{10}$$

2. Compare the numerators. Since **7** is greater than **6** then:

$$\frac{6}{10} \, (<) \, \frac{7}{10}. \text{ So, } \frac{3}{5} \, (<) \, \frac{7}{10}$$

Compare each pair of fractions. Write <, >, or =.

3. $\frac{2}{3} \bigcirc \frac{1}{6}$ $\frac{3}{8} \bigcirc \frac{3}{4}$ $\frac{1}{5} \bigcirc \frac{1}{10}$ $\frac{1}{3} \bigcirc \frac{2}{9}$

4. $\frac{3}{8} \bigcirc \frac{1}{4}$ $\frac{1}{3} \bigcirc \frac{5}{9}$ $\frac{5}{6} \bigcirc \frac{1}{2}$ $\frac{4}{6} \bigcirc \frac{2}{3}$

Write the fractions in order from the least to the greatest.

5. $\frac{1}{2}, \frac{3}{8}, \frac{1}{4}, \frac{0}{2}, \frac{4}{4}, \frac{7}{8}$ _____, _____, _____, _____, _____, _____

6. $\frac{1}{3}, \frac{5}{6}, \frac{2}{3}, \frac{1}{6}, \frac{1}{2}$ _____, _____, _____, _____, _____

Problem Solving Reasoning   Solve.

7. Compare $\frac{1}{12}$ and $\frac{1}{15}$ without finding equivalent fractions. Explain how you know which fraction is greater.

_____

_____

Test Prep ★ Mixed Review

 8 What number is the common factor of both 14 and 28?

    A 3   C 7

    B 4   D 8

9 Which fraction represents the shaded portion of the model?

    F $\frac{1}{3}$ H $\frac{1}{2}$

    G $\frac{3}{6}$ J $\frac{4}{6}$

You can estimate where to place fractions on a number line.

Place $\frac{4}{6}$ between **0** and **1** on a number line.

1. Divide the number line into six equal parts.

2. Then count to $\frac{4}{6}$.

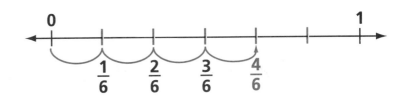

Estimate. Place the fractions on the number line.

1. $\frac{1}{4}$ $\frac{2}{4}$ $\frac{3}{4}$

2. $\frac{2}{5}$ $\frac{3}{5}$ $\frac{4}{5}$

3. $\frac{1}{8}$ $\frac{4}{8}$ $\frac{7}{8}$

4. $\frac{1}{6}$ $\frac{5}{6}$ $\frac{3}{6}$

5. $\frac{3}{8}$ $\frac{2}{8}$ $\frac{5}{8}$

6. $\frac{1}{10}$ $\frac{4}{10}$ $\frac{7}{10}$

Where would you place $\frac{1}{4}$ on this number line?

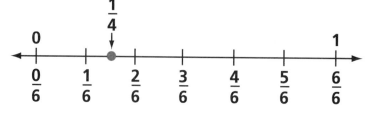

$\frac{1}{4}$

0   1

$\frac{0}{6}$ $\frac{1}{6}$ $\frac{2}{6}$ $\frac{3}{6}$ $\frac{4}{6}$ $\frac{5}{6}$ $\frac{6}{6}$

Estimate. Place the fractions on the number line.

7. $\frac{1}{4}$ $\frac{5}{6}$ $\frac{3}{8}$

0   1

8. $\frac{3}{4}$ $\frac{1}{3}$ $\frac{5}{8}$

0   1

Problem Solving Reasoning

Place each fraction on the number line. Then explain.

9. $\frac{1}{3}$

0   1

$\frac{1}{4}$ $\frac{2}{4}$ $\frac{3}{4}$

_____

10. $\frac{1}{4}$

0   1

$\frac{1}{5}$ $\frac{2}{5}$ $\frac{3}{5}$ $\frac{4}{5}$

_____

 Quick Check

Write >, <, or =.

11. $\frac{1}{3}$ ◯ $\frac{1}{4}$ **12.** $\frac{2}{5}$ ◯ $\frac{4}{10}$ **13.** $\frac{3}{4}$ ◯ $\frac{5}{8}$

Work Space.

Write the letter of the point that shows the position of each fraction on the number line.

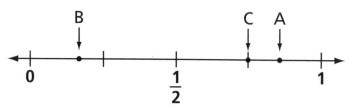

B   C   A

0          $\frac{1}{2}$ 1

14. $\frac{3}{4}$ _____   **15.** $\frac{5}{6}$ _____   **16.** $\frac{1}{5}$ _____

Name _____

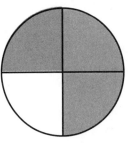

You can use models to add fractions with like denominators.

In the figure, the region shaded red represents the fraction $\frac{1}{4}$. The region shaded gray represents the fraction $\frac{2}{4}$. The total shaded region is $\frac{3}{4}$.

$$\frac{1}{4} + \frac{2}{4} = \frac{3}{4}$$

Use one color to shade the first addend and another color for the second addend. Then find each sum.

1.
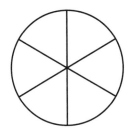
$$\frac{2}{6} + \frac{3}{6} = \underline{\quad}$$

2.
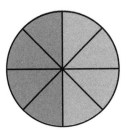
$$\frac{4}{8} + \frac{4}{8} = \underline{\quad}$$

3.
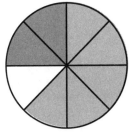
$$\frac{2}{8} + \frac{5}{8} = \underline{\quad}$$

4.
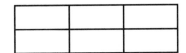
$$\frac{1}{6} + \frac{5}{6} = \underline{\quad}$$

5.
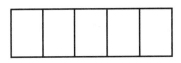
$$\frac{2}{5} + \frac{2}{5} = \underline{\quad}$$

6.

$$\frac{1}{3} + \frac{1}{3} = \underline{\quad}$$

7.
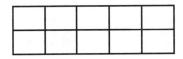
$$\frac{2}{10} + \frac{3}{10} = \underline{\quad}$$

8.

$$\frac{1}{2} + \frac{1}{2} = \underline{\quad}$$

9.
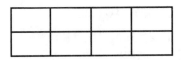
$$\frac{2}{8} + \frac{5}{8} = \underline{\quad}$$

Shaded regions can help you find a missing addend or sum.

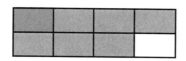

$\frac{2}{6} + \underline{\quad ? \quad} = \frac{6}{6}$

$\frac{1}{8} + \underline{\quad ? \quad} = \frac{7}{8}$

$\frac{3}{10} + \frac{4}{10} = \underline{\quad ? \quad}$

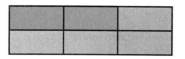

$\frac{2}{6} + \frac{4}{6} = \frac{6}{6}$

$\frac{1}{8} + \frac{6}{8} = \frac{7}{8}$

$\frac{3}{10} + \frac{4}{10} = \frac{7}{10}$

Find the missing addend.

10.

$\frac{1}{4} + \underline{\qquad} = \frac{3}{4}$

11.

$\frac{2}{5} + \underline{\qquad} = \frac{4}{5}$

Find the missing addend or sum.

12. $\frac{1}{6} + \frac{3}{6} = \underline{\qquad}$ $\quad$ $\frac{1}{4} + \underline{\qquad} = \frac{4}{4}$ $\quad$ $\frac{3}{8} + \frac{4}{8} = \underline{\qquad}$ $\quad$ $\frac{3}{10} + \underline{\qquad} = \frac{8}{10}$

Problem Solving Reasoning

Solve. Draw a picture if you need to.

13. Mike walked $\frac{3}{16}$ mile to one store. Then he walked $\frac{4}{16}$ mile to another store. How far did he walk altogether? $\underline{\qquad}$

14. Kim lives between Rick and Peter. She lives $\frac{3}{8}$ mile from Rick and $\frac{2}{8}$ mile from Peter. How far does Rick live from Peter? $\underline{\qquad}$

Test Prep ★ Mixed Review

15 Which group of numbers shows all the factors of 18?

A 1, 2, 3, 6, 9, 18

B 1, 2, 4, 8, 18

C 2, 8, 9, 10, 16

D 1, 2, 3, 8, 16, 18

16 Which fraction is equivalent to $\frac{4}{12}$?

F $\frac{1}{8}$

G $\frac{1}{4}$

H $\frac{2}{6}$

J $\frac{1}{2}$

Subtracting Like Fractions

You can use models to subtract fractions.

Find $\frac{6}{9} - \frac{4}{9}$.

$\frac{6}{9}$ — $\frac{4}{9}$ = $\frac{2}{9}$

6 shaded figures   cross out **4** shaded figures   **2** shaded figures left

Find $\frac{5}{8} - \frac{2}{8}$.

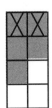

$\frac{5}{8}$ — $\frac{2}{8}$ = $\frac{3}{8}$

5 shaded parts   cross out **2** shaded parts   **3** shaded parts left

---

Find each difference.

1.
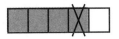

$\frac{4}{5} - \frac{1}{5} = \frac{}{5}$ $\frac{4}{7} - \frac{3}{7} = $ _____ $\frac{5}{10} - \frac{5}{10} = $ _____

2.

$\frac{4}{6} - \frac{2}{6} = $ _____ $\frac{5}{6} - \frac{2}{6} = $ _____ $\frac{6}{8} - \frac{4}{8} = $ _____ $\frac{2}{3} - \frac{1}{3} = $ _____

Subtract.

3. $\frac{8}{8} - \frac{7}{8} = $ _____ $\frac{4}{5} - \frac{3}{5} = $ _____ $\frac{5}{6} - \frac{3}{6} = $ _____ $\frac{3}{7} - \frac{2}{7} = $ _____

4. $\frac{1}{3} - \frac{1}{3} = $ _____ $\frac{3}{4} - \frac{2}{4} = $ _____ $\frac{6}{6} - \frac{1}{6} = $ _____ $\frac{4}{8} - \frac{1}{8} = $ _____

Subtract.

5. $\dfrac{4}{9} - \dfrac{3}{9} =$ _____ $\dfrac{6}{8} - \dfrac{1}{8} =$ _____ $\dfrac{3}{4} - \dfrac{1}{4} =$ _____ $\dfrac{2}{2} - \dfrac{1}{2} =$ _____

6. $\dfrac{5}{8} - \dfrac{4}{8} =$ _____ $\dfrac{3}{5} - \dfrac{1}{5} =$ _____ $\dfrac{7}{9} - \dfrac{5}{9} =$ _____ $\dfrac{3}{4} - \dfrac{3}{4} =$ _____

Add or subtract.

7. $\dfrac{0}{4} + \dfrac{3}{4} =$ _____ $\dfrac{3}{9} - \dfrac{1}{9} =$ _____ $\dfrac{2}{7} + \dfrac{4}{7} =$ _____ $\dfrac{5}{8} - \dfrac{2}{8} =$ _____

8. $\dfrac{2}{4} - \dfrac{2}{4} =$ _____ $\dfrac{3}{12} + \dfrac{2}{12} =$ _____ $\dfrac{2}{9} + \dfrac{3}{9} =$ _____ $\dfrac{4}{15} + \dfrac{7}{15} =$ _____

Problem Solving Reasoning   **Solve.**

9. Eddie was making cookies. The recipe called for $\dfrac{3}{4}$ cup milk and $\dfrac{1}{4}$ cup honey. How much more milk than honey did Eddie add?

_____

10. The sum of two fractions is $\dfrac{7}{12}$. There difference is $\dfrac{1}{12}$. They have the same denominator. What are the two fractions?

_____

 Quick Check

Solve.   **Work Space.**

11. $\dfrac{1}{3} + \dfrac{1}{3}$ _____   **12.** $\dfrac{6}{8} + \dfrac{1}{8}$ _____

13. $\dfrac{3}{6} + \dfrac{2}{6}$ _____   **14.** $\dfrac{4}{7} + \dfrac{2}{7}$ _____

15. $\dfrac{2}{3} - \dfrac{1}{3}$ _____   **16.** $\dfrac{7}{8} - \dfrac{6}{8}$ _____

17. $\dfrac{5}{6} - \dfrac{1}{6}$ _____   **18.** $\dfrac{8}{9} - \dfrac{3}{9}$ _____

Name _____

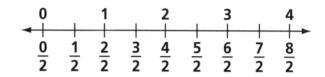
Mixed Numbers
STANDARD

Some fractions name numbers between **0** and **1**. Other fractions name numbers equal to or greater than **1**.

Some fractions name whole numbers. This number line is labeled with whole numbers and fractions.

To show **2** halves in **1**, write $\frac{2}{2} = 1$.   To show **8** halves in **4**, write $\frac{8}{2} = 4$.

Some fractions name numbers between whole numbers.

The number halfway between **1** and **2** is **3** halves or $\frac{3}{2}$.

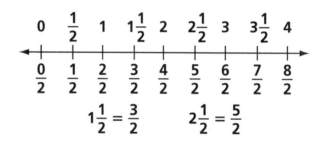

Mixed numbers are another way of writing fractions greater than **1**. A **mixed number** has a whole number part and a fraction part. This number line is labeled with whole numbers, fractions, and mixed numbers.

Write the missing whole numbers, fractions, and mixed numbers.

1.

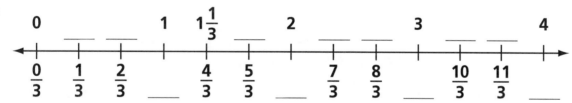

Write mixed numbers for the shaded regions.

2.

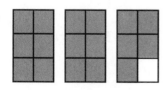

_____ wholes and _____ sixths

_____

3.

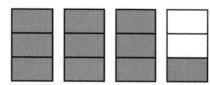

_____ wholes and _____ third

_____

Write a mixed number and a fraction for the shaded parts.

4.

_____ _____

5.

_____ _____

6.

_____ _____

7.

_____ _____

Write a mixed number for the fraction.

8. $\dfrac{9}{4}$ _____ $\dfrac{14}{6}$ _____ $\dfrac{11}{2}$ _____ $\dfrac{17}{3}$ _____

9. $\dfrac{23}{10}$ _____ $\dfrac{17}{8}$ _____ $\dfrac{18}{5}$ _____ $\dfrac{11}{4}$ _____

| Problem Solving |
| Reasoning |

Solve. Draw pictures if you need to.

10. There are **3** pizzas. Each one is cut into **8** slices. Write a fraction to show the total number of eighths.

_____

11. Of the **3** pizzas, you eat **3** slices. Write a mixed number to show the amount of pizza that remains.

_____

Test Prep ★ Mixed Review

12 Which of the following is a prime number?

A 36

B 21

C 18

D 2

13 A total of 2,707,588 people bought tickets to see a movie on its opening weekend. What is the number rounded to the nearest hundred thousand?

F 3,000,000   H 2,070,00

G 2,700,000   J 2,007,000

Adding and Subtracting Mixed Numbers

STANDARD

You can add and subtract with mixed numbers.

Find: $3\frac{3}{5} + 1\frac{1}{5}$.

1. Add fractions.   **2.** Add whole numbers.

$3\frac{3}{5}$
$+ 1\frac{1}{5}$
_____
$\frac{4}{5}$

Think:
3 fifths
+ 1 fifth
_____
4 fifths

$3\frac{3}{5}$
$+ 1\frac{1}{5}$
_____
$4\frac{4}{5}$

Find: $3\frac{3}{5} - 1\frac{1}{5}$.

1. Subtract fractions.   **2.** Subtract whole numbers.

$3\frac{3}{5}$
$- 1\frac{1}{5}$
_____
$\frac{2}{5}$

Think:
3 fifths
− 1 fifth
_____
2 fifths

$3\frac{3}{5}$
$- 1\frac{1}{5}$
_____
$2\frac{2}{5}$

Add.

1.

$4\frac{1}{3}$
$+ 2\frac{1}{3}$

$5\frac{3}{6}$
$+ 2\frac{1}{6}$

6
$+ 3\frac{5}{8}$

$7\frac{3}{4}$
$+ 1$

$8\frac{1}{5}$
$+ \frac{2}{5}$

$\frac{3}{10}$
$+ 2\frac{4}{10}$

Subtract.

2.

$7\frac{5}{8}$
$- 1\frac{2}{8}$

$9\frac{3}{5}$
$- 2\frac{1}{5}$

$4\frac{5}{6}$
$- 3$

$5\frac{1}{3}$
$- 2\frac{1}{3}$

$6\frac{3}{4}$
$- \frac{3}{4}$

$8\frac{5}{10}$
$- 5\frac{4}{10}$

Add or subtract. Watch the signs.

3.

$3\frac{3}{9}$
$+ 1\frac{5}{9}$

$7\frac{4}{5}$
$- 5\frac{3}{5}$

$8\frac{2}{6}$
$+ 4\frac{2}{6}$

$7\frac{2}{3}$
$- 3\frac{1}{3}$

4
$+ 4\frac{2}{3}$

$9\frac{4}{5}$
$- 9\frac{4}{5}$

4.

$3\frac{3}{4}$
$- 1\frac{2}{4}$

$6\frac{1}{4}$
$+ 3\frac{2}{4}$

$7\frac{1}{3}$
$- \frac{1}{3}$

$8\frac{1}{12}$
$+ 2\frac{4}{12}$

$1\frac{3}{4}$
$- \frac{1}{4}$

$2\frac{3}{8}$
$+ 4\frac{4}{8}$

Problem Solving | Reasoning Solve.

5. Damon had $9\frac{1}{4}$ feet of string. He used $7\frac{1}{4}$ feet of the string to tie up a package. How much string was left?

_____

6. Sandy was $5\frac{2}{4}$ feet tall last year. This year he is $5\frac{3}{4}$ feet tall. How much has he grown since last year?

_____

7. Marilyn mailed a package that contained a book. The book weighed $2\frac{4}{8}$ pounds. The entire package weighed $2\frac{7}{8}$ pounds. How much did the mailing materials weigh? _____

8. Julie bought $8\frac{2}{4}$ yards of red fabric and $6\frac{1}{4}$ yards of blue fabric. How many yards of fabric did Julie purchase altogether?

_____

✓ Quick Check

Write each whole number or mixed number as a fraction.

Work Space.

9. $1\frac{1}{4}$ _____ **10.** 6 _____ **11.** $2\frac{2}{3}$ _____

12. $2\frac{1}{4}$ _____ **13.** $2\frac{2}{3}$ _____ **14.** 2 _____

Add or subtract.

15. $1\frac{1}{3} + 1\frac{1}{3}$ _____ **16.** $2\frac{1}{5} + 1\frac{2}{5}$ _____

17. $3\frac{3}{6} + 2\frac{2}{6}$ _____ **18.** $2\frac{4}{5} - 1\frac{1}{5}$ _____

19. $3\frac{2}{3} - 2\frac{1}{3}$ _____ **20.** $5\frac{5}{8} - 2\frac{3}{8}$ _____

Sometimes you may need to decide how to
express a remainder to solve a problem.

- You may need to
  include the remainder
  in your answer.

  You have **$7** to buy notebooks. Each notebook costs
  $2.00. How many can you buy? How much money is left?
  7 ÷ 2 = 3 R1 ➝ 3 notebooks, **$1.00** left

- You may need
  to drop the
  remainder.

  You have **17** oranges to put in bags of **4.** How many
  complete bags can you make?
  17 ÷ 4 = 4 R1 ➝ 4 complete bags

- You may need to write
  the answer as the
  next whole number.

  A van seats **7** people. There are **18** people going on a
  trip. How many vans do they need?
  18 ÷ 7 = 2 R4 ➝ 3 vans for **18** people

- You may need to
  write the remainder
  as a fraction.

  There are **5** apples to share with **4** friends. How much
  will each friend receive?

$$1\frac{1}{4}$$
$$4\overline{)5}$$
$$\underline{4}$$
$$1$$

The remainder
is the numerator.
The divisor is the
denominator.

$1\frac{1}{4}$ apple for each.

Tips to Remember:

> **1. Understand   2. Decide   3. Solve   4. Look back**

- Try to remember a real-life situation like the one described
  in the problem. What do you remember that might help
  you find a solution?
- Ask yourself: Does the answer use the remainder correctly?

Solve.

1. At a picnic, you have **10**
sandwiches to divide equally
among **8** people. How many
sandwiches will each person get?

Think: What would you do with
the **2** extra whole sandwiches?

_____

_____

Answer _____

2. A restaurant has a bowl of candy
at the checkout. You can buy **4**
pieces for a quarter. How much
will **1** piece cost?

Think: How do stores round their
prices?

_____

_____

Answer _____

Solve.

3. Three juice boxes come in a package. You need **32** juice boxes for a class party. How many packages should you buy?

_____

4. Six boys equally shared **32** ounces of orange juice. How many ounces did each boy get?

_____

5. Martin bought **4** pairs of socks for $5. How much did he pay for each pair?

_____

6. A group of **26** students are going on a field trip by car. Each car can fit **4** students. How many cars are needed?

_____

7. A bakery packages left-over bagels for sale the next day at a discounted price. Each package holds **6** bagels. One day, **43** bagels were left over at the end of the day. How many complete packages could be made?

_____

8. There are **18** cars on a ferris wheel. Each car can hold **3** people. For this ride there are **56** people waiting in line. How many people will have to wait until the next ride?

_____

9. Seventy-eight people attended a lecture. There were **10** rows of seats with **7** seats in each row. Did everybody have a seat?

_____

10. A restaurant makes burgers that weigh exactly **6** ounces. How many burgers will be made from **32** ounces of meat? How many ounces will be left over?

_____

Extend Your Thinking

11. Go back to problem **5**. Explain how you solved the problem.

_____

_____

_____

_____

12. Write and solve a word problem for which it would make sense to write the remainder as a fraction.

_____

_____

_____

_____

Fractions with different denominators are called **unlike fractions.** You can add unlike fractions.

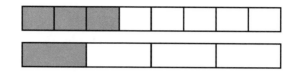

Find $\dfrac{3}{8} + \dfrac{1}{4}$.

1. Write both fractions with like denominators. Find an equivalent fraction.

$$\dfrac{1 \times 2}{4 \times 2} = \dfrac{2}{8} \;\longrightarrow\; \dfrac{3}{8} + \dfrac{2}{8}$$

2. Then add the numerators. Write the denominator.

$$\dfrac{3}{8} + \dfrac{2}{8} = \dfrac{5}{8}$$

Think: 3 eighths + 2 eighths

A fraction is in simplest form when **1** is the only number that will divide both the numerator and the denominator evenly.

Simplest Form	Not in Simplest Form
$\dfrac{5}{6}$ $\dfrac{3}{4}$ $\dfrac{1}{3}$	$\dfrac{4}{6}$ $\dfrac{2}{4}$ $\dfrac{8}{10}$

Add. Write the answer in simplest form.

1. $\dfrac{1}{2} + \dfrac{1}{4}$

$\underline{\quad} + \dfrac{1}{4} = \underline{\quad}$

2. $\dfrac{1}{3} + \dfrac{3}{6}$

$\underline{\quad} + \dfrac{3}{6} = \underline{\quad}$

3. $\dfrac{5}{12} + \dfrac{2}{6}$

$\dfrac{5}{12} + \underline{\quad} = \underline{\quad}$

4. $\dfrac{1}{3} + \dfrac{2}{9}$

$\underline{\quad} + \dfrac{2}{9} = \underline{\quad}$

5. $\dfrac{2}{4} + \dfrac{1}{8}$

$\underline{\quad} + \dfrac{1}{8} = \underline{\quad}$

6. $\dfrac{3}{5} + \dfrac{2}{10}$

$\underline{\quad} + \dfrac{2}{10} = \underline{\quad}$

7. $\dfrac{2}{8} + \dfrac{3}{4}$

$\dfrac{2}{8} + \underline{\quad} = \underline{\quad}$

8. $\dfrac{5}{12} + \dfrac{1}{6}$

$\dfrac{5}{12} + \underline{\quad} = \underline{\quad}$

Add. Write the answer in simplest form.

9. $\dfrac{3}{8} = \underline{\quad}$
$+ \dfrac{1}{4} = + \underline{\quad}$

10. $\dfrac{2}{10} = \underline{\quad}$
$+ \dfrac{2}{5} = + \underline{\quad}$

11. $\dfrac{5}{15} = \underline{\quad}$
$+ \dfrac{1}{5} = + \underline{\quad}$

12. $\dfrac{3}{8} = \underline{\quad}$
$+ \dfrac{2}{4} = + \underline{\quad}$

Add. Write the answer in simplest form.

13. $\dfrac{1}{6} =$ ___
$+\dfrac{2}{3} = +$___

14. $\dfrac{3}{12} =$ ___
$+\dfrac{2}{4} = +$___

15. $\dfrac{2}{5} =$ ___
$+\dfrac{3}{10} = +$___

16. $\dfrac{3}{6} =$ ___
$+\dfrac{2}{12} = +$___

17. $\dfrac{2}{3} =$ ___
$+\dfrac{1}{9} = +$___

18. $\dfrac{1}{4} =$ ___
$+\dfrac{5}{12} = +$___

19. $\dfrac{1}{8} =$ ___
$+\dfrac{3}{4} = +$___

20. $\dfrac{2}{5} =$ ___
$+\dfrac{5}{10} = +$___

21. $\dfrac{4}{10} + \dfrac{3}{5} =$ _____ $\dfrac{5}{9} + \dfrac{1}{3} =$ _____ $\dfrac{4}{10} + \dfrac{1}{2} =$ _____

22. $\dfrac{1}{9} + \dfrac{1}{3} =$ _____ $\dfrac{8}{12} + \dfrac{1}{3} =$ _____ $\dfrac{5}{12} + \dfrac{1}{2} =$ _____

| Problem Solving |
| Reasoning |

 Solve.

23. Sandy walked $\dfrac{1}{2}$ mile to the pet store and
$\dfrac{4}{10}$ mile to the crafts store.
How far did she walk? _____

Test Prep ★ Mixed Review

24 What number is the common factor of both 18 and 24?

A 4

B 6

C 8

D 9

25 Which mixed number represents the shaded portion of this model?

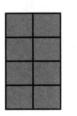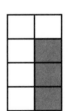

F $2\dfrac{3}{8}$ H 3

G $2\dfrac{5}{8}$ J $3\dfrac{3}{8}$

Subtracting Unlike Fractions

You also can subtract unlike fractions. Subtracting unlike fractions is similar to adding unlike fractions.

Find $\dfrac{3}{8} - \dfrac{1}{4}$.

1. Find an equivalent fraction. Write both fractions with like denominators.

$$\dfrac{1 \times 2}{4 \times 2} = \dfrac{2}{8} \;\rightarrow\; \dfrac{3}{8} - \dfrac{2}{8}$$

2. Then subtract the numerators. Write the denominator.

$$\dfrac{3}{8} - \dfrac{2}{8} = \dfrac{1}{8}$$

Think: 3 eighths − 2 eighths

Subtract. Write the answer in simplest form.

1. $\dfrac{1}{2} - \dfrac{1}{4}$

$\downarrow$

$\dfrac{2}{4} - \dfrac{1}{4} = $ ___

2. $\dfrac{2}{3} - \dfrac{3}{6}$

$\downarrow$

$\dfrac{4}{6} - \dfrac{3}{6} = $ ___

3. $\dfrac{3}{4} - \dfrac{3}{8}$

$\downarrow$

$\dfrac{6}{8} - \dfrac{3}{8} = $ ___

4. $\dfrac{7}{8} - \dfrac{2}{4}$

$\downarrow$

$\dfrac{7}{8} - \dfrac{4}{8} = $ ___

5. $\dfrac{4}{5} - \dfrac{5}{10}$

$\downarrow$

$\dfrac{8}{10} - \dfrac{5}{10} = $ ___

6. $\dfrac{1}{3} - \dfrac{3}{12}$

$\downarrow$

$\dfrac{4}{12} - \dfrac{3}{12} = $ ___

7. $\dfrac{11}{12} - \dfrac{1}{6}$

$\downarrow$

$\dfrac{11}{12} - \dfrac{2}{12} = $ ___

8. $\dfrac{3}{4} - \dfrac{3}{12}$

$\downarrow$

$\dfrac{9}{12} - \dfrac{3}{12} = $ ___

Subtract. Write the answer in simplest form.

9. $\dfrac{3}{4} = $ ___
$-\dfrac{1}{2} = $ ___

10. $\dfrac{1}{2} = $ ___
$-\dfrac{1}{6} = $ ___

11. $\dfrac{6}{10} = $ ___
$-\dfrac{1}{2} = $ ___

12. $\dfrac{5}{6} = $ ___
$-\dfrac{2}{3} = $ ___

13. $\dfrac{3}{4} = $ ___
$-\dfrac{1}{8} = $ ___

14. $\dfrac{2}{3} = $ ___
$-\dfrac{4}{9} = $ ___

15. $\dfrac{3}{6} = $ ___
$-\dfrac{3}{12} = $ ___

16. $\dfrac{8}{10} = $ ___
$-\dfrac{3}{5} = $ ___

Subtract. Write the answer in simplest form.

17.
$$\frac{3}{5} = \underline{\hspace{1cm}}$$
$$-\frac{1}{10} = -\underline{\hspace{0.5cm}}$$

18.
$$\frac{2}{3} = \underline{\hspace{1cm}}$$
$$-\frac{2}{9} = -\underline{\hspace{0.5cm}}$$

19.
$$\frac{3}{8} = \underline{\hspace{1cm}}$$
$$-\frac{1}{4} = -\underline{\hspace{0.5cm}}$$

20.
$$\frac{7}{12} = \underline{\hspace{1cm}}$$
$$-\frac{2}{6} = -\underline{\hspace{0.5cm}}$$

21. $\frac{11}{12} - \frac{1}{2} = \underline{\hspace{1cm}}$ $\qquad$ $\frac{6}{9} - \frac{2}{3} = \underline{\hspace{1cm}}$ $\qquad$ $\frac{7}{10} - \frac{1}{5} = \underline{\hspace{1cm}}$

22. $\frac{1}{2} - \frac{1}{8} = \underline{\hspace{1cm}}$ $\qquad$ $\frac{1}{3} - \frac{1}{9} = \underline{\hspace{1cm}}$ $\qquad$ $\frac{4}{5} - \frac{1}{10} = \underline{\hspace{1cm}}$

Find the missing addend. Use subtraction.

23. $\frac{1}{2} + \underline{\hspace{1cm}} = \frac{3}{4}$ $\qquad$ $\frac{1}{3} + \underline{\hspace{1cm}} = \frac{4}{9}$ $\qquad$ $\frac{2}{5} + \underline{\hspace{1cm}} = \frac{7}{10}$

24. $\frac{2}{3} + \underline{\hspace{1cm}} = \frac{5}{6}$ $\qquad$ $\frac{1}{2} + \underline{\hspace{1cm}} = \frac{9}{10}$ $\qquad$ $\frac{1}{6} + \underline{\hspace{1cm}} = \frac{7}{12}$

Problem Solving Reasoning | **Solve.**

25. Flo swam $\frac{1}{2}$ mile in the morning. She swam $\frac{3}{4}$ mile in the evening. How much farther did she swim in the evening?

_____

 Quick Check

Add or subtract. | | **Work Space.**

26. $\frac{2}{3} + \frac{1}{6}$ ____ $\qquad$ **27.** $\frac{1}{10} + \frac{3}{5}$ ____

28. $\frac{3}{8} + \frac{1}{2}$ ____ $\qquad$ **29.** $\frac{7}{8} - \frac{1}{4}$ ____

30. $\frac{11}{12} - \frac{5}{6}$ ____ $\qquad$ **31.** $\frac{8}{10} - \frac{1}{2}$ ____

Problem Solving Strategy: Draw a Picture

Drawing a picture can help you solve some problems.

It can also help you check an answer to a problem you have solved using computation.

Problem

Taylor rides his bike to and from school every day. The round trip is $\frac{3}{4}$ mile. How many miles does Taylor ride in a 5-day school week?

---

1 Understand   As you reread, ask yourself questions.

- What facts are you given in the problem?

    Taylor rides $\frac{3}{4}$ of a mile each day.

    Taylor rides every day during the school week.

- What do you need to find out?

_____

---

2 Decide   Choose a method for solving.

Try the strategy Draw a Picture.

- What should your picture show?

_____

---

3 Solve   Draw a number line divided into fourths.
Skip-count five times by three fourths.

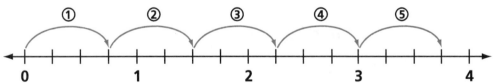

- Write a mixed number to show the point on the number line where you stopped.

_____

---

4 Look back   Write the answer to the problem below.

Answer _____

- How might you have solved this problem using addition?

_____

Solve. Use the Draw a Picture strategy or any other strategy you have learned.

1. Christy cut a $7\frac{1}{2}$ foot piece of ribbon into pieces that were each $1\frac{1}{2}$ feet long. How many pieces were there?

Think: What fraction is the same as $1\frac{1}{2}$?

_____

Answer _____

2. Kim lives $3\frac{1}{4}$ miles from the town library. She decides to walk to the library. After walking $1\frac{3}{4}$ miles, she stops for a break. How far is Kim from the library when she stops?

Think: How could you label the number line to help solve the problem?

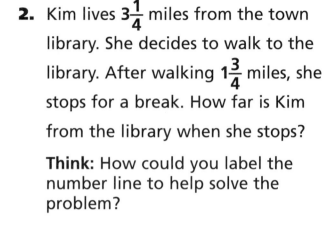

Answer _____

3. Mrs. Lorenz is putting a fence along the back of her yard. The fence will be **72** feet long. There will be a post every **8** feet and a post on each end. How many posts will there be?

_____

4. Grant made a punch by mixing $2\frac{3}{4}$ gallons of orange juice with $1\frac{3}{4}$ gallons of ginger ale. How many gallons of punch did he make?

_____

5. Write the next number in this sequence.

$1\frac{1}{2}$, $1\frac{3}{4}$, 2, $2\frac{1}{4}$, $2\frac{1}{2}$, _____

6. You want to cut a piece of rope into **5** pieces. How many cuts do you need to make?

_____

7. The sum of two numbers is **47**. Their difference is **17**. What are the two numbers?

_____

8. Roberta is thinking of a number. If you add **9** and then multiply the sum by **3**, the result is **45**. What is Roberta's number?

_____

Complete each list of multiples. Circle the common multiples.

1. Multiples of 3:   21, 24, _____, _____, _____, _____, 39, _____, _____, _____

     Multiples of 4:   _____, _____, _____, _____, 36, _____, _____, _____

Write an equivalent fraction in simplest form.

2. $\frac{10}{16}$ _____   **3.** $\frac{4}{20}$ _____   **4.** $\frac{4}{8}$ _____   **5.** $\frac{6}{10}$ _____

Compare. Write <, >, or =.

6. $\frac{2}{3} \bigcirc \frac{3}{5}$ **7.** $\frac{3}{4} \bigcirc \frac{6}{8}$ **8.** $\frac{7}{8} \bigcirc \frac{3}{4}$ **9.** $\frac{1}{12} \bigcirc \frac{1}{3}$

Write the fractions in order from least to greatest.

10. $\frac{7}{8}$ $\frac{1}{4}$ $\frac{2}{3}$ $\frac{1}{2}$ _____   **11.** $\frac{1}{2}$ $\frac{1}{10}$ $\frac{2}{5}$ $\frac{2}{10}$ _____

Write the number as a fraction.

12. 6 _____   **13.** $2\frac{5}{6}$ _____   **14.** $3\frac{2}{3}$ _____   **15.** $3\frac{1}{7}$ _____

Add or subtract. Write your answer in simplest form.

16. $\begin{array}{r} \frac{4}{6} \\ -\ \frac{2}{6} \\ \hline \end{array}$ **17.** $\begin{array}{r} \frac{2}{5} \\ +\ \frac{4}{5} \\ \hline \end{array}$ **18.** $\begin{array}{r} 1\frac{2}{8} \\ +\ 4\frac{3}{8} \\ \hline \end{array}$

19. $\begin{array}{r} 6\frac{4}{6} \\ -\ 2\frac{2}{6} \\ \hline \end{array}$ **20.** $\begin{array}{r} \frac{1}{3} \\ +\ \frac{1}{6} \\ \hline \end{array}$ **21.** $\begin{array}{r} \frac{5}{8} \\ -\ \frac{1}{4} \\ \hline \end{array}$

Solve. Check that your answer is reasonable.

22. Richard brought **6** oranges to the computer club as a snack. If Richard and **3** club members share the oranges equally, what portion will each person get?

_____

23. A pizza had **8** slices. James said, "I ate $\frac{1}{2}$ of $\frac{1}{2}$ of $\frac{1}{2}$ of the pizza." How many slices did James eat?

_____

Name _____

1 Joanna and Rachel make 20 necklaces to sell at an arts-and-crafts fair. They use 37 beads for each necklace. How many beads do they use in all?

A 7,400   C 640   E NH

B 740   D 57

2 A dripping faucet leaks 4 gallons of water a day. If no one fixes it, how many gallons will it leak in 28 days?

F 96   H 128   K NH

G 112   J 132

3 Painters finished $\frac{1}{2}$ of a house on Wednesday. They finished $\frac{3}{8}$ more of the house on Thursday. How much of the house was finished?

A $\frac{1}{8}$ C $\frac{5}{8}$ E NH

B $\frac{1}{4}$ D $\frac{3}{4}$

4 Which fraction is equivalent to $2\frac{3}{4}$?

F $\frac{6}{4}$ H $\frac{11}{4}$

G $\frac{8}{4}$ J $\frac{12}{4}$

5 Which fraction is in simplest form?

A $\frac{4}{5}$ C $\frac{2}{4}$

B $\frac{6}{9}$ D $\frac{3}{6}$

6 You and 3 friends share 30 books evenly. How many books will you each get?

F 10   H 7   K NH

G 8   J 5

7 What number should go in the ☐ to make the number sentence true?

$$16 \times 4 = (\boxed{} \times 2) \times 4$$

A 4   C 8

B 6   D 16

8 Four students in the choir practice singing at home. Which lists the students in order from the least time to the most time spent practicing?

Name	Time Spent Practicing
Maria	$\frac{1}{3}$ hour
George	$\frac{1}{2}$ hour
Frank	$\frac{3}{4}$ hour
Susan	$\frac{2}{3}$ hour

F Maria, George, Susan, Frank

G Maria, George, Frank, Susan

H Frank, Susan, George, Maria

J George, Maria, Frank, Susan

UNIT 6 • TABLE OF CONTENTS

Geometry

Dear Family,

During the next few weeks, our math class will be learning about geometry.

You can expect to see homework that provides practice with naming polygons and space figures. Here is a sample you may want to keep handy to give help if needed.

We will be using this vocabulary:

point a location in space

line a figure made up of a set of points that extends without end in both directions

line segment a part of a line having two endpoints

ray a part of a line with one endpoint

angle a figure formed by joining two rays that have a common endpoint

Identifying Polygons and Space Figures

A polygon is a closed plane figure made up of line segments that meet only at their end points. A space figure is a figure that takes up space. Here are some examples of polygons and space figures.

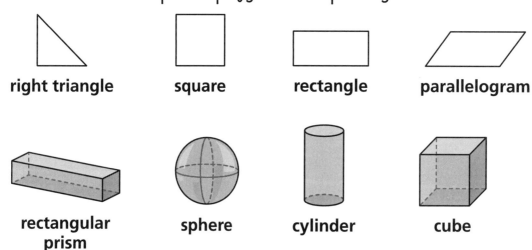

right triangle   **square**   **rectangle**   **parallelogram**

rectangular prism   **sphere**   **cylinder**   **cube**

Explore your home with your child and try to find examples of each figure shown. You might also look for polygons and space figures while driving or shopping.

During this unit, students will need to continue practicing identifying polygons and space figures, as well as determining congruence and symmetry in figures.

Sincerely,

Name _____

STANDARD

A **point** is a location in space. A capital letter is used to name a point. The name of this point is **point B**, or just **B**.

• B

You can draw a **line** through any two points. This line is drawn through points **B** and **C**. The arrows show that a line extends in both directions without end.

A line is named by any two points on the line. This is line **BC** or line **CB**. This is how to write line **BC** or line **CB**:

$$\overleftrightarrow{BC} \quad \overleftrightarrow{CB}$$

A **line segment** is part of a line that has two **endpoints**. A line segment is named for its endpoints. This is line segment **BC** or **CB**.

This is how to write line segment **BC** or line segment **CB**:

$$\overline{BC} \quad \overline{CB}$$

Name the line, line segment, or point.

1.

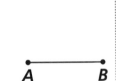
A   B
____

2.

• F

• E
____

3.

T
Q
____

4.

• K
____

5.
R

S
____

6.

• D
____

7.

O   P
____

8.

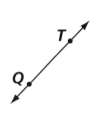
U
V
____

9.

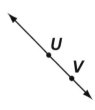
X
Y
____

10.

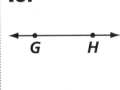
G   H
____

Use a straight edge. Draw the figure.

11.

point **A**

12.

$$\overleftrightarrow{BD}$$

13.

$$\overline{GT}$$

14.

$$\overleftrightarrow{UV}$$

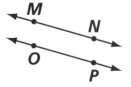 $\overleftrightarrow{DE}$ is a horizontal line.

A **horizontal line** is a straight line that extends left and right.

 $\overleftrightarrow{KL}$ is a vertical line.

A **vertical line** is a straight line that extends up and down.

$\overleftrightarrow{MN}$ and $\overleftrightarrow{OP}$ are parallel lines.

Parallel lines never meet because the distance between them is always the same.

Write: $\overleftrightarrow{MN} \parallel \overleftrightarrow{OP}$

$\overline{AB}$ and $\overline{CD}$ are parallel line segments.

Parallel line segments are parts of parallel lines.

Write: $\overline{AB} \parallel \overline{CD}$

The symbol ‖ means "is parallel to."

Identify the figure.

15.

_____

16.

_____

17.

_____

18.

_____

19.

_____

20.

• R

_____

Use a straight edge. Draw the figure.

21.

Horizontal line segment AB

22.

Parallel line segments AB and CD

23.

Vertical line AB

142   Unit 6 Lesson 1

Name _____

Line **AB** and line **CD** cross each other.

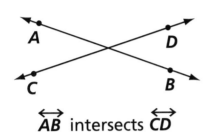

$\overleftrightarrow{AB}$ intersects $\overleftrightarrow{CD}$

Lines that meet or cross are **intersecting lines**.

Line **EF** and line **GH** intersect to form square corners or right angles. Lines that intersect to form square corners are called **perpendicular lines**.

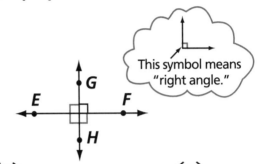

This symbol means "right angle."

$\overleftrightarrow{EF}$ is perpendicular to $\overleftrightarrow{GH}$.

Write: $\overleftrightarrow{EF} \perp \overleftrightarrow{GH}$

The symbol $\perp$ means "is perpendicular to."

Use a straight edge. Draw the figure.

24. $\overleftrightarrow{AB} \perp \overleftrightarrow{DE}$ | **25.** $\overleftrightarrow{CD}$ intersects $\overleftrightarrow{EF}$ | **26.** $\overleftrightarrow{EF} \parallel \overleftrightarrow{GH}$

Test Prep ★ Mixed Review

27 Which of the following is a prime number?

A 7   C 15

B 9   D 27

28 A pizza parlor cuts every pizza into 8 slices. Children at a birthday party finish 4 pizzas. Which fraction shows the number of pizzas the children ate?

F $\frac{32}{4}$ H $\frac{8}{4}$

G $\frac{32}{8}$ J $\frac{4}{8}$

Name _____

The figure below is a **ray**. A ray has only one endpoint.
When you name a ray, always name its endpoint first.

A •————————————————• B ————▶

This is ray **AB**. Another way to write ray **AB** is:

$$\overrightarrow{AB}$$

A **ray** is part of a line with only one endpoint.

Name the ray.

1.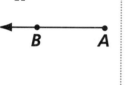

____

2.

____

3.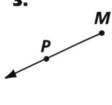

____

4.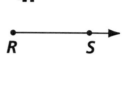

____

5.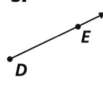

____

Name the line, line segment, or ray.

6.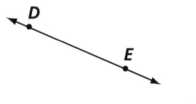

____

7.

____

8.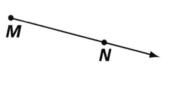

____

9.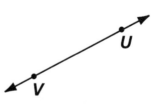

____

10.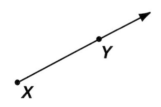

____

11.

____

This figure is an **angle**. It is made up of two rays with a common **endpoint**. Point **O** is the common endpoint. You say angle **JOL** and write ∠**JOL**. You can also name it ∠**LOJ**.

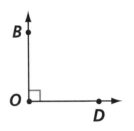

When you write the name of an angle, the common endpoint is always the middle letter. The common endpoint is also called the **vertex**.

A short way to write ∠**JOL** or ∠**LOJ** is ∠**O**.

This is a **right angle**. A right angle is sometimes called a square corner.

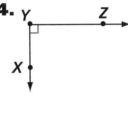

Write two different names for the angle. Circle the right angles.

12.

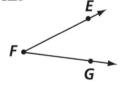

_____

_____

13.

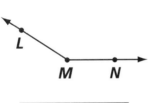

_____

_____

14.

_____

_____

15.

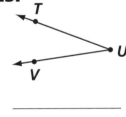

_____

_____

16.

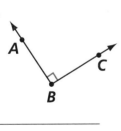

_____

_____

17.

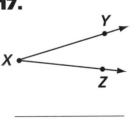

_____

_____

18.

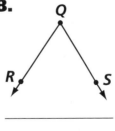

_____

_____

19.

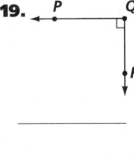

_____

_____

Use a straight edge. Draw and label each angle.

20. ∠*MOP*

. . . . . .
. . . . . .
. . . . . .
. . . . . .

21. ∠*RAN*

. . . . . .
. . . . . .
. . . . . .
. . . . . .

22. right angle *CAR*

. . . . . .
. . . . . .
. . . . . .
. . . . . .

Problem Solving Reasoning Solve.

23. How many different angles can you find in this figure? _____ Name the angles.

_____

_____

What vertex do the angles share? _____

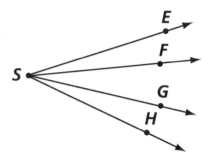

24. Use three letters to name each right angle in square *ABCD*.

_____

_____

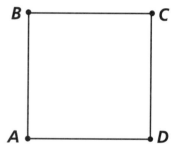

Test Prep ★ Mixed Review

25 Which fraction is in simplest form?

A $\frac{1}{4}$

B $\frac{2}{8}$

C $\frac{2}{6}$

D $\frac{4}{6}$

26 Which mixed number is equivalent to $\frac{7}{3}$?

F $7\frac{1}{3}$

G $2\frac{2}{3}$

H $2\frac{1}{3}$

J $1\frac{2}{3}$

146 Unit 6 Lesson 2

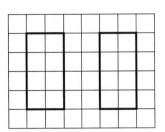

Figures that are the same size and the same shape are **congruent** figures.

These two figures are congruent.

Follow these steps to find whether the red and gray figures are congruent.

1. Trace and cut out one of the figures.

2. Place it on top of the other figure.

3. If the sides and angles match, then the figures are congruent.

---

1. Shade the figures below that are congruent to figure *H*. Trace and cut out figure *H* if you need to.

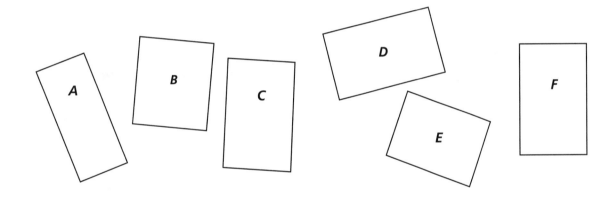

---

2. Match the congruent figures. Write the letter on the congruent figure in the bottom row.

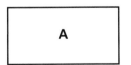
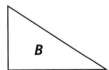
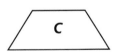

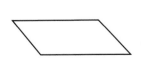

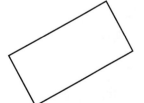
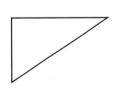

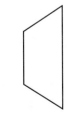

Sometimes different parts of the same figure are congruent. Look at figure **ABCD**.

$\overline{BC}$ is congruent to $\overline{CD}$. $\overline{AB}$ is congruent to $\overline{AD}$.

$\angle B$ is congruent to $\angle D$.

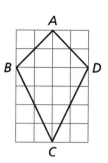

Write *Yes* or *No* to answer each question.
Make a tracing if you need to.

3.

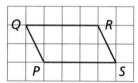

Is $\overline{AB}$ congruent

to $\overline{BC}$? _____

to $\overline{AC}$? _____

Is $\angle A$ congruent

to $\angle B$? _____

to $\angle C$? _____

4.

Is $\overline{PQ}$ congruent to

$\overline{QR}$? _____

$\overline{RS}$? _____

Is $\angle P$ congruent

$\angle Q$? _____

$\angle R$? _____

✓ Quick Check

Identify the figure.

Work Space.

5.

_____

6.

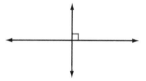

_____

7.

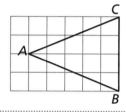

_____

8.

_____

Write the letters of the congruent figures.

9.

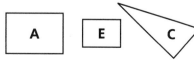

_____

148 Unit 6 Lesson 3

Name _____

Sometimes the best way to solve a problem is to act it out.

Problem

Can the four figures to the left be arranged to form a figure congruent to this square below?

....

1 Understand   Be sure you understand what the words in the problem mean.

• What are congruent figures?

Congruent figures have the same _____

and same _____.

....

2 Decide   Choose a method for solving.

Try the strategy Act it Out.

• Trace each of the **4** small figures and cut them out.

....

3 Solve   Try to arrange the figures so that they fit inside the large square without overlapping.

• Did you find a way to make all the figures fit

inside the larger square? _____

• Draw line segments in the square above to indicate where you placed each piece.

....

4 Look back   Write the answer to the problem below.

Answer _____

• If you take the **4** figures and arrange them to form a triangle, would the triangle be congruent to the large square? Why or why not?

_____

Solve. Use the Act it Out strategy or any other strategy you have learned.

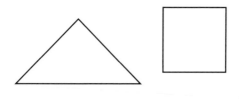

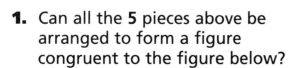

1. Can all the **5** pieces above be arranged to form a figure congruent to the figure below?

Think: Which shapes have sides of the same length as other shapes?

_____

_____

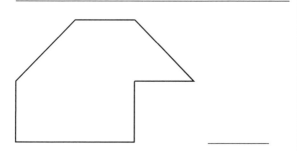

_____

2. Can the **5** pieces above be arranged to form a figure congruent to this figure?

Think: Will the shapes make a figure with **4** square corners the size of the large rectangle?

_____

_____

3. Use **12** toothpicks to form **4** congruent squares. Draw the shape.

4. Use **12** toothpicks to form **6** congruent triangles. Draw the shape.

5. Petra and Cecelia are sisters. Petra is $4\frac{1}{2}$ feet tall. Cecelia is $3\frac{3}{4}$ feet tall. How much taller is Petra than Cecelia?

_____

6. Naomi put her dog on a diet. It lost **3** pounds the first month and gained **2** pounds the second month. It then weighed **25** pounds. How much did the dog weigh when it started the diet?

_____

The size or opening of an angle is measured in a unit called a **degree** (°). The figure shown is a **right angle**. A right angle forms a square corner.

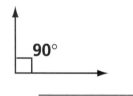

90°

| All **right angles** measure **90** degrees or **90°**. |

right angle

This angle measures **45°**. Its measure is less than a right angle. It is called an **acute angle**.

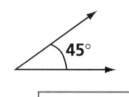

45°

| All angles less than **90°** are **acute angles**. |

acute angle

This angle measures **120°**. Its measure is greater than a right angle. It is called an **obtuse angle**.

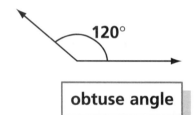

120°

| All angles greater than **90°** are **obtuse angles**. |

obtuse angle

Look at the angle. Write *right*, *acute*, or *obtuse*.

1.

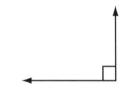

_____

2.

_____

3.

_____

4.

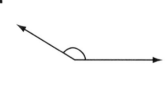

_____

5.

_____

6.

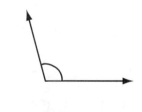

_____

Answer the question next to the figure.

7.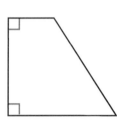

How many right angles? _____

How many acute angles? _____

How many obtuse angles? _____

8.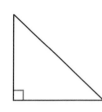

How many right angles? _____

How many acute angles? _____

How many obtuse angles? _____

9.

How many right angles? _____

How many acute angles? _____

How many obtuse angles? _____

10.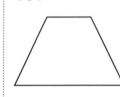

How many right angles? _____

How many acute angles? _____

How many obtuse angles? _____

Use a straight edge. Draw the figure.

11. acute angle

12. right angle

13. obtuse angle

Problem Solving / Reasoning **Solve.**

14. Name two times when the hour and minute hands of a clock form a right angle.

_____

Test Prep ★ Mixed Review

15 Which shows all the factors of 32?

  A 1, 2, 4, 8, 16, 32

  B 30, 2

  C 1, 2, 3, 4, 9, 32

  D 2, 4, 8, 16

16 What number is the common factor of both 15 and 27?

  F 9

  G 6

  H 5

  J 3

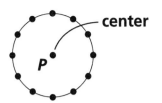

A **circle** is a set of all points that are the same distance from a given point, called the **center**. Point **P** is the center of the circle shown. The points shown on this circle are the same distance from point **P**.

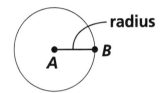

Any line segment joining any point on the circle with its center is called a **radius** (plural: **radii**). Point **A** is the center of the circle shown. $\overline{AB}$ or $\overline{BA}$ is a radius.

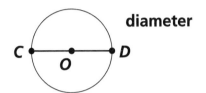

Any line segment that passes across the circle through the center is called a **diameter**. Point **O** is the center of this circle. $\overline{CD}$ or $\overline{DC}$ is a diameter. $\overline{CO}$ and $\overline{OD}$ are radii.

Use a straight edge and the points given to draw the radius.

1.

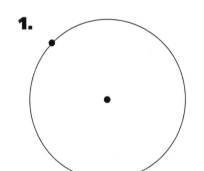

2.

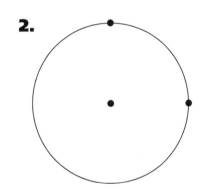

3.

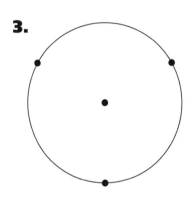

Use a straight edge and the points given to draw the diameter.

4.

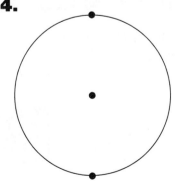

5.

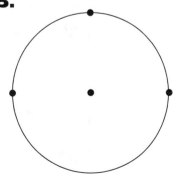

6.

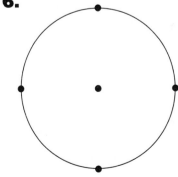

A circle measures **360°**. You can turn an object around the point that is the center of a circle.

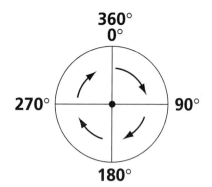

Each turn is measured from the start position. The start position is the **0°** mark.

A **quarter turn** is **90°**.   A **half turn** is **180°**.   A **three-quarter turn is 270°.**   A **full turn** is **360°**.

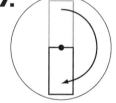 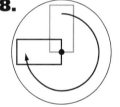 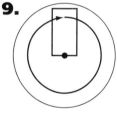 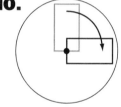

Name the kind of turn and its measure.

7.

turn _____

degrees _____

8.

turn _____

degrees _____

9.

turn _____

degrees _____

10.

turn _____

degrees _____

Solve.

11. Is the diameter of a circle always twice as long as its radius? Explain.

_____

_____

Test Prep ★ Mixed Review

12 Which are parallel line segments?

  A   **B**   **C**   **D**

13 Which fraction represents the shaded part of the model?

F $\frac{1}{4}$ **H** $\frac{1}{2}$

G $\frac{3}{8}$ **J** $\frac{3}{4}$

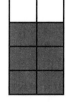

A figure has a **line of symmetry** if it can be folded so that its two parts match precisely. When the two parts of a figure match precisely, the fold line is called the **line of symmetry**.

A figure that has a line of symmetry is called a **symmetric figure**. Some symmetric figures have only one line of symmetry. Others have more than one line of symmetry.

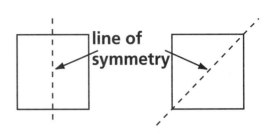
line of symmetry

> A **symmetric figure** is a figure that has one or more lines of symmetry.

Is the dashed line a line of symmetry? Circle *Yes* or *No*.

1.
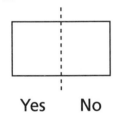
Yes   No

2.
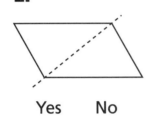
Yes   No

3.

Yes   No

4.
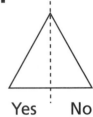
Yes   No

5.
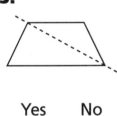
Yes   No

6.

Yes   No

7.
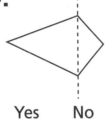
Yes   No

8.
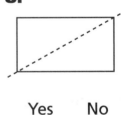
Yes   No

Use a straight edge. Draw all of the lines of symmetry for the figure.

9.

10.

11.
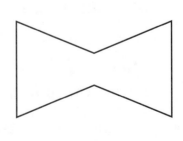

A figure has **rotational symmetry** if you can rotate it about a point less than a full turn and the figure looks the same as it did before the rotation.

quarter turn

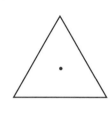

half turn

three-quarter turn

Does the figure have rotational symmetry? Circle *Yes* or *No*.

12.

Yes   No

13.

Yes   No

14.

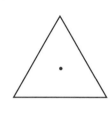

Yes   No

15.

Yes   No

| Problem Solving |
| Reasoning |

Solve.

16. Can you fold a circle anywhere to show a line of symmetry? Explain.

_____

_____

✓ **Quick Check**

Tell if the angle is right, acute, or obtuse.

Work Space.

17.

_____

18.

_____

19.

_____

Use the figures shown to answer the question.

20. Write the letters that identify the diameter of the circle shown. Then

identify the radius._____

21. Does the figure shown have line symmetry?

Does it have turn symmetry? _____

Name _____

Figure **ABC** is a triangle. A **triangle** is a figure with three line segments and three angles.

Triangles can be classified by the length of their sides.

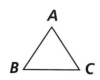

An **equilateral triangle** has all three sides the same length.

equilateral

An **isosceles triangle** has at least two sides the same length.

isosceles

A **scalene triangle** has three sides that are all a different length.

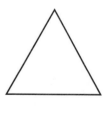

scalene

Write whether the triangle is *equilateral, isosceles,* or *scalene.*

1.

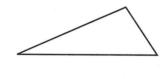

_____

2.

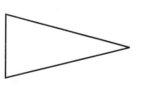

_____

3.

_____

4.

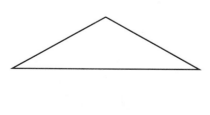

_____

5.

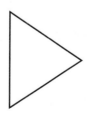

_____

6.

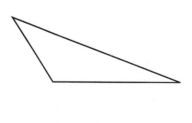

_____

Angle **E** in triangle **DEF** is a right angle. Triangles that have a right angle are called **right triangles**.

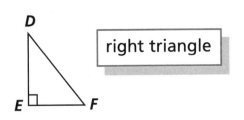

right triangle

Circle the right triangles.

7.

Draw the triangle.

8. equilateral triangle

9. isosceles triangle

10. scalene triangle

Solve.

11. How many different triangles can you find in this figure? _____

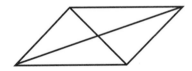

Test Prep ★ Mixed Review

12 Asa practices the piano for $\frac{1}{2}$ an hour each day. Her piano teacher tells her to practice $\frac{1}{3}$ hour more. How much time will she practice in all each day?

  A $\frac{5}{8}$ hour   C $\frac{3}{4}$ hour

  B $\frac{2}{3}$ hour   D $\frac{5}{6}$ hour

13 Which group of numbers shows all the factors of 12?

  F 1, 2, 8, 11, 12

  G 1, 6, 9, 12

  H 1, 2, 3, 4, 6, 12

  J 1, 4, 5, 7, 12

Name _____

A **polygon** is a closed figure that is made up of line segments.

Any polygon with **4** sides is a **quadrilateral**.

Some quadrilaterals have other names.

A **square** has four congruent sides and four right angles.

A **rhombus** has four congruent sides and two pairs of parallel sides.

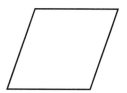

A **trapezoid** has only one pair of parallel sides.

A **rectangle** has two pairs of parallel sides and four right angles.

A **parallelogram** has two pairs of congruent sides and two pairs of parallel sides.

Write the name that best describes the figure.

1.

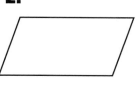

_____

2.

_____

3.

_____

4.

_____

5.

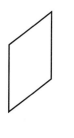

_____

6.

_____

7.

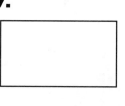

_____

8.

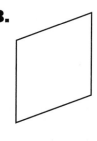

_____

These polygons are called **pentagons**. A pentagon has **5** sides and **5** angles.

These polygons are called **hexagons**. A hexagon has **6** sides and **6** angles.

Complete the charts for the figures shown.

Figure	Sides	Right angles	Pairs of parallel sides
hexagon			
square			

Figure	Sides	Right angles	Pairs of parallel sides
rectangle			
pentagon			

Problem Solving Reasoning Solve. Write *Yes* or *No*.

9. Is a quadrilateral with four right angles always a square? _____

10. Are all of the angles of a rectangle congruent? _____

✓ **Quick Check**

Write the name of the figure.

Work Space.

11.

_____

12.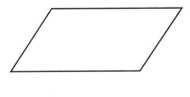

_____

13.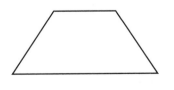

_____

14.

_____

A **space figure** is a figure that takes up space. This space figure is called a **cube.**

Each side of the cube is called a **face.** The place where two faces meet is called an **edge.** Each corner is called a **vertex** (plural: *vertices*).

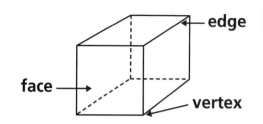

edge

face →

vertex

Here are some different types of space figures. Notice that spheres, cylinders, and cones have curved surfaces. Cones and cylinders have flat bases.

Cube

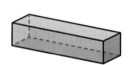

Rectangular Prism

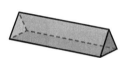

Triangular Prism

Rectangular Pyramid

Triangular Pyramid

Sphere

Cone

Cylinder

Tell what space figure the object suggests.

1.

_____

2.

_____

3.

_____

4.

_____

5.

_____

6.

_____

7.

_____

8.
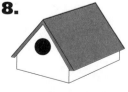
_____

Match the space figure to its name.

9. rectangular prism

cone

cube

triangular pyramid

cylinder

rectangular pyramid

sphere

triangular prism

Name space figures that have one or more faces shaped like each figure below.

10.
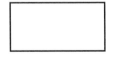

_____

_____

_____

11.

_____

_____

_____

12.

_____

_____

_____

13.

_____

_____

_____

162 Unit 6 Lesson 10

Name _____

Complete the chart.

14.

Space figure	Number of faces	Number of edges	Number of vertices
cube			
triangular pyramid			
rectangular prism			
triangular prism			
rectangular pyramid			

Problem Solving Reasoning Solve.

15. Can one or more faces of a cube be a rectangle?

Explain. _____

_____

Test Prep ★ Mixed Review

16 Which shape is congruent with the square shown?

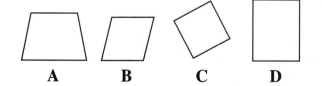

A   **B**   **C**   **D**

17 What is line segment *y*?

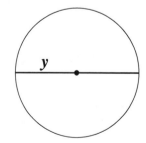

F diameter   **H** parallel lines
G ray   **J** radius

STANDARD

This pattern is called a **net**. You can use nets like this to make space figures. If you cut out this net and fold it on the dotted lines, it will make a cube.

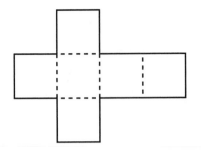

Circle each net that can be folded to make a cube.

1.

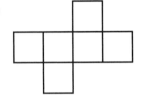 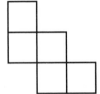 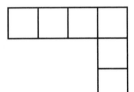

Match the space figure with the correct net.

2.

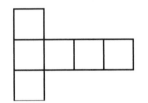

triangular pyramid

square pyramid

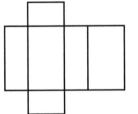

rectangular prism

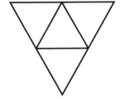

triangular prism

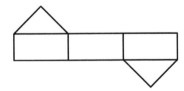

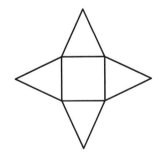

Name _____

Complete the net for the space figure.

3.

rectangular prism

4.

square pyramid

Draw a net for the space figure.

5.

cube

Solve.

6. How can you tell this net cannot be folded into a cube?

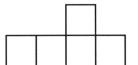

_____

_____

 Quick Check

Answer the question.

7. A cube has how many congruent faces? _____

How many vertices? _____

8. A sphere has how many curved surfaces? _____

How many vertices? _____

9. Which of these nets can be folded to make a cube? Write the letter.

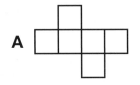 A

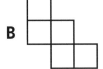 B

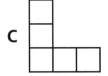 C

_____

Work Space.

Name _____

At a dinner, each person selected a main course. The circle graph shows the choices.

You will use circle graphs to solve the problems in this lesson.

A **circle graph** shows the parts of a whole.

Tips to Remember:

| 1. Understand | 2. Decide | 3. Solve | 4. Look back |

- Reread the problem. Circle important words and numbers.
- Compare the labels on the graph with the words and numbers in the problem. Find the facts you need from the graph.
- Try more than one strategy on the same problem. If one doesn't work, try another.

Main Courses Selected

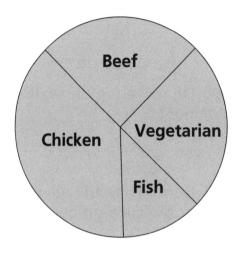

Beef

Chicken   Vegetarian

Fish

Solve. Use the circle graph above.

1. Did more people choose chicken or beef?

   Think: What parts of the graph do you need to compare? How could you compare them?

   _____

   _____

   _____

   Answer _____

2. Can you use the graph to find the total number of people at the dinner?

   Think: What information do you need to find the total?

   _____

   _____

   Answer _____

   _____

3. Which two meals were chosen by the same number of people? What fraction of the circle do they each represent?

   _____

   _____

4. Suppose **40** people chose the chicken and **10** people chose fish. Then how many people chose the vegetarian main course? Explain.

   _____

   _____

This circle graph shows how the students in Mrs. Mason's class travel back and forth to school.

How Students Travel to School

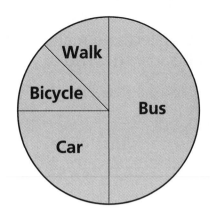

Solve. Use the circle graph above.

5. Do more people walk or take the bus?

_____

6. Do more people go home by car or bicycle?

_____

7. Do more than half of the students in the class go home by car?

_____

8. Suppose there were **24** students in the class. How many students would be going home by bus?

_____

9. If there were **12** students taking the bus, how many students would be going home by car?

_____

10. Suppose **4** students were going home by bicycle. How many students would be walking home?

_____

Extend Your Thinking

11. What fractional part of the whole does each section of the circle graph represent?

_____

12. What fraction represents the combined total of students who walk and students who ride a bicycle?

_____

13. Explain the method you used to solve problem **8**.

_____

_____

_____

14. Explain why this circle graph cannot show data about a class that has a total of **29** students.

_____

_____

_____

Identify the figure.

1.

2.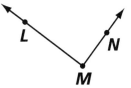

3.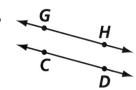

4.

_____   _____   _____   _____

Which figures are congruent?

 A   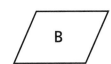 B   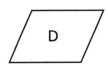 C   D   E    F

5. _____ and _____   **6.** _____ and _____

Tell if the angle is right, acute, or obtuse.

7.   **8.** 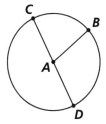   **9.**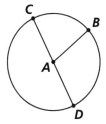

_____   _____   _____

Use the circle to answer the question.

10. Name a radius. _____

11. Name the diameter. _____

Name the kind of turn and its measure.

12.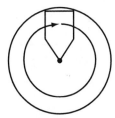

13.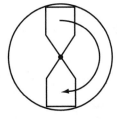

14.

15.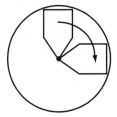

turn _____   turn _____   turn _____   turn _____

degrees _____   degrees _____   degrees _____   degrees _____

Name the figure.

16.

17.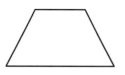

18.

19.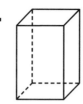

_____ _____ _____ _____

Is the dashed line on the figure a line of symmetry for the figure? Circle *Yes* or *No*.

20.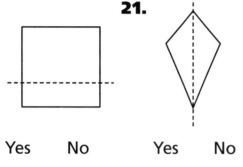

21.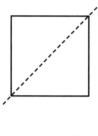

22.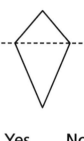

23.

Yes   No   Yes   No   Yes   No   Yes   No

Complete the net for the space figure.

24.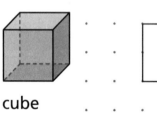

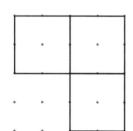

cube

Use the graph to answer the question.

Favorite Sport

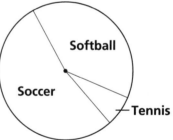

Softball

Soccer

Tennis

25. Which sport did about half the students say was their favorite?

_____

Use the Act it Out Strategy to solve the problem.

26. Can **3** of the **4** figures shown be arranged to form a rectangle? Explain.

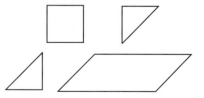

_____

1 A bakery sells 250 muffins in one day. How many muffins does the shop sell in a week?

  A 1,750   **C** 1,450   **E** NH

  B 1,500   **D** 1,400

2 What fraction of a circle is the right angle shown?

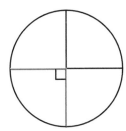

  F $\frac{3}{4}$ **H** $\frac{1}{3}$

  G $\frac{1}{2}$ **J** $\frac{1}{4}$

3 Employees at a music store unpack 12 cartons of CDs. There are 128 CDs in each carton. How many CDs did they unpack in all?

  A 1,524   **C** 1,548   **E** NH

  B 1,536   **D** 1,560

4 Which figure has the same shape as your math textbook?

  F Triangle   **H** Pentagon

  G Rectangle   **J** Hexagon

5 At a volleyball tournament, 87 students divided into teams with 6 students on each team. How many extra students were there?

  A 0   **C** 2   **E** NH

  B 1   **D** 3

6 The angles shown below are grouped together because they are similar.

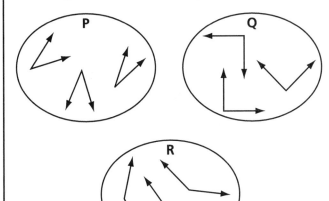

Which angle belongs with group R?

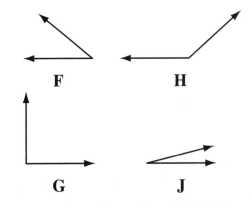

7 Which fraction is in simplest form?

  A $\frac{5}{12}$ **C** $\frac{3}{9}$

  B $\frac{4}{10}$ **D** $\frac{2}{6}$

8 The diameter of Mike's bicycle wheel is 22 inches. What is the radius?

F 44 in.

H 11 in.

G 22 in.

J 2 in.

9 Four students ran different distances. The distances are shown below.

Name	Distance Run
Jamail	$\frac{5}{6}$ mile
Kim	$\frac{1}{4}$ mile
Frank	$\frac{2}{3}$ mile
Elena	$\frac{11}{12}$ mile

Which lists the students in order from the *longest* distance run to the *shortest* distance run?

A Frank, Kim, Elena, Jamail

B Kim, Frank, Jamail, Elena

C Elena, Jamail, Kim, Frank

D Elena, Jamail, Frank, Kim

10 What number is equal to
$(6 \times 100,000) + (9 \times 10,000) + (7 \times 1,000) + (6 \times 1)$?

F 6,970,600

H 697,060

G 6,097,006

J 697,006

11 Which mixed number represents the shaded portion of this model?

A $3\frac{14}{6}$

C $3\frac{4}{6}$

B 4

D $3\frac{2}{6}$

12 Which of the following is a prime number?

F 15

H 22

G 17

J 25

13 Averil runs every day. He has run $7\frac{1}{4}$ miles so far this week. If he runs $1\frac{1}{4}$ miles on Friday, how far will he have run all together?

A $7\frac{1}{2}$

D $9\frac{1}{2}$

B $8\frac{1}{4}$

E NH

C $8\frac{1}{2}$

UNIT 7 • TABLE OF CONTENTS

Measurement

Dear Family,

During the next few weeks, our math class will be learning about and practicing measurement.

You can expect to see homework that provides practice with finding perimeter. Here is a sample you may want to keep handy to give help if needed.

Finding Perimeter

When you find the perimeter of an object, you are finding the distance around it. To find the perimeter of a rectangle, use the formula $P = 2 \times (l + w)$ where P = perimeter, l = the length of the rectangle, and w = the width of the rectangle.

Example Find the perimeter of rectangle **ABCD**.

$P = 2 \times (l + w)$ Write the formula.
$P = 2 \times (10 + 5)$ Substitute for l and w.
$P = 2 \times (15)$ Start inside parentheses.
$P = 30$ in.   Multiply. Label the answer.

Another way to find the perimeter of a figure is to add the measure of its sides.

Example Find the perimeter of square **WXYZ**.

$P = s + s + s + s$ s = the length of one side
$P = 12 + 12 + 12 + 12$
$P = 48$ cm

During this unit, students will need to continue practicing multiplication and addition facts.

Sincerely,

Name _____

The **centimeter** is a unit of length in the **metric system.**
This ruler is a centimeter ruler. The space between each
number on the ruler measures one centimeter.

This line segment is **8** centimeters long.
A short way of writing centimeters is **cm**.
So you can write: **8 cm** long.

**Measure the line segment with a centimeter ruler
or use the one below.**

1. ├─────────────────┤   _____ centimeters (cm)

2. ├──────────────────────────────┤   _____ cm

3. ├────────────┤   _____ cm

4. ├──────────────────┤   _____ cm

5. ├──────────────────────────────────────┤   _____ cm

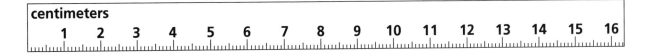

**Use a centimeter ruler to measure each side of the figure.
Then add to find the total distance around the figure.**

6.

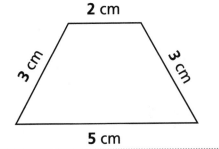
2 cm
3 cm   3 cm
5 cm   _____

7.

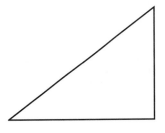
_____

8.

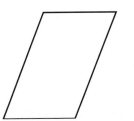
_____

9.

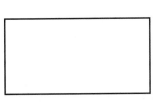
_____

The **millimeter** is a unit of length in the metric system that is smaller than the centimeter.

> **10** millimeters = **1** centimeter

The short way of writing millimeter is **mm**.   **10 mm = 1 cm**

The small marks on the ruler show millimeters.
The black line segment is **7 mm** long,
the red line segment is **23 mm** long, and
the paper clip is **40** mm, or **4** cm, long.

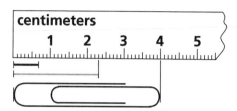

Measure the line segment in millimeters.

10. |————————————| _____ millimeters (mm)

11. |——————————————————| _____ mm

12. |——————————| _____ mm

Complete.

13. **1** cm = _____ mm   **30** mm = _____ cm   **6** cm = _____ mm

14. **90** mm = _____ cm   **12** cm = _____ mm   **60** mm = _____ cm

---

| Problem Solving |
| Reasoning |

Use a centimeter ruler with millimeter markings to draw the following.

15. A line segment **8** cm long.

16. A line segment **55** mm long.

Test Prep ★ Mixed Review

17 Which of the following is a prime number?

  A 17   C 25

  B 21   D 32

18 Which fraction is equivalent to $3\frac{2}{5}$?

  F $\frac{19}{5}$ H $\frac{15}{5}$

  G $\frac{17}{5}$ J $\frac{6}{5}$

Name _____

The decimeter, meter, and kilometer are other metric units of length. In the metric system, **1 decimeter (dm)** is the same as **10 centimeters**.

1 decimeter = 10 centimeters
1 dm = 10 cm

This ruler is marked in centimeters. It shows **10 centimeters** or **1 decimeter.**

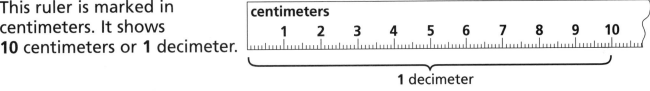

1 decimeter

The **meter (m)** is the basic unit of length in the metric system. It is used to measure length or distance.

1 meter = 100 centimeters	1 meter = 10 decimeters
1 m = 100 cm	**1 m = 10 dm**

The **kilometer (km)** is used to measure greater distances.

1 kilometer = 1,000 meters	1 kilometer = 10,000 decimeters
1 km = 1,000 m	**1 km = 10,000 dm**

Circle the better estimate.

1. thickness of a book	width of a door	width of your classroom
2 cm 2 dm	1 dm 1 m	8 m 8 dm
2. length of a pencil	height of a tree	height of an adult
1 cm 1 dm	15 m 15 km	2 dm 2 m
3. length of a board	length of a bicycle	width of a hand
1 m 1 km	2 dm 2 m	8 cm 8 dm

Complete.

4. If **1** meter is **100** centimeters, then **7** meters is _____ centimeters.

5. If **100** centimeters is **1** meter, then **800** centimeters is _____ meters.

6. If **1** kilometer is **1,000** meters, then **5** kilometers is _____ meters.

7. If **1,000** meters is **1** kilometer, then **8,000** meters is _____ kilometers.

Write the equivalent measure.

8. **3** km = _____ m   **5,000** m = _____ km   **6** dm = _____ cm

9. **8** m = _____ cm   **100** cm = _____ dm   **3,000** m = _____ km

10. **50** km = _____ m   **20** dm = _____ m   **6** m = _____ dm

---

Estimate the measurement. Then measure to the nearest centimeter, decimeter, or meter.

	Estimated Length	Actual Length
11. Length of your shoe		
12. Height of your desk		
13. Width of your desk		

Problem Solving Reasoning Solve.

14. Which is the greater number, the width of your classroom in decimeters, or in meters? Why?

_____

_____

Test Prep ★ Mixed Review

15 A drama club raises $275 to see a play. A theater sells student tickets for $7 each. How many tickets can the drama club buy?

A 36   C 38

B 37   D 39

16 Which fraction is equivalent to $\frac{6}{8}$?

F $\frac{1}{2}$ H $\frac{8}{6}$

G $\frac{3}{4}$ J $\frac{4}{3}$

Name _____

Capacity is the amount of liquid a container will hold.
The **liter** and **milliliter** are metric units of capacity.

Liters (L) are used to measure greater amounts of capacity.
A cube **10** cm on each side holds **1** liter of water.

Milliliters (mL) are used to measure lesser amounts of
capacity. A cube **1** cm on each side holds **1** mL of water.

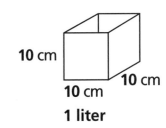

10 cm
10 cm
10 cm
1 liter

1 cm
1 cm
1 cm
1 milliliter

1,000 milliliters = **1** liter
1,000 (mL) = **1** (L)

**Tell if you would use liters (L) or milliliters (mL)
to measure the capacity of each object.**

1. small juice glass _____   bathtub _____

2. milk pitcher _____   glass _____

3. water bucket _____   bowl _____

4. bottle cap _____   aquarium _____

5. tea cup _____   pail _____

Circle the better estimate.

6. medicine dropper	aquarium	waste basket	soup spoon
1 mL 1 L	30 mL 30 L	20 mL 20 L	15 mL 15 L

Write the equivalent measure.

7. 2 L = _____ mL   1,000 mL = _____ L   4,000 mL = _____ L

8. 5 L = _____ mL   0.5 L = _____ mL   100 mL = _____ L

9. 1,500 mL = _____ L   1.5 L = _____ mL   2,500 mL = _____ L

10. 9 L = _____ mL   3,000 mL = _____ L   6 L = _____ mL

You measure the mass of an object by weighing it.
The **gram** and **kilogram** are metric units of mass.

The **kilogram (kg)** is used to measure large objects. A baseball bat has a mass of about 1 kilogram.

1 kilogram = **1,000** grams
1 (kg) = 1,000 (g)

The **gram (g)** is used to measure small objects. A paper clip has a mass of about **1** gram.

Circle the best estimate.

11. television   **16 g**   **16 kg**   pen   **10 g**   **10 kg**   apple   **200 g**   **200 kg**

Write the equivalent measure.

12. 3 kg = _____ g   5,000 g = _____ kg   2 kg = _____ g

13. 0.5 kg = _____ g   1,500 g = _____ kg   4,000 g = _____ kg

---

✓ Quick Check

Use a metric ruler to measure each line to the nearest centimeter. Then measure to the nearest millimeter.

Work Space.

14.

|—————| |———————————|

nearest cm _____   nearest cm _____

nearest mm _____   nearest mm _____

Write the equivalent measure.

15. 20 dm = ☐ m   **16.** ☐ km = 8,000 m

17. ☐ dm = 50 m   **18.** 4,000 m = ☐ km

Compare. Write >, <, or =.

19. 4 L ☐ 3,500 mL   **20.** 7 L ☐ 7,000 mL

21. 2 kg ☐ 1,750 g   **22.** 3 kg ☐ 4,000 g

Name _____

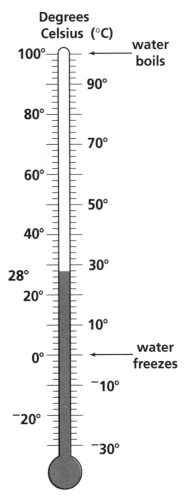

You measure temperature with a **thermometer**.

A **degree Celsius (°C)** is a metric unit used to measure temperature. The scale on this thermometer shows degrees Celsius. Each mark represents **2** degrees Celsius.

The red shading in this thermometer shows that the temperature is **28°C,** or **28** degrees Celsius.

Read the scale on the thermometer.

• Find **0°C**. Water freezes at **0°C**.

• Find **100°C**. Water boils at **100°C**.

Numbers less than **0** are called **negative numbers**. Temperatures colder than **0°** are represented with negative numbers. Two degrees below **0°C** is written as ⁻**2°C** and read as "minus two degrees Celsius."

• Find ⁻**10°C**. If the temperature is ⁻**10°C**, it is a very cold day.

Use arrows to mark each temperature on the thermometer above.

1. 32°C   ⁻8°C   70°C   ⁻4°C   22°C   48°C   ⁻22°C

Circle the warmer temperature.

2. 10°C   32°C | 32°C   36°C | 50°C   68°C | ⁻10°C   ⁻20°C

3. 5°C   ⁻5°C | 72°C   82°C | 0°C   ⁻8°C | 15°C   12°C

Circle the best estimate of temperature.

4. ice   boiling water   a snowy day   a very hot day

12°C   0°C | 90°C   100°C | ⁻5°C   25°C | 38°C   88°C

A **line graph** organizes and displays data that change during a period of time. This line graph shows how the temperature changed on Saturday.

Saturday's Temperatures

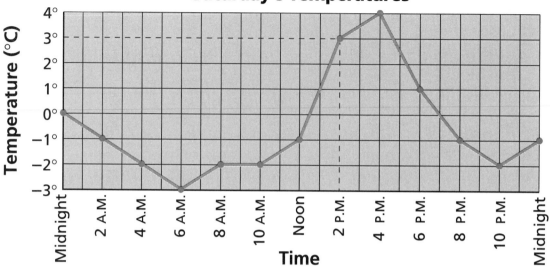

To find the temperature at **2 P.M.**, follow these steps.

• Find **2 P.M.** on the horizontal (left-to-right) axis.

• Trace a line up from **2:00 P.M.** until you reach a point on the graph.

• Trace a straight line from that point to the vertical (up-and-down) axis to find the temperature, **3°**. The temperature at **2 P.M.** was **3°C.**

Use the graph to answer the questions.

5. What was the warmest temperature on Saturday? _____

   At what time did that temperature occur? _____

6. What was the coldest temperature? _____

   At what time did that temperature occur? _____

7. When was the temperature **–1°C**? _____, _____, _____

8. For how many hours was the temperature less than **–2°C**? _____

Test Prep ★ Mixed Review

9 What is line segment *Q*?

   A Ray   **C** Diameter

   B Radius   **D** Chord

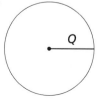

10 There are **360°** in a circle. **What is the degree measure of the angle shown?**

   F 60°   **H** 180°

   G 90°   **J** 270°

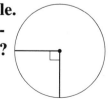

Name _____

Problem Solving Strategy:
Make a Table

STANDARD

In this lesson, you will learn to make a table to help you solve a problem.

Problem

Beginning at 6:30 A.M., buses leave to go to the airport. A bus leaves every **45** minutes. The trip takes $1\frac{1}{2}$ hours. If Marcia takes the second bus of the day, what time will she get to the airport?

❶ Understand   As you reread, ask yourself questions.

• What facts do you know?
The first bus leaves at **6:30** A.M.

Buses leave every _____ minutes.

The trip takes _____ hours.
• What do you need to find out?

_____

• What will you need to find out first?

_____

❷ Decide   Choose a method for solving.

Try the strategy Make a Table.

Bus	Leaves	Arrives
1		
2		

❸ Solve   Find the times you need. Write them in the table.

• What time can you fill in first?

_____

• Find the time the second bus leaves.

6:30 A.M. $\xrightarrow{\textbf{+30} \text{ min}}$ _____ A.M. $\xrightarrow{\textbf{+15} \text{ min}}$ _____ A.M.

• Find the time the second bus arrives at the airport.

7:15 A.M. $\xrightarrow{\textbf{+1} \text{ hr}}$ _____ A.M. $\xrightarrow{\textbf{+30} \text{ min}}$ _____ A.M.

❹ Look back   Write the answer to the problem. _____

• Why is it not necessary to complete the entire table?

_____

Copyright © Houghton Mifflin Company. All rights reserved.

Unit 7 Lesson 5 **183**

Solve. Use the Make a Table strategy or any other strategy you have learned.

1. At an amusement park, a musical show starts every **35** minutes and lasts for **20** minutes. If the first show is at **9:30** A.M., what time does the third show end?

Think: What could you label the columns and rows of a table?

_____

Answer _____

2. T-shirts are on sale, buy **2**–get one free. If one T-shirt costs **$6**, how much will Mrs. Simon pay for **7** shirts?

Think: How would you set up a table to help you solve the problem?

_____

Answer _____

3. Move **4** toothpicks to make **3** congruent squares.

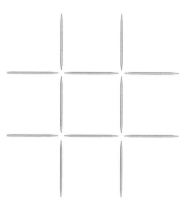

4. Are these two figures congruent?

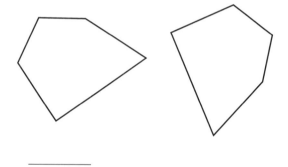

_____

5. A movie lasts **90** minutes. The movie is shown at **1:30** P.M., **3:25** P.M., **5:20** P.M., **7:15** P.M., and **9:05** P.M. Sarah can get from the theater to her house in **15** minutes. What is the latest show Sarah can go to and still be home by **8:30** P.M.?

_____

6. Sean bowled three games. His scores were **79, 76,** and **83**. What score will he need to get in the next game to have an average of exactly **80**?

_____

7. The sum of two numbers is **60**. Their difference is **12**. What are the two numbers?

_____

8. Write the next number in this sequence.

$5\frac{1}{3}$, $6\frac{2}{3}$, 8, $9\frac{1}{3}$, $10\frac{2}{3}$, _____

In the **customary system** of measurement, the **inch (in.)** is a standard unit of length. This ruler is marked with inches and half inches.

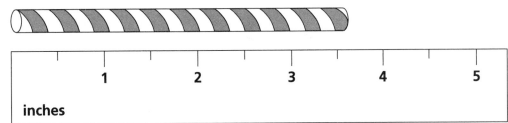

inches

- You can use a ruler to measure to the **nearest inch**. The straw is between **3** and **4** inches long. Because it is nearer to **4** inches than to **3** inches, the length of the straw is **4 inches to the nearest inch**. If the object you are measuring is **halfway** between two whole inches, use the greater number.

- You can also measure to the **nearest half inch**. The straw is between $3\frac{1}{2}$ and **4** inches long. But it is nearer to $3\frac{1}{2}$ inches, so the length of the straw is $3\frac{1}{2}$ **inches to the nearest half inch**.

Measure the pen to the nearest inch or half inch.

1. Pen **A** is about _____ inches long.

Pen **B** is about _____ inches long.

Pen **C** is about _____ inches long.

Pen **D** is about _____ inches long.

A

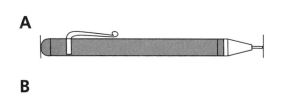

C

B

D

2. Pen **A** is _____ to the nearest half inch.

Pen **B** is _____ to the nearest half inch.

3. Pen **C** is _____ to the nearest half inch.

Pen **D** is _____ to the nearest half inch.

The units on this ruler are whole inches, half inches, and quarter inches. The straw is $3\frac{3}{4}$ inches long, **to the nearest quarter-inch.**

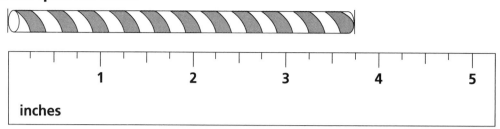

Complete.

4. What is the length of this pencil to the nearest inch? _____

to the nearest half inch? _____

to the nearest quarter inch? _____

Measure the line to the nearest quarter inch.

5. |————————————————————————| _____

6. |————————————————| _____

Problem Solving Reasoning Solve.

7. Is it more accurate to measure to the nearest quarter inch, half inch, or inch? Explain.

_____

_____

Test Prep ★ Mixed Review

8 What number is a common factor of both 14 and 28?

    A 7   **C** 4

    B 6   **D** 3

9 The distance from Brian's house to the park is 3,000 meters. What is the distance in kilometers?

    F 3   **H** 300

    G 30   **J** 30,000

Name _____

Customary Units of Length: Foot, Yard, Mile

The standard units of length in the customary system are the **inch, foot, yard,** and **mile**.

Customary Units of Length

1 foot (ft) =	**12** inches (in.)
1 yard (yd) =	**3** feet (ft) or **36** in.
1 mile (mi) =	**5,280** feet (ft)
1 mile (mi) =	**1,760** yards (yd)

Write the customary unit you would use to measure the following.

1. the length of a car _____

2. the length of a soccer field _____

3. the distance from Canada to Mexico _____

4. the length of a caterpillar _____

5. the height of a tree _____

6. the diameter of the Earth _____

7. cloth for making curtains _____

8. the length of a pencil _____

Choose the best unit for each measurement.
Write *inches*, *feet*, *yards*, or *miles*.

9. The pencil is **7** _____ long.   A football field is **100** _____ long.

10. The room is **20** _____ wide.   The trip was **150** _____ each way.

11. The door is **7** _____ high.   The basketball player is **7** _____ tall.

12. The plane is **5** _____ high.   It is **350** _____ from one city to another.

13. The desk is **42** _____ wide.   A swimming pool is **9** _____ deep.

Circle the correct measure.

14. the length of a room   the height of a bookcase   the length of a river

   24 miles   **24** feet   **6** yards   **6** feet   **25** miles   **25** inches

Complete the table.

15.

Feet	1	2	3	4	5	6	7	8
Inches	12							

16.

Yards	1	2	3	4	5	6	7	8
Feet	3							

Complete.

17. **5** yd = _____ ft   **36** in. = _____ yd   **2** yd = _____ in.

18. **3** mi = _____ yd   **5,280** ft = _____ mi   **2** ft = _____ in.

Problem Solving
Reasoning

Solve.

19. How many **4**-foot lengths of string can be cut from a piece of string **3** yards **1** foot long? _____

✔ Quick Check

Circle the better estimate of temperature.

Work Space.

20. To make a snowman   **21.** To boil soup

   A. 30°C   B. 10°C   A. 100°C   B. 40°C

Use a customary ruler to measure each line to the nearest half inch and nearest quarter inch.

22. ⊢————————⊣   **23.** ⊢————————⊣

   nearest half inch _____   nearest half inch _____

   nearest quarter inch _____   nearest quarter inch _____

Circle the better estimate.

24. height of a chair   **25.** length of your leg

   A. 4 ft   B. 4 yd   A. 2 in.   B. 2 ft

26. width of a bridge   **27.** height of a house

   A. 50 ft   B. 50 mi   A. 7 ft   B. 7 yd

Customary Units of Capacity and Weight

Customary units of liquid capacity include the **cup, pint, quart,** and **gallon.**

Units of Capacity

2 cups (c)	= **1** pint (pt)
2 pints (pt)	= **1** quart (qt)
4 quarts (qt)	= **1** gallon (gal)

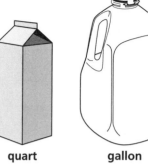

cup   pint   quart   gallon

Circle each item that is measured in units of liquid capacity.

1. peaches   milk   cereal   apples   paint

  sugar   oil   vinegar   gravel   gasoline

  nuts   potatoes   water   soup   lumber

Complete the chart.

2.

Quarts	1	2	3	4	5	6	7	8
Pints	2							
Cups	4							

Complete.

3. 1 pt = _____ c   4 gal = _____ qt   6 c = _____ pt

4. 8 qt = _____ gal   2 qt = _____ gal   _____ pt = $\frac{1}{2}$ gal

5. _____ c = 3 qt   _____ gal = 16 pt   32 qt = _____ gal

6. 6 c = _____ qt   _____ c = 5 pt   _____ p = $2\frac{1}{2}$ qt

---

A unit of quantity is the **dozen (doz).**

1 dozen (doz) = 12

Complete.

7. $\frac{1}{2}$ dozen = _____   3 dozen = _____   12 dozen = _____

8. 2 dozen = _____   10 dozen = _____ $1\frac{1}{2}$ dozen = _____

Customary units of weight include the **ounce, pound**, and **ton**.

Units of Weight

1 pound (lb) = 16 ounces (oz)
1 ton = 2,000 pounds (lb)

Complete.

9. 16 oz = _____ lb   2 tons = _____ lb   32 oz = _____ lb

10. 8,000 lb = _____ tons   4 lb = _____ oz   16 tons = _____ lb

11. _____ oz = 3 lb   _____ lb = 80 oz   _____ tons = 4,000 lb

12. 6 lb = _____ oz   _____ lb = 10 tons   10 lb = _____ oz

Write the equivalent measure.

13. 7,000 lb = _____ tons _____ lb   21 oz = _____ lb _____ oz

14. 13,000 lb = _____ tons _____ lb   18 oz = _____ lb _____ oz

15. 18,000 lb = _____ tons _____ lb   34 oz = _____ lb _____ oz

16. 5,622 lb = _____ tons _____ lb   25 oz = _____ lb _____ oz

Problem Solving
Reasoning
Solve.

17. Mrs. Chapman bought **2** qt of chocolate, **1** qt of strawberry, and **6** pt of vanilla ice cream. How many quarts of ice cream did she buy in all? How many pints?

_____

Test Prep ★ Mixed Review

18 **Which group of numbers shows all the factors of 28?**

A 2, 8, 9, 14

B 1, 2, 4, 7, 14, 28

C 1, 2, 4, 7, 8, 28

D 2, 4, 7, 14

19 **Which fraction is equivalent to $2\frac{3}{8}$?**

F $\frac{24}{8}$

G $\frac{21}{8}$

H $\frac{19}{8}$

J $\frac{16}{8}$

Fahrenheit Temperature and Negative Numbers

In the Customary System, temperature is measured in **degrees Fahrenheit (°F)**. Each mark on this thermometer is **1°F**. Temperatures below 0° are written with a negative sign (⁻).

Read the scale.

Find **32°F**. Water freezes at **32°** Fahrenheit.

Water boils at **212°F**.

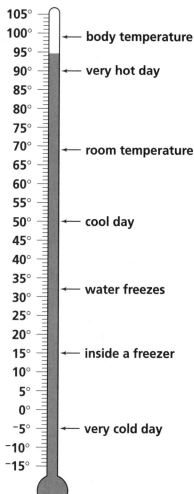

Fahrenheit Temperature and Negative Numbers

105°
100° ← body temperature
95°
90° ← very hot day
85°
80°
75°
70° ← room temperature
65°
60°
55°
50° ← cool day
45°
40°
35°
30° ← water freezes
25°
20°
15° ← inside a freezer
10°
5°
0°
⁻5° ← very cold day
⁻10°
⁻15°

Read the thermometer to find the temperature.

1. the inside of a freezer _____

2. body temperature _____

3. room temperature _____

4. a very cold day _____

5. a very hot day _____

6. a cool day _____

Draw an arrow pointing to the temperature on the thermometer.

7. **85°F**   **20°F**   **58°F**   **23°F**

8. **⁻10°F**   **17°F**   **⁻3°F**   **⁻14°F**

Circle the colder temperature.

9. **83°F or 73°F**   **16°F or 26°F**   **10°F or 0°F**

10. **⁻4°F or 0°F**   **⁻8°F or 8°F**   **⁻6°F or ⁻12°F**

Circle the best estimate.

11. ice cubes	12. hot soup	13. a day at the beach
32°F 80°F 50°F	230°F 125°F 70°F	49°F 99°F 149°F
14. a glass of cold water	**15.** water in a swimming pool	**16.** snowballs
72°F 40°F 95°F	114°F 84°F 34°F	20°F 52°F 81°F

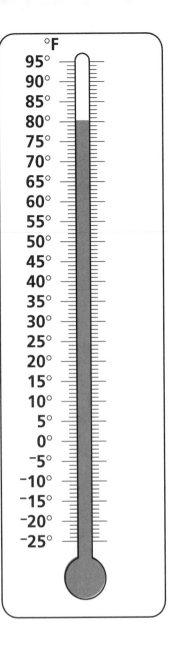

°F
95°
90°
85°
80°
75°
70°
65°
60°
55°
50°
45°
40°
35°
30°
25°
20°
15°
10°
5°
0°
−5°
−10°
−15°
−20°
−25°

You can think of a thermometer as a vertical **number line**.

You can use the number line to find the difference between two temperatures.

The temperature was **10°F**. Later, it was **⁻5°F**. What was the difference in temperature?

Use the thermometer. Find **10°F**. Count down on the number line until you reach **⁻5°F**. How many degrees did you count?

The difference between **10°F** and **⁻5°F** is **15** degrees.

Count on the thermometer to find the answer.

17. What temperature is **10 degrees** above **0°F**? _____

18. What temperature is **10 degrees** below **0°F**? _____

19. How many degrees is it from **0°F** to **20°F**? _____

20. How many degrees is it from **0°F** to **⁻20°F**? _____

21. What temperature is **5 degrees** warmer than **⁻10°F**? _____

22. What temperature is **5 degrees** colder than **⁻10°F**? _____

23. What temperature is **5 degrees** warmer than **25°F**? _____

Find the number of degrees from one temperature to the other.

24. **55°F** and **65°F** _____   **25°F** and **65°F** _____   **10°F** and **18°F** _____

25. **0°F** and **32°F** _____   **⁻10°F** and **0°F** _____   **⁻10°F** and **10°F** _____

26. **⁻20°F** and **20°F** _____   **⁻12°F** and **10°F** _____   **⁻5°F** and **25°F** _____

27. **⁻5°F** and **⁻10°F** _____   **⁻25°F** and **⁻5°F** _____   **⁻13°F** and **⁻6°F** _____

Write the temperature. Use the thermometer if you need to.

28. Was **10°F**. Increased **20** degrees. _____

29. Was **75°F**. Increased **12** degrees. _____

30. Was **62°F**. Decreased **8** degrees. _____

31. Was **32°F**. Decreased **7** degrees. _____

32. Was **0°F**. Decreased **6** degrees. _____

33. Was **0°F**. Increased **16** degrees. _____

34. Was **10°F**. Decreased **10** degrees. _____

35. Was **5°F**. Decreased **15** degrees. _____

36. Was ⁻**10°F**. Increased **15** degrees. _____

37. Was ⁻**5°F**. Decreased **5** degrees. _____

38. Was ⁻**16°F**. Increased **12** degrees. _____

39. Was ⁻**6°F**. Decreased **8** degrees. _____

°F
95°
90°
85°
80°
75°
70°
65°
60°
55°
50°
45°
40°
35°
30°
25°
20°
15°
10°
5°
0°
-5°
-10°
-15°
-20°
-25°

| Problem Solving |
| Reasoning |

Solve.

40. At midnight the temperature was ⁻**4°F**. Three hours later the temperature was **10** degrees colder. What was the temperature? _____

41. At dawn the temperature was ⁻**7°F**. By noon the temperature had risen **15** degrees. What was the noon temperature? _____

Test Prep ★ Mixed Review

42 Which is the most likely temperature outside when Angel is swimming?

A 93° C

B 38° C

C 10° C

D 0° C

43 The width of Glenda's room is 24 feet. What is the width in yards?

F 3

G 6

H 8

J 12

Name _____

STANDARD

Sometimes you can use a diagram to solve a problem.

You can use a number line to help you work with negative numbers. You have seen negative numbers used to show temperatures less than 0°. You can also use negative numbers to represent money that is owed, and in many different problem solving situations.

In this lesson, you will use a number line to keep track of changes and to compare numbers.

Tips to Remember:

1. Understand	2. Decide	3. Solve	4. Look back

- Picture the situation described in the problem. Tell what is happening in your own words.
- When you can, make predictions about the answer. Then compare your answer and your prediction.
- Compare the numbers on the number line with the words and numbers in the problem.

Solve. Use the number line.

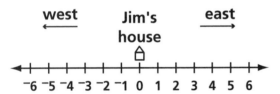

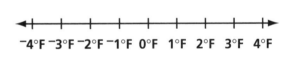

1. Jim is at his house. He walks **3** blocks west. Then he walks **4** blocks east and **6** blocks west. What point on the number line shows where Jim is then?

Think: At what point is Jim after he walks **4** blocks east? How did you use the number line to help you?

_____

_____

Answer _____

2. Monday's temperature was **2**° F. Tuesday's temperature was **1**°F higher than Monday's. Wednesday's temperature was **4**°F lower than Tuesday's. What was Wednesday's temperature?

Think: Where on the number line should you begin?

_____

Answer _____

```
 ◄──┼──┼──┼──┼──┼──┼──┼──┼──┼──┼──┼──┼──┼──►
   ⁻6  ⁻5  ⁻4  ⁻3  ⁻2  ⁻1   0  ⁺1  ⁺2  ⁺3  ⁺4  ⁺5  ⁺6
```

Solve. Use the number line.

3. Adrienne has **$6**. She tells Eric she will give him **$8**. If she gives him all her money, how much more does she owe?

Think: Where on the number line should you begin?

_____

Answer _____

4. A stock price gained **2** points in one day. On the next day, it lost **1** point. On the third day, it lost **2** more points. What was the total gain or loss over the **3** days?

Think: How can you use the number line to help solve this problem?

_____

Answer _____

5. Sylvia opens a savings account with **$5**. She then deposits **$1**. Then she withdraws **$4** and deposits **$3**. How much does she then have in the account?

Answer _____

6. Cara gets on an elevator at the fourth floor. The elevator goes up **2** floors and then down **5** floors. Then it goes up **4** more floors and Cara gets out. What floor is she on?

_____

7. Aaron has saved **$3**. He gets **$3** more for his allowance. He spends **$4** for a yo-yo. He gets another allowance of **$3**. Does Aaron have enough money to buy a **$7** game?

_____

8. Sam walks from school to Larry's house, which is **4** blocks east of the school. Sam then walks **7** blocks west to his own house. How many blocks is Sam from school?

_____

Extend Your Thinking

9. Go back to problem **7**. After Aaron bought the yo-yo, how much money did he have left? How did you decide?

_____

_____

10. Go back to problem **6**. How could Cara have made the same trip by going in only one direction?

_____

_____

Perimeter

Mr. Everett wants to build a fence around his garden. He wants to know how many meters of fence he will need.

> The distance around a figure is its **perimeter (P)**.

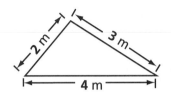

To find the perimeter, add the length of the sides.

$$2\text{ m} + 3\text{ m} + 4\text{ m} = 9\text{ m}$$

The perimeter is **9** meters. The garden needs **9** meters of fence.

Find the perimeter (P) of the figure.

1.
3 m
1 m ☐ 1 m
3 m

P = _____

2.
5 cm
5 cm ☐ 5 cm
5 cm

P = _____

3.
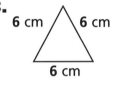
6 cm   6 cm
6 cm

P = _____

4.
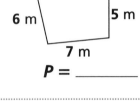
8 m
6 m   5 m
7 m

P = _____

5.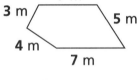
7 m
3 m
5 m
4 m
7 m

P = _____

6.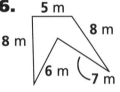
5 m
8 m   8 m
6 m   7 m

P = _____

7.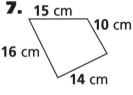
15 cm
10 cm
16 cm
14 cm

P = _____

8.
4 cm
14 cm   15 cm
21 cm

P = _____

Since all four sides of a square are the same length, you can multiply the length of one side by 4 to find the perimeter.

$$P = 2\text{ cm} + 2\text{ cm} + 2\text{ cm} + 2\text{ cm} \text{ or } 8\text{ cm}$$

$$P = 4 \times 2\text{ cm or } 8\text{ cm}$$

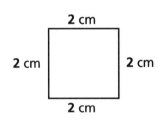
2 cm
2 cm   2 cm
2 cm

For any **square** with side s, $P = 4 \times s$

Find the perimeter of the square. Use $P = 4s$.

9. $s = 3$ cm _____

10. $s = 5$ m _____

11. $s = 10$ in. _____

12. $s = 25$ yd _____

Name _____

The **length (*l*)** of this rectangle is **4** cm.
The **width (*w*)** is **3** cm.
To find the perimeter, add the lengths of the four sides:

P = **4** cm + **4** cm + **3** cm + **3** cm or **14** cm

P = **2** × **4** + **2** × **3** or **14** cm

For any rectangle with length *l* and width *w*,
$P = (2 × l) + (2 × w)$

4 cm

3 cm   3 cm

4 cm

Use a formula to find the perimeter.

13. a rectangle **4** m long

and **2** m wide _____

14. a rectangle **15** cm long

and **10** cm wide _____

15. a square **6** mm on each side _____

16. a square **23** m on each side _____

 Quick Check

Compare. Write >, <, or =.

17. 1 lb ☐ 19 oz

18. 4,400 lb ☐ 2 T

19. 1 gal ☐ 5 qt

20. 2 pt ☐ 1 qt

Work Space.

Solve.

21. When would it be warm enough to swim outside? Circle the better estimate of temperature.

A. 40°F   B. 90°F

22. The temperature was ⁻3°F at dawn. By noon, it was 10°F. How much did the temperature rise?

_____

23. Find the perimeter of the rectangle shown.

4 feet

8 feet

_____

STANDARD

Area is the number of square units in a region.
The area of this region is **6** square units.

A **square centimeter** can be used to measure
area. A square centimeter is a square with
1 cm sides.

1 cm

1 cm

A rectangle has two dimensions: length (*l*) and
width (*w*). The rectangle at the right has a length
of **2** centimeters, a width of **1** centimeter,
and an area (*A*) of **2** square centimeters.

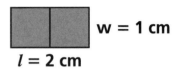

w = 1 cm

l = 2 cm

A = **2** square centimeters

Find the area in square units.

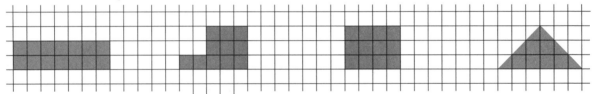

1.

_____   _____   _____   _____

Find the area in square centimeters.

2.

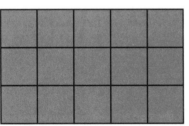

A = _____

3.

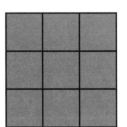

A = _____

4.

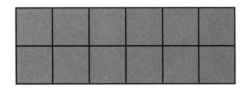

A = _____

5.

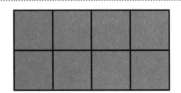

A = _____

Name _____

The rectangular region at the right has a length of **6** centimeters and a width of **4** centimeters. You can find the area (**A**) of the rectangular region by multiplying its length by its width.

A = **6** units × 4 units or **24 square cm**

4 cm

6 cm

> For any rectangular region with length **l** and width **w**,
> **A = l × w.**

Other units of area include the square millimeter, square meter, square kilometer, square inch, square yard, and square mile.

Find the area of the figure.

6.

19 cm

14 cm

A = _____

7.

25 cm

37 cm

A = _____

8.

15 cm

29 cm

A = _____

9.

5 in.

12 in.

A = _____

10.

15 yd

15 yd

A = _____

11.

23 km

12 km

A = _____

12.

27 m

18 m

A = _____

13.

10 ft

50 ft

A = _____

14.

30 in.

30 in.

A = _____

Find the area of the region.

Region	Equation	Answer
15. 8 feet long and **3** feet wide		
16. 12 inches square		
17. 7 feet long and **4** feet wide		
18. 15 centimeters square		

Find the area and perimeter of the region.

19.

6 ft

13 ft

$P =$ _____

$A =$ _____

20.

16 m

16 m

$P =$ _____

$A =$ _____

21.

33 mm

12 mm

$P =$ _____

$A =$ _____

Problem Solving Reasoning Solve.

22. Which regions have the same area, but a different perimeter? _____

23. Which regions have the same perimeter, but a different area? _____

A

B C

Test Prep ★ Mixed Review

24 Which fraction is equivalent to $\frac{9}{12}$?

A $\frac{12}{9}$ C $\frac{2}{3}$

B $\frac{3}{4}$ D $\frac{3}{6}$

25 Which one of the following fractions is greater than $\frac{3}{5}$?

F $\frac{7}{10}$ H $\frac{5}{12}$

G $\frac{1}{2}$ J $\frac{5}{16}$

Name _____

STANDARD

You can find the **perimeter** of this figure by adding the length of each side.

3 in. + **4** in. + **3** in. + **8** in. + **6** in. + **12** in. = **36** in.

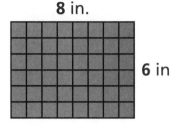

8 in.

3 in.

4 in.

3 in.

6 in.

12 in.

You can also find the **area** of the figure by first dividing it into two rectangles.

Find the area of both rectangles.

Use $A = l \times w$.

Rectangle 1: **4** in. × **3** in. = **12** square in.

Rectangle 2: **8** in. × **6** in. = **48** square in.

Then add the areas of the two rectangles to find the total area of the figure:

48 square in. + **12** square in. = **60** square in.

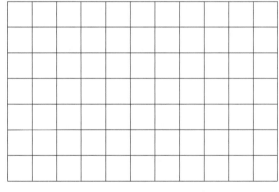

8 in.

4 in.

3 in.

6 in

Rectangle 1   **Rectangle 2**

Find the perimeter for each figure.
Draw the figure as two rectangles to find the area.

1.

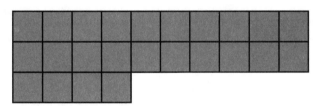

Perimeter = _____ units

Area = _____ square units

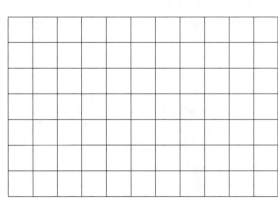

2.

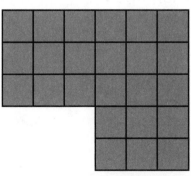

Perimeter = _____ units

Area = _____ square units

Find the area of this figure.

3.

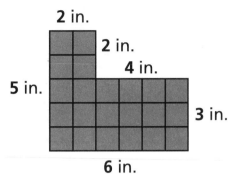

2 in.

2 in.

4 in.

5 in.

3 in.

6 in.

A = _____

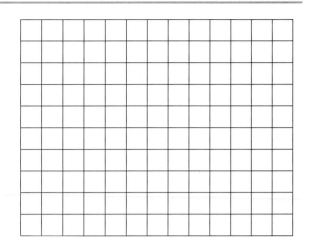

Solve.

4. What is the perimeter of this figure?

_____

5. What is the area of this figure?

_____

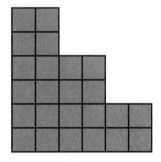

✓ **Quick Check**

6. Find the area of the rectangle shown. Give the measurement in square units.

Work Space.

7 cm

3 cm

_____

7. Find the perimeter of the figure shown. Then find the area. Write the measurement for area in square units.

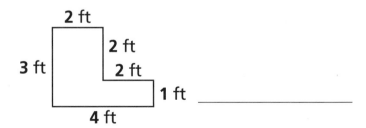

2 ft

2 ft

3 ft

2 ft

1 ft _____

4 ft

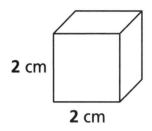
Surface area is the sum of the areas of all the faces of a space figure. A cube has **6** faces. The surface area of a cube is the sum of the areas of its **6** faces.

To find the surface area of a cube, first find the area of one face of the cube.

2 cm × **2** cm = **4** square cm

Since all **6** faces of a cube are **congruent**, or the same size and shape, you can add the area of one face six times to find the surface area.

4 + 4 + 4 + 4 + 4 + 4 = 24 square cm

Or, you can multiply the area of one face by **6**.

6 × 4 square cm = 24 square cm

2 cm
2 cm

_____

Find the surface area for each cube.

1.

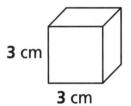
3 cm
3 cm

surface area _____

. . . .

2.

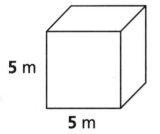
5 m
5 m

surface area _____

. . . .

3.

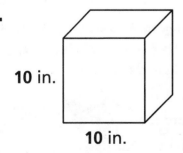
10 in.
10 in.

surface area _____

A rectangular prism also has **6** faces. But the faces are not all congruent. To find the surface area of a rectangular prism, first make a drawing of what the rectangular prism would look like if it was unfolded.

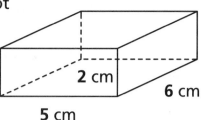

2 cm

5 cm

6 cm

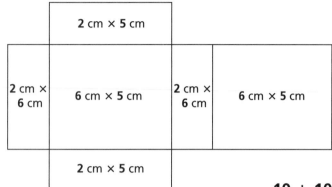

2 cm × 5 cm

2 cm × 6 cm | 6 cm × 5 cm | 2 cm × 6 cm | 6 cm × 5 cm

2 cm × 5 cm

Find the area of each face.

Then add the areas.

10 + 10 + 12 + 12 + 30 + 30 = 104 square cm

Find the surface area of this rectangular prism.

4.

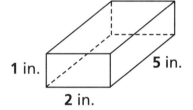

1 in.   5 in.

2 in.

$A =$ _____

Problem Solving Reasoning   Solve.

5. Look at the rectangular prism above. How many

pairs of faces are congruent? _____

Test Prep ★ Mixed Review

6 You return a library book that is exactly 4 weeks overdue. The fine is $.12 a day. How much do you owe?

   A $33.36

   B $3.36

   C $.84

   D $.48

7 Frank's vegetable garden is 15 feet wide and 10 feet long. What is the area of his garden?

   F 25 square feet

   G 50 square feet

   H 150 square feet

   J 200 square feet

Volume is the amount of space inside a space figure.

You can find the volume of this rectangular prism by counting the unit cubes it would take to fill it.

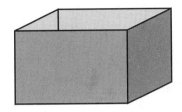

The volume of this rectangular prism is **12 cubic units**.

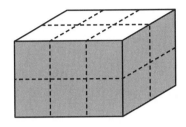

A standard unit that is used for measuring volume is a cube with each edge **1** centimeter long. This unit is called a **cubic centimeter**.

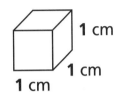

1 cm
1 cm
1 cm

1 cubic centimeter

A rectangular prism has three dimensions, length (*l*), width (*w*), and height (*h*). You can find its volume (*V*) by multiplying these dimensions.

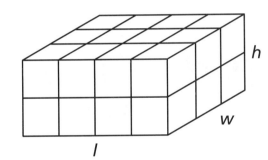

$V = l \times w \times h$
$V = \mathbf{4}$ cm $\times$ **3** cm $\times$ **2** cm
$V = \mathbf{24}$ **cubic cm**

Name the volume in cubic units.

1.

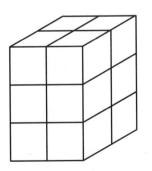

$V =$ _____

2.

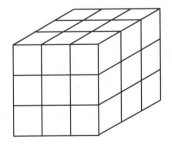

$V =$ _____

Write a number sentence to describe the volume. Then name the volume.

3.

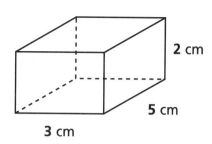

2 cm

5 cm

3 cm

4.

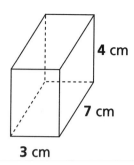

4 cm

7 cm

3 cm

number sentence: _____

volume: _____

number sentence: _____

volume: _____

Problem Solving Reasoning Solve.

5. Betty filled a box with **5** layers of centimeter cubes. Each layer had **6** rows with **4** cubes in each row. How many cubes were in the box?

_____

6. A box of candies had **3** layers. Each layer had **8** rows with **6** candies in each row. How many candies were in the box?

_____

 Quick Check

Solve.

Work Space.

7. Find the surface area of the cube shown. Write the measurement in square units.

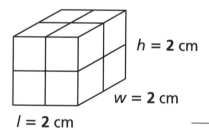

h = 2 cm

w = 2 cm

l = 2 cm

_____

8. Find the volume of the rectangular prism shown. Write the measurement in cubic units.

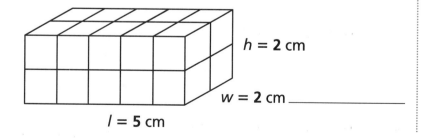

h = 2 cm

w = 2 cm

l = 5 cm

_____

Name _____

Use a ruler to measure the length of this segment to the nearest inch and to the nearest half inch.

1. •————————————————•

_____   _____

Use a ruler to measure the length of this segment to the nearest centimeter and to the nearest millimeter.

2. •————————————•

_____   _____

Circle the better estimate.

3. mass of a textbook

1 kg   1 mg

4. capacity of a spoon

5 L   5 mL

5. weight of a coin

1 oz   1 lb

6. capacity of a drinking glass

1 qt   1 pt

Name the equivalent measure.

7. 2 kg = _____ g

8. 5 cm = _____ mm

9. 4,000 mL = _____ L

10. 1,000 m = _____ km

11. 6,000 mg = _____ g

12. 2 L = _____ mL

13. 8 yd = _____ ft

14. 3 gal = _____ qt

15. 6 lb = _____ oz

16. 24 pt = _____ gal

17. 2 T = _____ lb

18. 2,640 ft = _____ mi

Write the letter that indicates the temperature.

19. 4°C _____

20. ⁻1°C _____

Write the letter that indicates the temperature.

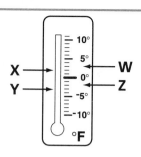

21. 2°F _____

22. ⁻2°F _____

Find the perimeter and area of the figure.

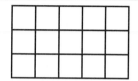

23. Perimeter = _____ units

24. Area = _____ square units

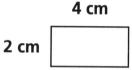

25. Perimeter = _____ cm

26. Area = _____ square cm

4 cm

2 cm

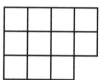

27. Perimeter = _____ units

28. Area = _____ square units

Find the surface area and volume of each rectangular prism.

29. Surface area = _____ square units

30. Volume = _____ cubic units

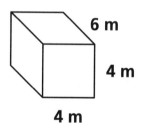

31. Surface area = _____ square m

32. Volume = _____ cubic m

6 m

4 m

4 m

Solve.

33. Which two letters on this number line are **6** units apart?

_____

34. A **90**–minute long movie begins showing in a theater at **10:30** A.M. every morning. Between movies there is a **30**-minute break. What time will the second movie of the day end?

_____

1 A contest has 5 winners. Each winner gets $7,600 in prize money. What is the total amount of prize money?

A $34,600 C $36,600 E NH

B $35,000 D $38,000

2 Which phrase describes the intersection of Green Street and Maple Street?

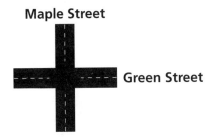

Maple Street

Green Street

F Perpendicular lines

G Vertical lines

H Parallel lines

J Horizontal lines

3 Waiters at a restaurant put two rectangular tables together. One table is $4\frac{1}{3}$ feet long. The second table is $5\frac{1}{3}$ feet long. They place these tables end to end to make one long table. How long a table will they make?

A $9\frac{2}{3}$ feet C 9 feet E NH

B $9\frac{1}{3}$ feet D $8\frac{2}{3}$ feet

4 Suppose you folded each of these letters in half. Which could you fold to show line symmetry?

F G H J

5 A field has 33 rows of tomato plants. Each row has 25 plants. How many plants are in the field?

A 825 C 800 E NH

B 815 D 750

6 The Celsius thermometers show the temperature at noon and at midnight. How many degrees colder was the temperature at midnight?

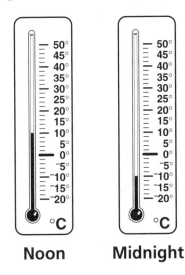

Noon **Midnight**

F 26° C H 12° C

G 20° C J 10° C

7 Which angle shown is less than a right angle?

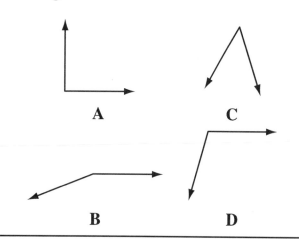

A

B

C

D

8 Four students record the time it takes them to finish eating their lunch.

Name	Time Spent Eating Lunch
Jackson	$\frac{1}{4}$ hour
An	$\frac{1}{8}$ hour
Maria	$\frac{1}{2}$ hour
Bernard	$\frac{3}{8}$ hour

Which lists the students in order from the *least* time to the *most* time spent eating lunch?

F An, Jackson, Bernard, Maria

G Maria, Jackson, Bernard, An

H Maria, Bernard, Jackson, An

J An, Jackson, Maria, Bernard

9 Choose the shape that answers this riddle.

> I have exactly 3 sides that are the same length. What shape am I?

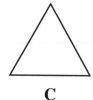

A

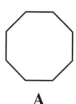

C

B

D

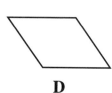

10 Which mixed number is equivalent to $\frac{17}{4}$?

F $4\frac{1}{4}$ **H** $5\frac{3}{4}$

G $4\frac{1}{2}$ **J** $17\frac{1}{4}$

11 What number is a common factor of both 18 and 42?

A 9   **C** 7

B 8   **D** 6

12 Lorraine rode her bicycle $\frac{3}{4}$ of a mile. Joanne rode her bicycle $\frac{5}{8}$ of a mile. How much farther did Lorraine ride her bicycle?

F $\frac{1}{2}$ mile   **H** $\frac{1}{4}$ mile   **K** NH

G $\frac{3}{8}$ mile   **J** $\frac{1}{8}$ mile

Decimals

Dear Family,

During the next few weeks, our math class will be learning about decimals.

You can expect to see homework that provides practice with comparing and ordering decimals. Here is a sample you may want to keep handy to give help if needed.

Comparing and Ordering Decimals

To put decimals such as **2.04**, **1.9**, **3.1**, and **2.77** in order from least to greatest, you can use place value.

First, align the decimal points in each number.

2.04
1.9
3.1
2.77

Compare the digits in each column starting at the greatest place value. The digit in the ones place has the greatest value in each of these decimals. Since **3** has the greatest value, **3.1** is the greatest number. Since **1** has the least value, **1.9** is the least number. The other two numbers are between **1.9** and **3.1**.

↓
2.04
1.9
3.1
2.77

Both of the numbers have **2** in the ones place. So, you need to compare their digits in the next column, the tenths place. Compare these digits. Since **7** is greater than **0**, **2.77** is greater than **2.04**.

↓
2.04
1.9
3.1
2.77

Once all the numbers have been compared, you can put them in order from least to greatest.

least → **greatest**
1.9   2.04   2.77   3.1

During this unit, students will need to continue practicing addition and subtraction facts.

Sincerely,

Each of these squares is divided into **10** equal parts.

The mixed number $1\frac{4}{10}$ represents the shaded regions.

You can write the mixed number $1\frac{4}{10}$ like this: **1.4**

⬆ ⎿⎽⎽⎽ decimal point

Read **1.4** as "one **and** four tenths." Say "and" for the decimal point.

Numbers such as **1.4**, **3.5** (three and five tenths), and **0.8** (eight tenths) are called **decimals**.

Circle the decimal that represents the shaded regions.

1.    3.2   2.3   2.5

2.   6.1   2.6   1.6

3.   2.7   1.7   7.2

4.   9.0   0.9   1.9

Write a mixed number and a decimal for the shaded regions.

5. 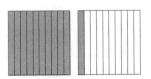 ___ ___   ___ ___

6. 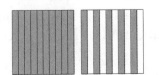 ___ ___   ___ ___

You can show decimals on a number line. Notice that the distance between **0** and **1** on the number line below is **10** times as great as the distance between each tenth.

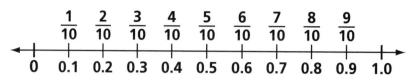

Write the missing decimals and fractions on the number line.

7.

Write the fraction or mixed number as a decimal.

8. $\dfrac{3}{10} =$ _____ $\dfrac{6}{10} =$ _____ $\dfrac{10}{10} =$ _____ $\dfrac{15}{10} =$ _____

9. $4\dfrac{2}{10} =$ _____ $2\dfrac{8}{10} =$ _____ $38\dfrac{7}{10} =$ _____ $55\dfrac{4}{10} =$ _____

Write the decimal as a fraction or mixed number.

10. 0.9 = _____   0.2 = _____   4.8 = _____   39.0 = _____

11. 0.7 = _____   1.3 = _____   7.4 = _____   8.2 = _____

Problem Solving
Reasoning

Solve.

12. Chet has a block of wood that measures **0.1** meter on each side. How many blocks would he need to make a row of blocks **1** meter long?

_____

Test Prep ★ Mixed Review

13 Angela is 60 inches tall. What is her height in feet?

   A 4   C 6
   B 5   D 7

14 A rectangle has an area of 36 square meters. Which of the following could be the measurement of its perimeter?

   F 72 meters   H 12 meters
   G 24 meters   J 8 meters

Name _____

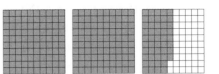

Each of these squares is divided into **100** equal parts. These parts are called hundredths.

You can show hundredths in mixed numbers, decimals, or words.

$2\frac{48}{100}$ ← mixed number

2.48 ← decimal

two **and** forty-eight hundredths ← words

Circle the decimal that represents the shaded parts.

1.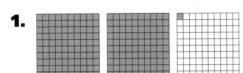

| 2.01 | 2.10 | 1.02 |

2.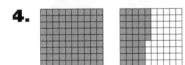

| 1.60 | 1.10 | 1.06 |

3.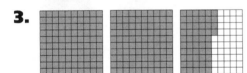

| 2.05 | 2.54 | 2.45 |

4.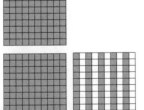

| 1.45 | 1.40 | 1.54 |

Write a mixed number and a decimal for the shaded parts.

5.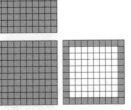

_____ _____

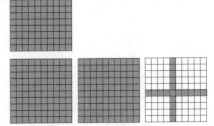

_____ _____

6.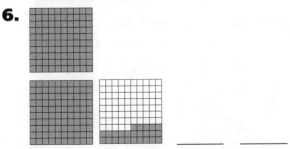

_____ _____

_____ _____

A number line can show how fractions, mixed numbers, and decimals are related. Write the missing fractions, mixed numbers, and decimals on the number line below.

7.

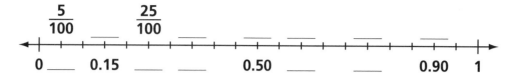

8.

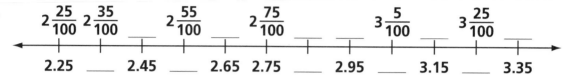

Write the number as a decimal and as a mixed number.

9. three and two tenths   seven and seven hundredths

_____   _____

Write the decimal in words.

10. 4.6 _____

11. 0.7 _____

12. 5.09 _____

| Problem Solving |
| Reasoning |

Solve.

13. Jorge said **0.1** mile is **10** times as far as **0.01** mile. Is he correct? Use a number line to show why.

_____

14. Helen said **0.4** is less than **0.40**. Peter said the numbers were equal. Who is correct? Use shaded squares to show why.

_____

Test Prep ★ Mixed Review

15 Which fraction is in simplest form?

A $\frac{7}{8}$ C $\frac{6}{10}$

B $\frac{4}{12}$ D $\frac{4}{6}$

16 Which group of fractions is in order from *greatest* to *least*?

F $\frac{3}{4}, \frac{2}{3}, \frac{1}{2}, \frac{1}{4}$ H $\frac{2}{3}, \frac{3}{4}, \frac{1}{2}, \frac{1}{4}$

G $\frac{1}{4}, \frac{1}{2}, \frac{2}{3}, \frac{3}{4}$ J $\frac{1}{4}, \frac{1}{2}, \frac{3}{4}, \frac{2}{3}$

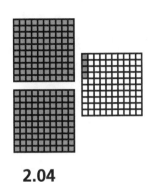
One way to compare decimals is to use models.

These models show **2.1** and **2.8**.

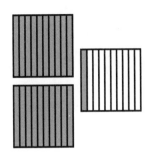 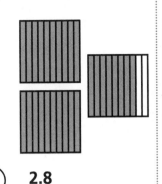

These models show **2.05** and **2.04**.

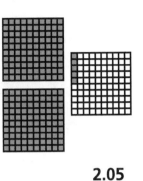 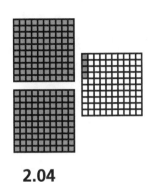

2.1 ⟨ **<** ⟩ **2.8**

2.05 ⟨ **>** ⟩ **2.04**

Another way to compare decimals is to use a number line.

Compare 2.73 and 2.68.

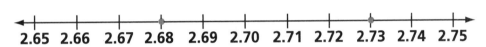

- Locate each decimal on the number line.

- Compare. The decimal farther to the left is less.
  The decimal farther to the right is greater.

    2.73 ⟨ > ⟩ 2.68

- Write >, <, or =.

Compare. Write >, <, or =.

1. 1 ◯ 0.1   0.3 ◯ 0.7   0.8 ◯ 0.80

2. 2.35 ◯ 2.26   3.46 ◯ 3.46   5.37 ◯ 5.4

Compare these decimals. Then write them in
order from least to greatest.

| 8.03 | 3.80 | 3.08 | 4.56 | 4.05 | 5.00 |

3. _____   _____   _____   _____   _____   _____
   least   greatest

| 9.10 | 12.1 | 10.9 | 1.10 | 9.12 | 1.29 |

4. _____   _____   _____   _____   _____   _____
   least   greatest

You can also use place value to compare decimals.

1. Align the decimal points. You may have to add zeros so each decimal has the same number of decimal places.

3.10
3.15

2. Compare the digits in each place. Start with the greatest place value. Work to the right until you find the digits that are different.

↓
3.10
3.15
↑

3. Write >, <, or =.

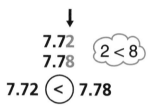

3.1 (<) 3.15

Other Examples

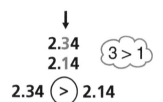

↓
2.34
2.14
(3 > 1)
2.34 (>) 2.14

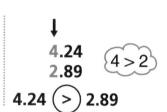

↓
4.24
2.89
(4 > 2)
4.24 (>) 2.89

↓
7.72
7.78
(2 < 8)
7.72 (<) 7.78

Is the statement True or False? Write *T* or *F*.

5. 4.78 < 5.79 _____   49.08 = 49.80 _____   11.3 < 10.8 _____

6. 52.71 > 25.71 _____   260.7 = 260.07 _____   201 > 20.19 _____

7. 68.46 > 684.60 _____   831.45 < 543.47 _____   72.98 = 72.980 _____

✓ Quick Check

Write a fraction and decimal for the shaded part.

Work Space.

8.   _____ _____

9. _____ _____

10. _____ _____

11. 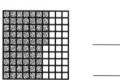 _____ _____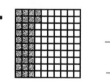

Compare. Write >, <, or =.

12. 0.2 ◯ 0.20   **13.** 0.23 ◯ 0.21   **14.** 0.45 ◯ 0.4

15. 6.45 ◯ 2.89   **16.** 7.05 ◯ 7.03   **17.** 9.46 ◯ 9.48

218 Unit 8 Lesson 3

To find the missing number in a sequence, you need to look for a pattern and find the rule.

Problem

What would be the next number in this sequence?
0.26, 0.36, 0.46, 0.56, 0.66, 0.76, _?_

❶ Understand As you reread, ask yourself questions.

• What information do you have?
  The first six numbers in a sequence:
  0.26, 0.36, 0.46, 0.56, 0.66, 0.76

• What do you need to find out?

_____

❷ Decide Choose a method for solving.

Try the strategy Find a Pattern.

• Look at how each number is related to the next number.

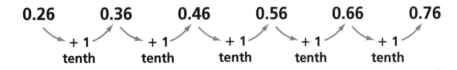

| 0.26 | 0.36 | 0.46 | 0.56 | 0.66 | 0.76 |
| + 1 tenth | + 1 tenth | + 1 tenth | + 1 tenth | + 1 tenth | |

❸ Solve What is the pattern?

• How does each number change?

_____

Use the pattern to find the missing number.

0.76 _____ = _____

❹ Look back Check your answer. Write the answer below.

Answer _____

• Why was it important to try the pattern with all the numbers?

_____

_____

Solve. Use the Find a Pattern strategy or any other strategy you have learned.

1. What is the missing number in this sequence?

　_?_ , 0.15, 0.25, 0.35, 0.45

Think: Why would working backward help with this problem?

_____

Answer _____

2. What is the missing number in this sequence?

4.3, _?_ , 4.2, 4.15, 4.1, 4.05, 4.00

Think: What is the relationship between each number and the next ?

_____

Answer _____

3. Use **9** toothpicks to form **5** triangles. Draw a picture.

4. The distance around a bicycling course is $1\frac{3}{4}$ mi. Danusa rode around the course **3** times. How many miles did she ride?

_____

5. Luann needs **20** minutes to get dressed, eat breakfast, and get ready for school. It takes her **15** minutes to walk to school. If school starts at **8:30** A.M. and Luann likes to arrive **10** minutes early, what time should she get up?

_____

6. The distance Alex jogs follows a pattern. On Sunday, he jogs **1.5** mi, on Monday **1.75** mi, on Tuesday **2** mi, and on Wednesday **2.25** mi. If he continues this pattern, how many miles will Alex jog on Saturday?

_____

7. Use the clues to find Katherine's favorite number.

- It is less than **20**.
- When you divide it by **3**, the remainder is **1**.
- When you divide it by **4**, the remainder is **3**.
- When you divide it by **5**, the remainder is **2**.

_____

8. At a certain grocery store, the amount you save increases according to a pattern. On the first visit, you save **$.25**. On the second visit you save **$.50**, On the third visit you save **$.75**, and so on. How much will you save on your fifth visit?

_____

Name _____

A number line can help you write a fraction as a decimal.
Study the number line below.

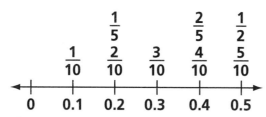

Equivalent fractions can be used to write fractions as decimals.

Write $\frac{1}{5}$ as a decimal.

Rewrite $\frac{1}{5}$ as a fraction with a denominator of **10**.

$\frac{1 \times 2}{5 \times 2} = \frac{2}{10}$; and $\frac{2}{10} = 0.2$

Write $\frac{3}{4}$ as a decimal.

Rewrite $\frac{3}{4}$ as a fraction with a denominator of **100**.

$\frac{3 \times 25}{4 \times 25} = \frac{75}{100}$; and $\frac{75}{100} = 0.75$

Write the missing fractions and decimals on each number line.

1.

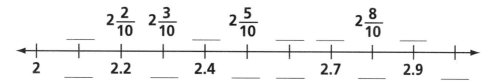

2.

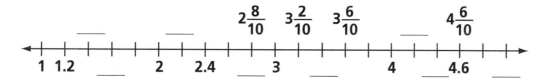

Write a decimal for the fraction or mixed number.

3. $\frac{3}{10} = $ _____ $\frac{1}{2} = $ _____ $2\frac{1}{5} = $ _____ $3\frac{9}{10} = $ _____

4. $\frac{2}{4} = $ _____ $5\frac{2}{5} = $ _____ $3\frac{7}{10} = $ _____ $7\frac{3}{5} = $ _____

Write a fraction or mixed number for the decimal.

5. $0.8 = $ _____ $0.9 = $ _____ $4.2 = $ _____ $1.3 = $ _____

6. $0.5 = $ _____ $1.6 = $ _____ $0.7 = $ _____ $0.4 = $ _____

Is the statement True or False? Write *T* or *F*.

7. Decimals and fractions both show parts of a whole. _____

8. You can write **0.7** as a fraction in more than one way. _____

9. There is only one way to write a decimal such as **7.5** as a mixed number. _____

10. On the number line there are only 2 decimal numbers between **0.2** and **0.5**. _____

Circle the equivalent decimal for the fraction. (Hint: Write the decimals as fractions, then simplify if possible.)

11. $\frac{6}{25}$ 0.06 0.24

12. $\frac{3}{20}$ 0.15 0.60

13. $1\frac{9}{25}$ 1.70 1.36

14. $\frac{3}{12}$ 0.25 0.24

15. $\frac{3}{15}$ 0.15 0.20

16. $\frac{16}{20}$ 1.80 0.8

Problem Solving Reasoning Solve.

17. Chris knows that $\frac{1}{4}$ equals **0.25**, $\frac{2}{4}$ equals **0.50**, and $\frac{3}{4}$ equals **0.75**. What pattern can he use to write a decimal that equals $\frac{5}{4}$? What decimal does he write?

_____

_____

Test Prep ★ Mixed Review

18 The length of a desk is 2 meters. What is the length of the desk in centimeters?

A 0.2   C 24
B 20   D 200

19 An athlete ran a 200-meter race 0.03 seconds faster than she ran this distance the day before. What is 0.03 in words?

F Thirty   H Three tenths
G Three   J Three hundredths

You can use a number line to help round decimals to the nearest whole number.

Round **4.8** to the nearest whole number.

Since **4.8** is closer to **5** than to **4**, **4.8** rounds to **5**.

Round **9.4** to the nearest whole number.

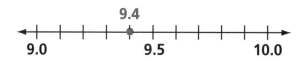

Since **9.4** is closer to **9** than to **10**, **9.4** rounds to **9**.

> When a decimal number is halfway between two whole numbers, round up to the next whole number. For example, **7.5** rounds to **8**.

You can also use place value to help round decimals.

Round **5.78** to the nearest tenth.	Round **12.79** to the nearest whole number.
• First look at the digit in the hundredths place.	• First look at the digit in the tenths place.
5.78	**12.79**
• If it is equal to or greater than **5**, round up. **8 > 5**, so **5.78** rounds to **5.8**.	• If it is equal to or greater than **5**, round up. **7 > 5**, so **12.79** rounds to **13**.

Round the decimal to the nearest whole number.
Use a number line if you need to.

1. 3.7 _____   0.9 _____   4.7 _____   13.8 _____   17.0 _____

2. 10.1 _____   0.1 _____   0.5 _____   4.5 _____   1.90 _____

Round the decimal to the nearest tenth.

3. 0.39 _____   0.22 _____   1.09 _____   34.92 _____   0.67 _____

4. 6.48 _____   12.00 _____   0.15 _____   5.55 _____   9.09 _____

You can use rounding to estimate sums and differences.
Estimate by rounding to the nearest whole number.

5.   5.78   rounds to   __   5.38   rounds to   __ $12.07
      + 6.89   rounds to   + __   − 1.07   rounds to   − __   + $5.01

6.   9.38   0.44   88.00   34.75 $3.54 $14.36
      + 4.55   − 0.20   − 4.02   +   9.4   + $6.14   − $6.92

Problem Solving
Reasoning   Solve.

7. Greg bought lunch at the school
cafeteria. He spent **$3.75** for a
sandwich and **$.75** for a drink.
Dessert cost **$1.25**. To the nearest
dollar, how much did he spend?

_____

8. Three friends are going to the
movies. Tickets cost **$6.75** each.
They expect to pay about **$21** for
the **3** tickets. Is this reasonable?
Explain.

_____

_____

✔ Quick Check

Find the point on the number line that represents
the fraction or decimal. Write the letter next to the
fraction or decimal.

Work Space.

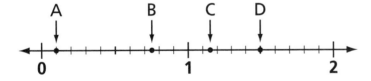

9. 1.5 _____   **10.** $\frac{3}{4}$ _____   **11.** $\frac{1}{10}$ _____   **12.** 1.15 _____

Round the decimal to the nearest whole number.

13. 2.7 _____   **14.** 7.2 _____   **15.** 6.5 _____

Round the decimal to the nearest tenth.

16. 3.67 _____   **17.** 10.85 _____   **18.** 1.77 _____

Name _____

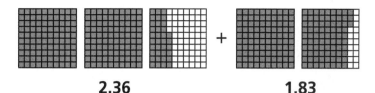

STANDARD

You can use what you know about adding whole numbers to add decimals.

Find 2.36 + 1.83.

2.36   +   1.83

---

1. Line up the decimal points. Add as you would whole numbers.

$$\begin{array}{r} 2.36 \\ + 1.83 \\ \hline 4.19 \end{array}$$

2. Write the decimal point in the answer.

$$\begin{array}{r} \overset{1}{2}.36 \\ + 1.83 \\ \hline 4.19 \end{array}$$
↑

3. Use estimation to check your answer.

$$\begin{array}{r} \overset{1}{2}.36 \\ + 1.83 \\ \hline 4.19 \end{array}$$ rounds down → rounds up →

$$\begin{array}{r} 2 \\ + 2 \\ \hline 4 \end{array}$$

Since **4.19** is close to **4**, the answer is reasonable.

Whenever you add decimals:

• Place a decimal point in the answer.

• Use estimation to check if your answer is reasonable.

Use estimation to place the decimal point in the answer.

1. 5.46 + 3.56 = 9 0 2   0.03 + 1.2 = 1 2 3   4.39 + 3.0 + 1 = 8 3 9

2. 0.34 + 0.3 = 0 6 4   288 + 3.4 = 2 9 1 4   1.38 + 20.4 + 13 = 3 4 7 8

Find the sum. Estimate to help make sure your answer is reasonable.

3.
$$\begin{array}{r} 2.35 \\ + 4.55 \\ \hline \end{array}$$
$$\begin{array}{r} 8.42 \\ + 0.20 \\ \hline \end{array}$$
$$\begin{array}{r} 8.00 \\ + 4.02 \\ \hline \end{array}$$
$$\begin{array}{r} 54.05 \\ + 9.4 \\ \hline \end{array}$$
$$\begin{array}{r} 5.54 \\ + 5.84 \\ \hline \end{array}$$

4.
$$\begin{array}{r} 15.05 \\ + 8.61 \\ \hline \end{array}$$
$$\begin{array}{r} 4.11 \\ + 0.99 \\ \hline \end{array}$$
$$\begin{array}{r} 6.81 \\ + 0.04 \\ \hline \end{array}$$
$$\begin{array}{r} 4.89 \\ + 7.12 \\ \hline \end{array}$$
$$\begin{array}{r} 8.32 \\ + 9.41 \\ \hline \end{array}$$

Find the sum. Estimate to help make sure your answer is reasonable.

5.
13.01	6.72	7.99	15.9	4.33
1.66	3.61	2.09	5.77	2.41
+ 4.9	+ 8.52	+ 5.77	+ 8.32	+ 0.31

Find the sum. Be sure to line up the decimal points.

6. 35.9 + 25.44 _____   0.38 + 23.95 _____

7. 14.79 + 3.56 _____   7.39 + 6.2 _____

8. 1.24 + 4.5 + 1.02 _____   8.25 + 7.55 + 0.29 _____

Problem Solving
Reasoning

Solve.

9. Jeff rode **13.75** kilometers on his bike one month and **12.4** kilometers the next month. What was the total number of kilometers he rode in both months?

_____

10. Ellen has **3.5** yards of ribbon for a project. She buys **4.75** yards more. She estimates she now has about **9** yards of ribbon in all. Is her estimate greater or less than the actual amount she has? Explain.

_____

_____

_____

Test Prep ★ Mixed Review

11 A square has a perimeter of 24 feet. Which of the following could be the measurement of its area in square feet?

  A 36   **C** 24

  B 28   **D** 18

12 Manuel rode his bicycle $3\frac{1}{4}$ kilometers. What decimal is equivalent to $3\frac{1}{4}$?

  F 3.41   **H** 3.20

  G 3.25   **J** 3.14

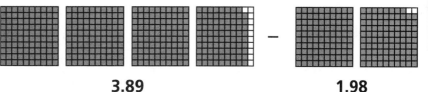

You can use what you know about subtracting whole numbers to help subtract decimals.

3.89   1.98

Find 3.89 − 1.98.

1. Line up the decimal points. Subtract as you would whole numbers.

$$\begin{array}{r} 3.89 \\ -\,1.98 \\ \hline 1\,91 \end{array}$$

2. Write the decimal point in the answer.

$$\begin{array}{r} \overset{2}{\cancel{3}}.\overset{18}{\cancel{8}}9 \\ -\,1.98 \\ \hline 1.91 \end{array}$$
↑

3. Use estimation to check your answer.

$$\begin{array}{r} \overset{2}{\cancel{3}}.\overset{18}{\cancel{8}}9 \\ -\,1.98 \\ \hline 1.91 \end{array}$$

rounds up → 4
rounds up → −2
____
2

Since **1.91** is close to **2**, the answer is reasonable.

Whenever you subtract decimals:

• Place a decimal point in the answer.

• Use estimation to check if your answer is reasonable.

Use estimation to place the decimal point correctly in the answer.

1. 6.43 − 0.26 = 6 1 7   8.77 − 0.9 = 7 8 7   45.0 − 1.9 = 4 3 1

2. 67.34 − 3.2 = 6 4 1 4   9.62 − 8.4 = 1 2 2   9.7 − 2.5 = 7 2

Find the difference. Estimate to be sure your answer is reasonable.

3.
$$\begin{array}{r} 9.75 \\ -\,3.55 \\ \hline \end{array}$$
$$\begin{array}{r} 6.32 \\ -\,0.60 \\ \hline \end{array}$$
$$\begin{array}{r} 9.90 \\ -\,7.04 \\ \hline \end{array}$$
$$\begin{array}{r} 84.04 \\ -\,7.16 \\ \hline \end{array}$$
$$\begin{array}{r} 10.24 \\ -\,8.04 \\ \hline \end{array}$$

4.
$$\begin{array}{r} 9.66 \\ -\,8.51 \\ \hline \end{array}$$
$$\begin{array}{r} 3.91 \\ -\,0.39 \\ \hline \end{array}$$
$$\begin{array}{r} 2.21 \\ -\,0.24 \\ \hline \end{array}$$
$$\begin{array}{r} 5.49 \\ -\,3.77 \\ \hline \end{array}$$
$$\begin{array}{r} 4.38 \\ -\,3.21 \\ \hline \end{array}$$

Find the difference. Estimate to be sure your answer is reasonable.

5.
7.6 − 4.2	9.41 − 3.54	12.00 − 2.99	8.77 − 0.02	3.21 − 0.91

Find the difference. Be sure to line up the decimal points.

6. 21.9 − 20.44 _____   82.9 − 81.95 _____

7. 14.12 − 7.50 _____   8.32 − 7.8 _____

8. 1.24 − 1.03 _____   33.22 − 10.29 _____

9. 6.4 − 4.7 _____   14.1 − 6.05 _____

Problem Solving Reasoning Solve.

10. Josh saved **$5.89** one week. The next week he saved **$4.75**. How much more did he save the first week?

_____

11. Maria ran **1** mi in **8.7** minutes. Her friend Teresa ran the same distance in **7.9** minutes. Is the difference in minutes more or less than **1** minute?

_____

✓ **Quick Check**

Solve.

Work Space.

12.
1.53
+ 2.33

13.
2.78
+ 2.13

14.
3.45
+ 3.67

15.
3.69
− 1.43

16.
4.52
− 2.37

17.
5.47
− 1.79

228 Unit 8 Lesson 8

Name _____

Problem Solving Application:
Too Much or Too Little
Information

Some problems give more facts than you need.
You need to decide which facts are necessary.

Some problems do not give enough facts. In this
lesson, you will decide what fact or facts you need
to solve a problem.

Tips to Remember:

| 1. Understand | 2. Decide | 3. Solve | 4. Look back |

- Read each problem more than once. Circle the
  important words and numbers. Cross out the words
  and numbers that you don't need.
- Think about each fact in the problem. Ask yourself:
  Is this an extra fact? Or do I need it to find a
  solution?
- Predict the answer. Then solve the problem.
  Compare your answer with your prediction.

Cross out the extra information. Then solve the
problem. If information is missing, name the fact
or facts needed on the answer lines.

1. In Florida, the highest monthly
average temperature is **91.7** °F. The
lowest monthly average is **39.9** °F.
The highest temperature ever
recorded in Florida is **109** °F. What
is the difference between the
highest and lowest monthly
temperatures?

Think: How does the question help
you decide what facts are needed?

_____

_____

Answer _____

_____

2. The population of the state of
New Jersey is **7,945,298**. It has an
average of **1065.4** people per
square mile. Massachusetts has an
average of **770.7** people per
square mile. What is the difference
in the populations of the two
states?

Think: What two numbers do you
need to compare?

_____

_____

Answer _____

_____

Cross out the extra information. Then solve the problem. If information is missing, name the fact or facts that you need.

3. California has more public schools than any other state. California has **1,481** more public schools than Texas, which has **4,185**. Illinois has **4,032** and New York has **4,032**. How many more public schools does California have than New York?

_____

_____

4. New Mexico is the fifth largest state. The land area of New Mexico is **121,364** square miles. Its water area is **234** square miles. What is the total area of New Mexico?

_____

_____

5. Here are the populations of the major cities in Nebraska.

Bellevue	30,982
Grand Island	39,386
Kearney	24,396
Lincoln	191,972
Omaha	335,795

What is the population of Nebraska?

_____

_____

6. Alaska and Hawaii were the last two states to become part of the United States. Alaska became the forty-ninth state on January **3, 1959**. Hawaii became the fiftieth state in August of the same year. For how many days did the United States have exactly **49** states?

_____

_____

Extend Your Thinking

7. Explain the method you used to solve problem **3**.

_____

_____

_____

_____

8. Make up a word problem using facts from this lesson. Solve the problem.

_____

_____

_____

_____

Write the decimal in words.

1. 2.08 _____

2. 0.4 _____

Write the fraction or mixed number as a decimal.

3. $\frac{3}{4}$ _____

4. $7\frac{1}{10}$ _____

5. $\frac{1}{2}$ _____

6. $8\frac{3}{100}$ _____

Write the decimal as a fraction or mixed number.

7. 0.3 _____

8. 13.01 _____

9. 6.7 _____

Compare. Write >, <, or =.

10. 0.03 $\bigcirc$ 0.21

11. 1 $\bigcirc$ 0.72

12. 9.2 $\bigcirc$ 9.1

13. 5.3 $\bigcirc$ 5.35

Write these decimals in order from greatest to least.

1.14, 0.8, 2.3, 0.9

2.15, 2.05, 2.75, 2.09

14. _____ _____ _____ _____

15. _____ _____ _____ _____

Round the decimal to the nearest tenth.

16. 3.61 _____

17. 7.66 _____

18. 13.55 _____

19. 8.12 _____

Round the decimal to the nearest whole number.

20. 4.76 _____

21. 17.07 _____

22. 7.51 _____

23. 8.43 _____

Find the sum or difference.

24. 8.3
 + 14.02

25. 5.05
 + 9.1

26. 4.72
 − 2.31

27. 6.4
 − 3.66

Solve. Which number comes next in the sequence?

28. 0.8, 0.85, 0.9, 0.95, 1.0, 1.05 _____

Cross out the extra information. Then solve the problem.

29. In a class of **24** students, **11** girls and **9** boys like to play soccer. How many students in the class like to play soccer? _____

1 Which are parallel line segments?

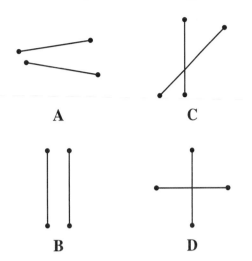

2 Four students timed how long they waited for the bus one morning.

Student	Time Spent Waiting
Steven	**7.55** minutes
Emily	**6.97** minutes
Sarah	**7.7** minutes
Ralph	**7.35** minutes

Which lists them in order from the *greatest* to the *least* time waiting?

F Emily, Ralph, Steven, Sarah

G Sarah, Steven, Emily, Ralph

H Sarah, Steven, Ralph, Emily

J Steven, Sarah, Ralph, Emily

3 Arthur's family drove 72.9 miles on Saturday. What is this distance rounded to the nearest mile?

A 70 miles   C 73 miles   E NH

B 72 miles   D 74 miles

4 Which angle shown is greater than a right angle?

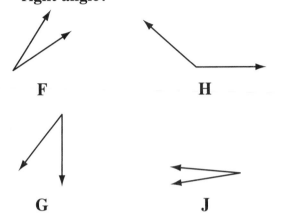

5 Amanda added $\frac{1}{3}$ c milk and $\frac{1}{2}$ c water to a recipe. How much liquid did she add in all?

A $\frac{3}{6}$ c   C $\frac{3}{4}$ c   E NH

B $\frac{2}{3}$ c   D $\frac{5}{6}$ c

6 The Fahrenheit thermometers show the temperature in the morning and in the afternoon. How many degrees warmer was the temperature in the afternoon?

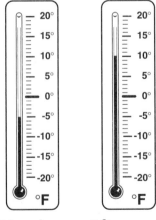

Morning   Afternoon

F 3°F   H 15°F

G 5°F   J 20°F

UNIT 9 • TABLE OF CONTENTS

Division with 2-Digit Divisors

UNIT 9 • TABLE OF CONTENTS

We will be using this vocabulary:

dividend the number that is divided
divisor the number that is divided by
quotient the answer to a division problem

Dear Family,

During the next few weeks, our math class will be learning and practicing division of whole numbers by **2**-digit numbers.

You can expect to see homework that provides practice with dividing whole numbers by **2**-digit numbers. Here is a sample you may want to keep handy to give help if needed.

Four-Digit Dividends

Divide: $61\overline{)1{,}285}$

1. $61\overline{)1{,}285}^{\,?}$ Not enough thousands to divide.

2. $61\overline{)1{,}285}^{\,?}$ Not enough hundreds to divide.

3. $\begin{array}{r} ? \\ 61\overline{)1{,}285} \\ -1\,22 \\ \hline 6 \end{array}$ Divide tens. Think: $60\overline{)120}^{\,2}$

4. $\begin{array}{r} 2\ ? \\ 61\overline{)1{,}2\,8\,5} \\ -1\,2\,2 \\ \hline 6\,5 \\ -6\,1 \\ \hline 4 \end{array}$ Divide ones. Think: $60\overline{)60}^{\,1}$

5. Write the answer using a remainder. $61\overline{)1{,}285}^{\,21\ R4}$

During this unit, students will need to continue practicing division and multiplication facts.

Sincerely,

Name _____

You can use estimation to help you know where to place the first digit in a quotient.

Divide 83 by 38.

1. Estimate. Round the divisor and the dividend. Try **2**. Write it in the ones place in the quotient.	2. Try the estimate. Multiply. Subtract. Write the remainder in the quotient.
$38\overline{)83}$ with ? above — rounds to → $40\overline{)80}$ with ? above. Think: $4\overline{)8}$ gives 2. Then $40\overline{)80}$ gives 2.	$38\overline{)83}$ with 2 R7 above $-76 \leftarrow 2 \times 38$, remainder 7

Estimate to place the digit in each quotient. Then divide.

Estimate.

1. $31\overline{)94}$ rounds to: $30\overline{)90}$ with ? above

Try **3**.

2. $39\overline{)89}$ rounds to: $40\overline{)90}$ with ? above

Try **2**.

3. $41\overline{)84}$ rounds to: $\overline{)}$ with ? above

Try _____.

4. $54\overline{)78}$ rounds to: $\overline{)}$ with ? above

Try _____.

5. $39\overline{)94}$ rounds to: $\overline{)}$ with ? above

Try _____.

6. $28\overline{)81}$ rounds to: $\overline{)}$ with ? above

Try _____.

7. $19\overline{)74}$ rounds to: $\overline{)}$ with ? above

Try _____.

8. $22\overline{)93}$ rounds to: $\overline{)}$ with ? above

Try _____.

Divide.

9. $33\overline{)54}$ $19\overline{)45}$ $21\overline{)93}$ $55\overline{)84}$

10. $36\overline{)82}$ $54\overline{)65}$ $69\overline{)77}$ $24\overline{)32}$

11. $39\overline{)83}$ $28\overline{)87}$ $18\overline{)82}$ $43\overline{)93}$

12. $37\overline{)89}$ $19\overline{)83}$ $41\overline{)93}$ $52\overline{)79}$

Problem Solving Reasoning   Solve.

13. If **24** apples can fit in a tray and there are **89** apples altogether, how many trays can be filled? How many apples will be left over?

_____

14. If **32** potatoes can fit in a sack and there are **74** potatoes altogether, how many sacks can be filled? How many potatoes will be left over?

_____

Test Prep ★ Mixed Review

15 Sam's sneakers have a mass of 2 kilograms. What is the mass of his sneakers in grams?

  A 20

  B 200

  C 2,000

  D 20,000

16 The course for the bicycle race is 27.75 kilometers long. What is this distance rounded to the nearest tenth?

  F 27.5 kilometers

  G 27.7 kilometers

  H 27.8 kilometers

  J 28 kilometers

Sometimes when you divide, your first estimate will be too large.

Divide: $34\overline{)62}^{?}$

1. Estimate.

$$30\overline{)60}^{\,2}$$

Try **2**.

2. Divide.

$$34\overline{)62}^{\,2}$$
$$\underline{-\ 68}$$
↑
Too large. Try **1**.

3. Adjust.

$$34\overline{)62}^{\,1\ \textbf{R28}}$$
$$\underline{-\ 34}$$
$$28$$

Check:
$$\begin{array}{r} 34 \\ \times\ 1 \\ \hline 34 \\ +48 \\ \hline 62 \end{array}$$

Divide: $24\overline{)64}^{?}$

1. Estimate.

$$20\overline{)60}^{\,3}$$

Try **3**.

2. Divide.

$$24\overline{)64}^{\,3}$$
$$\underline{-\ 72}$$
↑
Too large. Try **2**.

3. Adjust.

$$24\overline{)64}^{\,2\ \textbf{R16}}$$
$$\underline{-\ 48}$$
$$16$$

Check:
$$\begin{array}{r} 24 \\ \times\ 2 \\ \hline 48 \\ +16 \\ \hline 64 \end{array}$$

---

1. Estimate.

Think:

$$30\overline{)90}^{\,3} \qquad 32\overline{)94}^{\,3}$$
$$\phantom{32\overline{)94}}\underline{-96}$$
$$\phantom{32\overline{)94}}↑$$

Try **3**.   Too large.

Try _____.

$$32\overline{)94}$$

2. Estimate.

Think:

$$40\overline{)80}^{\,2} \qquad 41\overline{)81}^{\,2}$$
$$\phantom{41\overline{)81}}\underline{-82}$$

Try **2**.

Try _____.

$$41\overline{)81}$$

---

3. $23\overline{)66}$

Estimate.   Divide.

4. $12\overline{)73}$

Estimate.   Divide.

---

5. $44\overline{)87}$

Estimate.   Divide.

6. $24\overline{)69}$

Estimate.   Divide.

Sometimes your first estimate will be too small.

Divide: $16\overline{)84}^{\;?}$

Estimate.   Check.   Divide.
Try **5**.

Think:
$20\overline{)80}^{\;4}$

$$16\overline{)84}^{\;4} \\ \underline{-\;64} \\ 20$$
↑

$$16\overline{)84}^{\;5\;R4} \\ \underline{-\;80} \\ 4$$

Try **4**.

The remainder is
greater than the
divisor. Try again.

Find: $15\overline{)62}^{\;?}$

Estimate.   Check.   Divide.
Try **4**.

Think:
$20\overline{)60}^{\;3}$

$$15\overline{)62}^{\;3} \\ \underline{-\;45} \\ 17$$
↑

$$15\overline{)62}^{\;4\;R2} \\ \underline{-\;60} \\ 2$$

Try **3**.

The remainder is
greater than the
divisor. Try again.

> **Remember:** The remainder must always be less than the divisor.

Estimate to place the digit in each quotient. Then divide.

7. Estimate.   Try _____.

$30\overline{)50}$ $26\overline{)53}^{\;1} \\ \underline{-\;26} \\ 27$ $26\overline{)53}$

Try **1**.   Too large.

8. Estimate.   Try _____.

$20\overline{)70}$ $18\overline{)73}^{\;3} \\ \underline{-\;54} \\ 19$ $18\overline{)73}$

Try **3**.

9. $28\overline{)84}$

Estimate.   Divide.

10. $16\overline{)33}$

Estimate.   Divide.

11. $36\overline{)74}$

Estimate.   Divide.

12. $16\overline{)84}$

Estimate.   Divide.

Name _____

Estimate to place the digit in each quotient. Then divide.

13. $31\overline{)96}$ $41\overline{)86}$ $12\overline{)74}$

14. $18\overline{)93}$ $34\overline{)89}$ $17\overline{)87}$

15. $40\overline{)78}$ $45\overline{)93}$ $27\overline{)82}$

Problem Solving
Reasoning

Solve.

16. A librarian had **84** books to pack in boxes. Each box held **16** books. How many boxes were filled? How many books were left over?

17. Henry uses **12** oranges to make one pint of juice. How many pints can he make from **75** oranges? How many oranges will not be used?

Test Prep ★ Mixed Review

18 Choose the shape that answers this riddle.

I have more than **2** sides that are parallel. What shape am I?

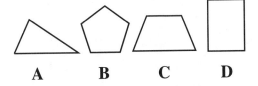

A   B   C   D

19 Which of these models shows fifty-five hundredths shaded?

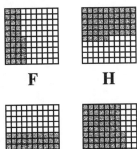

F   H

G   J

You can use the same steps to divide with **3**-digit dividends as you would with **2**-digit dividends.

Divide: $19\overline{)187}^{\,?}$

Estimate. Round to the nearest **10**. Then divide.

$$20\overline{)190}^{\,?} \qquad 19\overline{)187}^{\,9\ R16}$$

Try **9**.

$$\begin{array}{r} -\ 171 \end{array} \leftarrow 9 \times 19$$
$$16$$

$9 \times 20 = 180$

Divide: $64\overline{)203}^{\,?}$

Estimate. Round to the nearest **10**. Then divide.

$$60\overline{)200}^{\,?} \qquad 64\overline{)203}^{\,3\ R11}$$

Try **3**.

$$\begin{array}{r} -\ 192 \end{array} \leftarrow 3 \times 64$$
$$11$$

$3 \times 60 = 180$

Remember: Check your answer.

Estimate to place the digit in each quotient. Then divide.

1. $54\overline{)221}$

2. $43\overline{)194}$

3. $54\overline{)110}$

4. $44\overline{)134}$

5. $62\overline{)321}$

6. $31\overline{)198}$

7. $37\overline{)219}$

8. $23\overline{)118}$

9. $18\overline{)161}$

To divide **105** by **54**, you can estimate first. Since you know that **100 ÷ 50 = 2**, then you know that the first digit of the quotient of **105 ÷ 54** will be in the ones place.

Divide: $54\overline{)105}^{\ ?}$

1. Estimate.

$50\overline{)100}^{\ 2}$ $54\overline{)105}^{\ 2}$
$\phantom{54\overline{)}}-\ 108$
$\phantom{54\overline{)}}\uparrow$

Try **2.**   Too large.

2. Adjust. Try 1. Then divide.

$\phantom{54\overline{)10}}1\ \text{R}51$
$54\overline{)105}$
$\phantom{54\overline{)}}-\ 54$
$\phantom{54\overline{)}}\ \ 51$

3. Check.

54
$\underline{\times\ 1}$
54
$\underline{+\ 51}$
105

Divide: $17\overline{)104}^{\ ?}$

The remainder must always be less than the divisor.

1. Estimate.

$20\overline{)100}^{\ 5}$ $17\overline{)104}^{\ 5}$
$\phantom{17\overline{)}}-\ 85$
$\phantom{17\overline{)}}\ \ 19$
$\phantom{17\overline{)}}\ \ \uparrow$

Try **5.**   Too large.

2. Adjust. Try 6. Then divide.

$\phantom{17\overline{)10}}6\ \text{R}2$
$17\overline{)104}$
$\phantom{17\overline{)}}-\ 102$
$\phantom{17\overline{)}}\ \ \ 2$

3. Check.

17
$\underline{\times\ 6}$
102
$\underline{+\ 2}$
104

Estimate to place the first digit in the quotient. Then divide.

10. $22\overline{)163}$

11. $32\overline{)151}$

12. $82\overline{)732}$

13. $43\overline{)341}$

14. $45\overline{)431}$

15. $57\overline{)461}$

Estimate to place the first digit in the quotient. Then divide.

16. 28)205   18)156   32)284   56)472

17. 16)107   66)635   83)762   44)336

18. 48)460   31)202   43)294   17)137

 Problem Solving Reasoning   Solve.

19. Billy had **156** stamps in his collection. He pasted **16** stamps on each page of his album. How many pages were filled? How many stamps were left over?

✓ Quick Check

Estimate to place the digit in each quotient. Then divide.

Work Space.

20. 37)82   **21.** 23)75   **22.** 45)93

23. 23)42   **24.** 33)96   **25.** 44)86

26. 17)121   **27.** 43)227   **28.** 62)394

Name _____

2-Digit Quotients

When you divide by a **2**-digit number, you may need to place the first digit in the quotient in the tens or ones place.

Divide 533 by 23.

1. Divide the hundreds.

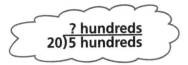

Not enough hundreds. Regroup to tens.

$$23\overline{)533}$$

2. Regroup hundreds as tens. Estimate. Divide.

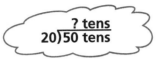

Try **2.**
$$
\begin{array}{r}
2 \\
23\overline{)533} \\
-46 \\
\hline
7
\end{array}
$$

3. Regroup tens as ones. Bring down the ones digit. Divide.

Try **3.**
$$
\begin{array}{r}
23 \text{ R4} \\
23\overline{)533} \\
-46 \\
\hline
73 \\
-69 \\
\hline
4
\end{array}
$$

Divide.
$$
\overset{?}{24\overline{)879}}
$$

1. Estimate. Try **4.** Divide.

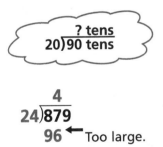

$$
\begin{array}{r}
4 \\
24\overline{)879} \\
96
\end{array}
$$
← Too large.

2. Adjust. Try **3.** Bring down the next digit.

$$
\begin{array}{r}
3 \\
24\overline{)879} \\
-72 \\
\hline
159
\end{array}
$$

3. Multiply. Subtract. Write the remainder in the quotient.

$$
\begin{array}{r}
36 \text{ R15} \\
24\overline{)879} \\
-72 \\
\hline
159 \\
-144 \\
\hline
15
\end{array}
$$

4. Check.

$$
\begin{array}{r}
24 \\
\times 36 \\
\hline
144 \\
+720 \\
\hline
864
\end{array}
$$

Divide and check.

1. $36\overline{)823}$ $21\overline{)657}$ $42\overline{)913}$ $18\overline{)624}$

2. $43\overline{)814}$ $14\overline{)683}$ $12\overline{)732}$ $33\overline{)864}$

Divide and check.

3. $27\overline{)865}$ $26\overline{)891}$ $17\overline{)734}$ $16\overline{)641}$

4. $15\overline{)344}$ $26\overline{)834}$ $18\overline{)942}$ $17\overline{)689}$

5. $24\overline{)729}$ $14\overline{)637}$ $19\overline{)854}$ $49\overline{)938}$

6. $12\overline{)562}$ $35\overline{)421}$ $28\overline{)663}$ $50\overline{)748}$

Problem Solving Reasoning   **Solve.**

7. A theater holds **892** people. There are **27** rows of seats. All the rows except **1** have the same number of seats. How many seats are in each row?

8. Betty has **521** flowers. She uses **15** flowers to make a bouquet. How many bouquets can she make? How many flowers will she have left over?

Test Prep ★ Mixed Review

9 A square has a perimeter of 48 meters. Which could be the measurement of its area?

A 12

B 24

C 80

D 144

10 What number should go in the ☐ to make the number sentence true?

$$\frac{1}{2} = 0.50$$
$$\frac{3}{4} = \boxed{}$$

F 0.25   H 0.5

G 0.34   J 0.75

Name _____

When you divide, you may need to write a zero in the quotient.

Divide 595 by 56.

1. Not enough hundreds. Regroup hundreds as tens. Divide.

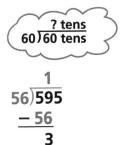

? tens
60)60 tens

$$
\begin{array}{r}
1 \\
56)\overline{595} \\
-56 \\
\hline
3
\end{array}
$$

2. Regroup tens as ones. Bring down the next digit. Divide.

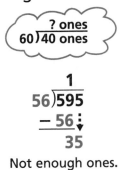

? ones
60)40 ones

$$
\begin{array}{r}
1 \\
56)\overline{595} \\
-56 \downarrow \\
\hline
35
\end{array}
$$

Not enough ones.

3. Write a **0** in the quotient. Write the remainder.

$$
\begin{array}{r}
10 \text{ R35} \\
56)\overline{595} \\
-56 \\
\hline
35 \\
-0 \\
\hline
35
\end{array}
$$

4. Check:

$$
\begin{array}{r}
56 \\
\times 10 \\
\hline
560
\end{array}
$$

$$
\begin{array}{r}
560 \\
+35 \\
\hline
595
\end{array}
$$

Divide and check.

1. 24)741   32)658   13)922   17)462

2. 26)785   39)806   24)752   27)830

3. 23)920   17)863   16)851   36)720

4. 44)469   32)355   18)850   35)710

Divide and check.

5. $17\overline{)584}$ $28\overline{)391}$ $36\overline{)857}$ $13\overline{)661}$

6. $21\overline{)473}$ $32\overline{)931}$ $18\overline{)972}$ $29\overline{)654}$

7. $15\overline{)762}$ $12\overline{)467}$ $23\overline{)926}$ $33\overline{)993}$

Problem Solving
Reasoning

Solve.

8. Tony has **124** video tapes. Each shelf in his video cabinet holds **12** tapes. How many shelves will he fill? How many tapes will be left over?

_____

_____

9. Maria has a collection of **285** CDs. She wants to show her collection on shelves that hold **14** CDs each. How many shelves does she need? Explain.

_____

_____

Test Prep ★ Mixed Review

10 What number is a common factor of both 12 and 24?

   A 12

   B 10

   C 9

   D 8

11 Which fraction is equivalent to $\frac{8}{12}$?

   F $\frac{1}{4}$

   G $\frac{1}{2}$

   H $\frac{2}{3}$

   J $\frac{3}{4}$

Problem Solving Application: Solving Multi-Step Problems

Sometimes you need to use several steps in order to solve a problem.

Try to break the problem into parts. Write simpler problems that will help you find each fact you need. Solve each simpler problem. Then use the answers to solve the original problem.

Tips to Remember:

1. Understand	2. Decide	3. Solve	4. Look back

- Try to remember a real-life situation like the one described in the problem. What do you remember that might help you find a solution?
- Think about the action in the problem. Is there more than one action? Which operation best represents each action—addition, subtraction, multiplication, or division?
- When you can, make a prediction about the answer. Then compare your answer and your prediction.

Solve.

1. A wall-to-wall carpet costs **$15** per square yard. Mrs. Sullivan paid **$630** to carpet a room **6** yards long. What was the width of the room?

Think: What do you need to find first? How can you find it?

_____

_____

Answer _____

2. A shoe box **11** inches long and **4** inches high has a volume of **330** cubic inches. What is the width of the shoe box?

Think: How do you find the volume of a rectangular prism?

_____

_____

Answer _____

3. A square garden has a perimeter of 48 ft. What is the area?

_____

4. Jim doubled the length of his square garden to 24 ft. What is the area now?

_____

5. A certain custom frame costs **$.75** per inch. How much will it cost Carla to frame an oil painting **26** inches by **18** inches?

_____

6. You can buy a school lunch for **$1.75** or you can buy **5** lunch tickets for **$7.50**. How much can you save on each lunch by using a ticket?

_____

7. A full-year family membership to the Museum of Science costs **$79**. A one-day visit costs **$9** for adults and **$7** for children. If the LeBlanc family has **2** adults and **2** children, how many times would they need to visit the museum in a year for the family membership to be a good value?

_____

8. Package A weighs **2.43** pounds. Package B weighs **4$\frac{3}{4}$** pounds. Package C weighs **1.6** pounds. Package D weighs **1.2** pounds. Is the total weight of the four packages more than **10** pounds?

_____

9. Mrs. Li and **15** other people equally share the cost of dinner in a restaurant. The total bill, including tip is **$192**. If Mrs. Li puts in a **$20** bill, how much change should she take out?

_____

10. Chelsea wants to buy **3** books. One costs **$3.99**, one costs **$2.75**, and one costs **$4.98**. She has **8** dollars, **15** quarters, **9** dimes, and **7** nickels. Does Chelsea have enough money to buy the books?

_____

Extend Your Thinking

11. Go back to problem **5**. Carla wants to use the same kind of frame for a square painting. It turns out that the price will be the same as for the rectangular painting. How long is each side of the square painting?

_____

12. Describe the method you used to solve problem **10**. Tell whether you used exact calculations or estimates.

_____

_____

_____

_____

You can use what you know about dividing **3**-digit numbers to divide **4**-digit numbers.

Divide: $29\overline{)1,948}$

1. Divide the thousands.

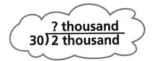

$29\overline{)1,948}$

Not enough thousands.

2. Regroup thousands as hundreds.

$29\overline{)1,948}$

Not enough hundreds.

3. Regroup hundreds as tens. Divide.

$$
\begin{array}{r}
6 \\
29\overline{)1,948} \\
-1\,74 \\
\hline
20
\end{array}
$$

4. Regroup tens as ones. Bring down the next digit. Divide the ones.

$$
\begin{array}{r}
67 \text{ R5} \\
29\overline{)1,948} \\
-1\,74 \\
\hline
208 \\
-203 \\
\hline
5
\end{array}
$$

Remember to multiply and add to check your answer.

Divide and check.

1. $38\overline{)2,371}$ $45\overline{)3,056}$ $23\overline{)2,164}$

2. $19\overline{)1,073}$ $52\overline{)3,134}$ $61\overline{)4,892}$

3. $72\overline{)4,103}$ $57\overline{)4,980}$ $67\overline{)5,042}$

4. $52\overline{)4,187}$ $83\overline{)6,014}$ $17\overline{)1,092}$

Divide and check.

5. $16\overline{)8,384}$ $82\overline{)9,430}$ $14\overline{)8,614}$

6. $71\overline{)9,236}$ $46\overline{)9,755}$ $55\overline{)6,380}$

Problem Solving
Reasoning

Solve.

7. Jose's family traveled **4,200** miles during their **12**-day vacation. If they traveled the same number of miles each day, how many miles each day did they travel?

8. Judy's Nursery planted **1,216** flower bulbs. They planted **4** dozen bulbs in each row. How many rows did they plant? How many bulbs were left over?

☑ Quick Check

Divide and check.

Work Space.

9. $23\overline{)356}$ **10.** $54\overline{)657}$ **11.** $41\overline{)953}$

12. $36\overline{)724}$ **13.** $17\overline{)693}$ **14.** $24\overline{)965}$

15. $21\overline{)1,019}$ **16.** $37\overline{)2,523}$ **17.** $58\overline{)3,617}$

Name _____

A quotient can sometimes contain one or more zeros.

Divide: $37\overline{)7{,}646}^{\ ?}$

1. Not enough thousands to divide. Regroup thousands as hundreds. Divide.

? hundreds
$40\overline{)80\text{ hundreds}}$

$$\begin{array}{r} 2 \\ 37\overline{)7{,}646} \\ -74 \\ \hline 2 \end{array}$$

2. Regroup hundreds as tens. Bring down the next digit.

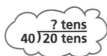

? tens
$40\overline{)20\text{ tens}}$

$$\begin{array}{r} 20 \\ 37\overline{)7{,}646} \\ -74 \\ \hline 24 \end{array}$$

Not enough tens. Write a zero in the quotient.

3. Regroup tens as ones. Divide. Write the remainder in the quotient.

? ones
$40\overline{)250\text{ ones}}$

$$\begin{array}{r} 206\text{ R24} \\ 37\overline{)7{,}646} \\ -74 \\ \hline 246 \\ -222 \\ \hline 24 \end{array}$$

Check your answer. Multiply and add.

Divide and check.

1. $31\overline{)8{,}756}$ $26\overline{)5{,}983}$ $19\overline{)5{,}834}$

2. $16\overline{)8{,}457}$ $56\overline{)4{,}487}$ $72\overline{)7{,}421}$

3. $71\overline{)2{,}852}$ $47\overline{)5{,}082}$ $32\overline{)6{,}489}$

Divide and check.

4. $35\overline{)1{,}482}$ $68\overline{)1{,}164}$ $56\overline{)3{,}928}$

5. $28\overline{)3{,}248}$ $17\overline{)4{,}309}$ $27\overline{)5{,}623}$

6. $52\overline{)5{,}324}$ $35\overline{)2{,}352}$ $43\overline{)8{,}781}$

Problem Solving Reasoning Solve.

7. Niles has a puzzle with **2,496** pieces. If he puts **24** pieces together a day, how many days will it take to finish the puzzle?

_____

8. The total attendance for **12** performances of a play was **1,860** people. The same number of people attended each performance. How many people attended each performance?

_____

Test Prep ★ Mixed Review

9 What is the area in square feet of the figure shown?

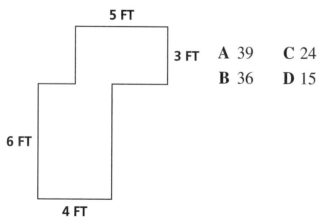

5 FT

3 FT

6 FT

4 FT

A 39   C 24
B 36   D 15

10 Which of these shows thirty-four hundredths shaded?

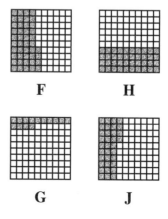

F   H

G   J

252   Unit 9 Lesson 8

Name _____

One way to estimate a quotient is to round the dividend and divisor. Another way to estimate a quotient is to use compatible numbers.

Compatible numbers are numbers that are easy to divide mentally.

Examples of Compatible Numbers		
2 and 4	3 and 9	7 and 35
4 and 16	8 and 24	9 and 36

With **1**-digit divisors, find a compatible number for the dividend.

Estimate: $7\overline{)431}$

1. Find a number for the dividend compatible with **7**.

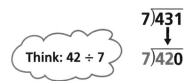

2. Estimate.

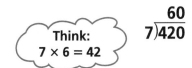

With **2**-digit divisors, find compatible numbers for both the dividend and the divisor.

Estimate: $62\overline{)192}$

1. Find the compatible numbers.

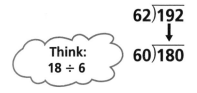

2. Estimate.

Estimate each quotient using compatible numbers. Then circle the correct answer.

1. $7\overline{)492}$ $7\overline{)490}^{70}$ 7 R2   700 R2   70 R2

2. $21\overline{)336}$ $20\overline{)400}^{20}$ 1 R20   108 R16   16

3. $57\overline{)582}$ $57\overline{)570}$ 101 R12   10 R12   1 R12

4. $76\overline{)795}$ $\overline{)}$ 1 R48   104 R48   10 R35

5. $52\overline{)4,546}$ $\overline{)}$ 8 R22   807 R22   87 R22

Estimate each quotient using compatible numbers. Then circle the correct answer.

6. $24\overline{)539}$ $25\overline{)}$ **200 R2**   **22 R11**   **70 R11**

7. $41\overline{)7,962}$ $40\overline{)}$ **194 R8**   **94 R8**   **294 R8**

8. $78\overline{)5,617}$ $80\overline{)}$ **177 R5**   **17 R5**   **72 R1**

9. $39\overline{)3,440}$ $40\overline{)}$ **903 R1**   **10 R5**   **88 R8**

| Problem Solving |
| Reasoning |

Solve.

10. A tool company shipped **3,672** small tools in **18** boxes. Each box contained the same number of tools. About how many tools were in each box?

_____

11. A toy company shipped **3,914** marbles in **38** boxes. Each box contained the same number of marbles. About how many marbles were in each box?

_____

 Quick Check

Divide and check.

12. $17\overline{)3,521}$ **13.** $26\overline{)7,956}$ **14.** $14\overline{)8,537}$

Work Space.

Estimate the quotient using compatible numbers.

15. $240 \div 63$ _____   **16.** $3,627 \div 92$ _____

17. $4,243 \div 74$ _____

Problem Solving Strategy: Solve a Simpler Problem

STANDARD

Sometimes using simpler numbers can make it easier to decide what steps you need to take to solve a problem.

Problem

Mr. Kim is driving his car a total distance of **3,339** miles. He used **58** gallons of gasoline to drive the first **1,218** miles. How many gallons of gasoline will he need to complete the trip?

---

1 Understand As you reread, ask yourself questions.

• What do you need to find out? _____

---

2 Decide Choose a method for solving.

Try the strategy Use a Simpler Problem.

• Find simpler numbers to use. One way to make a simpler number is to replace all the digits, except the first digit, with zeros.

Original number	3,339	58	1,218
Simpler number	3,000	50	_____

---

3 Solve Solve the simpler problem and the original problem.

• Break the simpler problem into parts and solve.
  a. Find the miles per gallon (mpg).

  1,000 ÷ _____ = _____ mpg

  b. Find the number of miles left.

  3,000 − _____ = _____ mi

  c. Find the number of gallons needed.

  _____ ÷ _____ = **100** gal

• Now use the same steps for the original problem.

  a. Find the miles per gallon (mpg). _____ mpg

  b. Find the number of miles left. _____ miles

  c. Find the number of gallons needed. _____ gallons

---

4 Look back Write the answer to the problem. _____

Solve. Use the Use a Simpler Problem strategy or any other strategy you have learned.

1. Mr. Kay bought **3** shirts for **$15.99** each. Mrs. Kay bought **2** shirts for **$29.50** each. How much more money did Mrs. Kay spend than Mr. Kay?

   Think: How can you round dollars and cents?

   _____

   Answer _____

2. Mr. Johnson cut a **25**-foot rope into **12** equal-sized pieces. How many cuts did he make?

   Think: What numbers could you choose that would be simpler?

   _____

   Answer _____

3. Write the missing number in this sequence.

   2.34, 2.44, 2.43, 2.53, _____, 2.62

4. Find the missing digits.

   ```
          4□7
   2□)9,□61
   ```

5. To celebrate a shopping mall's **fifteenth** anniversary, a cake **15** feet long and **15** feet wide will be served. How many square pieces with **3**-inch sides can be cut from the cake?

   _____

6. Six people at a party all shake hands with each other. How many handshakes is that? (Hint: Try solving the problem for fewer people. Look for a pattern.)

   _____

7. The Kleiner family is making a trip to Connecticut. The total distance is **364** miles. So far they have driven **208** miles in **4** hours. If they continue at the same speed, how many hours will it take them to complete the trip?

   _____

8. A special fundraiser concert is being held in the school gym. Tickets cost **$12** each. Ticket sales so far total **$3,768**. Chairs for all ticket holders plus **50** extra chairs will be set up. Each row will have **14** chairs. How many rows will there be?

   _____

9. The choir is standing on steps in a specific pattern. The bottom step has **18** people. The next step has **15** people, then **12** people and so on. How many people are in the choir?

   _____

10. A local play is offering a special discount rate on tickets: **2** tickets for **$12**. A class of **18** students can use the special discount rate or a special student rate of **3** tickets for **$15**. Which is cheaper?

   _____

Name _____

Divide.

1. $12\overline{)84}$　　　　**2.** $41\overline{)68}$　　　　**3.** $29\overline{)93}$　　　　**4.** $32\overline{)197}$

5. $27\overline{)763}$　　　　**6.** $17\overline{)680}$　　　　**7.** $26\overline{)785}$　　　　**8.** $17\overline{)688}$

9. $64\overline{)3,306}$　　　　**10.** $35\overline{)7,245}$　　　　**11.** $84\overline{)7,057}$　　　　**12.** $12\overline{)8,530}$

Use compatible numbers to estimate each quotient.

13. $41\overline{)451}$

Estimate _____

14. $67\overline{)556}$

Estimate _____

15. $25\overline{)2,197}$

Estimate _____

16. $51\overline{)3,526}$

Estimate _____

Solve.

17. During a grand opening, a store gave every fourth customer a discount coupon. Every tenth customer was given a discount coupon and a free gift. During the grand opening, **240** people visited the store. How many coupons and gifts were given away?

_____

_____

18. A **20**-foot length of ribbon is to be cut in half. Each length will then be cut into **5** equal lengths. How many equal lengths of ribbon will there be altogether?

_____

_____

Name _____

1 At track practice, 4 students ran different distances.

Student	Distance Run
Amanda	**2.65** meters
Wilson	**2.75** meters
Robert	**2.6** meters
Alexia	**2.8** meters

Which lists the students in order from the *shortest* distance run to the *longest* distance run?

A Amanda, Robert, Wilson, Alexia

B Robert, Amanda, Wilson, Alexia

C Robert, Amanda, Alexia, Wilson

D Alexia, Wilson, Amanda, Robert

2 The Celsius thermometers show the temperature at noon on Monday and the temperature at noon on Tuesday. How many degrees colder was the temperature on Tuesday?

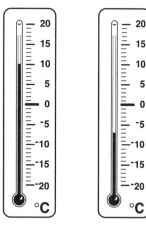

Monday   Tuesday

F 17° C   H 10° C

G 12° C   J 7° C

3 The Lawsons are driving 1,235 miles to visit relatives in Colorado. If they drive 65 miles an hour, how many hours will the trip take?

A 15 hours   C 19 hours   E NH

B 17 hours   D 21 hours

4 Which shape is congruent with the triangle shown?

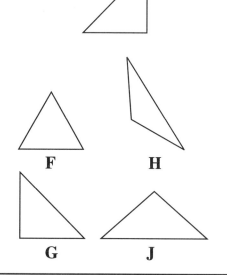

F   H

G   J

5 What decimal should go in the ☐ to make the number sentence true?

$$\frac{3}{10} = 0.30 \qquad \frac{1}{2} = \boxed{}$$

A 0.75   C 0.25

B 0.50   D 0.1

6 An employee is arranging 170 CDs on a display rack. Each shelf of the rack holds 15 CDs. How many shelves will he use to display all the CDs?

F 10 shelves H 12 shelves K NH

G 11 shelves J 13 shelves

UNIT 10 • TABLE OF CONTENTS

Data, Statistics, and Probability

We will be using this vocabulary:

mean a way of describing numerical data; to find the mean or average (6) of 4, 5, and 9, find the sum of the numbers, and then divide by the number of addends.

outcome a result of an experiment

probability the chance of an event occurring

line graph a way to describe how data change during a period of time

Dear Family,

During the next few weeks, our math class will be learning about data, statistics, and probability.

You can expect to see homework that provides practice with describing sets of data. Here is a sample you may want to keep handy to give help if needed.

Finding Median, Mode, and Range

To find the median of the set of data {3, 9, 4, 2, 9, 16, 5}:

First arrange the numbers from least to greatest or from greatest to least.

2 3 4 5 9 9 16

The median is the middle number. The median is **5**.

2̶ 3̶ 4̶ **5** 9̶ 9̶ 1̶6̶
          ↑

If a set of data has two middle data numbers, the median is the number halfway between the two middle numbers.

To find the mode of the set of data {3, 9, 4, 2, 9, 16, 5}:

Look for the number or numbers that occurs most often. The mode is **9**.

3 9 4 2 9 16 5

To find the range of the set of data {3, 9, 4, 2, 9, 16, 5}:

Subtract the greatest number from the least. The range is **14**.

3 9 4 2 9 16 5
    16 − 2 = 14

During this unit, students will need to continue practicing working with data, as well as addition and subtraction facts.

Sincerely,

When you conduct a **survey**, you collect **data** or facts.

• Record the data in a table.

• Make a tally mark each time a choice is made.

• After all the people have been surveyed, find the total number of the tallies in all the choices.

Survey question: "What is your favorite color for a car?"

Title →
Column Headings →
Categories {

Favorite Color for a Car		
Color	Tally	Total
Blue	ЖII III	8
Green	ЖII ЖII II	12
Red	ЖII III	8

Number of people surveyed

8 + 12 + 8 = 28

Conduct a survey. Use the table to record your data.

1. Choose an idea for your survey. Write a question to ask that has **3** possible responses.

2. Make a table with a title, headings, and three choices.

3. Survey **20** people. Tally the results.

4. Count the tally marks for each choice.

5. Which choice received the most tallies? The least?

_____

_____

Title:		
	Tally	Total

A **line plot** is a way to show the frequency of data. This line plot shows the number of books members of the book club have read this month.

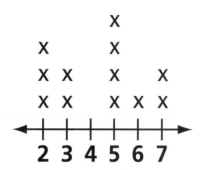

Number of Books Read

Number of Books Read	
Jan	3
Paul	5
Steve	7
Karen	6
Mia	3
Kim	2
Tara	5
Andy	7
Kris	2
Tim	5
Roland	5
Juan	2

The four X's above **5** mean that four members of the book club have read **5** books. One X above **6** means that one member has read **6** books.

Use the line plot to answer each question.

6. How many members of the book club read exactly **2** books this month? _____

7. A total of _____ club members read **8** books this month.

8. In all, there are _____ club members.

9. How many club members read at least **5** books? _____

10. What was the least number of books read this month? _____

Test Prep ★ Mixed Review

11 Which shows all the factors of 28?

A 3, 4, 6, 19

B 1, 2, 6, 8, 28

C 1, 2, 4, 7, 14, 28

D 2, 4, 7, 14

12 The course for a cross-country skiing race is 20.13 kilometers long. What is this distance rounded to the nearest tenth?

F 21 kilometers

G 20.2 kilometers

H 20.1 kilometers

J 20 kilometers

Number of Apples Eaten Last Week

Person	Chris	Pat	Ann	Mark	Andy	Doug	Angela	Susan	Erin	Shelly
Apples	1	3	2	4	9	1	1	0	3	6

In a set of data, the **mode** is the number in the data that occurs most often. If no number occurs more than once, there is no mode.

Use the line plot. There are more X's above **1** than above any other number. The mode is **1**.

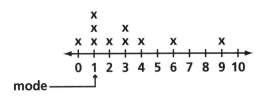

You can also find the range. The **range** is the difference between the greatest value and the least value in the set of numbers.

To find the range, subtract the least number from the greatest number.

9 − 0 = 9   The range is **9**.

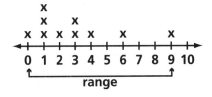

An **outlier** is a number in the data that is much greater or much less than the other numbers. In this set of data, **9** is an outlier.

The **mean**, or average, is the sum of the numbers divided by the number of addends.

0 + 1 + 1 + 1 + 2 + 3 + 3 + 4 + 6 + 9 = 30   **30 ÷ 10 = 3**

In this set of data, **3** is the mean.

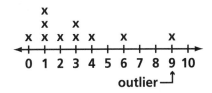

The middle number in the data is called the **median**.

Write the numbers in order from least to greatest.

0, 1, 1, 1, 2, 3, 3, 4, 6, 9

This set of data has **10** numbers, so it has two middle numbers. The middle numbers are **2** and **3**. The median is the mean of the two middle numbers:

2 + 3 = 5   **5 ÷ 2 = 2$\frac{1}{2}$**

In this set of data, **2$\frac{1}{2}$** or **2.5** is the median.

Use the line plot to answer the question.

1. How many responses are shown in this survey? _____

2. What is the mode? _____

3. What is the range? _____

4. What is the median? _____

5. What is the mean? _____

6. Is there an outlier? _____
   If so, what is it? _____

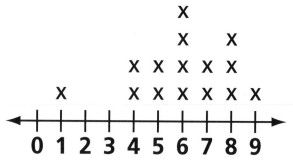

Amount of Money Spent Last Week

Number of Dollars

Find the mean, range, median, mode, and outlier of the set of data.

7. 1, 1, 1, 3, 3, 4, 6, 6, 11   range: _____   median: _____

   mean: _____   mode: _____   outlier: _____

8. 3, 3, 4, 4, 4, 4, 5, 6, 7, 7, 8   range: _____   median: _____

   mean: _____   mode: _____   outlier: _____

9. 22, 22, 23, 25, 25, 26, 26, 26, 39   range: _____   median: _____

   mean: _____   mode: _____   outlier: _____

10. 1, 18, 18, 19, 20, 20, 20, 21, 21, 22   range: _____   median: _____

    mean: _____   mode: _____   outlier: _____

Arrange the data in order from least to greatest. Then find the range, median, mode, and outlier.

11. 4, 8, 5, 2, 2, 5, 5, 9, 15, 5 _____

    range: _____ median: _____ mode: _____ outlier: _____

12. 3, 1, 4, 3, 6, 4, 7, 5, 8, 6, 3, 7 _____

    range: _____ median: _____ mode: _____ outlier: _____

13. 7, 14, 2, 1, 7, 19, 28, 7, 4, _____

    range: _____ median: _____ mode: _____ outlier: _____

Name _____

In sets without numbers, the mode depends on the group you select.

This set of buttons is grouped by color.

The mode color of this set is **red**.
Red is the group with the most buttons.

Use the set of buttons above to answer each question.

Draw the buttons grouped in another way.

14. How did you group them?

_____

15. What is the mode?

_____

| Problem Solving Reasoning | Solve. Use this set of buttons to answer problems 14–16. |

16. What is the mode number of holes in this set?

_____

17. What is the mode shape of this set?

_____

18. What is the mode color of this set?

_____

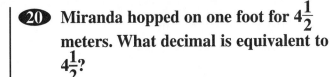

Test Prep ★ Mixed Review

19 An Olympic athlete runs 200 meters in 19.75 seconds. What is 19.75 in words?

A Nineteen and seventy hundredths

B Nineteen and seven tenths

C Nineteen and seventy-five hundredths

D Nineteen and seventy-five tenths

20 Miranda hopped on one foot for $4\frac{1}{2}$ meters. What decimal is equivalent to $4\frac{1}{2}$?

F 4.05

G 4.12

H 4.21

J 4.50

STANDARD

Sometimes you will need to use the information in a table in order to solve a problem.

Molly and Katy worked together on a project. They collected information about three brands of oatmeal-raisin cookies. All the cookies were about the same size. They made this table to show the number of cookies in each bag and the cost of each bag.

	Price per bag	Number of cookies
Granny's Best	$5.50	50
Just Like Home	$3.60	20
Uncle Erno's	$3.50	25

Tips to Remember:

1. Understand	2. Decide	3. Solve	4. Look back

- Think about what the problem is asking you to do. What information does the problem give you? What do you need to find out?
- Try to break the problem into parts.
- Do you need to use both addition and subtraction to show what is happening? Which should you use first?

Solve. Use the table above.

1. Which brand of cookies was most expensive?

Think: How would you find the cost of **1** cookie?

_____

_____

Answer _____

2. You want to buy **200** of Granny's Best cookies. How much will they cost?

Think: How would you find the number of bags you need?

_____

Answer _____

3. Write the unit price of the cookies in order from least to greatest.

4. How much would **100** cookies from Uncle Erno's cost?

Name _____

Molly and Katy took **5** cookies from each bag and counted the number of raisins in each cookie. This table shows their results.

Number of raisins					
	1	**2**	**3**	**4**	**5**
Granny's Best	6	5	4	8	7
Just Like Home	9	8	9	10	9
Uncle Erno's	10	10	18	11	12

Solve. Use the table above.

5. Which brand had the greatest range in the number of raisins?

_____

6. For which brand does the data not have a mode?

_____

7. For which brand does the data have an outlier? What is it?

_____

8. What is the median number of raisins for Just Like Home?

_____

9. What is the median number of raisins for Uncle Erno's?

_____

10. What is the mean number of raisins for Granny's Best?

_____

Extend Your Thinking

11. Go back to problem **10**. Suppose the number of raisins in the first cookie were different. What number of raisins would have to be in the first cookie for the mean to be **7** raisins? Explain how you solved this problem.

_____
_____
_____
_____

12. The line plot below shows data for **10** cookies of one brand. Which brand do you think the data is for? Explain your thinking.

Number of Raisins

_____
_____
_____

STANDARD

You can use a **line graph** to show how data change during a period of time. This graph shows how the temperature outside changed during twelve hours.

The vertical scale should always start at 0. You can save space by using a jagged line to show a gap.

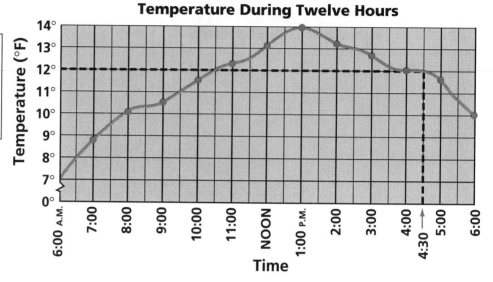

Temperature During Twelve Hours

To find the temperature at **4:30** P.M. follow these steps:

• Find **4:30** P.M. on the Time scale.

• Trace a straight line up from **4:30** P.M. until you reach a point on the line segment.

• Trace another line from that point to the Temperature scale to find the temperature, **12°F.**

You can show the temperature at **4:30** P.M. by writing this coordinate: **(4:30** P.M., **12°F).**

Use the graph to answer the question.

1. What was the greatest temperature? _____

2. At what time did the greatest temperature occur? _____

3. When was the temperature **10°F**? _____ and _____

4. What time was the temperature **13°F**? _____ and _____

5. Describe how the temperature changed between **6:00** A.M. and **1:00** P.M. _____ By how much? _____

6. Would you expect the temperature at **7:00** P.M. to be greater or less than **10°F**? Explain. _____

_____

Name _____

Monthly Balloon Sales at Helium Joe's	
June	$100
July	$300
August (Aug.)	$100
September (Sept.)	$100
October (Oct.)	$600
November (Nov.)	$500

Follow these steps to make a line graph of the sales data in the table.

1. Write the months on one scale. Use abbreviations. Label it *Months*.

2. Write the number of dollars using multiples of **100** on the other scale. Label it *Dollars*.

3. Plot the amount of money for each month on the graph. Here's how June was plotted.
   - Find June on the Month scale.
   - Find **100** on the Dollars scale.
   - Place a point where both lines meet.

4. Connect the points with line segments.

Monthly Balloon Sales

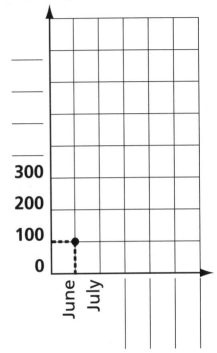

Complete.

7. Which month had the greatest

sales? _____

8. In which three months were the

sales **$100**? _____

_____

9. Between June and November, which month had the greatest decrease in sales?

_____

10. What is the difference in sales between the least point and the greatest point on the graph?

_____

11. What might have caused the sales during August to be so low?

_____

Unit 10 Lesson 4 **269**

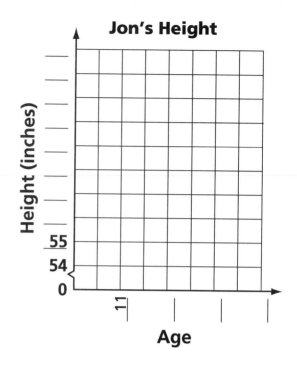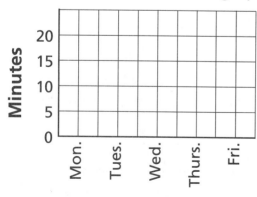

12. Use this data to make a line graph.

Jon's Height from Ages 11 to 14	
Age	Height (inches)
11	55
12	59
13	62
14	63

✓ Quick Check

13. The tally chart shows results of a survey. How many more people liked orange juice than liked cherry juice? _____

Favorite Juices		
Apple	Orange	Cherry
卌 卌 II	卌 卌 IIII	卌 II

Work Space.

14. The ages of people at a family dinner were **12, 15, 20, 21, 48, 51, 78, 81**. Find the range of ages.

_____

15. Manuel records how long he spends walking to school every morning: Monday, **10** min.; Tuesday, **15** min.; Wednesday, **9** min.; Thursday **15** min.; Friday **18** min. Show this data on the line graph below.

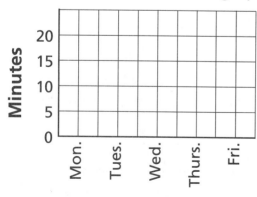

Name _____

OUTCOMES:
Red, gray, white

A **prediction** uses as many facts as possible to describe what is likely to happen.

An **experiment** is an activity you do to gather data. An **outcome** is a result of an experiment.

You can conduct an experiment and record the outcomes to make a prediction.

The tally chart and the line plot show the outcomes of an experiment:

	Tally	Total
Red	|||	3
Gray	卌|	6
White			1

• Without looking, a cube was removed from the bag.

• The cube's color was recorded with a tally mark, and it was put back in the bag.

• Ten draws were made from the bag. The chart shows **10** tally marks.

What color will be picked on the eleventh draw?

To predict the outcome of the next draw, study the data. Since **6** out of **10** cubes chosen were gray, you can predict that the next cube chosen most likely will be gray.

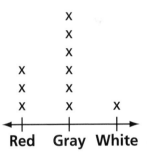

A bag has 10 slips of paper in it. Each slip has one letter on it. Aimee chose one slip, recorded the letter, then put the slip back. She recorded her data in a line plot.

1. What are the possible outcomes?

_____

2. Predict whether there are more T's or more H's in the bag. Explain your prediction.

_____

_____

3. Which letter do you think is on the most slips? Explain.

_____

_____

Problem Solving Reasoning Solve.

4. Ricky put several cubes in a bag and conducted an experiment. He used a tally of his results to make this bar graph.

Of the cubes in the bag, do you think the least number were red? If not, explain.

Experiment Results

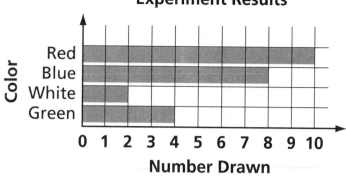

_____

Spinner Results

Color	Tally

5. The tally chart shows the results of an experiment with a spinner. What do you predict you will spin next? Explain.

_____

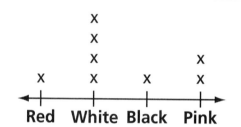

6. This line plot shows the results of an experiment. Circle the bag of cubes that may have been used. Then explain your choice.

_____
_____
_____
_____

 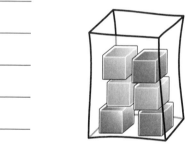 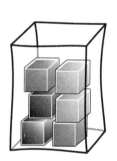

Test Prep ★ Mixed Review

7. A warehouse is packing an order for 3,264 books. If each box holds 24 books, how many boxes will the warehouse need?

A 130   C 134

B 132   D 136

8. The area of a square is 64 square meters. What is the length of one side?

F 16 meters

G 12 meters

H 8 meters

J 4 meters

The possible results of an experiment can be described in words or in numbers.

Will you choose a green cube?

- There are **0** chances out of **6**, or $\frac{0}{6}$, to choose a green cube from the bag.

- It is **impossible** to choose a green cube from this bag.

Will you choose a gray or red cube?

- There are **6** chances out of **6**, or $\frac{6}{6}$, to choose a red or a gray cube from the bag.

- It is **certain** that either a red or gray cube will be chosen from this bag.

Will you choose a gray cube?

- There are **2** chances out of **6**, or $\frac{2}{6}$, to choose a gray cube from the bag.

Will you choose a red cube?

- There are **4** chances out of **6**, or $\frac{4}{6}$, to choose a red cube from the bag.

Are you more likely to choose a red or a gray cube?

- There are more red than gray cubes. Red is a greater part of the whole.

- Since $\frac{4}{6} > \frac{2}{6}$, you are **more likely** to choose a red cube than a gray cube.

4 red cubes
2 gray cubes

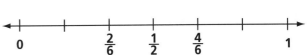

Suppose the spinner is spun once.

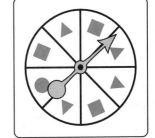

1. What is the chance that the spinner will point to a square?

   _____ out of _____, or _____

2. What is the chance that the spinner will point to a triangle?

   _____ out of _____, or _____

3. Compare the fractions you found in exercises 1–2.

   _____ ◯ _____

4. Predict whether you are more likely to spin a triangle or a square.

   _____

The spinner shown is the same as on p. 273. Suppose it is spun once.

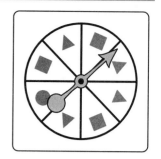

5. What is the chance that the spinner will point to a circle?

_____ out of _____ or _____

6. What is the chance that the spinner will point to a pentagon? A pentagon is a five-sided figure.

_____ out of _____ or _____

| Problem Solving Reasoning | Solve. Choose the spinner that describes the statement. |

7. For which spinner is W an impossible outcome? Explain.

_____

8. For which spinner is there a $\frac{1}{5}$ probability of pointing to Y?

Explain. _____

_____

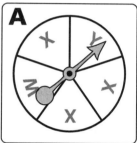

9. In which spinner is there a $\frac{1}{4}$ probability of pointing to X? Explain. _____

_____

10. Which spinner is more likely to point to X than to Y? Explain. _____

_____

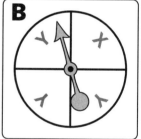

Test Prep ★ Mixed Review

11. Which group of numbers shows all the factors of 18?

A 1, 2, 9, 18   C 3, 9, 18

B 1, 2, 3, 6, 9, 18   D 18, 36, 54

12. A class trip costs a total of $682 for 22 students. How much does it cost for each student?

F $29   H $33

G $31   J $35

You are deciding what to wear. You have **1** pair of jeans, but you have a choice of a red or blue T-shirt and sneakers or hiking boots. How many different outfits could you wear?

You can use a **tree diagram** to show all the possible outcomes.

1. Write down *jeans*. It will be the trunk of the tree.

2. Draw two branches from the trunk. Label one *red shirt* and the other *blue shirt*.

3. Draw two branches from each shirt. Label one *sneakers* and the other *hiking boots*.

4. Count the number of branches made in step **3**. This is the number of possible outcomes.

Tree Diagram

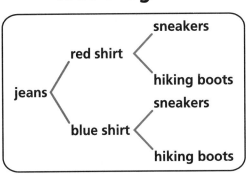

4 possible outcomes

You could wear four different outfits:

Jeans, red shirt, sneakers   Jeans, red shirt, hiking boots

Jeans, blue shirt, sneakers   Jeans, blue shirt, hiking boots

---

The tree diagram shows choices for wrapping a present. Use it to answer each question.

1. How many different ribbon colors are there to choose from? _____

2. How many different kinds of wrapping papers are there to choose from? _____

3. How many different possible outcomes are there so far? _____

4. Extend the tree diagram to show two different colors of bows.

5. How many different possible outcomes are there now? _____

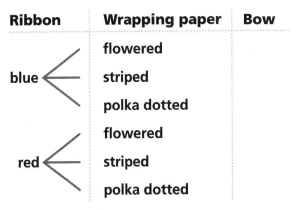

Make a tree diagram to solve the problem.

6. A restaurant has round and square tables. It has 3 kinds of tablecloths: red, blue or white. The vases on the table have a rose or a daisy. Show all of the possible combinations.

table	tablecloth	flower

✓ **Quick Check**

Answer each question.

Work Space.

7. There are **12** cubes in a bag. Four are red, **2** are yellow, and **6** are green. Which color will you probably pick most often? _____

8. What are the chances of the spinner stopping on red? Write your answer both in words and as a fraction. _____

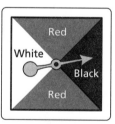

White   Red   Black   Red

9. You flip a coin three times. How many ways could the coin flips turn out? _____
Complete the tree diagram shown.

H   T

276   Unit 10 Lesson 7

Problem Solving Strategy: Make a List

In the last lesson, you used a tree diagram to show possible outcomes. Another way to show possible outcomes is to make an organized list.

Problem

Mia bought a pair of blue jeans and a pair of black jeans. She also bought a red shirt, a white shirt, and a yellow shirt. How many different outfits can she make?

---

1 Understand   As you reread, ask yourself questions.

- What information do you have?

    Mia bought _____ jeans and _____ jeans.

    Mia bought a _____ shirt, a _____ shirt, and

    a _____ shirt.

- What do you need to find out?

    _____

---

2 Decide   Choose a method for solving.

Try the strategy Make a List.

- First list all the outfits with the blue jeans.

    blue jeans—red shirt

    blue jeans—white shirt

    blue jeans—yellow shirt

- Then list all the outfits with the black jeans.

    black jeans—red shirt

    _____ jeans—_____ shirt

    _____ jeans—_____ shirt

---

3 Solve   Count the number of outfits in the list.

Mia can make _____ outfits with the blue jeans.

Mia can make _____ outfits with the black jeans.

Mia can make _____ outfits altogether.

---

4 Look back   Check your answer. Write the answer below.

Answer _____

- Why was it helpful to list the items in the same order as they are given in the problem?

    _____

Solve. Use the Make a List strategy or any other strategy you have learned.

1. Mrs. Norton is making sandwiches. She has white bread and whole wheat bread. She has turkey and ham and she has Swiss cheese and American cheese. Each sandwich will have one kind of bread, one kind of meat, and one kind of cheese. How many different kinds of sandwiches can she make?

Think: How many different sandwiches can she make with white bread?

_____

Answer _____

2. At the department store, you can have your purchase gift-wrapped. The store has blue, gold, and silver paper. It has white, blue, and green ribbon. You want to get a package wrapped. You can choose one color paper and one color ribbon. How many different combinations are available?

Think: How many different ways are available using blue paper?

_____

Answer _____

3. You have **12** square tiles. Each tile measures **1** foot on each side. How many noncongruent rectangles can you make? Each rectangle must use all **12** tiles.

_____

4. Three boys – Andrew, Jamie, and Sean – are lining up for a picture. If they stand in a row, how many different ways can they line up?

_____

5. List all **2**-digit numbers for which the sum of the digits is **5**.

_____

6. List all **3**-digit numbers for which the sum of the digits is **3**.

_____

7. How many strips of paper **4** inches long and **1** inch wide can be cut from a piece of paper **8** inches long and **6** inches wide?

_____

8. How many strips of wood **4** inches long and **1** inch wide can be cut from a piece of board **8** inches long and **36** inches wide?

_____

9. Mrs. Washington purchased a refrigerator that is **6** feet high, **3** feet deep and **4** feet wide. How much floorspace does she need to fit the refrigerator?

_____

10. There are **60** people in a line for a local concert. Every third person will be given a ticket so they can sit on the stage. How many people will be sitting on the stage?

_____

Name _____

**Arrange the data in order from least to greatest.
Then find the range, median, and mode.**

1. **49, 34, 43, 63, 50, 26, 2, 50** _____

range: _____ median: _____ mode: _____

2. **17, 15, 22, 25, 14, 22, 19** _____

range: _____ median: _____ mode: _____

Use the table to make a line graph on the grid.

3. Use a scale of **0, 5, 10, 15, 20, 25, 30** to complete
the vertical axis.

4. Complete the horizontal axis by writing a
number for each week.

5. Graph the height of the tomato plant for each
week. Connect the points with line segments.

6. When was the tomato plant **15** inches tall?

_____

7. Describe how the height of the tomato plant
changed between Week **2** and Week **3**.

_____

Tomato Plant Growth	
Week	**Height (in.)**
1	0
2	5
3	10
4	15
5	25
6	30

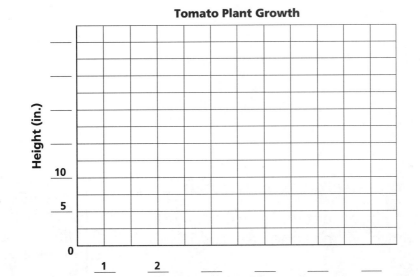

Tomato Plant Growth

Use the spinner to answer each question.

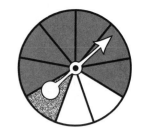

8. What is the chance that the spinner will point to a red section? A gray section? A white section? Express each outcome as a word and as a fraction.

_____

9. Which outcome is more likely to occur: the spinner pointing to a gray section or to a white section?

_____

Make a tree diagram to show all the possible lunch combinations. The sandwich is chicken. The salad is vegetable, potato, or fruit. The drinks are spring water or fruit juice.

10.   **Sandwich**   **Choice of Salad**   **Choice of Drink**

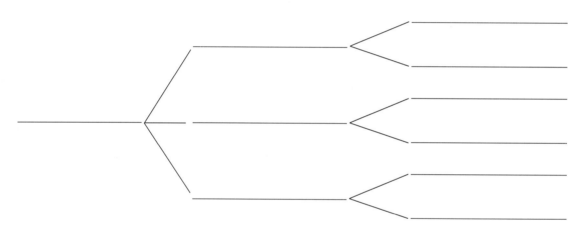

11. How many different lunch combinations are there?

_____

Solve.

12. List all **4**-digit whole numbers whose digits have a sum of **2**.

_____

_____

Use the table of prices to answer the question.

13. Maria wants to buy a hat and scarf. If sales tax is **$1.17**, how much will her purchase cost?

_____

Clothing Sale	
hat	$ 9.00
sweater	$25.99
scarf	$12.50

Name _____

1 Amelia has 113 raffle tickets. She wants to divide them equally among 9 people. How many tickets will she have left over?

A 2   C 6   E NH

B 4   D 8

2 The line graph shows the number of visitors to a new museum. How many more people visited the museum in August than in June?

Museum Visitors

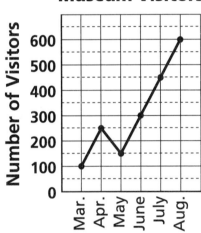

F 300   H 450

G 400   J 500

3 A room is 24.56 meters long. What is 24.56 in words?

A twenty-four and six hundredths

B twenty-four and fifty hundredths

C twenty-four and fifty-six hundredths

D twenty-four and sixty-five hundredths

4 Students recorded the hours that they spent doing their homework each week. They displayed the results on a line plot.

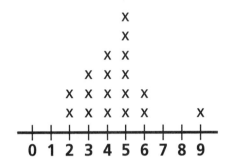

What is the range of hours that students spent on homework?

F 4   H 7

G 5   J 9

5 The chart shows rainfall for one storm in 4 different California cities.

City	Amount of Rain Fallen
Monterey	1.8 inches
Salinas	1.71 inches
Santa Cruz	1.9 inches
San Jose	1.29 inches

Which lists the cities in order from the *greatest* amount of rain to the *least* amount of rain fallen?

A San Jose, Salinas, Santa Cruz, Monterey

B Santa Cruz, Salinas, Monterey, San Jose

C San Jose, Salinas, Monterey, Santa Cruz

D Santa Cruz, Monterey, Salinas, San Jose

6 Melissa's books have a mass of 6 kilograms. What is the mass of her books in grams?

F 60

G 600

H 6,000

J 60,000

7 What decimal should go in the ☐ to make the number sentence true?

$$\frac{7}{10} = 0.70$$
$$\frac{1}{2} = 0.50$$
$$\frac{1}{4} = \boxed{}$$

A 0.80

C 0.25

B 0.4

D 0.14

8 Which of these decimal models shows seventy-eight hundredths shaded?

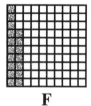

F

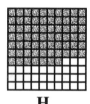

H

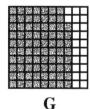

G

J

9 Which fraction is equivalent to $\frac{4}{16}$?

A $\frac{2}{3}$

C $\frac{1}{2}$

B $\frac{4}{8}$

D $\frac{1}{4}$

10 Which fraction is in simplest form?

F $\frac{4}{6}$

H $\frac{7}{8}$

G $\frac{8}{10}$

J $\frac{14}{16}$

11 The distance between two towns is 76.78 kilometers. What is this distance rounded to the nearest tenth?

A 77 kilometers

B 76.8 kilometers

C 76.7 kilometers

D 76 kilometers

12 A school is planning a field trip for 288 students. Each school bus holds 36 students. How many buses will the school need?

F 6

G 8

H 10

J 12

K NH

UNIT 11 • TABLE OF CONTENTS

Algebra: Variables and Coordinate Graphing

Dear Family,

During the next few weeks, our math class will be learning about variables and coordinate graphing.

You can expect to see homework that provides practice using words to describe relationships. Here is a sample you may want to keep handy to give help if needed.

Finding a Rule

A table can be used to show the relationship between the number of automobiles and the number of wheels.

automobiles (a)	wheels (w)
1	4
2	8
3	12
4	16

In words, the relationship can be described as: *Four times the number of automobiles is the number of wheels.*

The algebraic rule that describes this relationship is: $4 \times a = w$.

A table can be used to show the relationship between the number of pounds and the number of ounces.

pounds (p)	ounces (o)
1	16
2	32
3	48
4	64

In words, this relationship can be described as: *Sixteen times the number of pounds is the number of ounces.*

The algebraic rule that describes this relationship is: $16 \times p = o$.

During this unit, students will need to continue practicing finding rules and relationships as well as working with variables.

Sincerely,

The word phrase "three more than Nancy's age" can be written as an arithmetic phrase or **expression.**

$$\square + 3$$
↑
unknown number

An unknown number can also be represented by a letter.

A letter that represents an unknown number is called a variable.

$$n + 3$$
↑
variable

This phrase is called an **algebraic expression.** An algebraic expression is a math phrase that contains at least one variable. It can also include one or more numbers and symbols of operations.

Name the variable in the algebraic expression.

1. $5 + w$ _____ $p - 8$ _____ $16 \div r$ _____

2. $(11 + x) \div 3$ _____ $7 \times (r + 2)$ _____ $(9 - h) + 5$ _____

3. $7 \times y$ _____ $(4 + n) \times 2$ _____ $(3 - j) \times 6$ _____

Match the word phrase with an algebraic expression.

4. _____ r subtract 7   A. $4 + w$

5. _____ 8 divided by x B. $y + 9$

6. _____ the sum of **4** and w C. $p \times 5$

7. _____ **6** less than h D. $r - 7$

8. _____ **9** greater than y E. $7 - r$

9. _____ p times **5**   F. $8 \div x$

10. _____ **7** decreased by r G. $h - 6$

Choose a letter to represent the unknown number.
Then write an algebraic expression for the word phrase.

Word Phrase	Variable	Algebraic Expression
11. **6** less than a number	_____	_____
12. the product of **8** and a number	_____	_____
13. a boy's age divided by **7**	_____	_____
14. **5** more than a number	_____	_____
15. the sum of **11** and a number	_____	_____
16. double a number	_____	_____

Problem Solving
Reasoning

Solve.

17. Bryan is **8** years older than Tracey.

    a. Write an algebraic expression to represent Bryan's age.

       Use *t* as the variable. _____

    b. If Tracey is **12** years old, how old is Bryan? _____

    c. If Bryan is **10** years old, how old is Tracey? _____

18. Cory is *twice* Mai's age.

    a. Write an algebraic expression to represent Cory's age.

       Use *m* as the variable. _____

    b. If Mai is **14** years old, how old is Cory? _____

    c. If Cory is **18** years old, how old is Mai? _____

Test Prep ★ Mixed Review

19 Lisa can jump rope 109 times a minute. At this rate, how many jumps would she make in 11 minutes?

    A 399

    B 1,130

    C 1,199

    D 1,356

20 Which of the following is a prime number?

    F 21

    G 27

    H 29

    J 33

A mathematical sentence with an equals sign (=) is called an **equation**.

4 + 2 = 6

An equation is balanced when the value on one side of the equals sign is the same as the value on the other side.

You can think of a balance scale.

4 + 2 marbles on the left side → ← **6 marbles on the right side**

4 + 2 = 6 is a balanced equation.

If you add the same number to both sides of a balanced equation, the equation stays balanced.
Add **3** to both sides of **4 + 2 = 6**.

(4 + 2) + 3 or 9 marbles on the left side → ← **(6 + 3) or 9 marbles on the right side**

4 + 2 + 3 = 6 + 3 is a balanced equation.

A balanced equation is a number sentence that is true.

Write *Yes* if the equation is balanced. Write *No* if it is not balanced.

1. 6 + 4 = 10 _____   6 + 4 + 2 = 10 + 2 _____

2. 2 + 5 + 7 = 6 + 7 _____   3 + 4 + 8 = 7 + 4 _____

3. 3 + 8 = 12 _____   3 + 8 + 4 = 11 + 4 _____

Complete the equation so that it is balanced.

4. 4 + 5 + 2 = 9 + ___   3 + 1 + 7 = ___ + 7   8 + 5 + 9 = 8 + ___

5. 7 + ___ + 1 = 10 + 1   11 + 4 + ___ = 15 + 6   ___ + 8 + 11 = 13 + 11

6. 10 + ___ + 5 = 16 + 5   8 + 2 + 9 = 8 + ___   ___ + 16 + 1 = 23 + 17

7. 34 + 15 + 7 = 49 + ___   37 + 11 + 8 = ___ + 8   68 + 5 + 19 = 73 + ___

8. 80 + ___ + 16 = 100 + 16   10 + 90 + 18 = ___ + 18   23 + 18 + 12 = 23 + ___

A balanced equation stays balanced if you multiply both sides by the same number.

This is a balanced equation:
3 + 1 = 4

Now multiply both sides by **2**.

(3 + 1) × 2 →
8 marbles on
the left side

← 4 × 2
8 marbles on
the right side

(3 + 1) × 2 = 4 × 2 is a balanced equation.

Write *Yes* if the equation is balanced. Write *No* if it is not balanced.

9. (5 + 4) × 2 = 9 × 2 _____

(6 + 6) × 2 = (6 + 5) × 2 _____

10. (1 + 5) × 2 = 6 _____

(2 + 3) × 2 = 5 × 2 _____

Complete the equation so that it is balanced.

11. (4 + 3) × 2 = _____ × 2

(8 + 1) × 7 = _____ × 7

12. (5 + 6) × 2 = 11 × _____

(7 + 5) × 2 = 12 × _____

| Problem Solving |
| Reasoning |

Solve.

13. Lyle has **4** red and **6** green marbles. Jane has **10** blue marbles. If they each doubled the number of marbles they have, who would have the greater number?

Explain. _____

_____

Test Prep ★ Mixed Review

14 Which shows all the factors of 34?

A 2, 4, 9, 18   C 1, 6, 9

B 2, 17   D 1, 2, 17, 34

15 A boat is sailing a distance of 3,315 miles. If the boat sails 65 miles a day, how many days will the trip take?

F 49   H 51

G 50   J 53

Name _____

The word sentence, "The length of a rug decreased by **12** feet is **32** feet.", can be written as an **algebraic equation.**

$$y - 12 = 32$$

An algebraic equation contains an equals sign and at least one variable, number, and operation.

Write the letter of the algebraic equation that matches the word sentence.

1. _____ If a number is decreased by **5**, it is **10**.

2. _____ If a number is increased by **5**, it is **10**.

3. _____ Six more than a number is **13**.

4. _____ Six less than a number is **13**.

5. _____ A number divided by **2** is **10**.

6. _____ Ten divided by a number is **2**.

A. $n - 6 = 13$

B. $n \div 2 = 10$

C. $n + 6 = 13$

D. $n - 5 = 10$

E. $10 \div n = 2$

F. $n + 5 = 10$

Write an algebraic equation for the word sentence. Use n for the variable.

7. Tim's age doubled is **24**.

_____

8. Twelve less than the number of rocks is **14**.

_____

9. Thirteen dollars less than the price of a baseball bat is **$8**.

_____

10. The length of a rug increased by 5 meters is **15** meters.

_____

To solve an equation, you need to find a value for the variable that balances the equation.

$4 + n = 6$

$4 + n$ marbles on the left side.  **6** marbles on the right side.

The value of n must be **2**.
Replace n with **2** in the equation.
$$4 + 2 = 6$$
The equation is balanced.

Circle the value for the variable that makes the equation balanced.

11. $8 - t = 3$ 2   4   5   **12.** $y + 7 = 15$ 6   8   10

13. $5 \times n = 45$ 6   9   11   **14.** $16 - r = 11$ 5   8   9

Find the value of the variable that makes the equation balanced.

15. $p + 7 = 18$, $p =$ _____   **16.** $r + 10 = 23$, $r =$ _____

17. $t \times 8 = 48$, $t =$ _____   **18.** $2 + m = 44$, $m =$ _____

19. $j \div 7 = 8$, $j =$ _____   **20.** $64 \div 8 = k$, $k =$ _____

 Quick Check

Write an algebraic expression for the word phrase.

21. 7 more than a number   **22.** 6 less than a number

_____   _____

Complete the equation so it is balanced.

23. $2 + 3 + 6 = 7 + \boxed{}$ **24.** $(2 + 7) \times 2 = 9 \times \boxed{}$

Write an algebraic equation for the word sentence. Use n for the variable.

25. 10 less than the number of students is 25. _____

26. Triple Ellen's age is 33. _____

Name _____

In this lesson, you will write
equations to solve word problems.

You will use a variable in the
equation to represent the number
you want to find in order to solve
the problem.

Problem

Stephanie wants to buy some red nail
polish. Nail Glo costs twice as much as
Supershine. Nail Glo costs **$6**. How much
does Supershine cost?

---

1 **Understand**   As you reread, ask yourself questions.

- What information do you have?

    Nail Glo costs _____ as much as Supershine.

    Nail Glo costs _____.

- What do you need to find out?

    _____

---

2 **Decide**   Choose a method for solving.

Try the strategy Write an Equation.

- Draw a circle around the equation that could be
  used to represent the problem.

    $2 \times 6 = s$ $2 \times s = 6$

---

3 **Solve**   Solve the equation.

- Use a related equation.

    $6 \div 2 = s$ is the related equation.

    The solution of $6 \div 2 = 3$ so, $s = 3$.

- Check. $2 \times s = 6$ $2 \times$ _____ $= 6$ True.

---

4 **Look back**   Check your answer. Write the answer below.

Answer _____

Read the problem again. Check your answer.

- Why was it important to go back and reread the
  problem to check your answer?

    _____

    _____

Solve. Use the Write an Equation strategy or any other strategy you have learned.

1. Mr. Vesprini bought **6** dozen muffins. How many muffins was that?

Think: Circle the equation that can help you solve the problem.

$6 \times 12 = m$ $\qquad$ $6 \times m = 12$

Answer _____

2. The total cost of a hot dog and a carton of orange juice is **$3.25**. The hot dog cost **$1.75**. How much was the orange juice?

Think: Circle the equation that can help you solve the problem.

$\$1.75 + j = \$3.25$ $\quad$ $\$3.25 + \$1.75 = j$

Answer _____

3. The area of a rectangular hallway is **24** square feet. The width of the hallway is **3** feet. What is the length of the hallway?

_____

4. You need $\frac{3}{4}$ cup of corn meal to make one pan of cornbread. How many cups of corn meal would you need to make **3** pans of cornbread?

_____

5. A restaurant has four pizza toppings: pepperoni, sausage, green pepper, and mushrooms. How many different two-topping pizzas can be made?

_____

6. The perimeter of a rectangle is **16** feet. The area of the rectangle is **15** square feet. The length is greater than the width. What are the length and width?

_____

7. There is a bus stop in front of Luann's house. A bus arrives at the stop every **45** minutes and goes into town. The first bus comes at **7:15** A.M. If the bus trip takes **12** minutes, what is the latest bus Luann can take in order to get to town by **1:00** P.M.?

_____

8. Rachel is **50** inches tall. Alyssa is **2** inches shorter than Rachel. Benjamin is **3** inches taller than Alyssa. Spencer is **5** inches taller than Benjamin. How much taller is Spencer than Alyssa?

_____

9. A square kitchen has an area of **100** square feet. What is the kitchen's perimeter?

_____

10. Jenny has some money in her pocket. Sharon gave her **$13** more. Then Jenny had **$15**. How much money did Jenny start with?

_____

You can use a table to show the relationship between the number of tricycles and the number of wheels.

tricycles (t)	wheels (w)
1	3
2	6
3	9
4	w

← **1** tricycle has **3** wheels.
← **2** tricycles have **6** wheels.
← **3** tricycles have **9** wheels.
← **4** tricycles have **w** wheels.

Look for a pattern in the table. Describe the pattern as a rule.

Three times the number of tricycles is the number of wheels.

You can write the rule as an algebraic equation. $3 \times t = w$

This means that if you know the number of tricycles (**t**), you can use the equation to find the number of wheels (**w**).

How many wheels do **4** tricycles have?

Replace **t** with **4**. $3 \times 4 = w$
Find the product. $12 = w$

There are **12** wheels when there are **4** tricycles.

Describe the rule using words. Then complete the tables.

1. _____   _____

_____   _____

bicycles (b)	wheels (w)
1	2
2	4
3	6
4	

cups (c)	ounces (n)
1	8
2	16
3	
4	

2. _____   _____

length (l)	width (w)
5	8
6	9
7	
8	

side (s)	perimeter (p)
1	4
2	8
3	
4	

Describe the rule using words. Complete the table.
Then write the rule as an algebraic equation using the variables given.

3. _____

_____

plants (p)	flowers (f)
1	6
2	12
3	18
4	

Algebraic equation: _____

4. _____

_____

clarinets (c)	trumpets (t)
3	6
6	9
9	
12	

Algebraic equation: _____

5. _____

_____

feet (f)	inches (i)
2	24
4	48
6	
8	

Algebraic equation: _____

6. _____

_____

yards (y)	feet (f)
1	3
2	6
3	
4	

Algebraic equation: _____

7. _____

_____

x	y
2	1
4	3
6	
8	

Algebraic equation: _____

8. _____

_____

x	y
11	12
12	13
13	
14	

Algebraic equation: _____

Test Prep ★ Mixed Review

9 A clothing company is shipping an order for 246 sweaters in boxes. If each box holds 12 sweaters, how many boxes will be needed?

A 22   C 20

B 21   D 18

10 What number could go in the ☐ to make the equation true?

$$(4 + 3) + y = y + \boxed{}$$

F 3   H 6

G 4   J 7

You can use a grid to locate points on a map.

The location of the open book from the tree can be described in words.

Go **3** squares right, then **4** squares up.

The location of the book can also be described using an **ordered pair**. An ordered pair is a pair of numbers that describes a location.

(3, 4)

The first number tells how many squares to move to the right. The second number tells how many squares to move up.

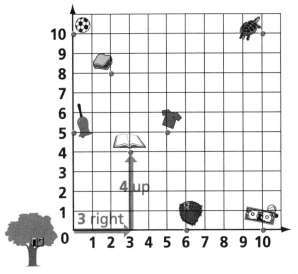

Start at the treehouse. Write words or numbers to complete the directions and ordered pair for the object.

1. To find 💵

   a. Walk _____ squares right, then **0** squares up.

   b. (10, _____)

2. To find 👕

   a. Walk _____ squares right,

      then _____ squares up.

   b. (_____)

3. To find 🥪

   a. _____

     _____

   b. _____

4. To find 🔔

   a. _____

     _____

   b. _____

5. To find ⚾

   a. _____

     _____

   b. _____

6. Which treasure can be found by walking **0** squares right, then **10** squares up?

   _____

7. Draw a treasure on the grid. **4** squares right, then **8** squares up. Label it **(4, 8)**.

Write the letter for the ordered pair.

8. (3, 0) ____

9. (2, 2) ____

10. (5, 3) ____

11. (3, 5) ____

12. (4, 1) ____

13. (1, 4) ____

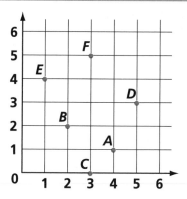

Write the ordered pair for the point on the grid.

14. G ____

15. H ____

16. J ____

17. K ____

18. L ____

19. M ____

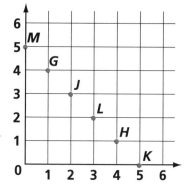

20. Connect the points on this graph. What shape did you make? _____

✓ Quick Check

21. Complete the table. Describe the rule using words. Then write the rule as an algebraic equation.

x	y
8	4
16	12
24	
30	

Work Space.

Words: _____

_____

Algebraic equation:

_____

22. Do (5, 1) and (1, 5) both represent the same point on a grid? Why or why not?

_____

_____

You can use ordered pairs and a **coordinate grid** to locate points.

A coordinate grid has a horizontal line, called the *x*-axis, and a vertical line, called the *y*-axis.

Each axis is labeled like a number line. The point where the *x*-axis and *y*-axis meet is called the origin.

Ordered pairs are used to locate points on the grid. The origin is at point **(0, 0)**.

In an ordered pair
- the first number tells how far to move right along the *x*-axis. It is called the *x*-coordinate.
- the second number tells how far to move up the *y*-axis. It is called the *y*-coordinate.

Locate the point **(4, 5)**
1. Start at the origin.
2. Move **4** units right, along the *x*-axis.
3. Move **5** units up, along the *y*-axis.

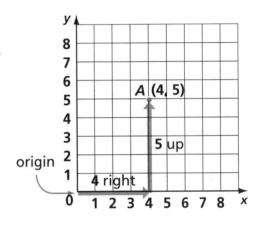

Complete the set of directions that describes the location of each ordered pair.

1. (2, 6) move _____ 2, move _____ 6

2. (7, 1) move _____ _____, move _____ _____

Locate and label each point.

3. *A* (8, 4)   *B* (8, 3)   *C* (7, 2)

   D (6, 1)   *E* (5, 2)   *F* (4, 3)

   G (4, 4)   *H* (4, 5)   *I* (5, 6)

   J (6, 7)   *K* (7, 6)   *L* (8, 5)

4. Using line segments, connect the points from exercise **3** in alphabetical order. What figure is formed?

_____

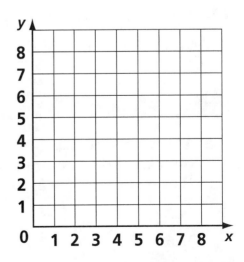

Name all the sums for 5. Write the addends as ordered pairs. Then graph the ordered pairs.

Addends $x + y = 5$	Ordered pairs (x, y)	Graph the ordered pairs on this grid.
5. $0 + $ _____ $= 5$	$(0, $ _____ $)$	
6. _____ $+ 4 = 5$	$($ _____ $, 4)$	
7. _____ $+$ _____ $= 5$	$($ _____ $, $ _____ $)$	
8. _____ $+$ _____ $= 5$	$($ _____ $, $ _____ $)$	
9. _____ $+$ _____ $= 5$	$($ _____ $, $ _____ $)$	
10. _____ $+$ _____ $= 5$	$($ _____ $, $ _____ $)$	

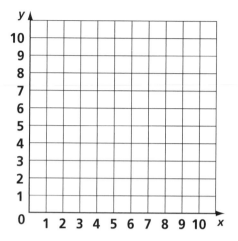

11. Connect the points. What do you have?

_____

Problem Solving
Reasoning

Solve.

12. **a.** How many units long is $\overline{AB}$? _____ units

b. Find the difference of the *x*-coordinates of *A* and *B*. _____ Does the difference equal the length of $\overline{AB}$? _____

13. **a.** How many units long is $\overline{AC}$? _____ units

b. Find the difference of the *y*-coordinates of *A* and *C*. _____ Does the difference equal the length of $\overline{AC}$? _____

14. Explain two ways to find the length of a vertical line on a grid. _____

_____

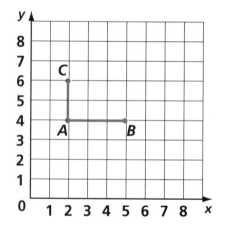

$\overline{AB}$ is a **horizontal line.**
$\overline{AC}$ is a **vertical line.**

Test Prep ★ Mixed Review

15 A movie theater has 141 seats. Each row except the first row has 9 seats. How many seats are in the first row?

A 8   C 4

B 6   D 2

16 Carlos hiked 8,648 yards in 4 hours. What is the average number of yards he hiked each hour?

F 216   H 2,262

G 2,162   J 22,312

You can use words or symbols to write a rule about the numbers in an ordered pair.

(3, 5)

Words: Add **2** to the first number to get the second number.

Symbols: $x + 2 = y$

Use the rule to write more ordered pairs. The table shows different numbers for **x**. It also shows how to get numbers for **y** using the rule.

Write the ordered pairs from the table.

(1, 3)   (2, 4)   (3, 5)   (4, 6)   (5, 7)

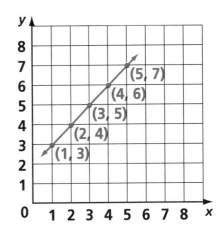

first number x	rule x + 2	second number y
1	1 + 2	3
2	2 + 2	4
3	3 + 2	5
4	4 + 2	6
5	5 + 2	7

Use the coordinate grid to graph the ordered pairs.

The graph of these ordered pairs forms a straight line.

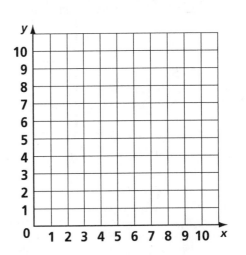

Complete the table. Write the ordered pairs. Then graph and connect the points on the grid.

1.

x	x − 1	y
1	1 − 1	
2	2 − 1	
3	3 − 1	
4	4 − 1	
5	5 − 1	

Ordered Pairs

(1, _____)

(2, _____)

(3, _____)

(4, _____)

(5, _____)

Complete the function table. Write the ordered pairs. Then graph and connect the ordered pairs on the grid.

2.

x	x + 1	y
1	1 + 1	
2		
3		
4		
5		

Ordered Pairs

(_____, _____)

(_____, _____)

(_____, _____)

(_____, _____)

(_____, _____)

3.

x	x × 2	y
1	1 × 2	2
2	× 2	
3	× 2	
4	× 2	
5	× 2	

Ordered Pairs

(_____, _____)

(_____, _____)

(_____, _____)

(_____, _____)

(_____, _____)

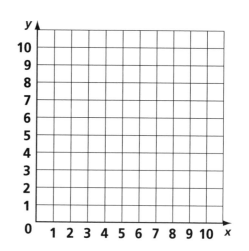

4.

x	x × 1	y
2		
3		
5		
6		
8		

Ordered Pairs

(_____, _____)

(_____, _____)

(_____, _____)

(_____, _____)

(_____, _____)

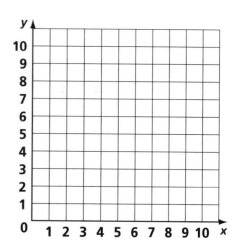

Name _____

In the equation $x - 5 = y$, you can find the value of the y-coordinate when you know the value of the x-coordinate.

Find the value of y when $x = 9$.

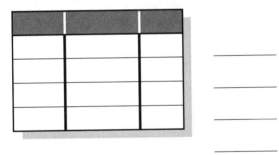

$x - 5 = y$

$9 - 5 = 4$

For the equation $x - 5 = y$, when $x = 9$, $y = 4$.

One ordered pair for $x - 5 = y$ is (9, 4).

Use the equation to find the values of y for the given values of x. Write the ordered pairs. Then graph and connect them on the grid.

5. $x + 7 = y$ $x = 0, 1, 2,$ and **3**

_____

_____

_____

_____

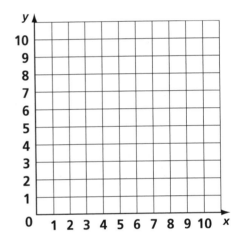

6. $(x \times 2) - 6 = y$ $x = 3, 5, 7,$ and **8**

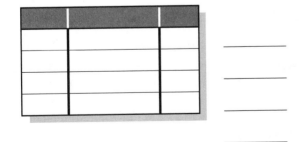

_____

_____

_____

_____

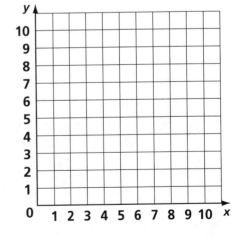

Problem Solving Reasoning Solve.

7. Find the lengths of these line segments by finding the difference of the *x*- or *y*-coordinates.

$\overline{AH}$ _____ $\overline{EH}$ _____

$\overline{BC}$ _____ $\overline{DK}$ _____

$\overline{AG}$ _____ $\overline{CJ}$ _____

8. What is the perimeter of rectangle *BFLG*? Explain how you found it.

_____

_____

_____

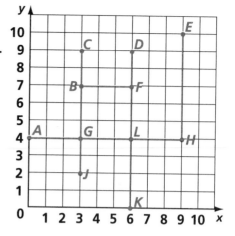

✓ Quick Check

9. Name all the sums for **4** using the given equation. Write the addends as ordered pairs. Then graph and connect the ordered pairs.

Work Space.

$x + y = 4$	(x, y)
$0 +$ _____ $= 4$	$(0,$ _____ $)$
$1 +$ _____ $= 4$	$(1,$ _____ $)$
$2 +$ _____ $= 4$	$(2,$ _____ $)$
$3 +$ _____ $= 4$	$(3,$ _____ $)$
$4 +$ _____ $= 4$	$(4,$ _____ $)$

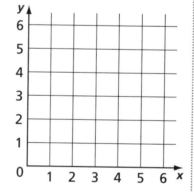

10. Complete the function table. Write the ordered pairs. Then graph the ordered pairs on the grid.

x	x + 2	y
1		
2		
3		
4		

(_____)
(_____)
(_____)
(_____)

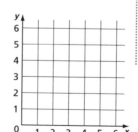

Some problems give more facts than you need. You need to decide which facts are necessary.

Some problems do not give enough facts. In this lesson, you may need to tell what fact or facts you need to solve a problem.

Tips to Remember:

1. Understand	2. Decide	3. Solve	4. Look back

- Read each problem more than once. Circle the important words and numbers. Cross out the words and numbers that you don't need.
- Try to remember a real-life situation like the one described in the problem. What do you remember that might help you find a solution?
- When you can, make a prediction about the answer. Then compare your answer and your prediction.

Cross out the extra information. Then solve the problem. If information is missing, name the fact or facts needed on the answer lines.

1. The Barker family drove to Orlando, Florida. They drove the total distance, **1044** miles, in **3** days. Their average speed was **51** miles per hour. What was the average number of miles they traveled per day?

Think: How does the question help you decide what facts are needed?

_____

_____

Answer _____

_____

2. When they arrived in Orlando, the Barkers stayed at a large hotel. There were **350** guest rooms and **2** restaurants. Their room cost **$85** (tax included) per night. What was their total room bill?

Think: What information do you need to find the total room bill?

_____

_____

Answer _____

_____

Cross out the extra information. Then solve the problem. If information is missing, name the fact or facts that you need.

3. Yosemite National Park is **300** miles north of Los Angeles and **200** miles east of San Francisco. The Chin family drove to Yosemite. They drove at an average speed of **50** miles per hour. How many hours did the trip take?

_____

_____

4. There is an observatory on the **86**th floor of the Empire State Building. On a clear day, you can see for **80** miles. A ticket to go up to the observatory costs **$3.75**. How much will **3** tickets cost?

_____

5. Elevator ticket prices at the Eiffel Tower vary. To go to the first level (**188** feet), the cost is **$3.50**. To go to the second level (**380** feet), the cost is **$7.30**. To go to the highest level (**1,060** feet), the cost is **$9.90**. What is the difference in price between the highest level and the first level?

_____

6. About **3** million people visit the Statue of Liberty each year. The statue weighs **225** tons and is **151** feet high. The Dori family climbed up from the ground level to the crown and then climbed down. It took them a total of **3** hours and **20** minutes. How many steps did they climb altogether?

_____

_____

Extend Your Thinking

7. Go back to problem **4**. Complete the graph below to show the cost of tickets to the observatory.

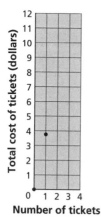

Do all the points lie on a line?

_____

8. Go back to problem **5**. Use the information in the problem to complete the graph below.

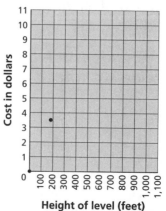

Do all the points lie on a line?

_____

Choose a variable for each unknown number.
Then write an algebraic expression for the
word phrase.

Word Phrase	Variable	Algebraic Expression
1. 4 more than a number	_____	_____
2. the product of **6** and a number	_____	_____
3. a person's height doubled	_____	_____

Complete the equation so that it is balanced.

4. $4 + 5 + 4 = 9 +$ _____

5. $11 + 8 + 3 =$ _____ $+ 3$

6. $(7 + 5) \times 2 =$ _____ $\times 2$

7. $(6 + 5) \times 3 = 11 \times$ _____

Circle the value for the variable that makes the
equation balanced.

8. $12 - t = 7$ 2   4   5

9. $y + 6 = 14$ 6   8   10

10. $8 \times n = 48$ 6   9   11

11. $21 - r = 9$ 30   14   12

Solve the equation.

12. $j \times 7 = 70$ $j =$ _____

13. $y + 13 = 53$ $y =$ _____

Write an algebraic equation for the word sentence.
Then find the solution. Use *n* for the variable.

14. Five more than some number is **18**. What is the
number?

_____

15. The sum of Rick's test score and **15** is **100**. What was
Rick's score?

_____

16. A number divided by **6** is **4**. What is the number?

_____

Complete the table. Describe the rule using words. Then write the rule as an algebraic equation using the variables given.

m	n
4	8
6	12
17. 8	
18. 10	

19. Words: _____

_____

20. Algebraic rule: _____

_____

Complete the function table for the rule and the values of x listed. Write the ordered pairs. Then graph and connect them on the grid.

x	x − 4	y
4	4 − 4	0
21. 5		
22. 6		
23. 7		

Ordered Pairs

(4, 0)

_____

_____

_____

24. If you connected the points on the graph, what would you draw?

_____

Solve.

25. Luke is **12** years old and **4** years older than his sister Erica. What number sentence could be used to find Erica's age? How old is Erica?

_____

Cross out the extra information. Then solve the problem.

26. A museum was visited by **1,290** people on Friday, **3,615** people on Saturday, and **2,753** people on Sunday. How many people did not visit the museum on Friday?

_____

306 Unit 11 Review

1 The line graph shows the high temperature each day for a week. How much warmer was the temperature on Friday than on Thursday?

High Temperatures for a Week

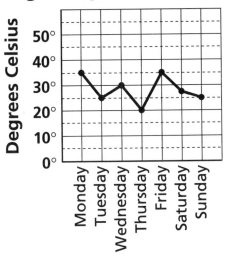

Day of the Week

A 15° C

C 7° C

B 10° C

D 5° C

2 Find the rule for the function table shown below. Choose the algebraic expression that states the rule.

p	n
5	25
8	40
11	55
13	65

F $p + 20$

H $p + 32$

G $p \div 5$

J $p \times 5$

3 Plot the points (3, 6) and (6, 6) on the coordinate grid. Draw lines to connect these points to the other points shown. What shape did you make?

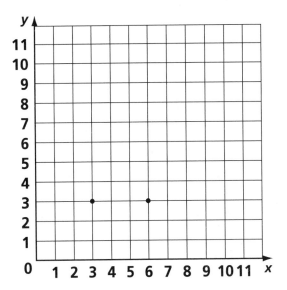

A Triangle

C Square

B Circle

D Hexagon

4 Students recorded the number of people in their families. They displayed the results on a line plot.

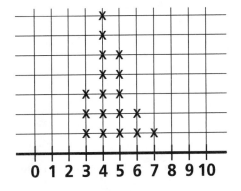

What is the median number of people in these families?

F 4

H 6

G 5

J 18

5 Choose the shape that answers this riddle.

I have exactly 2 sides that are parallel. What shape am I?

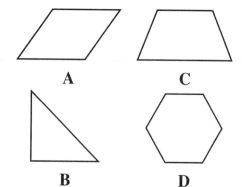

A   C

B   D

6 At a sports arena, there are 122 seats in every row. There are 93 rows. How many seats are in the stadium all together?

F 1,244   H 10,246   K NH

G 1,464   J 11,346

7 What is line segment *z*?

A Diameter   C Ray

B Radius   D Chord

8 What number could go in the ☐ to make the equation true?

$$15 + x = (\boxed{} + 8) + x$$

F 6   H 8

G 7   J 9

9 Find the rule for the function table shown below. Choose the algebraic expression that states the rule.

x	y
37	43
18	24
48	54
13	

A $x + 6$ C $y \div 3$

B $x \times 7$ D $x + 8$

10 Mr. O'Connell's driveway is 45 yards long. What is the length of his driveway in feet?

F 540   H 270

G 450   J 135

11 A rectangle has a perimeter of 26 feet. Which of the following could be the measurement of its area?

A 42 square feet

B 32 square feet

C 26 square feet

D 18 square feet

Tables of Measures

Metric System

Prefixes

kilo (k)	=	1,000
hecto (h)	=	100
deka (da)	=	10
deci (d)	=	$\frac{1}{10}$
centi (c)	=	$\frac{1}{100}$
milli (m)	=	$\frac{1}{1,000}$

Length

1 kilometer (km)	=	1,000 meters (m)
1 meter	=	10 decimeters (dm)
1 decimeter	=	10 centimeters (cm)
1 meter	=	100 centimeters (cm)
1 centimeter	=	10 millimeters (mm)
1 meter	=	1,000 millimeters

Capacity and Mass

1 liter	=	1,000 milliliters (mL)
1 kilogram	=	1,000 grams (g)
1 gram	=	1,000 milligrams (mg)

Customary System

Length

1 foot (ft)	=	12 inches (in.)
1 yard (yd)	=	3 feet
1 yard	=	36 inches
1 mile (mi)	=	5,280 feet
1 mile	=	1,760 yards

Capacity

1 cup (c)	=	8 fluid ounces (fl oz)
1 pint (pt)	=	2 cups
1 quart (qt)	=	2 pints
1 gallon (gal)	=	4 quarts

Weight

1 pound (lb)	=	16 ounces (oz)
1 ton (T)	=	2,000 pounds

Other Measures

Time

1 minute (min)	=	60 seconds (s)
1 hour (h)	=	60 minutes
1 day	=	24 hours
1 week (wk)	=	7 days
1 month (mo)	≈	4 weeks
1 year (yr)	=	12 months
1 year	=	52 weeks
1 year	=	365 days
1 leap year	=	366 days
1 decade	=	10 years
1 century	=	100 years

Counting

1 dozen (doz)	=	12 things
1 score	=	20 things
1 gross (gro)	=	12 dozen
1 gross	=	144 things

Geometric Formulas

Rectangle	Square	Rectangular Prism	Cube

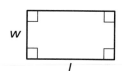

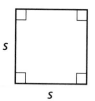

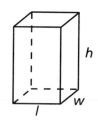

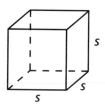

Rectangle

Perimeter:
$P = 2 \times (l + w)$

Area:
$A = l \times w$

Square

Perimeter:
$P = 4 \times s$

Area:
$A = s \times s$

Rectangular Prism

Surface Area:
$SA = 2 \times (l \times w) + (w \times h) + (l \times h)$

Volume:
$V = l \times w \times h$

Cube

Surface Area:
$SA = 6 \times (s \times s)$

Volume:
$V = s \times (s \times s)$

310

Glossary

A

acute angle An angle whose measure is less than 90°.

addend A number to be added in an addition expression.

adding zero property Adding zero to any number does not change the number.
Examples:
$7 + 0 = 7; n + 0 = n$

A.M. A symbol used for times from midnight to noon.

angle A geometric figure formed by two rays with a common endpoint.

angle *ABC*

area A measure of the number of square units in a region. The area of the region shown below is 6 square centimeters.

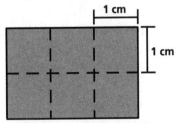

associative property of addition (also called the *grouping property of addition*) Changing the grouping of the addends does not change the sum.
Example:
$(7 + 5) + 6 = 7 + (5 + 6)$

associative property of multiplication (also called the *grouping property of multiplication*) Changing the grouping of the factors does not change the product.
Example:
$(7 \times 5) \times 2 = 7 \times (5 \times 2)$

average (or mean) The sum of given numbers, divided by the number of addends used in finding the sum.
Example: The average of 4, 5, and 9 is 6.

axis (see *x*-axis, *y*-axis) A reference line on a coordinate grid or graph.

B

bar graph A pictorial representation of data that uses lengths of bars to show the information.

base A side or face in a plane or space figure.

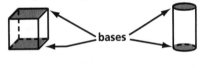
bases

C

capacity The maximum amount of liquid that a container can hold.

Celsius temperature scale (°C) The temperature scale in the metric system in which the freezing temperature of water is 0°C and the boiling temperature of water is 100°C.

circle A plane figure that has all of its points the same distance from a given point called the *center*.

center

circle graph A pictorial representation of data that uses sections of a circle to show the information.

common factor A number that is a factor of two or more whole numbers.
Example: 1, 2, 3, and 6 are common factors of 12 and 18.

common multiple A number that is a multiple of two or more whole numbers.
Example: Common multiples of 3 and 4 are 12, 24, 36, . . .

commutative property of addition (also called the *order property of addition*) Changing the order of the addends does not change the sum.
Example: $3 + 4 = 4 + 3$

commutative property of multiplication (also called the *order property of multiplication*) Changing the order of the factors does not change the product.
Example:
$3 \times 5 = 5 \times 3$

compatible numbers
Numbers used to make estimates. They are easy to work with mentally and are close to the given numbers.

composite number A number that has more than two factors.
Example: 9 is composite, because its factors are 1, 3, and 9.

cone A space figure with one flat, circular surface and one curved surface.

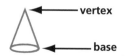

congruent figures Figures that have exactly the same size and shape.

coordinates An ordered pair of numbers that locate a point on a coordinate grid. The first number represents how many units to move across. The second number represents how many units to move up.

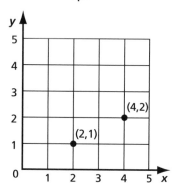

coordinate grid A grid with number lines used to locate points in a plane.

cube A rectangular prism whose faces are all congruent squares.

customary system The system of measurement that uses units such as foot, quart, pound, and degrees Fahrenheit.

cylinder A space figure with two congruent circular bases joined by a single curved surface.

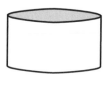

D

data Numerical information.

decimal A number that uses place value to indicate parts of a whole. The decimal point separates the whole number digits from the digits representing parts of a whole.
Examples: 1.6, 3.67

decimal point A symbol used to separate tenths and hundredths from whole numbers. It is also used to separate dollars and cents.
Example:

3.67 $5.10

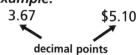
decimal points

degree A unit of measure of temperature or of an angle.

denominator The digit written below the fraction bar in a fraction. It tells how many parts are in the whole.
Example:
$\frac{1}{5}$ ← denominator

diameter A line segment passing through the center and joining any two points on a circle.

difference The answer to a subtraction problem.

digit Any of the symbols 1, 2, 3, 4, 5, 6, 7, 8, 9, and 0.

distance The length of a path between two points.

distributive property The product of a number and the sum of two numbers is equal to the sum of the two products.
Example:
3 × (20 + 7) =
(3 × 20) + (3 × 7)

dividend The number that is divided in a division problem.

divisible When a number can be divided by another number without a remainder.
Example: 4, 16, and 64 are all divisible by 4.

divisor The number by which the dividend is divided in a division problem.

E

edge A line segment where two faces of a space figure meet.

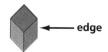

elapsed time The time that passes between the beginning and end of an event.
Example: The elapsed time between 9:30 A.M. and 2:15 P.M. is 4 hours 45 minutes.

endpoint A point at the end of a line segment or ray.

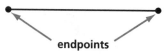
endpoints

equation A number sentence in which an equal sign is used.
Example: 3 + 7 = 10
3 + n = 10

equilateral triangle A triangle with three congruent sides.

equilateral triangle

equivalent fractions Two or more fractions that represent the same number.
Example:
$$\frac{1}{2} \rightarrow \frac{2}{4} \rightarrow \frac{3}{6} \rightarrow \frac{4}{8}$$

equivalent measures Two or more measures that represent the same amount.
Example: 2 gal = 8 qt

estimate To find an approximate solution by using rounded numbers.

even number A whole number that is divisible by 2.

event Any outcome or set of outcomes of an experiment.

expanded form A number written as the sum of the value of its digits.
Example: The expanded form of 2,316 is $2,000 + 300 + 10 + 6$.

expression A number, symbol, or combination of numbers and symbols that represent a quantity.
Examples:
$(7 + 3) \div 5$ or $6 \times n$

F

face A flat surface that is a side of a space figure.

face

factor A number to be multiplied in a multiplication expression.

factor (of a number) A number that divides exactly into another number.
Example: The numbers 1, 2, 3, 4, 6, and 12 are all factors of 12.

Fahrenheit temperature scale (°F) The temperature scale in the customary system in which the freezing temperature of water is 32°F and the boiling temperature of water is 212°F.

formula An equation that expresses a mathematical relationship.
Example: A formula for area A of a rectangle with length l and width w is $A = l \times w$

fraction A number that names a part of a region or set.
Examples: $\frac{1}{2}$ or $\frac{3}{4}$

H

hexagon A polygon that has six sides.

horizontal line A straight line on a grid that goes across, rather than up.

I

impossible event In probability, an event that cannot take place. The probability of an impossible event is expressed as 0.

inequality A number sentence that states that two numbers or expressions are greater than (>), less than (<), or not equal to (≠) each other.
Examples: $3 + 6 < 10$
$5 + 7 \neq 10$

intersecting lines Line segments that cross each other.

inverse operation An operation that undoes the results of another operation.
Example: $3 \times 8 = 24$
$24 \div 3 = 8$

isosceles triangle A triangle with at least two congruent sides.

K

key (of a pictograph) A part of a pictograph that tells what each symbol on the graph represents.

L

line A set of points that extends endlessly in two opposite directions.

line *AB* or $\overleftrightarrow{AB}$

line graph A pictorial representation of data that uses line segments to show changes over time.

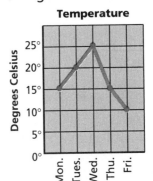

line plot A pictorial representation of data along a number line.

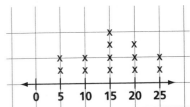

line segment A part of a line that has two endpoints.

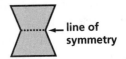

line symmetry A figure has line symmetry when it can be folded to make two parts that match exactly.

line of symmetry

Glossary 313

M

mass The amount of matter in an object. Some units of mass are gram and kilogram.

mean *See* average.

median The middle point of a set of data, arranged from least to greatest.
Example: The median of 2, 4, 5, 6, 7 is 5.

metric system An international system of measurement that uses the meter, liter, gram, and degrees Celsius as the basic units of measure.

mixed number A number, such as $2\frac{2}{3}$ that is made up of a whole number and a fraction less than one.

mode The number (or numbers) that occurs most often in a set of data. If every number occurs only once, the data has no mode.
Example: The mode of 2, 4, 5, 5 is 5.

multiple The product of the number and any whole number.
Example: The multiples of 4 are 0, 4, 8, 12, 16, . . .

multiplying by 1 property Multiplying any number by 1 is equal to that number.
Example: $8 \times 1 = 8$

multiplying by 0 property Multiplying any number by 0 is equal to 0.
Example: $8 \times 0 = 0$

N

negative number A number that is less than zero.
Example:

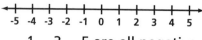

$-1, -3, -5$ are all negative numbers.

net A flat pattern that folds into a space figure.

number line A line that has its points labeled with numbers.

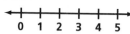

number sentence A statement showing how numbers in an operation are related.
Example: $9 \times 3 = 27$

numerator The number written above the bar in a fraction. It tells how many parts of the whole.
Example:

$\frac{3}{5}$ ← numerator

O

obtuse angle An angle whose measure is greater than 90° and less than 180°.

obtuse angle

octagon A polygon that has 8 sides.

odd number A whole number that is not divisible by 2.

open sentence A number sentence that contains a variable.
Example: $10 + n = 17$

order of operations The rules that define the order in which the operations in an expression are to be evaluated.

Order of Operations
1. Do operations in parentheses first.
2. Multiply and divide from left to right.
3. Add and subtract from left to right.

outcome A result in a probability experiment.

outlier An item of data that is significantly greater or less than the other items of data.

P

parallel lines Two lines in the same plane that do not intersect.

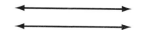

parallelogram A quadrilateral in which both pairs of opposite sides are parallel.

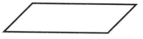

parentheses Symbols used in number sentences to show what part of a problem to solve first.
Example:
$(7 \times 3) \times 2 = 21 \times 2$

pentagon A polygon with five sides.

perimeter The distance around a polygon. It is found by adding the lengths of all the sides.

period Each group of three digits seen in a number written in standard form.
Example: In 306,789,245, the millions period is 306, the thousands period is 789, and 245 is the ones period.

perpendicular lines Two lines that intersect to form right angles.

pictograph A pictorial representation of data that uses symbols to represent quantities.

Class A	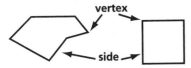
Class B	
Key 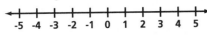 = 5 votes	

place-value system A system of numeration in which the value of a digit depends on its position in the number.
Example: In 8,756, the digit 7 is in the hundreds place.

plane A flat surface that extends in all directions without end.

plane figure A figure whose points are all in the same plane.

point A location in space. It is represented by a dot.

polygon A plane figure composed of line segments that meet only at their endpoints. The segments must form a closed figure.

vertex
side

positive number A number that is greater than zero.
Example:

-5 -4 -3 -2 -1 0 1 2 3 4 5

1, 3, and 5 are all positive numbers.

prediction In a probability experiment, a guess about an outcome that is based on earlier events.

prime number A whole number greater than 1 that has exactly two factors, itself and 1.
Example: $2 = 2 \times 1$

prism A space figure that is named for the shape of its two parallel bases.

triangular prism

probability The chance that an event will occur; probability is expressed using a number from 0 to 1.

product The answer to a multiplication problem.

pyramid A space figure whose base is a polygon and whose other faces are triangles that share a common vertex. A pyramid is named by the shape of its base.

Q

quadrilateral A polygon that has four sides.

quotient The answer in a division problem.

R

radius A segment from any point on a circle to its center; also the length of this segment.

6 cm
radius

range The difference between the least and greatest number in a set of data.
Example: In the data set 2, 4, 5, 5 the range is 3 $(5 - 2 = 3)$.

ray A part of a line that has one endpoint. When naming it, the endpoint is used first.

endpoint   *A*   *B*   ray *AB*

rectangle A parallelogram that has four right angles.

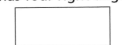

rectangular prism A space figure having six rectangular faces.

region The space inside a closed figure.

regular polygon A polygon that has all sides congruent and all angles congruent.

remainder The number that is left over in a division problem.

rhombus A parallelogram that has all of its sides congruent.

right angle An angle whose measure is 90°.

90°

rounding Changing a number up or down to the nearest 10, 100, 1,000, and so on.
Examples:
12,501 rounded to the nearest hundred is 12,500.
4.38 rounded to the nearest tenth is 4.3.

S

scalene triangle A triangle that has no congruent sides.

sequence Numbers arranged according to some pattern or rule.

side A line segment forming part of a figure.

simplest form A fraction whose numerator and denominator have no common factor greater than 1.
Example: $\frac{1}{2}$ is the simplest form of $\frac{5}{10}$.

space figure A figure that is not entirely in one plane such as a sphere, a rectangular prism, or a pyramid.

sphere A space figure that has all of its points the same distance from the center.

square A rectangle that has all its sides congruent.

standard form A number that is expressed using digits and a base 10 place-value system.
Example: 3,126 is the standard form of the number three thousand, one hundred twenty-six.

sum The answer to an addition problem.

surface area The total area of all the faces or surfaces of a space figure.

survey An approach to collecting data that involves asking many people the same question or questions.

Symmetric figure A figure that has one or more lines of symmetry.

T

trapezoid A quadrilateral that has exactly one pair of parallel sides.

tree diagram An organized way of listing all the possible outcomes of an experiment.

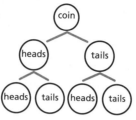

triangle A polygon that has three sides.

turn (rotation) The rotation of a figure around a point.

turn symmetry (rotational symmetry) When a figure still looks exactly the same after being rotated less than a full turn around a point.

U

unit A fixed quantity used as a standard for length, area, volume, weight, and so on.

unit price The cost of a single unit of an item.
Example: $3 for each pound of hamburger meat.

V

variable A letter that is used to represent one or more numbers.

vertical line A straight line on a grid that goes up and down, rather than across.

vertex (plural: vertices) The common point where two sides or edges meet.

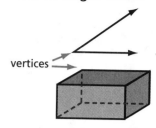

volume A measure of the space within a closed figure in space.

W

whole number Any of the numbers 0, 1, 2, 3, . . .

X

x-axis The horizontal number line on a coordinate grid.

Y

y-axis The vertical number line on a coordinate grid.

Symbols

=	is equal to
≠	is not equal to
<	is less than
>	is greater than
$n, \square$	placeholders
+	add
−	subtract
×	multiply
÷	divide
$\overline{)0}$	divide
$\angle$	angle
$\overline{AB}$	line segment AB
$\overrightarrow{AB}$	ray AB
$\overleftrightarrow{AB}$	line AB